Psychoanalysis Through the Life Cycle

Psychoanalysis Through the Life Cycle

Selected Papers of Martin Silverman

VOLUME 1

IPBOOKS.net
International Psychoanalytic Books
International Psychoanalytic Books (IPBooks)
New York • www.IPBooks.net

IPBooks Inc
International Psychoanalytic Books (IPBooks)
Queens, NY
Online at: www.IPBooks.net

Interior book design by Maureen Cutajar, gopublished.com

ISBN: 978-1-949093-56-8

Silverman, M.A., & Neubauer, P.B. (1971). The Use of the Developmental Profile for the Pre-Latency Child. In: *The Unconscious Today*, edited by Mark Kanzer. New York: International Universities Press, pp.363–380.

Silverman, M.A. (1971). The Growth of Logical Thinking: Piaget's Contribution to Ego Psychology. *Psychoanaytic. Quarterly*, 40:317–341.

——— Rees, K., & Neubauer, P.B. (1975). On a Central Psychic Constellation. *Psychoanalytic. Study Child* 30:127–156.

——— (1981). Cognitive Development and Female Psychology. *Journal of the American Psychoanalytic Association* 29:581–605.

——— (1978). The Developmental Profile. In: *Child Analysis and Therapy*, edited by Jules Glenn, Northvale, NJ/London: Jason Aronson, pp. 109–127.

——— (1986). The Male Superego. *Psychoanalytic Review* 73:(40)23–40.

——— & Bernstein, P.P. (1993). Gender Identity Disorder in Boys. *Journal of the American Psychoanalytic Association* 41:729–742.

——— (1982). The Voice of Conscience and the Sounds of the Analytic Hour. *Psychoanalytic Quarterly* 51:196–217.

——— (1982). A Nine-Year-Old's Use of the Telephone: Symbolism in *Statu Nascendi*. *Psychoanalytic Quarterly* 51:598–611.

——— (1985). Progression, Regression, and Child Analytic Technique. *Psychoanalytic Quarterly* 54:1–19.

——— (1985). Sudden Onset of Anti-Chinese Prejudice in a Four-Year-Old Girl. *Psychoanalytic Quarterly* 54:615–619.

——— (1986). Identification in Healthy and Pathological Character Formation. *International Journal of Psycho-Anaysis*, 86:181–191.

——— (1989). Power, Control, and the Threat to Die in a Case of Asthma and Anorexia. In: *Psychosomatic Symptoms. Psychodynamic Treatment of the Underlying Personality Disorder*. Edited by C. Philip Wilson, M.D., and Ira L. Mintz, M.D. Northvale, NJ/London: Jason Aronson, pp. 351–364.

——— (2002). Homosexuality in Two Women Treated from the Age of Nine Years. *Psychoanalytic Inquiry* 22 (2):259–277.

——— (1993). Working with Parents at the Beginning of Treatment. In: *The Treatment of Neurosis in the Young: A Psychoanalytic Perspective.* Edited by M. Hossein Etezady, M.D. Northvale, NJ/London: Jason Aronson, pp. 9–17.

——— (2004). Insecurity and Fear of Attachment in a Troubled Adoption: A Clinical Example. *Journal of Infant, Child, and Adolescent Psychotherapy* 3:313–328.

——— (1985). Countertransference and the Myth of the Perfectly Analyzed Analyst. *Psychoanalytic Quarterly* 54:175–199.

——— (1987). Clinical Material. In: How Theory Shapes Technique: Perspectives on a Clinical Study, Edited by Sidney E. Pulver, with Philip J. Escoll and Newell Fischer. *Psychoanalytic Inquiry* 147–166.

——— (1987). The Analyst's Response. From: *How Theory Shapes Technique Perspectives on a Clinical Study,* edited by Sidney E. Pulver, with Philip J. Escoll and Newell Fischer. *Psychoanalytic Inquiry* 7(2):277–287.

——— (1998). Discussion of "What Is This Movie Doing in This Psychoanalytic Session?" by Marshall Edelson. *Journal of Clinical Psychoanalysis* 7:54–66.

——— (2007). Psychoanalytic Ethics and Psychoanalytic Competence: Lessons from the Biographies of Masud Khan. *Psychoanalytic Quarterly* 76:1019–1026.

——— (2007). The Psychoanalyst as a New Old object, an Old New Object, and a Brand New Object: Reflections on Loewald's Ideas about the Role of Internalization in Life and in Psychoanalytic Treatment *Psychoanalytic Quarterly.*

——— (2010). Psychoanalysis and the Treatment of Psychosis. *Psychoanalytic Quarterly* 79:795–817.

——— (2012). On Myths and Myth-Making: Psychoanalytic Theorizing about Mother-Daughter Relationships and the "Female Oedipus Complex." *Psychoanalytic Quarterly* 81:955–968.

——— (2016). The Sorrows of Young Werther and Goethe's Understanding of Melancholia. *Psychoanalytic Quarterly* 85:199–209.

——— (2018). Death as the Ultimate Castration. *Psychoanalytic Inquiry* 38:59–75.

AN INTRODUCTION BY EUGENE MAHON

The collected papers of a psychoanalyst may not be autobio-graphical in the strictest sense but they do illuminate multiple facets of the analyst's clinical experience, his reading experience and his experience with the flux of life itself over many decades; and therefore, in a relative sense, can be called autobiographical. Dr. Silverman wrote articles for fifty years and as Book Editor of the *Psychoanalytic Quarterly,* he read books and reviewed them for many decades. The articles in this collection have emerged out of an immersion in clinical encounters with children and adults, and his book essays have been the product of very close and serious encounters with the many books he has reviewed. When George Seferis was asked what were the influences that shaped him, he said, "A lion is the product of all the lambs he has eaten, and I have been reading all my life."

His gastronomic definition of influence is poetically comic but it illustrates the point I wish to make about Dr Silverman: he continued to devour experience with analysands and books— and life itself—throughout his analytic career, and that makes his collected papers the exciting and partially autobiographical story of his professional life of over half a century. This is a great span of time and it is reflected in the vast scope and depth of these brilliant contributions to psychoanalysis.

Any reader who, prior to reading the book cover to cover, ponders the array of chapter titles, cannot but be impressed by the collection's range and depth: e.g.,

Chapter 2: The Growth of Logical Thinking: Piaget's Contribu-tion to Ego Psychology;
Chapter 3: On a Central Psychic Constellation;

The issues grappled with in this book (and I have only listed a few of them) have been engaged with in great depth and sensitivity and no reader who accompanies Dr. Silverman on this intellectual odyssey can come away without having his/her mind challenged by the scope of insight and original thinking contained in these disparate chapters. Each chapter features a mind in total engagement with an analytic idea that troubles him, fascinates him and will not let him rest until he has learnt all that can be learnt from the intellectual encounter. I will focus briefly on only two or three such issues: (1) in a delightful presentation of a four year girl who suddenly develops an anti-Chinese prejudice based on the confusion of vagina and China Dr. Silverman shows us what alert psychoanalytic sleuthing in the clinical vineyards of childhood imagination can stumble upon and discover.

(2) In a most significant contribution to Psychoanalytic developmental psychology Dr Silverman suggests that there is a central

psychic constellation that is already a stable entity as early as age 3 or 4. In other words the ego is already quite stable in its identity as it looks back, so to speak, on the achievements of the first years of preoedipal development and looks ahead to the challenges of Oedipal development relatively secure in its capacity to manage nascent triadic complexity as competently as it has engaged with the dyadic.

(3) In his study of two homosexual women analyzed from age 9 Dr. Silverman shows us how unique and varied are the dynamics of each patient, suggesting that homosexuality, like heterosexuality, emerges out of a complex polymorphous sexual matrix before it differentiates into each unique expression that clinicians encounter. To pigeonhole or categorize homosexuality, or indeed heterosexuality, too narrowly may well diminish their richness and complexity, in the service of a limiting and even prejudiced nosology. I have merely scratched the surface of the riches of this book in these introductory remarks: like letters of introduction in "the old days" I hope they serve as character references and assurances that will commend the depth and quality of this brilliant book to the reader and make her/him eager to make its acquaintance. It is my considered conviction that such an informed reader will not only not be disappointed, but will be deeply informed and moved by the encounter.

CONTENTS

Section I:

---

*Psychoanalytically Informed
Early Intervention*

CHAPTER 1:

THE USE OF THE DEVELOPMENTAL PROFILE FOR THE PRELATENCY CHILD

Martin A. Silverman, M.D. and Peter B. Neubauer, M.D.
[from: Chapter 18 of Kanzer, M. Ed, (1971). *The Unconscious Today.*]

APPLICATION OF THE PROFILE

During the past two years we have been applying Anna Freud's Developmental Profile as a tool for organizing information in a long-term study of eight preschool children. Our eventual purpose is to try to construct an outline of the child's functioning at this period of life. The use of the profile enables us to pinpoint the areas of development for which appropriate data are already available, while at the same time exposing the areas that are as yet uncharted or require further exploration. Thus we consider the profile to be more than a mere instrument for data organization. We expect it to lead us to see important new correlations between psychic structure and functioning which clarify our basic understanding and assumptions. This, in turn, should suggest new questions to help us test metapsychology and review clinical findings within the framework of psychoanalytic theory.

Anna Freud's profile in Normality and Pathology in Childhood (1965) provides an over-all system of organization but leaves the future detailing to be determined according to the particular development period that is assessed. Over the years, the profile has been applied to various age groups, and appropriate modifications have been proposed to take account of the specific aspects of each developmental phase. In the case of the preschool child, however, because development proceeds in a series of small but significant steps of ever increasing complexity, many more than the usual number of details will have to be added if the profile is to carry the requisite information to allow us to draw the "developmental line" for this period.

Perhaps the most fruitful effect of our use of the profile so far has been the search for a new ordering of data that in the past has been subsumed under clinical considerations or in the discussion of the dynamic processes. A closer look, demanded by the outline, gave focus to new areas of exploration. Even at this comparatively early stage in our project, the material we have gathered has already suggested a number of topics for a fuller profile; for example, the area of individual variation in developmental progression, or differential reaction to different environmental stimulation, and fantasy-action balance. We needed to add the topic of affect because we have found it to be a major factor in the clinical diagnostic summary; the mood swing, elation or affective restriction, the depressive quality, and the level of anxiety appear to be significant orientation points for the statement of normality and pathology.

One topic which seems to be fundamental to the success of the entire project is the evaluation of the information sources, The younger the child, the more we are dependent on information from other than clinical sources, i.e., parents and teachers, etc., to give us the developmental history and the child's relationship to the environment in which he grows. The clinical interview and direct observation of the child, no matter how carefully undertaken and even when conducted over long periods of time, by themselves cannot give us enough data for a developmental assessment. Nor is the information available to us from therapy sufficient for the purpose, since at this age analytic treatment of the child has usually only just begun. Even when therapy can reveal the major constellations of conflicts, it cannot supply data on other aspects of development. The question, "What kind of information can be provided by which source?" therefore becomes a central issue, and a systematic appraisal of the data that each of the various sources of information could be expected to contribute to the development profile is essential.

In the course of our studies, we have found the developmental differences between boys and girls during the preschool period to be much greater than suspected. We therefore evaluated the available information indicating these differences in order to determine how they contribute to later phallic and oedipal formation. Significant differences were discovered in symptom clustering and rates of development. Variation of ego function and preferences in channelization were so revealing that we decided to make an assessment of sex characteristics before the phallic phase. The existence of significant sex differences during the preschool period obviously has important implications affecting the evaluation of criteria for the respective developmental expectations of boys and girls In the present paper, however, we will deal with these topics only insofar as they relate to that area we have selected for preliminary discussion here: namely, the progression-regression balance.

The very aim of the profile, to assess pathology and normality against a yardstick of development, constitutes a direct challenge to our ability to understand the process of regression, fixation, and progression. For our inherent difficulties in diagnosing the preschool age group stem precisely from the fluidity of the child's psychic organization during this period and from our consequent inability to make predictions. Certainly, where disorders are severe, diagnostic statements can be made, but when these statements are checked against the child's developmental capacity, new questions immediately arise for which at present no diagnostic category exists.

A fuller knowledge of the progression-regression balance is thus a prerequisite for valid developmental assessment.

Just as it was the application of the profile that originally pointed up the need for further studies in many areas, so the results of our exploration have, in their turn, indicated a need for the profile's enlargement to accommodate the new information. ft is not our intention, however, to. formulate specific recommendations at this stage of our project. The notes which follow are therefore in the nature of preliminary formulations and require further testing, not only by the study of more children but, more important, by the continued assessments of the same children throughout each succeeding phase of their development. Only when we are sure of what constitutes significant data in each phase of development, only when we know the range of individual variations, will we be in a position to make recommendations for the expansion of the profile.

EVALUATION OF DEVELOPMENTAL PROGRESSION AND REGRESSION

Anna Freud (1945) has demonstrated that diagnostic assessment of children is most meaningful when carried out according to developmental rather than symptomatic considerations. The hallmark of psychological health in the child is not freedom from symptoms, but optimal progression toward mature drive- and ego organization. Our longitudinal study at the Child Development Center of eight children between three and four-and-a-half years of age, in which we have been using Anna Freud's Diagnostic Profile (A. Freud, 1962, 1963, 1965; and Nagera, 1963), has led us to consider some of the difficulties in applying this developmental approach. to the very young child.

The following discussion will be limited to consideration of some general questions concerning the use of the Diagnostic Profile with

6

this age group and is divided into two parts: (1) discussion of the issues involved in identifying the pattern of over-all developmental progression in the very young child, and (2) examination of the specific problems involved in assessing fixation and regression at this age. It is our belief that the developmental fluidity characteristic of these children is responsible for most of the diagnostic difficulties and uncertainties. Methodological capacity to map out these fluid patterns facilitates the more specific tasks of identifying and evaluating the significance of fixations and regressions.

THE PROBLEM OF ASSESSING
DEVELOPMENTAL PROGRESSION

Development in the three- to four-and-a-half-year-old child is characterized by rapid, fluctuating changes in an evolving and as yet incompletely formed psychic apparatus. There is wide individual variation in drive and autonomous ego endowment and in rates of maturation and development. Patterns of drive and ego organization are characterized by shifting reorganization so that new configurations are observable at the same time as derivatives of previous drive- and ego-configurations are still in evidence. Development does not proceed in a smooth progression but in a series of irregular and overlapping progressive and regressive movements. Some investigators suggest that the pattern of expression of the various zonal consolidations is not only highly specific to each individual child, but is predetermined at birth. As Greenacre (1954a) has pointed out:

We are used to speaking of the oral, anal, phallic and genital phases as though they were a series of fairly discrete stages in a regular timetable of successive development. It is certainly recognized, however, that there is a great overlap in these phases of development, and that a certain flexibility of the schedule increases the adaptability of the organism.

It may be, however, that this overlap is even greater than we have customarily thought: that in fact all lines of activity are present in some degree at birth or soon thereafter, but rise to a peak of maturational activity at different rates of speed. It is the maturational peak and its relative prominence in the total activity of the individual organism which marks the phase; and the succession of the maturational peaks which creates the appearance of a succession of phases [p. 20].

The observer of the three- or four-year-old is confronted by a fuzzy picture of overlapping and oscillating organizational patterns, in contrast to the relatively clearer picture available at a later stage of development, when time has smoothed out the peaks and troughs of the various developmental curves. The younger the child at the time of observation, the less available (as a rule) are data on the forthcoming changes and crystallizations of the oedipal phase, and the more multipotential are the evolving organizational patterns. Autonomous ego endowments have not in all cases reached a stage of sufficient expression for their adequate appraisal. Stimulus-response patterns, preferred receptive and expressive channels, and Anlagen of later defensive modes are not always clearly definable. Developmental assessment bearing reasonable predictive value can nevertheless be carried out with a method combining historical, cross-sectional, and longitudinal approaches.

HISTORICAL DATA REQUIRED FROM THE PARENTS

Paradoxically, information on the first three years after birth is even more essential at three-and-a-half than it is at a later age, when greater crystallization has taken place and investigators can reconstruct earlier trends from their later effects. Hence, inferences drawn from direct observation and from data supplied by parents and teachers of necessity play a larger role in assessment than might be the case at a later time. Moreover, although psychoanalytic investigation has been carried out with a number of very young children, providing important data about early fantasies, object relations, defenses, etc., there are limitations to the investigator's ability to draw reconstructive conclusions from therapeutic work with very young children, so that it is worthwhile and necessary to supplement knowledge derived from analytic investigation with that derived from direct observation (Kestenberg, 1956).

From the parents, we need information on constitutional factors, the environmental circumstances within which the Anlagen have developed, and the modifications that have evolved. If we have these data, we can draw inferences from certain quantitative or qualitative variations which might present themselves in different areas. For example, evidence of a significant intensification or shift in certain patterns in response to specific maturational or environmental influences will alert us to possible points of fixation which threaten to impede progress or to persist as potential attraction points for future regressive movements. The following clinical example illustrates how early variations can serve as danger signals of later disorders.

F., a three-and-a-half-year-old boy, had been a subject in an infant study, the report of which included an isolated reference to low frustration tolerance, motor perseveration, and toeing outward in the earliest months. F.'s parents also disclosed that, between the ages of 10 and 24 months, he had sporadically become very interested in opening and closing doors, and that between two and two-and-a-half years he had a tendency, when tired or irritable, to bump into walls and trip over his feet. These data, extracted from a profusion of historical information, alerted us to the possibility of an organic disturbance, despite the absence of any clinical evidence of organicity at three-and-a-half years. Careful observation and study over the next six months revealed a neurologically very mild but developmentally highly significant aphasic disorder. Painstaking identification of the specific components of this disorder not only clarified certain puzzling aspects of F.'s development, but led to specific remedial intervention in the educational process.

After early historical data have been gathered, the next step is to compile a cross-sectional profile of current patterns of functioning. Inasmuch as this can be done with the combination of observation, interview, and psychological testing ordinarily used in child-study today, no detailed discussion of the process is required here.

STUDY OF THE MUTUAL INFLUENCES
IN THE PARENT-CHILD INTERACTION

Because of the preschool child's special vulnerability to influence from his objects, we have to pay particular attention to his environment and to his object relationships. The ego's attitude to the id, while derived from multiple sources, is still significantly related to the need to comply with parental standards of behavior and performance in order to ensure the love of the primary objects. It is necessary, therefore, to scrutinize the interaction between the child and his objects so as to elucidate all the factors which influence the balance between progressive and regressive forces. We need, for instance, to determine the way in which parents ally themselves with their children's progressive and regressive trends. Parents do not react the same way to different lines of activity in their children. They encourage advancement in some areas and exert an infantilizing effect in others. They also have varying reactions to the same lines of development during different phases in the child's development (M. Kris, 1957). The following case illustrates how information on the psychological state of the parents during different phases of their child's development assisted us in pinpointing developmental interferences influencing the child's later structural configurations.

C. , a three-year-old girl, presented a pattern of marked ego restriction, overcontrol, unusually intense visual activity, and eating disturbances which persisted (with some modification) over the next The early impression of inactivity resulting from not enough information and lack of appreciation of the style of ego functioning was thus rectified on the basis of additional information gathered during the second investigative period.

A final comment on the interpretation of the data is required. It is clear that the conclusions we can draw during this stage of the child's life are in the nature of inferences about certain trends within the over-all developmental timetable. Awareness of these trends guides the investigator in determining the areas in which additional or more specific data are required before more specific diagnostic conclusions bearing predictive value can be reached. Assessment, for this age group in particular, is not a static process, but is always a dynamic and open one, in which each new clarification points the way toward the gathering of additional information which will illuminate still another aspect of the child's development.

THE PROBLEM OF ASSESSING FIXATION AND REGRESSION

As has been stated, manifestations of early drive- and ego-configurations coexist in this age group with those reflecting higher levels of organization. Delays in development, persistence of early forms, and regression to earlier levels signify pathological trends only when they interfere with the development of the total personality, or of some of its components, so as to impede adaptational processes. It should be emphasized that the individual timetable of development needs to be mapped out before meaning can be ascribed to any cross-sectional data. For children in the three- to four-and-a-half-year age group, general norms of progression exist only in very broad terms, and the range of individual variation is so wide that each child must, to a large extent, serve as his own control.

Examination of the correspondence among the different rates of progression of the various lines of development (A. Freud, 1963), allowing for each child's individual range of progressive/regressive fluctuation, provides us with a picture of the degree of evenness or unevenness of developmental progression. Significant developmental unevenness alerts us to the possibility of defects in ego equipment, which are not necessarily congenital, as "equipment is not a static but a dynamic force" (E. Kris, quoted by M. Kris, 1957), maturational imbalances, environmental interferences which partially inhibit development, and fixation of regression. Uniform lag in progression of all modalities indicates an unusually slow, although not necessarily foreboding, rate of over-all progression.

Fixation points need to be identified, as Nagera (1964) has pointed out, not only in terms of the developmental level involved, but with regard to the specific form that the fixation takes:

> We speak of fixation to a given component instinct, to a phase of libidinal and aggressive development, to a type of object choice, to a type of object relationship, and to a traumatic experience. We further know that all these different forms of fixations are expressions of similar and somewhat equivalent phenomena.... Nevertheless, our clinical experience shows that there are differences among our cases with respect to where it is that the emphasis is placed in terms of fixation [p. 225].

Arrest of or disturbance in the development of particular ego functions is particularly important to identify because the clinical significance of a fixation depends in large measure upon the degree to which critical ego processes are implicated or affected.

The situation is similar with regard to the assessment of regressive movements. Again, we must concern ourselves with the specific form the regression takes. Regressive shifts involve specific component instincts, drives, forms, aspects of object relations, and ego functions. Identification of the specific aspects involved is necessary for an adequate understanding of the impact of the regression upon over-all functioning and progressive development. As with fixation, the structural aspects of the regressive process are most crucial. Regression in critical ego functions seems to exert the most deleterious effect upon over-all progression and are less well tolerated by the organism than regressive shifts primarily involving drive forms.

THE PROBLEM OF EVALUATING THE SIGNIFICANCE OF FIXATIONS

Adequate over-all progression does not require complete advance from earlier levels of organization to higher ones, nor is such total reorganization necessary (perhaps it is not even desirable). There is always partial adherence of drive energies to earlier' forms as the bulk of the available cathectic quantity moves on to new levels of organization. Anna Freud (1965) mentions "a specific characteristic of drive development, namely . . . that while libido and aggression move forward from one level to the next and cathect the objects which serve satisfaction on each stage no station on the way is ever fully outgrown" (p. 95; italics added). Fixation to early levels of organization can be considered pathological only when the economic effect is so great as to impede the general progressive movement of drive- and ego organization. Viewed in developmental terms, the pathological effect of fixations resides in the fact that "they have the function of binding and retaining drive energies and . . . thereby impoverish later drive functioning and object relations" (p. 96).

Not all fixations, however, exert such a depleting effect upon drive and ego development. Drive energy can persist in part at early stages of organization without necessarily preventing the child from functioning generally at age- and phase-adequate levels. Miss Freud (1954b) describes well-developed children of four or five, who are clean, intelligent, responsive, humorous, in excellent contact with their environment, with more than the beginnings of character and personality development. Their whole demeanor leaves no doubt that they have reached the phallic phase, or even entered the prelatency period. Yet, their favorite indulgence before going to sleep, when relaxing in tiredness, or under emotional strain, remains thumb-sucking. They may be solving a difficult intellectual or emotional problem at one moment, and be found the next with their finger in their mouth, soothing and lulling themselves in repetitive sucking activity. That part of their libido has been left behind at the oral stage is obvious. Yet this fixation seems to interfere remarkably little with the progress of libido development [p. 27].

In other words, fixation to early levels can exist without significantly influencing over-all progression. It is not enough, therefore, to diagnose the presence of a fixation in the very young child. We have to determine how and to what extent it interferes with adaptation and over-all development before we can determine whether or not a fixation can be considered pathological.

We would tend to agree, in fact, with Nagera's (1963) interesting speculation that, although in general the existence of strong fixation points is a potentially dangerous situation, there can be instances in which the attractive pull exerted by such strongly cathected points serves the forces of progression. Where massive regression involving the ego as well as the drives has led to disorganization of the whole personality, fixation points in stages of development higher than those to which the regressive movement has led may exert a forward pull on the libido and thus promote recovery. The fixations would thus prove to have been highly advantageous to the ultimate development of the personality.

THE PROBLEM OF EVALUATING THE SIGNIFICANCE OF REGRESSION

The problem of assessing the significance of regressive movements, i.e., return to earlier forms and modes, is an even more complicated one. First, it is often difficult to distinguish between persistence of earlier patterns into subsequent phases and regression to a previous phase. Then too, current conflicts and behavior can sometimes spread over from a dominant area to a related one so as to produce a spurious picture of apparent regression. An excellent example of this situation is provided by Frijling-Schreuder (1966):

A child negotiating with his mother about bowel control may be obstinate in regard to eating as well. In that case, we need not think that it has regressed to the oral level. We only diagnose regression to the oral level if the process of eating has the same libidinal cathexis as it had in the oral phase [p. 3651].

Backsliding of a function or modality from a higher to a lower level of organization does not necessarily indicate that pathological forces are at work. To a greater or lesser extent, regression is a mechanism which is regularly employed by the ego in the service of mastery (E. Kris, 1952). There is, of course, great variation from one child to another in the range of progressive/regressive swing consistent with healthy over-all progression. Some children progress relatively smoothly, with little apparent regression, even in fantasy, while other children regularly respond to maturational or environmental stress with wide regressive swings, from which they rebound to new heights. There are instances in which failure (i.e., inability) to regress in appropriate fashion portends difficulty later on. The following is an example of a child who regressed in response to stress, only to rebound to new ego achievements.

Re, the youngest child in her family, learned at age three that her mother was pregnant. There was no immediate behavioral effect discernible, but during the final trimester of her mother's pregnancy, she became increasingly whiny, clinging, and babyish, and lost some of her capacity for independent functioning. She grew more and more interested in the idea of a baby in "mommy's tummy" and began to wonder about babies in general. After the birth of her brother (when she was three and a half), her anxiety about separation disappeared, she became active as mother's helper in caring for the baby, and succeeded in recovering her ability to function independently. Not only did she regain the ground she had lost in the previous three months; the investigator was impressed with her improved social adaptation, newly acquired ability to draw representational human figures, and significantly increased intellectual curiosity and interest. Psychological testing revealed a striking cognitive advance and an increase of 11 1.Q. points over the score obtained before the pregnancy. Presumably, identification with the feeding, caring mother and a widening and sharpening of the body image (Schilder, 1950), the result of her thoughtful observation of her mother's progressive body changes and production of a baby from her insides, facilitated not only recovery from the libidinal and ego regression that had taken place, but advance to even higher levels of ego functioning.

THE ADAPTIVE FUNCTION OF REGRESSION

In some children, it would seem that a period of regression regularly precedes any new advance, a pattern which can be viewed as one developmental variation among many. Fraiberg (1952) reported such a case. Many children regress temporarily when confronted with an unfamiliar situation without showing any later untoward effects, so that this period of temporary reversion to old forms can be viewed as a harmless and, perhaps, beneficial preamble to mastery of new situations:

> Children in new situations may study the situation for a while without active participation. In this period many regressive autoerotic activities can be observed, thumb sucking, genital play, etc. At the same time, the child is busy exploring what is going on. Other children may throw themselves actively into new situations, but this active participation does not always lead to the best ultimate adaptation. In young children it often means identification with the aggressor and the underlying anxiety may lead to failure [Frijling-Schreuder, 1966, p. 365].

The children in our study at the Child Development Center showed various responses to entering nursery school for the first time. The vignette which follows illustrates the adaptive function of regression in a new and unfamiliar situation.

J., a boy of nearly four, during his first three months in the nursery school appeared to be lethargic, passive, and withdrawn. He declined to take part in group activities, spent a considerable amount of time lying down "resting," and altogether gave the appearance of a passive observer. As time wore on, he became increasingly active and assertive, began to woo one of the girls in a masculine, phallic-assertive way, and proved to possess unusually fine capacities for reasoning and problem-solving. At the end of the year, he was the only one of the group to be advanced beyond the next level to the oldest group, where he was observed to be the early leader in constructive and intellectual projects.

ASSESSMENT OF THE EFFECT OF A
REGRESSIVE MOVEMENT

We must follow the course of a regressive movement over a reasonable period of time before concluding that it has exerted a deleterious effect on the child's over-all development. Reversion to old modes of drive- or ego organization may represent temporary retreat from insoluble conflict followed by resumption of forward movement at a more propitious time. It may represent mobilization by the ego of old tools to assist in attempts to solve current conflicts. A newly strengthened ego may reach back in order to deal anew with earlier conflicts whose resolution had previously been beyond its power. This new attempt, which can be conceived of as a spontaneous effort at self-healing, may lead to the ego's further enrichment. The child who is unable to regress because of restriction of the ego's freedom of mobility suffers as much from ego weakness as the child who automatically swings into a deep regressive movement in response to stress. In either case, we are observing an ego lacking in resiliency, one bound to respond automatically, an ego which is passive, hence, weak (Rapaport, 1951a).

L., a three-and-a-half-year-old girl entering the nursery school, moved immediately into active participation in the program and seemed lively and competent. It gradually became apparent, however, that her display of competence and forthright independence was largely defensive in nature, serving to vigorously suppress an intense yearning for an exclusive, dependent relationship with the teacher, which conflicted with the role she was required TO play within her family. Her inability to depart from the stylized behavioral pattern that fulfilled her neurotic requirements for inner tranquility and supported her ideal self-image prevented her from forming close relationships with her teachers and peers. She remained somewhat on the fringe of the group, except when she could assume the role of a competent, matronly, caring figure, and consistently impressed all observers as inappropriately old beyond her years.

Identification of these various patterns of regression, each with its own diagnostic implications, depends upon observation of their effect upon the movement of other lines during and following the regressive period. Speaking of childhood development, Anna Freud (1965) says:

> In our clinical appraisal of regressions as ongoing processes, it is almost impossible to determine whether in a given child's case the dangerous step from temporary to permanent regression has already been taken or whether spontaneous reinstatement of formerly reached levels is still to be expected. Thus far, I know of no criteria for this, even though the entire decision about the child's abnormality may depend on this distinction [p. 106].

The significance of regressive movements can be judged according to three criteria: (1) reversibility of the regression; (2) the extent to which the various aspects of the personality are involved in the regression; and (3) the degree to which adaptation is affected by the regression (Frijling-Schreuder, 1966). Again, as with fixation, the significant issues revolve about economic (quantitative) and adaptive factors. The question of whether a regressive movement exerts a pathological effect on development depends upon the extent to which essential functions are implicated, the quantity of energies mobilized in the movement, and the degree to which the movement reverses itself. Hence, we can speak, in this regard, of "the economy of regression."[1]

Precocious development of certain functions to higher levels can also lead to pathological development (Hartmann, 1954). The role of premature activation of ego defenses against instinctual forces

---

[1] An apt term suggested by Miss Annie Hermann in a personal communication.

in disposing the child to later obsessional illness is well known (Freud, 1913b). The case of L. , quoted above, illustrates the disturbing effect that precocious independence can exert upon object relations.

Progression in the three- to five-year-old child is fluid and highly individual. It is therefore difficult to distinguish in this period between interference in over-all development and transient manifestations of patterns of response to stress characteristics of the psychic apparatus at particular points in the individual's developmental timetable. Applying the Developmental Profile to prelatency children, therefore, is an exceedingly complex task. The difficulty is highlighted by Anna Freud's (1965) remarks on progression and regression:

> An individual child's capacity to function on a comparatively high level is no guarantee that the performance will be stable and continuous. On the contrary: occasional returns to more infantile behavior have to be taken as a normal sign. . . . In fact, what we regard as surprising are not the relapses but occasional sudden achievements and advances. . . . convenient as such transformations may be for the child's environment, the diagnostician views them with suspicion and ascribes them not to the ordinary flow of progressive development but to traumatic influences and anxieties which unduly hasten its normal course. According to experience, the slow method of trial and error, progression and temporary reversal is more appropriate to healthy psychic growth [p. 99].

CHAPTER 2:

THE GROWTH OF LOGICAL THINKING— PIAGET'S CONTRIBUTION TO EGO PSYCHOLOGY[1]

[from 1971). *Psychoanalytic Quarterly*, 40:317–341]

For nearly half a century, Jean Piaget and his co-workers have been studying the line of development in the child from simple perceptual patterns and stimulus-bound, automatic, rigid, unidirectional motor behavior to the mobile, abstract, hypothetico-deductive operations that characterize mature intelligent thought. They have been able to demonstrate, through a series of brilliant observations and experiments, that this developmental achievement occurs by means of a complex epigenetic sequence in which each developmental stage is derived from and represents the outer limit of equilibrium of the previous stage.

The emphasis in Piagetian theory is on progressive coördination and internalization of experimental actions so that they become increasingly reversible, mobile, and independent of the immediate perceptual field. The central role ascribed to action is, in fact, an essential feature of Piagetian theory. Piaget emphasizes that it is through his actions that the child relates to the world and comes to understand it. He has made an essential contribution to epistemology by demonstrating that intellectual development does not consist in

---

[1] Inhelder, Bärbel, and Piaget, Jean: *The Early Growth of Logic in the Child: Classification and Seriation*. New York: The Norton Library, W.W. Norton & Co., Inc., 1969, 302 pp. (Originally appeared in French in 1959 with the title, *La Genese des structures logique elementaire: Classifications et seriations*.) English translation by E.A. Lunzer and D. Papert.

differentiations and reorganizations in the perceptual sphere alone, which had been the prevailing view prior to his researches. He has shown that although dependent upon maturational and social-experiential factors and intimately connected with perception, intellectual development can be described in terms of step-by-step re-equilibration of action patterns that are progressively internalized, abstracted, and coordinated. He defines thought, as did Freud, as internalized, symbolic trial action.

A brief summary of the over-all epigenetic sequence provides a contextual framework within which the work to be reviewed in this essay may be considered.[2]

The Sensorimotor Period (birth to 18 months)

The earliest period, extending to the second half of the second year, is characterized, according to Piaget, by the acquisition of what he terms 'sensorimotor intelligence'. The infant who was able to approach the world at first only by way of minimally coordinated, reflex perceptual and motor behavior develops the ability during this period to utilize rapid, experimental displacement of internalized mental representations for exploring the world about him.

Piaget divides this first period into six stages, the first of which subsumes the initial few weeks after birth. The neonate is equipped with perceptual and motor apparatuses that function in close unison with one another and are organized along hereditary, reflex lines. During the first months after birth, under the rhythmic impulsion of instinctual need, he comes into passive and active contact with a world that is not yet differentiated from

---

[2] In drawing this outline, I am largely following Piaget's summary presented in *The Psychology of Intelligence* (Paterson: Littlefield, Adams & Co., 1960; first published as *La Psychologie de l'intelligence* in 1947). Relevant sections of John A. Flavell's *The Developmental Psychology of Jean Piaget* (Princeton: D. Van Nostrand Co., 1963) provided welcome clarification of difficult or unclear points.

his own body. He is a long way from appreciating that the world consists of finite objects and identifiable phenomena, which he can comprehend, classify, and, to a significant extent, master.

During the course of his repeated and, in suitable circumstances, relatively consistent environmental contacts, sensorimotor habit patterns emerge (Stage 2) which, although they possess a certain degree of adaptive flexibility (accommodation), consist in relatively rigid, stimulus-bound, egocentric, repetitive actions, that show little capacity for successive variation. Through repeated practice, they are performed with increasing efficiency and skill (reproductive assimilation). As the elementary habit patterns evolve, they assimilate to themselves new experiential elements, so long as the latter resemble elements which are already familiar, and, at the same time, modify themselves somewhat so as to accommodate to these new elements. The habit patterns thus extend beyond their earliest objects to embrace new ones as well (generalizing assimilation). Situations begin to be discriminated from one another (recogitory assimilation) via these partially exploratory actions, which are intimately associated with perceptual experience.

The third stage begins with the visual-prehensive (eye-hand-mouth) coördination that appears between three and six months, most often at four and a half months. The infant becomes able to deliberately repeat actions connected with interesting events, situated increasingly farther from his own body, in the attempt to stimulate their reproduction. Although it can be demonstrated that this attempt does not yet reflect true means-end behavior, but represents a kind of reproductive assimilation, it does connote increasing generalization, coördination, and expansion of the field of perceptual-motor activity beyond the near space surrounding the child's body.

The complex sensorimotor schemata of the third stage become capable, at eight to ten months of age, of coördination among themselves so that some can serve as means and others as ends. At

23

this level, for example, a child for the first time will remove a screen placed before a desired object in order to retrieve the object. From this it can also be inferred that objects have acquired permanence of existence transcending their continuous availability in the immediate perceptual field. The child can now decide upon a goal before he has chosen the means for its attainment, which provides him with greatly improved mobility and generalizing ability in carrying out his sensorimotor investigations.

The fifth stage is marked by two related advances. First, the child's newly acquired investigative capacities are utilized for active experimentation, in which novelty is no longer merely tolerated accommodatively but is actively sought. In the second place, the child until now has only been able to apply familiar schemata to new objects, as though attempting to understand them by determining which schemata are applicable to them. For example, when presented with a new object, he might have grasped it, struck it, shaken it, bitten it. Now, however, utilizing his ability to coordinate means-end procedures for investigative purposes, he is capable of utilizing truly intelligent trial-and-error experimentation in order not only to apply familiar means but even to devise new means with which he might achieve his objectives. He might, for example, not only set aside a screen barring him from access to a desired object, but draw the object to him by means of the base on which it rests or pull on a string to which it is attached.

In the final stage, reaching its equilibrial peak somewhere in the middle of the second year, the child becomes capable of internalizing his active experimentation so that he is less bound to the perceptual field. This achievement derives from the ability to manipulate symbolic mental images in place of the actual objects which they represent. The child is now increasingly able to solve problems by internal displacement of mental images rather than by trial-and-error procedures with actual objects. The speed and range of problem-solving maneuvers are enormously increased. An eighteen-month-old child, for example, who has not had prior opportunity to experiment with sticks as possible implements with which he can obtain otherwise inaccessible objects, quickly perceives that they can be used for such a purpose. This contrasts sharply with the younger child's inability to make such a discovery without actual trial-and-error experimentation with the actual objects.

Piaget is not able to account fully for the appearance of symbolic mental images at this particular point in the child's development. One factor seems to be the capacity for imitative analogy. Piaget describes, for example, a child who interrupted his unsuccessful attempt to widen a matchbox opening by random action, looked carefully at the opening for a while, and then imitatively opened and closed his mouth. He defines symbolic imagery (or at least its formal aspects) as internal imitation growing out of external imitation and symbolic play.

The Preconceptual Period (18 months to 4 years)

The availability of symbolic imagery contributes to the beginnings of language and ushers in the period of symbolic or preconceptual intelligence extending from about eighteen months to about four years of age. With the aid of mental imagery, the child begins to form notions of the things with which he comes into contact and attaches these notions to the words he is learning to use. His mental images are closely tied to the actual perceptual configurations they represent. There is little understanding of the immutability of objects and relations over time and space as the permanence of individual objects does not yet extend beyond the field of immediate action and as there is not yet awareness that individual objects and phenomena exist in multiples and groups beyond his ken (egocentricity). To a two to three-year-old child, for example, it is not clear whether several objects of the same kind encountered during the course of a day are several individuals in the same class or a single individual that continually reappears. Objects appear to change their size and shape when they are viewed for a second time from a new perspective.

This period is characterized by perceptual collections rather than concepts. Reasoning, based on incomplete dovetailing, is performed by means of analogies rather than deductions. The child in this phase is midway between sensorimotor functioning and conceptual thought. As he collects and organizes his impressions and experiences into complex groups, he moves increasingly farther from empirical sensorimotor experimentation and closer to conceptual thinking based upon principles of generality, inclusiveness, and exclusiveness.

Intuitive Thought (4 to 7 years)

The period from four to seven years is a transitional one in which the rigid, unidirectional preoperational thinking described above becomes increasingly flexible, mobile, and reversible. The child is still bound to perceptual referents in his thinking, but there is an important advance. Whereas in the past the child was perseveratively bound to the perceptual aspect upon which his attention initially had been centered, he is now capable of correcting the distortions produced by that centration (all perception involves distortions emanating from centration errors) by shifting attention to other aspects. With this capacity to make serial adjustments or 'intuitive regulations', the child is increasingly able to consider multiple relations, a capacity necessary for the construction of stable concepts.

The child in this transitional phase, however, can consider multiple relations consecutively but not simultaneously. When he shifts his attention from one aspect to another, he frees himself from the centration error produced by the first focusing procedure but, in centering upon the second aspect, he becomes subject to the distorting effect of the second centration and cannot keep firm hold on the first aspect. With his lack of simultaneous access to multiple facets and relations so that he can reciprocally compare them, he still is not capable of conserving the whole set while working with the elements contained within it. This leads to significant logical errors in his appraisal of the world.

These logical errors are demonstrable by means of simple experiments. The child is presented, for example, with twenty beads all of which, he acknowledges, are made of wood. Most of the beads are brown and the few remaining are white. When asked whether there are more brown or wooden beads, the child under seven almost invariably replies that there are more brown—because there are only a few white ones. He persists in this assertion even after it has been demonstrated to him that some remain after the brown ones have been removed, but that removal of the wooden beads leaves none behind. Piaget's explanation is that in centering upon the brown, the child in this age group irreversibly destroys the representation of the whole, so that only the white portion can be used for numerical comparison. Differentiation cannot be made between 'all' and 'some'.

Concrete Operations (7 to 11–12 years)

With the passage of time, the successive intuitive regulations utilized by the preoperational child eventually reach a point at which they suddenly become organized so that all the different viewpoints in a given system are coordinated reciprocally and reversibly. The child now has at his command a well-integrated, flexible cognitive system in which multiple relations can be considered simultaneously by means of mobile, reversible mental displacements and simple hypothetical deductive experiments that are free of the effects of perseverative, centristic distortion.

Thinking is decentered and organized into stable yet mobile systems, which are no longer dominated by the need for perceptual orientation. The 'whole' no longer ceases to exist while its constituents are being compared and manipulated. By means of 'anticipations and reconstitutions' *(The Psychology of Intelligence, p. 142)*, the child can now compare a present configuration with what has come before and can use the two to some extent to aid him in planning future action. The child's thinking is no longer fragmented and contradictory. Two classes can now be combined into a superordinate one containing them and a large class can be subdivided into several smaller ones. Thought is free to make detours without losing the original goal and the system is not altered by these detours. Nullification allows hypotheses to be tested and rejected, followed by a return to the original starting point.

Such mobile, reversible, systematically organized mental activities are termed 'operations' by Piaget. Such operations permit organization of objects and phenomena into orderly classes and groups. The child is now able to construct stable concepts of numerical relationship, time, and space.

The operations of this period, however, are limited in their range and scope. They can be applied only to the actual, concrete here-and-now. Problems involving displacements, transformations, and re-organizations of actual objects and phenomena can be solved and increasingly complex real life issues are mastered. But it is not until the next and final phase that the child will be able to apply his powers of reasoning not only to the real *hic et nunc,* but to go beyond it to contemplate the possible and potential. Furthermore, his grasp of properties and relations is not fully coordinated. The child, for example, who understands at seven or eight that the quantity of two identical balls of dough remains equal if the shape of one of them is modified, does not recognize until he is nine or ten that their weight remains identical or until the age of eleven or twelve that their volume has been unchanged by the modification in shape.

Formal Operations (adolescence to adulthood)

In contrast to the younger child who can only contemplate the real and actual, the reasoning of the adolescent, from eleven or twelve years on, is truly reflective, hypothetico-deductive, and propositional. The adolescent looks beyond the immediate to its potential implications. He does not confine himself to operations that organize elements in reality, but reflects upon the results of these operations so as to theorize as to the potential limits within which the actual elements exist. He no longer confines his mental activity to manipulating raw data of reality but, out of the results of his concrete operations, constructs higher order propositions (i.e., operations performed upon operations), the relations among which he can still further classify and examine. He has now freed himself from the perceptual links with actual reality to which he was formerly bound and is able to reason theoretically and speculatively. He is in a position not only to understand but to master his environment.

THE EARLY GROWTH OF LOGIC IN THE CHILD

With this over-all outline in mind, let us turn to The Early Growth of Logic in the Child. In this volume, Inhelder and Piaget do not present anything that significantly departs from the basic Piagetian theory of 1947 that I have outlined. They do offer, however, a detailed, richly illustrated account of the steps through which the three to eleven-year-old child passes in his progress from pre-operational to concrete operational thinking, as epitomized in the development of logical classification and seriation. The book consists of a brief sixteen-page introduction and an equally brief fifteen-page concluding statement, between which is an account of the experiments carried out over an eight-year period upon which the conclusions are based. A total of 2,159 children participated; with an occasional exception, fewer than a hundred subjects took part in any one experiment.

The authors advise that it is sufficient to read the conclusions to understand the book, the remainder serving as reference material. My own recommendation would be to read the introduction, conclusions, and intervening experimental data in that order. A careful reading of the account of the experiments that were performed is well worth the effort as it greatly clarifies and illuminates the multiple facets of the complex, fascinating developmental sequence that is the subject of the book. I recommend it also for the beauty and simplicity of experimental design, so typical of Piaget's approach. The discerning reader will also be interested in assessing for himself whether the data support all the conclusions and whether alternative or additional inferences can be drawn.

The central thesis of the book is that—although maturational, linguistic, and perceptual factors play a role—the essential factor in the development of classification and seriation is the development, through progressive organizational re-equilibration, of operational structures out of sensorimotor schemata. No attempt is made to study maturational and linguistic factors, and their importance is disparaged and even questioned, a matter to which I will return. The perceptual factor, too, is relegated to a level of secondary importance. In the introduction, for example, one finds such statements as: 'The perceptual schema is never independent;

30

right from the start, perception is subordinated to action… Perceptions are no more than signals which enter into the construction of the schema (and they include proprioceptive signals)… In other words the subject does not perceive objects and his own movements separately; he perceives objects as things which are modified, or are capable of being modified by his own actions' (pp. 12–13). The area of inquiry is accordingly limited to the organizational aspects of classification and seriation. The results of the various experiments are interpreted in terms of progressive re-equilibrations in (progressively internalized) action schemata. Perception is depicted repeatedly as impeding progress and the need for thinking to free itself from perception is strongly emphasized.

Before proceeding to a critical evaluation of the book, I will summarize the authors' findings as to the stages in the development of classification and seriation (or at least of their formal, organizational aspect). Logical classification, they point out, depends upon differentiation between and coördination of the intension and extension of the members of hierarchically arranged groups or classes. Intension is defined as the properties common to the members of a class that set them off from non-members. Extension is defined as the set of individuals of which the group is comprised. Thus the former is a qualitative and the latter a quantitative factor.

Some appreciation of intension, based upon recognitive assimilation, is present from the start. The only kind of extension available before the age of five or six years, however, is that of spatial or graphic extension of a perceptual whole. Children in this age group, for example, when presented with figures of three shapes and three colors distributed variably among them, do not sort the figures in logical fashion. Instead, they make graphic collections or alignments according to spatial or temporal contiguity.

There is apposition according to similarity but in successive, linear fashion and with fluid criteria. When an initially chosen criterion for apposition is exhausted, the child merely shifts to a new criterion of similarity in order to continue the alignment. The original criterion is forgotten, so that is ceases to influence the structure of the alignment. The linear alignment that is formed is, therefore, unstable. In an attempt to preserve it, there is a strong tendency to shift into the use of more than one dimension and to construct a collective or complex object. The child may, for example, arrange the elements into 'a train' or 'a bridge'. There is oscillation between intension and extension which are neither clearly differentiated from nor coordinated with one another so that extension may determine intension.

Children from five or six to seven or eight years of age (Stage 2), however, shift from perceptually-bound, linear alignments to nongraphic collections. They differentiate small groups of elements according to similarities and differences and are increasingly free from graphic considerations as they do so. The key to understanding this development, according to the authors, is the progressive appearance of what they term 'hindsight and anticipation'. In constructing collections or collective objects, the Stage1 child performs each step independently of or in simple assimilation to the previous step, but all steps earlier than the previous step are forgotten and no longer available for consideration. As the child becomes increasingly capable of remembering and harking back to the first step in a sequence, however, he achieves coherence between the beginning and what comes after and is able to return to what he has already done and alter it in light of what has come after it. He begins to be able to look ahead and anticipate the result of his actions so that he can adhere to a set plan as he performs a series of trial and error displacements. In this manner, the child's experimental actions achieve the permanence and coherence that allow them to be increasingly internalized. He can shift back and forth in comparing the elements in a given set as he constructs a series or collection. This primitive form of reversibility consists in a series of regulations that will eventually evolve into mobile, reversible 'operations'.

It is only when the child has achieved a sufficient degree of hindsight and foresight to adhere to a set plan in a series of displacements that he begins to construct nongraphic collections based on similarity rather than on spatial or temporal configuration, to which he formerly had been bound by his inability to consider any groups the members of which could not be perceived simultaneously. The transition from Stage 1 to Stage 2 is shown in the following illustration:

> However, once it has been constructed, the total series obtained by continuing an alignment may induce the subject to go back and inspect the figure as a whole. When this happens, the relations are seen simultaneously, and the alterations which follow now lead the subject to Stage II, i.e., the juxtaposition of a number of qualitatively distinct logical collections. In this way, one of our subjects (Wal; 10), starts with a continued alignment involving a succession of different criteria (first a line of squares ending with a yellow square, then yellow figures ending with a semi-circle, then semi-circles of which the last is blue, and, finally, blue squares), but he then goes on to move the blue squares from the end of the row to the beginning. He therefore finishes with three homogeneous linear segments (squares, triangles and semi-circles). In spite of the linear arrangement, these are not far removed from non-graphic collections (p. 24).

There are two ways of constructing nongraphic collections, either of which may appear first but both of which are eventually employed. The child may start with small collections and combine them into larger ones with more general properties in common (the ascending method) or, alternately, he may start with larger collections and subdivide them into smaller ones (the descending method). What is typical of the Stage 2 child is that the ascending and descending series are not coordinated with one another. The construction of one type of series does not imply to the child that the reverse process is also possible. He carries out each process independently and does not appreciate their inverse relationship. The child at this preoperational stage can subdivide a collection, B, into two subcollections, A and A1, but this does not lead to the realization that both A and A1 are contained in B. For this reason, he is not capable of logical, hierarchical class-inclusion. The concepts of 'all', 'some', 'one', and 'none' are beyond his ken. There is greater accuracy and more precise grasp of relationships compared to the previous stage but intension and extension are not yet fully differentiated and coordinated. He has achieved hindsight and anticipation but can apply them only to simple sequences and not to transformations as a whole. If a child in this stage is confronted with multicolored beads, most of which are brown, or shown pictures of flowers, most of which are primulas, and asked whether there are more brown or wooden beads, or more primulas or other flowers, he makes logical errors because of false quantification of the predicate resulting from inability to define part/whole relations. This is the same experiment used earlier by Piaget to illustrate intuitive preoperational thinking.

As the child progresses in his ability to anticipate not only the static results of a unidirectional process, but to anticipate the stages of a sequence in reverse order as well, he moves toward Stage 3 (seven or eight to nine or ten years) which develops out of subdivisions of nongraphic collections. It is characterized by a mobile equilibrium in which the child can shuttle back and forth within a total classificatory system. Such mobility provides him with ability to appreciate unions and subdivisions simultaneously. The ability to add and subtract simultaneously and to recognize that one is the inverse of the other enables him to conserve the whole while he is manipulating parts of it. He can shift criteria so as to examine multiple relations within a set or system without losing sight of the whole system and, accordingly, becomes capable of constructing a hierarchical system of class-inclusions that is logically ordered and correctly quantified. The problem involving multicolored wooden beads or multiple kinds of flowers described above is now solved immediately and correctly. The transition from Stage 2 to Stage 3 is exemplified in the following illustration:

Pat (7; 3) still shows a trace of Stage II. 'Are all the red ones heavy?— *No, not all.*—Are all the heavy ones red?—*No, not at all, because all the red ones aren't heavy.*—Is it the same thing to say that all the red ones are heavy and that all the heavy ones are red?—*Yes ... Oh no! Because all the heavy ones are red and all the red ones aren't heavy.*—Are all the blue ones light?—*Yes.*—Are all the light ones blue?—*No, not all, there are light ones there also* (pile of red boxes)' (p. 87).

The Stage 3 child is relatively free from the distorting effects of the perceptual set and, able to coordinate his experimental mental actions, is free to choose criteria of classification that provide order and permanence through time and adhere to these criteria despite potential distorting influences. Utilizing freely mobile mental operations, he can organize the world into logical, hierarchical classes and relations. Intension and extension are differentiated and coordinated.

The development of logical seriation follows a course roughly parallel to that of classification. The major difference is that classification is significantly re-enforced by the syntactical structure of language, while seriation is less affected by language development and more closely related to perceptual cues.

A CRITICAL EVALUATION

Inhelder and Piaget conclude their presentation by conceding that maturation and education, including language, do play a part in the development of logical thinking but that 'the key to its explanation lies in the concept of equilibration, which is a wider notion than any of these and comprehends them all' (p. 292). They proceed to explain that their task has been limited to detailing the steps in the progressive coordination of actions that leads to operations, i.e., the organizational aspect of the development of logical thinking, and that they have not attempted to study the underlying forces that make such increasing organization possible. If this indeed has been their aim, then this reviewer's impression is that they have been brilliantly successful.

On the other hand, when I compare the introduction and conclusions and examine the book as a whole, I am forced to modify my appraisal. The aim given in the introduction is 'to elucidate the causal mechanism' (p. 1) of the evolution of logical structures and to assess the contributions of language, maturation, perceptual factors, and sensorimotor schemata. This goal has not been achieved. The relative importance of multiple factors cannot be assessed by examining but one of the factors.

Furthermore, a careful reading of the book leads to the impression that a polemic is contained within it. A hierarchical value system is constructed in which increasing organization of action patterns is placed in a position of overwhelming importance and all other factors are relegated to a level of minor significance. Memory, for example, is not even mentioned as a factor worthy of specific consideration. Perception, as I stated earlier, comes off particularly badly. It is repeatedly portrayed as structurally primitive, functionally subordinate to action, and serving to hinder progress by interfering with mobility of thought. The necessity for thought to overcome its dependence upon perceptual cues is repeatedly emphasized. A picture is not painted of a fluctuating balance of forces continually oscillating to and fro as it moves toward an increasingly stable dynamic state, but of an unceasing struggle on the part of action schemata to free themselves from the inhibiting effect of perception in order to realize their inherent disposition to increasingly organize themselves. The picture is of a struggle between a hero and a villain. Can it be that in concentrating on the sphere of action as the object of intense scrutiny inhelder and piaget have succumbed to a kind of centering error in which the relative importance of action schemata vis-à-vis other factors has been magnified and, hence, distorted? The experimental data presented in the book suggest, in fact, that perception and action are intimately connected and operate in a complex and conjoint fashion. There appear to be qualities of each that facilitate progression and other qualities of each that hinder it. Their effects at times appear to be additive and at other times they appear to oppose each other.

The distorting and perseverative effects of perceptual centering, which necessitate that thinking free itself from its initial dependence upon perceptual cues, have been amply demonstrated by Piaget and by others. What has not been the subject of scrutiny, although allusion is made to it in this volume, is that sensorimotor activity also has a perseverative and distorting effect. The alignments that children construct in the course of their attempts to order the phenomena confronting them, as Inhelder and Piaget have shown, for a long time are relatively weak and tend toward dissolution. The data suggest that the tendency toward dissolution arises in part from the perseverative, fragmenting effect of reproductive assimilation which operates conservatively. Once the child has accepted the task of dividing a number of objects into subgroups based on similarity, he tends to continue the process unidirectionally. When the original criterion of similarity is no longer available, accommodation is made to the altered circumstances and the motor sequence of combining 'similar' elements is maintained by simply shifting the criterion of 'similarity'. Thus, once the process of dissecting the whole into parts has been started, it is not simple matter to terminate and reverse the process in order to restore to the objects their original existence as a whole. The dissolution of the whole puts an obstacle in the way of logical classification, which consists essentially in ordering part-whole relations.

From the experimental data adduced in the early growth of logic in the child, it would seem that several avenues are open to the child by which he can extricate himself from his dilemma. On the one hand, he can ignore some of the elements available so as to reduce the field to one of smaller proportions, within which the fragmenting effect of reproductive assimilation can better be contained. An alternative method is to utilize perceptual cues to delimit the margins of the alignment being formed and bind the whole together. Some children shift from alignment to construction of complex objects. Some of the younger children delimit the field by accentuating either end of an alignment, e.g., by placing a vertical rectangle at either end of a series of otherwise horizontally placed rectangles. Some children utilize symmetry, invoke representational analogy ('that's a staircase'), or continually shift the direction of the alignment. They all seem to be utilizing perceptual aids in order to counteract the disorganizing effects of reproductive assimilation upon the whole set.

Such dependence on perceptual cues, however, subjects the child to all the distorting effects of perceptual centering. He must eventually devise a third means of preserving the whole, a means that will allow him to work with groups containing large numbers of members and that will not depend upon perceptual cues. This third means, of course, consists in hierarchical class inclusion through reversible mental operations. Until operational thinking has evolved, however, and, indeed, in order to facilitate its evolution, perception plays a critical role in maintaining the whole within which subgroups can be manipulated.

The importance of perception is repeatedly illustrated in the experimental data. Geometric shape, for example, is utilized as a stable referent for grouping long before color is made use of for that purpose (table ia, p. 64). Interestingly, this sequence resembles that of appreciation of conservation of quantity, a more plastic quality, before conservation of weight. (It would be interesting to repeat the experiments on classification of elements perceived by touch with the addition of texture to that of shape as an available criterion of differentiation.) apparently geometric shape, which lends itself to perceptual definition in more than one dimension, is a more useful referent than color, which is unidimensional. It would seem that for a long time form—possessing multiple perceivable qualities, the coordination of which indicates its finite existence—tends to be given preference as a stable referent for class inclusion. Young children seem to have difficulty recognizing that a color is an identifiable 'something' apart from the geometrically definable objects to which it is attached.

Another example is the group of experiments reported in chapter iii. In these experiments the weight of an object must be identified as the determinant of the depression of the pan of a scale on which it is placed rather than its size or color (see table iii, p. 88). Most children before nine years of age regularly invert the question 'are all the heavy ones red?' to 'are all the red ones heavy?', which is attributed by the authors to false quantification of the predicate (treating 'some' as though it were 'all'). the authors recognize that it is 'easier' (p. 88) for a child to think about a collection defined by color than by weight (which possesses even fewer graphic properties than color) and conclude that 'the development of understanding in relation to the true meaning of the quantifier "all" is very much bound up with imaginal properties in general' (p. 99). The data would seem to me to suggest the further possibility that the need for imagery may be related in part to the need to seize upon the most graphic criteria of differentiation possible, even at the price of loss of logical consistency, in order to protect the whole against the centrifugal effects of motor manipulations which have not yet achieved reversibility. The use of imagery, which provides graphic qualities to thought, regularly persists into adulthood as an aid to reasoning. We 'illustrate' our points, 'figure things out', construct diagrams and tables, etc.

In constructing matrices (chapter vi), the child at first achieves success by way of perceptual orientation. Only later does he shift to operational means of achieving that same success. In solving the problems involving the primulas, the children tend to place the flowers 'together' or 'in a field' in order to visualize them in a cohesive group (see pp. 94-97).

The hypothesis which I have been developing is that the achievement of reversibility, the essential element of operational structures, can be viewed in part in terms of overcoming the fragmenting effect upon the whole of the perseverative influence of assimilation; perception appears to play an important part in facilitating this development. In order to perform a series of alternating (i.e., reversible) ascending and descending movements, the child must be able to terminate the action of dividing and shift to the new action of uniting, which action must then be terminated so that return can be made to the action of dividing. Until this capability has been achieved, perceptual cues are utilized to help hold the parts together into a whole while they are being manipulated.

In other words, perception, despite its inherent distorting effects, serves an essential role in facilitating the development of a self-regulated, mobile, reversible operational equilibrium. It is just as accurate, therefore, to speak of the important role of perception in facilitating advance from rigid, unidirectional, perseverative reproductive assimilation to mobile operations as it is to speak of the importance of operational equilibria in freeing the child from the perseverative, distorting effect of perception. It would appear to me that exploration of the complex relations between perception and action is more fruitful than a tendentious discussion of the relative importance of one or the other.

Similarly, while the organizational aspect of intellectual development is undoubtedly of major significance, it is important also to study underlying and related factors and the relations among them. I would include among these: perception, motility, memory, education and other experiential influences, language, and, of enormous significance, drive energies and their vicissitudes, including sublimation. Defensive processes also deserve attention as they frequently exert a stimulating effect on intellectual development outlasting their period of activity. Multidimensional consideration of the mutual influences of multiple factors is as important for epistemology as is multidimensional consideration of the mutual influences of id, ego, and superego for psychoanalysis.

The Significance of Piaget's Work for Psychoanalysis

This brings us to a consideration of the relevance to psychoanalysis of the investigations of Piaget and his co-workers. Although Piaget does not address himself to the conflict situations that are the psychoanalyst's main concern, he has conducted careful research into an area of ego development that is of great theoretical and clinical import. His precise mapping out of the epigenetic sequences in the development of thought and cognition has made available to the psychoanalyst a collection of very valuable developmental data that deserves serious attention.

In the seventh chapter of the interpretation of dreams, Freud indicated that the efficiency of the mental apparatus derives from the increasing capacity to substitute 'exploratory thought-activity',[3] utilizing small quantities of mental energy in a flexibly mobile way,[4] for the imperative motor discharge of drive energies that is characteristic of the immature psyche. Considered from the economic and dynamic points of view, this shift consists in progressive taming and neutralization of drive energies by the evolving ego apparatuses, which then can utilize these energies for mastery of the drives in the service of adaptation to environmental demands, and for mastery of the environment in the service of gratification of the drives.

Considered from the structural point of view, this advance consists in the progressive differentiation, coordination, and organization of the various modalities that comprise the executive functions of the psychic apparatus. As Hartmann has pointed out,[5] there is a rank-order of ego functions with regard to the

---

[3] In addition, see Freud, *Formulations on the Two Principles of Mental Functioning* (1911). Standard Edition, XII.

[4] See, Merton Gill's clarification of the differentiation made by Freud between the presumably neutral, flexibly mobile (*mobil*) energy available in the system *Pcs* and the freely displaceable (*frei beweglich*) drive energy within the system *Ucs* (Topography and Systems in Psychoanalytic Theory. In: *Psychological Issues*, Vol. III, No. 2. New York: International Universities Press, 1963, pp. 13–14). Further on in his discussion, Gill reaches the following conclusion: 'It is probable that what Freud described as the function of the *Pcs cathexis* is what he later called the synthetic function of the ego. Presumably, most of the synthetic function is carried out by means of the "mobile" energy available to the ego, of which attention cathexisis only a part' (p. 74).

[5] See, Hartmann, Heinz: *Ego Psychology and the Problem of Adaptation* (1939). New York: International Universities Press, 1958, particularly pages 48–73.

degree to which they serve the adaptational needs of the organism. Within this, it is the synthetic function of the ego, says Hartmann, that eventually provides it with that degree of independent assertive will that frees it from regulation either by primitive drive demands or by the external world. The synthetic or integrative function consists, in turn, in the coordination of various ego apparatuses that appear at varying rates, so that as time goes on there appears a succession of increasingly efficient regulatory groups of coordinated functions at various levels of maturation.[6] The most efficient of these, according to Hartmann, consist in rational regulations by intelligent thought processes that take into account means-end relationships, causal relations, objectivation, abstract generalizations, and so on.

In the closing paragraphs of this monograph, Hartmann states: 'I stress again that no satisfactory definition of the concepts of ego strength and ego weakness is feasible without taking into account the nature and maturational stage of the ego apparatuses which underlie intelligence, will, and action' (Hartmann, Heinz: *Ego Psychology and the Problem of Adaptation* (1939). New York: International Universities Press, 1958, p. 107). manner in which the human organism frees itself from stimulus bound automatic reactivity and acquires a position of mastery over the inner and outer environments.[7]

---

[6] Hartmann states, for example, that 'ego development is a differentiation in which these primitive [reflex] regulating factors are increasingly replaced or supplemented by more effective ego regulations... Differentiation [of ego and id] progresses not only by the creation of new apparatuses to master new demands and new tasks, but also and mainly by new apparatuses taking over, on a higher level, functions which were originally performed by more primitive means' (Hartmann, Heinz: *Ego Psychology and the Problem of Adaptation*(1939). New York: International Universities Press, 1958, pp. 49–50).

[7] Hartmann puts it in the following way: 'Freud states that the ego, by interpolation of thought processes, achieves a delay of motor discharge. This process is part of an already discussed general evolution, namely, that the more differentiated an organism

Psychoanalytic theory rightfully emphasizes the transition from primary process to secondary process functioning in the psychic development of the individual.[8] in the earliest form of mental organization the accumulation of tension to a threshold level leads to immediate discharge upon an available object, hallucinatory evocation of a memory of a past gratification, and/or an undifferentiated affective reaction that has protective, emergency discharge value as well as communicational value. The ideational and affective discharge channels provide the organism with the capacity to temporarily reduce the level of tension below the threshold level so as to delay discharge in the absence of a suitable object in the environment. They are of limited adaptive value, however, in that they substitute for effective action without preparing the organism for such action.

Further development leads to a shift from a mental organization dominated by the necessity for indiscriminate discharge according to the pleasure principle to one in which the accumulation of drive

---

is, the more independent from the immediate environmental stimulation it becomes. Freud described thinking also as experimental action using small quantities of energy, and thereby elucidated both its biological function and its relation to action. It appears that in higher organisms, trial activity is increasingly displaced into the interior of the organism, and no longer appears in the form of motor action directed toward the external world. With this advance in evolution, human intelligence has reached that high point at which it affords man, whose somatic equipment is certainly in no way outstanding, his superiority over his environment. Intelligence involves an enormous extension and differentiation of reaction possibilities, and subjects the reactions to its selection and control. Causal thinking (in relation to perception of space and time), the creation and use of means-end relations, and particularly the turning of thinking back upon the self, liberate the individual from being compelled to react to the immediate stimulus' (Hartmann, Heinz: *Ego Psychology and the Problem of Adaptation* (1939). New York: International Universities Press, 1958, pp. 59–60).

[8] A brief but clear description of this transition can be found in Engel, G.: *Psychological Development in Health and Disease*. Philadelphia: W. B. Saunders Company, 1962, especially pp. 221–236. For a fuller exposition, see Rapaport, D.: The Structure of Psychoanalytic Theory. In: *Psychological Issues*, Vol. II, No. 6. New York: International Universities Press, 1960.

tension mobilizes structuralized control and delay mechanisms that include directed means-end activities to find a suitable object *in reality* upon which effective and efficient drive discharge can be carried out. This transition is mediated by the development of countercathectic mechanisms to impede drive pressures and the evolution of cognitive apparatuses which permit the individual to coordinate past and present perceptions and to anticipate, select, locate, and act upon objects in reality. Affect discharges become modulated, differentiated, and controlled by the developing ego apparatuses so that for the most part they are restricted to serving as signals for the mobilization of regulatory ego processes.

The central role of thought in facilitating the evolution from primary to secondary process functioning is highlighted by the persistent use of the terms 'primary process' and 'secondary process' not only to describe the ego's capacity to regulate cathectic discharge but also to define two different kinds of thought process. Many psychoanalysts apply the terms both to different modes of energic discharge *and* to different types of thinking, although there are those who adhere to the narrower view that they refer strictly to economic hypotheses.[9]

The countercathectic defense mechanisms employed by the maturing psychic apparatuses to impede drive discharge have been subjected to intensive study by psychoanalytic investigators. Although dynamic considerations have received the greatest emphasis, the sequence of appearance and shift in dominance of the various defense clusters (i.e., the developmental aspect) have been given increasing attention.[10] Although the progressive differentiation and

---

[9] The former opinion is exemplified in the dual definitions provided in Moore, B. E., and Fine, B. D., editors: *A Glossary of Psychoanalytic Terms and Concepts.* New York: The American Psychoanalytic Association, 1967. For the stricter point of view, see Arlow, J. A. and Brenner, C.: *Psychoanalytic Concepts and the Structural Theory.* New York: International Universities Press, 1964, pp. 84–102.

[10] Anna Freud has made important contributions in this area. See Freud, A.: *The Ego and*

taming of affects by the developing ego has been the subject of less intensive study, engel, jacobson, mahler, rapaport, schur, and others have made important contributions in this area.

The development of the cognitive structures that assume increasing importance as regulatory agencies has been the subject of relatively little psychoanalytic attention, however. Although Hartmann[11] and others have called attention to the importance of the intellectual sphere, the actual details of its development have not attracted a great deal of interest among psychoanalysts.[12] The work of piaget and his collaborators helps to fill the void. Their description of the stages in the development of logical thinking goes far toward elucidating the transition from thought organized according to primary process to that reflecting secondary process regulations. They have demonstrated, moreover, that the transition takes place very slowly, extending through most of childhood. In describing this transition in structural terms they add scope and dimension to the largely economic and dynamic formulations of psychoanalysis.

Their description of the thought of the preoperational child essentially approximates that made by the psychoanalyst of thinking organized along primary process lines. The thinking of piaget's stage 1 child is characterized by rapid, easy shift from one attribute

---

the *Mechanisms of Defense* (1936). New York: International Universities Press, 1946, and *Normality and Pathology in Childhood, Assessments of Development.* New York: International Universities Press, 1965. Her concept of developmental lines and comments about progression and regression in childhood are of particular significance.

[11] Hartmann's contributions are too numerous to list. In addition to the work already cited, most of the relevant papers can be found in his *Essays on Ego Psychology: Selected Problems in Psychoanalytic Theory.* New York: International Universities Press, 1964.

[12] A notable exception is Peter Wolff's thoughtful attempt to integrate Piaget's theories about cognitive development in the sensorimotor period (the first year and a half after birth) with the psychoanalytic theory of the early development of the psychic apparatus. See, Wolff, P.: The Developmental Psychologies of Jean Piaget and Psychoanalysis. In: *Psychological Issues,* Vol. II, No. 1. New York: International Universities Press, 1960.

to another as a criterion for association and categorization, condensation of elements into unstable, jerry-built images that loosely coordinate them, poor distinction between part and whole, simultaneous existence of mutually contradictory beliefs, and a highly fluid imagery that is close to concrete perception. Through progressive internalization of his exploratory manipulations in such a fashion that his thought processes can range increasingly widely and reversibly, the child gradually moves toward the logically organized, consistent and cohesive, reversible, mobile thought of stage 3 that approximates what analysts refer to as secondary process thinking. The equilibration reaches relative stability at about ten years of age. The detailed description of the evolution from stage 1 to stage 3 that inhelder and piaget have provided represents a rich source of information about the evolution of secondary process regulation and adds significantly to our understanding of the course of structuralization of the ego.

A familiar observation can serve as an illustration of the clinical relevance of piaget's findings. I am referring to the utilization by an analysand of different modes of thinking during a single analytic hour. During part of the session, thinking occurs in the form of words. At some point a shift takes place to pictorial images which have to be described to the analyst. At times such a shift signals a heightening of resistive forces that threatens to impede analytic progress. At other times, however, it does not interfere with the analytic work but seems to facilitate it.[13]

The data provided by inhelder and piaget can enhance our understanding of these observations. The experiments tracing the evolution of multiplicative classification (matrices) indicate that there exists a discontinuous sequence in which children below the age of six years make use of graphic means, involving visual symmetry, to

---

[13] I am grateful to Drs. Shelley Orgel and Jules Glenn for their helpful comments in discussion of this clinical phenomenon.

solve the problems with which they are confronted, while older children shift to an entirely different nonvisual, abstract approach that, nevertheless, leads them to the same results. There is a significant difference between the two methods. The initial graphic approach is an intuitive one that allows for considerable contradiction and illogicality. The abstract method, achieved through increased organization, demands consistency and adherence to logical order. Reversion from the more advanced mode to the earlier one involves an intrasystemic regression to a more loosely organized type of thinking that utilizes a more primitive form of logic. The aim of such a regression can vary. It is obvious that it lends itself well to the purpose of resistance. Shift is made to a mode of thinking and problem-solving in which contradiction and illogicality are permitted to prevail. The ego is enabled to reach workable syntheses and conclusions at the same time that it excludes from awareness details which it would rather not have to consider.

A shift from verbal to imaginal thinking during an analytic session does not always signal an increase in resistance, however. In fact more often it represents a regression in the service of the ego[14] that facilitates the forward progress of the analysis. What seems to be taking place in this instance is that the ego frees itself from the restrictions imposed upon it by the narrow bounds of logical consistency and reality-syntonicity by instituting a controlled, limited, reversible regression of some of its functions, by means of which it reverts to a more primitive mode of thinking that is intuitive and imaginative in nature.

When the regression is reversed and return is made to more highly differentiated and organized verbal thought, rules of logic and order are applied to the relatively free-ranging imaginative

---

[14] See, Kris, E.: *On Preconscious Mental Processes. This QUARTERLY, XIX, 1950, pp. 540–560.*

thoughts that emanated during the regressed state, which thus are integrated into the mainstream of thinking. It has long been recognized that this kind of oscillation between, and integration of, archaic forms of thinking and more highly differentiated and organized thought processes is an essential ingredient in fantasy formation, daydreaming, and creative processes in general. The data adduced by Inhelder and Piaget suggest that this kind of alternation between, and synthesis of, higher and lower forms of thinking plays an important role in certain kinds of problem-solving as well. It will be recalled that in the course of evolution of operational thinking, but before an operational equilibrium had been established, the stage 2 children whom they describe continually reverted to more archaic graphic modes to aid them whenever they ran into difficulty in their struggles to solve the problems before them. It would seem that development (including that which takes place in the course of psychoanalytic treatment) depends in part upon the ability to temporarily suspend higher forms of functioning and revert to earlier successful modes of problem-solving. The degree to which the regressive movement facilitates development, rather than inhibiting it, depends upon the degree of mobility and reversibility with which the ego is capable of carrying out the regressive process.[15]

It has long been clear that an essential feature of the analytic process is the recovery of repressed archaic memories and fantasies so that they can be subjected to reflection and judgment by a more mature ego than existed at the time the memory traces were established and the fantasies were elaborated. It is possible, however, to postulate an additional aspect of the therapeutic effect of psychoanalysis. In the process of repeatedly ranging back

---

[15] I have discussed this in another context in Silverman, M. A. and Neubauer, P.B.: The Use of the Developmental Profile for the Prelatency Child. In: *The Unconscious Today*, edited by M. Kanzer. New York: International Universities Press (in press).

and forth between archaic fantasies and the more mature thinking processes with which they are coordinated in the course of the
analytic work, the ego appears to take part in an exercise that has
the effect of progressively increasing the efficiency of its synthetic
or integrative functions. This takes place through increasingly
flexible and controlled alternation between regressive and progressive movements, with increasing integration of the results of
these movements. If this is so, then it cannot suffice for the analytic process to simply 'make the unconscious conscious'. It may
very well be equally important to facilitate improvement in the
various components of the analysand's synthetic function, i.e., to
effect a change in the ego itself.[16] This is a question that deserves
further consideration by psychoanalytic investigators.

Piaget's description of early structural development adds further
dimension to familiar psychoanalytic observations of the earliest
period of life. His demonstration, for example, that permanence of
an object representation transcending the availability of the actual
object in the immediate perceptual field, which appears at eight to
ten months of age, contributes to our understanding of the appearance of stranger anxiety (which depends upon the ability to
discriminate between mother and other persons) at precisely
that age. His observations provide an additional source of data to

---

[16] Hartmann states, for example, that 'the mere reproduction of memories in psychoanalysis can, therefore, only partly correct the lack of connection or the incorrect
connection of elements. An additional process comes into play here which may justly
be described as a scientific process. It discovers (and does not rediscover), according
to the general rules of scientific thinking, the correct relationships of the elements to
each other... Clearly, I do not concur with the often-voiced idea that the unconscious
basically 'knows it all' and that the task is merely to make this knowledge conscious by
lifting this defense' (*Ego Psychology and the Problem of Adaptation*, pp. 63-64). An
elaboration of this view can be found in Hartmann, H.: *Technical Implications of Ego
Psychology. This Quarterly*, XX, 1951, pp. 31-43. A further discussion of the technical
aspects of this point of view is available in Blanck, G. *Some Technical Implications of
Ego Psychology.* Int. J. Psa., XLVII, 1966, pp. 6–13.

help us understand the phenomena of pleasure in functioning and mastery through repetition. A detailed examination of these issues, however, would take us beyond the scope of this discussion. I raise them to further illustrate the heuristic value of Piaget's researches for psychoanalysis. Even if it were not for the areas of direct confluence, however, piagetian exploration and theory deserve attention for the light they shed on significant aspects of human development. A broad interest in the manifold aspects of development is essential in psychoanalysis, particularly if it is to aspire to the status of a general psychology exerting influence upon education, childrearing, characterology, and so on.

Even in the therapeutic psychoanalytic situation, however, familiarity with multiple facets of the human process facilitates the analyst's complex and difficult task. In the dawn of psychoanalysis, Freud used the image of a passenger in a railway carriage who has only indirect access to the window to illustrate the navigational problem of the analyst. With his usual parsimony and wisdom, he etched for us in this metaphor the essential limitation to our powers of observation.[17] He was not dissuaded from pursuing the task, but devoted himself among other things to the study and explication of the instruments at the analyst's disposal.

In the roughly three-quarters of a century that has elapsed since the beginning of our discipline, scientific exploration in all fields has exploded geometrically. We possess a mushrooming body of data regarding human development that is too valuable to be ignored. At a time when the jet age is hurtling toward the past, the complexity of our navigational task is becoming increasingly evident. At the same time, we are moving toward ever greater precision and accuracy. It is in the realm of ego psychology(including mutual influences of ego and id) that the most

---

[17] See, Lewin, B. D.: *The Train Ride: A Study of One of Freud's Figures of Speech. This Quarterly*, XXXIX, 1970, pp. 71–89.

stirring effects are being felt. In this regard, it can be said that the painstaking researches of Piaget and his co-workers have yielded data of inestimable value to the psychoanalytic investigator. In the complexity of space age navigation, the instrument panel grows wider and wider.

Section II:

Observations on Child Development

CHAPTER 3

ON A CENTRAL PSYCHIC CONSTELLATION

Martin A. Silverman, M.D., Katherine Rees and Peter B. Neubauer, M.D.

[from: (1975). *Psychoanalytic Study of the Child* 30:127–156]

In this paper, we shall describe the emergence of a central psychic constellation which is observable during the preoedipal period. Our observations were made in the course of a longitudinal study in which we utilized observational techniques, supplemented by therapeutic material, to investigate the course of development and fate of the conflicts and structures associated with the prelatency period. We shall try to demonstrate that this central constellation emerges by the age of 3 or 4 out of the coordination of certain key variables into a relatively stable, cohesive, psychic organization which persists as an influential factor and which seems to play an important role in codetermining the pattern of further development, including the form and early outcome of the struggles of the oedipal period. The constellation's stability derives from the organization of its constituent elements into a dynamic equilibrium which persists despite changes in the elements themselves as development proceeds.

Ever since Freud's momentous discovery of the role of the oedipus complex in human mental life, psychoanalysts have centered their attention upon oedipal conflicts and the ego's efforts to resolve them. Advances in ego psychology and research into the events of the preoedipal period have greatly broadened our perspective of development, but the knowledge thus gained has not yet been fully integrated into the mainstream of psychoanalytic theory and practice. There have been many contributions to our understanding of the preoedipal and oedipal periods and of the organization and functioning of the ego. This may be the time for psychoanalytic investigators to pull together the large quantity of information about early development that has been gathered over the years and to make use of it to enhance and refine our understanding of the origins, structure, and fate of the oedipus complex and further development. We hope in this communication to contribute to such an integration by describing what may be a significant aspect of the transition from preoedipal psychic organization to the developmental currents of the oedipal and latency periods.

In 1966, we embarked upon a long-range longitudinal study of eight children who at that time were between 3 and 3½ years of age. We set out to study the patterns of developmental change and evolution which were taking place. We were especially interested in the modifiability of early neurotic patterns and the ultimate fate of early patterns of conflict and conflict resolution.

We drew up a detailed Developmental Profile, derived from the outline devised by Anna Freud (1965), on each child twice yearly for three years and yearly thereafter. Our Profiles were based upon data obtained from multiple sources. In addition to the full clinical records available to us, we observed the children extensively in the classroom, paying attention to their relationships with the teachers and the other children, the fantasies expressed in their play and in their verbal communications, their physical activities and intellectual interests, and their involvement with the various people in their lives (including the investigators). The teachers kept a daily log on each child and met with us regularly to share their observations and impressions. The children and each of their parents were interviewed by one or more of the investigators and each child underwent a battery of psychological tests prior to each Profile.

For the first Profile, a detailed account of each child's personal and family history was compiled. In addition to our own research, we also had access to the data gathered in a lengthy study of each child before his acceptance to the nursery school. The majority of the children had older siblings who also had attended the Center nursery school, which provided an additional rich source of information about the family. Some of the older siblings also had been in treatment at the Center. A staff member regularly saw at least one of each child's parents during the first three years of the study. One of the children had been a subject of a detailed infant study, the raw data of which were made available to us. It is significant that the main patterns of family interaction observed for each child at the beginning of the study seemed to have remained quite stable throughout the course of the investigation.

THE CENTRAL CONSTELLATION

Although at the time of the first Profile, the children's development was marked by considerable fluidity and change, certain observations stood out quite clearly. There were plentiful derivatives from prephallic levels of libidinal organization, with wide variation from child to child. All the children showed evidence of having reached the phallic phase of libidinal development, but not all were firmly engaged in it. In most of the children there was little evidence of involvement in oedipal fantasies and conflicts at the time of the first Profile.

As we followed the children through the "oedipal period" and on into latency, we were increasingly impressed that in our initial Profiles we had described a constellation of central characteristics which had become organized in such a way as to have reached relative stability, so that it was bound to exert an important impact upon further development. There were wide individual variations in the relative significance of each of the constituent elements of the constellation. In general, however, the components could be grouped into four overall areas, the assessment of which provided a key to each child's readiness at 3 or 3½ to move in certain directions.

The areas which we have come to view as particularly significant are: the pattern of phase progression, drive balance and discharge patterns, the impact of early variations in ego equipment and organization, the self and object representations, and the modes of regulating self-esteem with which the latter are associated. When we watched the children progress into late latency, we were increasingly impressed by the finding that what had been basic in each of these areas at the beginning of the phallic-oedipal period continued to be observable, despite all the changes which took place thereafter.

By the time the children entered the phallic and oedipal period, the inherent tendency to consolidation and integration underlying the increasing efficiency of operation of the developing psychic apparatus seemed to have coordinated and organized these psychic components into a remarkably stable constellation of forces. As we followed the children into latency, we found that this central constellation played a highly significant role, in interaction with the effects of ongoing maturational and experiential influences, as a codeterminant of the form and content of the children's oedipal conflicts, the options available for their resolution (or failure thereof), and the personality organization observable in latency.

We do not view the constellation as constituting a binding together either of pathological components exclusively or only of components arising out of normal developmental sequences. We would rather describe the process as a binding together of "core" variables in which conflictual and nonconflictual elements combine to form a characteristic psychic organization.

THE COMPONENTS OF THE CENTRAL CONSTELLATION

The variables which we shall describe emerged from the assessment data as significant areas which seemed to be coordinated with one another into a developmentally meaningful, dynamic, interaction system. These variables are an expression of the developmental forces, drive expressions, ego functions, and patterns of object and self regulation which have crystallized by the fourth year of life.

PHASE PROGRESSION

When we correlated current observations with the historical data on each child, it became apparent that each child had his own style of developmental progression. There were individual variations in the pattern of progressive and regressive movements, including variations in intensity of conflict engagement, strength of the progressive pull, ease of regression, range of movement to and fro, degree of fluidity and overlap, and the extent to which various modalities were affected by regressive shifts (Silverman and Neubauer, 1971).

There was evidence of advance to the phallic level, but each child had his own particular combination of prephallic and phallic elements. The impact of conflict at earlier levels upon the course of the phallic phase varied from one child to another. The range included fixations which impeded advance to higher levels, fixations which served as potential attraction points for regression in some areas without greatly interfering with general progression, and contamination of phallic interests and activities by derivatives of earlier conflicts. A few children seemed to shift fluidly back and forth between oral and phallic or anal and phallic interests without dominance at either level of libidinal organization.

It is not possible to speak of drive progression without describing the ego attitudes which are correlated with drive organization. In addition to responding to the specific tasks imposed in each new psychosexual phase, the ego had developed a characteristic attitude toward libidinal or aggressive drive pressure in general, regardless of its phase-specific form. Historical data seemed to point to three sources of this ego attitude: the relative strength of the drives, the child's perception of the reliability of his environmental objects, and his capacity to tolerate drive tension and secure object gratification. In other words, by 3½, the ego of each child had developed a characteristic way of responding to the intensity of the drive demands imposed upon it, of assessing the availability of suitable environmental resources with which they might be satisfied, and of pursuing, capturing, and utilizing those resources.

DRIVE BALANCE AND DISCHARGE PATTERNS

Our data suggested that by the time they had reached the age of 3½, our children had reached a point of relative stability in the balance between libidinal and aggressive drive expression. The interplay between variations in drive endowment (Alpert et al., 1956) and crucial experiences during the first few years seemed to have determined the way in which libidinal and aggressive drive components had developed, intertwined, and fused with one another during the first three years in each child. The way in which each child's ego had experienced and executed drive demands during the first year or two seemed to have determined the pattern with which the ego sought and experienced pleasure thereafter. The form of aggressive drive expression and ambivalence conflicts seemed to have acquired relative stability as a result of passage through the oral and anal phases. The effect of defense systems, of course, played an important role.

Each child had experienced the onset of the capacity for independent assertion and execution of libidinal and aggressive drive demands differently during the toddler phase. These differences had greatly influenced his view of his ability both to assert himself independently and to move into and enjoy the focused, assertive, independent, competitive explorations and activities of the phallic phase. We saw that the children had come through the prephallic period with various quantities of aggressivity which had to be controlled. The degree to which aggressive drives had been tamed and neutralized (as well as the mechanisms employed for that purpose) also varied from one child to another at the beginning of the phallic phase.

We have seen that inability to mobilize aggressive energies in the pursuit of drive satisfaction in the prephallic period can be the harbinger of a restricted ability to be assertive and competitive during the phallic-oedipal period (an example will be described later on). Another child, Mark, possessed a strong, innate or congenital aggressivity, which enabled him vigorously to pursue libidinal objects during his second and third years despite the repeated loss of important objects. In the phallic phase, however, he was unable to restrain his aggressivity enough to hold on to his objects (and preserve his object representations against sadistic attack) once he had pursued and captured them. He was so terrified of driving off or destroying his objects, or of incurring terrible, punitive reprisal, that he was forced to abandon oedipal, rivalrous strivings and to turn to previously treasured inanimate objects onto which he could safely divert his aggressive attacks. He could not sufficiently engage himself in oedipal struggles to resolve them and move into latency. He was very intelligent and perceptive, but had little interest in learning for its own sake. He used his skills rather to charm and manipulate people, as well as to defeat and hurt them. In grade school, he used his intellectual abilities in the service of narcissistic withdrawal rather than employing them in the pursuit of knowledge.

THE DEVELOPMENTAL EFFECT OF EARLY VARIATIONS IN EGO EQUIPMENT AND ORGANIZATION

In each child we followed, a unique way of perceiving and responding to life situations and adaptational pressures had developed by the time of the first Profile. Although we did not directly study the children's development during the first three years, our data strongly suggested that these individual patterns derived in part from innate dispositions and equipmental variations which had been evident very early in their lives. The historical information we received (one child had also taken part in a thorough infant study, conducted by Annemarie Weil and Anneliese Riess) indicated that from the beginning each child had shown innate preferences for using certain modalities rather than others for relating to and interacting with the outside world. There was evidence of intrinsic variations in tension tolerance and in thresholds of response to external stimulation. The children differed in their perceptual sensitivities as well as in their patterns of assessing and integrating information. Motor activity patterns varied from one child to another and there were significant variations in motor control and in the rudiments of cognitive control apparatuses.

In each case, these variations were observed in early infancy and their impact upon behavior and personality characteristics was readily apparent during the first three years. However vague or unclear they may have been about other matters, nearly all the parents were unequivocally certain about these particular early observations. As we followed the children during the course of the study we were impressed with the ongoing consistency with which these individual characteristics remained observable and with the significant impact which they seemed to exert upon the developmental process.

The observation that variations in endowment, in interplay with environmental experience, contribute significantly to ongoing development is not a new one (Escalona, 1963), (1968); (Korner, 1964); (Thomas et al., 1963); (Weil, 1956), (1970). It is difficult to predict from infant studies alone what will be the eventual developmental impact of early variations (Escalona and Heider, 1959). Longitudinal study beyond the period of infancy is necessary before the meaning of congenital traits and characteristics can be appreciated (Ritvo et al., 1963). By the fourth year, enough structuralization and organization seem to have taken place to indicate which factors have been developmentally significant and to permit reasonable predictions about the fate of the structural and organizational elements to whose evolution they have contributed. Our own findings indicate that by the age of 3½, they have become organized into a relatively stable, central constellation which exerts an important influence upon psychic development thereafter. We do not mean to imply that no change occurs in the individual elements with further development. *The stability to which we refer is that of a dynamic interaction of interrelated factors within an organized, integrated, dynamic grouping or constellation which remains relatively stable despite changes in the constituent elements.*

An example may help to clarify this point. One child as an infant had been relatively inactive motorically but very alert and active perceptually, with precocious discriminative powers. Possessing a high degree of visual and tactile sensitivity, Karen had related to people largely through those modalities, quietly savoring contact in favorable circumstances, but closing her eyes and withdrawing into sleep when conditions were unsatisfactory. By the age of 3, she had developed a pattern of motor restriction, under aggressivity, vigilant avoidance of excessive stimulation, and defensive scotomization, coupled with exquisite perceptual sensitivity and a rich and active fantasy life. As we followed her development further, we were impressed both with the stability of this pattern and with the important role it played in her overall development.

In another of our children, Jack, we saw how from infancy, an unusual capacity to tolerate tension was combined with a particular perceptual style of slow, thorough observation and assessment of his objects and environment. Such attributes significantly influenced his ongoing development and contributed to the evolution of a psychic constellation which included low-keyed, measured interaction with objects, steady drive progression and integration, much problem-solving activity in the realm of fantasy, and a highly developed use of his intellect for careful observation, empathic understanding, the working over of drive demands, and scientific explorations. These individual variations in ego function became an important factor in his ongoing development.

SELF AND OBJECT REPRESENTATIONS AND THE REGULATION OF SELF-ESTEEM

In the process of passage through the normal autistic, symbiotic, and separation-individuation phases (Mahler, 1968), each child in the study appeared to have developed a unique set of self and object representations and a related group of mechanisms for preserving self-esteem and narcissistic well-being that greatly influenced his current and ongoing perception of himself and of the object world in general.

One aspect of this involved self-object differentiation (Jacobson, 1964). Disturbances in this area could be traced to regressions, the impact of endowment, the effect of certain conflicts, or environmental interferences. A second facet involved the nature of the self and object representations. We saw that the way in which the children viewed themselves and their main objects, consciously and unconsciously, affected the way they approached the tasks of the phallic-oedipal period in important ways.

A third aspect was the economic one. By the time a child had reached the age of 3 there might already have been a significant depletion in the narcissistic cathexis of the self-representation, an over idealization of his objects, or a pattern of narcissistic grandiosity, excessive self-preoccupation and withdrawal from objects. In such instances, the disturbances were carried over into the phallic and oedipal struggles, coloring their form and contents and imposing limitations upon their outcome. At the time of the first Profile, we already could see which aspects of the self representation received special narcissistic cathexis and we could discern certain aspects of the evolving ego ideals, including whether they contained demands which were excessively high or low.

Another item of importance involved the maintenance of self-esteem. It was significant whether or not self-esteem regulation was based upon realistic self and object representations and actual achievements. In some instances the ego had acquired confidence in its ability to maintain control over tension states, achieve independent mastery, and secure affection and approval from its objects. In others, for various reasons, self-esteem was dependent to a significant extent upon the provision of certain external supplies.

We could offer many examples of the significance of this developmental dimension. Mark, for example, who had difficulty regulating the expression of his aggressivity, had suffered a number of object losses (including that of his father) early in his life. His image of himself as dangerously destructive to his objects and of men as weak, disappointing, and helplessly vulnerable to illness and death contributed in an important way to his need hastily to give up his rivalrous oedipal ambitions and to the weakness of his striving toward a masculine identity.

Jeanette's alertness, superior intellectual endowment, high tension tolerance, adaptability, and unusual capacity for self-control and delay were quickly recognized by her dependent and ambitious but unsuccessful parents. In their eagerness to realize their ambitions vicariously through her, they actively reinforced her high self-expectations and fostered the development of a lofty ideal self to which she aspired. The central constellation observable in her fourth year was organized about the need to maintain this idealized self-representation. She easily advanced into a phallic libidinal organization, in which her fantasies included an all-powerful, illusory phallus. Yet, the need to be in continual command of an adulatory environment and her inability to risk defeat severely compromised Jeanette's ability to engage herself in oedipal, rivalrous struggles, and she entered latency as a haughty, lonely girl who was incapable of intense social relationships and hampered by the burden of unresolved oedipal and preoedipal conflicts.

A CLINICAL ILLUSTRATION OF THE CENTRAL CONSTELLATION

We have chosen a child in whom all four component areas of the central constellation are well defined and in whom the contribution of the constellation to oedipal and early latency development is particularly clear. The psychological makeup of this child also afforded us an unusually good view of her fantasy life and intellectual processes; she has received no psychological treatment to complicate the developmental process.

KAREN AT THE BEGINNING OF NURSERY SCHOOL

Karen was just 3 years old when she started in our nursery school. She stood out not only for her delicate prettiness, but even more for her sober demeanor and quiet aloofness. She keenly observed all the activities, but held back for a long time from direct participation. Although she obviously yearned for attention from the teachers, her overtures were so meek and tentative that they often went unanswered. She was happy when they responded in a friendly but low-keyed manner, but had to pull away when they were effusive with her. When her overtures were ignored, she was dejected and withdrew temporarily into a solitary reverie, accompanied at times by autoerotic activity.

Karen could more easily accept the friendly approaches of the other children, and gradually reached out for friendship with them, but she tended to withdraw whenever there was more than one other child in the play. She occupied herself mainly with simple, solitary activities that afforded her a good vantage point for observing the others. She alternated in her play between competitively making the tallest towers and constructing carefully tended buildings and enclosures, which she populated with people and animals.

In her individual interview with a male observer, Karen appeared to be very interested in him, but froze after she had taken two steps into the room. She stood there during the interview and poured out a stream of anxious, loosely organized chatter, the content of which concerned feelings of helplessness, conflicts overeating and biting, yearning for her father, who had just gone on a plane trip, fear of being overexcited sexually the way she had been at times with her father and brother, and guilt over masturbation and sex play with her brother. At home, Karen continued to compete actively with her brother for her mother's attention. She indicated repeatedly that she felt cheated (of attention, oral supplies, her father, and a phallus), but was unable to maintain an angry attack upon her mother without soon making up to her.

EARLY HISTORY

Karen had been conceived in the hope of saving a crumbling marriage. Her mother characteristically staved off anxiety and depression via flamboyant bravado, seductiveness, a stream of chatter, and immersion in a kaleidoscopic sea of sensation. Her father was charismatic, creative, and unpredictable. During Karen's infancy, her mother became increasingly anxious and depressed as the inevitability of a divorce became obvious. The father left the home when Karen was 8 months old, but he continued seeing the children three times a week until the divorce, when Karen was 2½, after which he temporarily left the state. Although his contact with the children was irregular thereafter, with absences of many months at a time, Karen remained loyally attached to him.

Karen was so motorically inactive during the first few days after her birth that her mother worried about her. She developed colic, which lasted for four months. She was noted from the very beginning to be unusually alert, perceptive, and visually observant. Like her older brother, Karen very early discriminated between men and women. She showed a clear preference for men, and made an early attachment to her father.

Blocked tear ducts had to be pressed out each day by her mother during her first year. They were finally probed free by the doctor when Karen was 12 months old. Teething, which took place quickly, was associated with a moderate amount of discomfort.

Karen's mother tended to offer the breast to her frequently as a universal panacea. When weaning was attempted at 6 months, Karen resolutely refused to accept a cup, and continued at the breast until it was abruptly removed at 10 months. She refused milk in any form for the next year and a half. Mrs. K. was intermittently depressed and anxious during Karen's first year. Most of the time, she responded appropriately to Karen's needs, but there were times when she was less available. At other times, apparently in response to her own needs, Mrs. K. picked Karen up to cuddle and feed her when she actually had been quietly asleep. Rather than protesting these ill-timed, intrusive stimulations, Karen responded by closing her eyes and "falling asleep."

Toilet training was begun at 2 years of age and took about a year to complete. On the toilet Karen showed anxiety that began with fear of falling in; the flushing also disturbed her. She made no protest against the toilet-training demands and did well for a while, but when her parents were divorced and her father moved away, a general ego regression took place, during which she wet herself intermittently day and night, and she tended periodically to retain her stool. Her father returned when she was 3 years old; she responded by recovering from her regressive episode and attaining complete control of toilet functions.

When she was about 2½ years old, she began to masturbate and was seduced by her 4½-year-old brother into mutual genital explorations, which continued intermittently thereafter with the mother's tacit approval. Karen's brother, the only sibling, was good looking, aggressive, and talented, and Mrs. K. scarcely concealed her preference for him.

DEVELOPMENTAL ASSESSMENT AT 3 YEARS

Phase Progression

At 3 years, Karen showed intense libidinal wishes and longings, with an adherent attachment to her aims and objects and intense fear both of overstimulation and of loss. Despite intermittent

69

temporary flight and emotional withdrawal, she maintained cathexis of her objects via vivid fantasy relationships to them even when they actually were absent or unavailable. Her persistent longings and her efforts to seek out new possibilities of finding the gratifying relationships for which she yearned encouraged continual psychosexual progression.

A fluid libidinal organization seemed to have emerged, in which persistent oral yearnings had become interwoven with powerful longings to receive a penis. These unified longings contributed to the yearning for a man as a rescuer and provider, although inability to risk the loss of her mother prevented Karen from pushing away from her. There was a capacity for fluid, progressive-regressive shifts within her drive organization, without firm closure and with only relative phallic primacy. There had been a weakness in her anal level engagement and in her ability to control and dominate her objects. The early sexual play with her brother seemed nevertheless to have promoted early vaginal awareness and fantasies (e.g., a lollypop was found in her vagina when she was 2½ years old) which, combined with her observations of her mother's coquettish interest in men and her early attachment to her father, had stimulated movement into phallic and oedipal interests.

Drive Balance and Discharge Patterns

Karen showed intense libidinal cathexis of object representations, accompanied by a relative inability to mobilize aggressive energies either to assert and secure possession of her objects or to do battle with them. The genetic roots seemed to include both innate and experiential factors.

Karen had been relatively inactive motorically as an infant, relating to the world largely via perceptual (especially visual and tactile) channels. She had possessed a considerable need for sensual contact from infancy on, enjoying the contact when it was presented in a comfortable fashion and withdrawing from it by tuning out and turning off contact when it was intensive or hyperstimulating. From the combination of innate inclinations and the effect of repeated experiences with objects who were inconsistent, often overstimulating, and difficult to control or influence, she had developed a pattern of pursuing objects by studying them, learning to anticipate their behavior, and adapting her own behavior to make herself pleasing to them, rather than aggressively demanding from them what she needed or complaining when they failed her.

The Developmental Effect of Early Variations in Ego Equipment and Organization

From earliest infancy, Karen had presented a striking combination of relative motor inactivity and a high degree of visual alertness and perceptual activity. She had tended to use tactile sensitivity and visual pursuit as her favored modalities for relating to the world around her. She also had tended from very early on to withdraw from ill-timed intrusions and experiences of overstimulation by closing her eyes and retreating into a sleeplike state. These early characteristics seemed to have developed from her particular endowment, reinforced by ongoing experiences (the pattern of feeding and maternal handling, the lacrymal duct probing, uncomfortable teething, maternal depression and anxiety, and her father's departures), especially during the first year.

An early tendency to employ a defensive style centering about flight, avoidance, and withdrawal, rather than mobilizing aggressive energies to demand gratification and fight off unwelcome intrusions, had persisted as a basic, ongoing characteristic. Karen had become particularly sensitive, empathic, and observant, but was continually on guard against the possibility of being overwhelmed by excessive stimulation. Associated with this was an ego attitude toward her own aggressive and libidinal impulses in which vivid, relatively undisguised fantasies could be tolerated, but their direct motor expression was prohibited. The ego avoided the possibility of their enactment, at the expense at times of an extensive restriction of ego activity in general.

Karen's learning capacity was enhanced by acute powers of observation, a ready capacity to absorb rote information, a vivid memory, and a fine sense of color and form. It was hindered, on the other hand, by her tendency to turn away from painful or disturbing stimuli, avoid the new and unknown, and reduce impinging stimuli by scotomizing the field of attention. Avoidance of competition and an inclination to hold on to what was already possessed, but not seek after more, completed the picture observable at 3 years.

Self and Object Representations and the Regulation of Self-Esteem

Karen's self and object representations centered about vivid images of idealized, loving, and protective objects whom she yearned to possess in reality, although she had little confidence that she might actually succeed in doing so. Although her past experiences had led her to view her objects as potential sources of pleasurable gratification, they also had led her to perceive them as unreliable, frequently elusive or unavailable, and often painfully overstimulating. Correspondingly, she viewed herself as being not quite desirable enough to attract her objects or as strong enough to catch, hold onto, and control them.

Karen's self representation had received insufficient narcissistic investment and she lacked the capacity to mobilize enough aggression to achieve full individuation from her objects. Since her self-esteem was still largely dependent upon the objects' response to her, she was cautious lest she alienate them. She suppressed angry, complaining feelings and made an effort to be good and pleasing to win their favor. Since her defensive style was organized about flight, avoidance, and restriction of activity, she was hindered in her ability to utilize reality experiences to modify either her fears or the contents of her self and object representations. This served to reinforce the tendency to withdraw from interaction with actual, new objects and to turn to her highly cathected, idealized, fantasy objects. She always returned, however, to an interest in the outside world, where she sought objects who might approximate the idealized object representations which she held so dear. This indicated to us that she did not give up hope, but maintained her object cathexis at times of disappointment and injury. It was possible, therefore, that if she were fortunate enough to find the right people, she would be capable of achieving meaningful change as a result of her interaction with these new objects.

THE CENTRAL CONSTELLATION AT 3 YEARS

The initial Profile contained evidence of the coordination of the key developmental factors we have described above into an internally coordinated constellation possessing a high degree of stability. As we have followed Karen's development, we have become increasingly convinced that this constellation has been an influence upon her ongoing development. A strong innate progressive push, reinforced by the forward pull exerted by a sexually stimulating environment, more than counteracted the retarding effects of oral fixations. Since her ego organization permitted wide progressive-regressive fluctuation and an unusual degree of fluidity and overlap, early fixations did not prevent developmental advance, but were carried along and woven into the higher levels of organization which progressively evolved.

Karen's relative inability to mobilize aggression interfered with her ability to take control of and possess her objects and interfered with certain aspects of individuation, but it also contributed to the preservation of her object cathexes at times of disappointment and narcissistic injury. This very sensual little girl's tendency to establish intense, discriminative cathexes and her ability to maintain her object cathexes in fantasy, even in the prolonged absence of her cathected object, helped preserve the availability of constant, positive object representations. Although her self-esteem remained dependent upon positive responses from her more or less idealized objects, she was able to seek out such responses and to use them in the service of developmental progression.

The ability to make restitutive use of fantasy at times of actual frustration and failure enabled her to retreat temporarily when confronted by overwhelming stress. Stemming partly from intrinsic variations in ego endowment and partly from the impact of early experiences of overstimulation and ego inadequacy, she seemed to have developed a well-organized defense system built around avoidance, temporary introversion and withdrawal, flight, and ego restriction. It served to control anxiety, although at the price of reduced ego flexibility and freedom of action, so that developmental progression could proceed. An important aspect of Karen's central constellation was the ability to make good use of environmental resources to facilitate developmental progression.

THE PHALLIC-OEDIPAL PHASE

There was steady movement forward between 3 and 6 years into increasing phallic and oedipal interests. Although phallic organization was attained, her libidinal organization remained fluid, with a plentiful admixture of oral fantasy and conflict and an ease of progressive-regressive alternation. Karen persistently wooed her father, who had returned to the city with his new wife, and there was evidence of intense genital excitement in his presence, associated with wishes to abandon herself to him. She was frightened by her excitement, however, particularly at times of natural regression, and was unable to spend the night at her father's apartment. She maintained an intense, visual, idealizing interest in him as well as vivid fantasies about him when she was not with him, but her activity was restricted in his presence and she had difficulty expressing appropriate anger at him.

There was evidence of intense anger at her mother and of attempts to push away from her, but Karen was inhibited in her expressions of resentment and hostility, which she was unable to sustain for long. There were indications of intermittent longing for closeness with her mother (which at times had to be warded off anxiously) and of inability to give her up as a source of narcissistic reinforcement and libidinal satisfaction. Karen was a fussy eater at school as well as at home and developed a number of transient food intolerances.

At school, Karen was increasingly assertive and capable of a certain amount of verbal aggression and sarcasm, but she continued to be relatively restricted, inhibited, and somewhat phobic. She became increasingly able to woo the attention of her favorite teachers, but remained quite cautious and overly sensitive to rebuff. Her learning and her peer relations progressed, but she was limited to a significant extent by her cautiousness, reluctance to explore the unknown, tendency to scotomize, and relative inability to be competitive. She grew increasingly interested in the male investigator who was following her progress, and gradually acquired the courage to approach him in the classroom and woo his attentions in competition with the other girls. When she finally dared to make physical contact with him, she reacted with excitement that necessitated prompt removal of herself from his presence. In her semiannual interviews with him, she initially showed a wistful yearning for him to be a prince charming who would like her, care for her, and provide her with the feeding breast she had lost and the phallus of which she had been cheated. This fantasy gradually faded and was replaced by increasingly exciting images of being taken for wild roller-coaster rides, being thrown down and run over, and being attacked and torn apart. Castration themes alternated with restitution themes in these fantasies. Retreat to peaceful scenes of mutual feeding became less and less prominent with each set of interviews until it finally disappeared.

THE LATENCY PERIOD

Karen moved into latency via resigned acceptance that she could not obtain from her parents all that she wanted from them. Her mother was absorbed increasingly in pursuing a career and social activities, with less and less time and energy available for the children. Her father remarried when Karen was 5½, and a year later had a son. This half brother aroused in Karen wistful envy of the lovingly fed baby and the fantasy of herself becoming father's bride.

Karen gradually shifted from her parents to her teachers as objects to be wooed and won. She was fortunate in that each year from 5 to 9 her teacher was a perceptive young woman who liked and appreciated Karen and was alert to her need for low-keyed interest, warmth, and approval. Their descriptions of Karen bore a striking resemblance to our original observation of her. They depicted her as a perceptive observer, sensitive to the responses of others, averse to exploring the unfamiliar, and reluctant to take the initiative, although she responded well to gentle encouragement.

Karen became excited but anxious in the presence of men. With familiar men, including her father, she was provocative and seductive, but she shunned direct physical contact (even at 9, she did not like to be kissed by her father). Her reaction to new men in her life was largely one of avoidance. The wildness of the boys and the excitement they aroused in her discomfited her. Her intense wish to be liked, her efforts to please, and her empathetic response to their needs made her very popular with her peers. Although her academic achievements and popularity did much to raise her self-esteem, she continued to feel uncertain of her successes and to worry about losing her place in her friends' affections, even when she was past the age of 9 years. She gradually became able to express anger and to register complaints against her mother (and brother), but she could do so only timidly. She developed a rather typical feminine superego organization, although with more dependence upon external approbation and fear of loss of approval and admiration than the average.

THE THEORETICAL SIGNIFICANCE OF THE CENTRAL CONSTELLATION

We have described the emergence by the age of 3 or 4 years of a relatively stable, organized, central psychic constellation which persists thereafter as an influential factor. Our conclusions are related to two fundamental propositions regarding human development. One is the notion that development proceeds via a process of sequential organization and reorganization in which new systems of psychic functioning periodically evolve to supersede previously existing systems as dominant, organizational configurations. The other is the proposal that increasing differentiation and hierarchy formation are accompanied in the developmental process by a tendency to internal coordination and cohesion which leads to stability and systemic integrity. To state the latter proposition another way, there is an intrinsic tendency toward synthesis and self-regulation which leads to a "bonding between the interacting components" (Sander, 1973).

The work of a number of investigators suggests that in the course of development there are certain nodal points at which critical reorganizations can be identified. Freud (1905), for example, reconstructed the existence of successive waves of libidinal reorganization in childhood, each of which centers about a particular erotogenic zone. Abraham (1925) defined the epigenetic nature of this sequence of libidinal reorganization. Erikson (1950) later expanded this point of view to include the psychosocial aspects of development and extended its application to the entire life cycle from birth to death.

Spitz (1959), (1965), Ritvo et al. (1963), and others have demonstrated that a sequence of progressive reorganizations can be observed in the first two years in which psychic elements periodically regroup themselves into a new, relatively stable, superordinate organization which supplants the previous one as the current *modus operandi* of adaptation. Each new organizational system has its own way of perceiving, processing, and responding to environmental stimuli and drive demands. The periodic regroupings, leading to new levels of psychic equilibrium, derive only partly from the appearance of new ego structures. In part, they derive from shifts in the coordination or patterning of already existing structures.

Piaget has shown that cognitive development proceeds by means of a complex, epigenetic sequence in which each developmental stage is derived from and represents the outer limit of equilibrium of the previous stage (Silverman, 1971). He has demonstrated that the process of reorganization in each stage leads to the crystallization of an end point of organizational patterning in which firm internal bonding provides relative stability. Cognitive development may be particularly well suited, in fact, to demonstrate the interplay of epigenetic reorganization and synthesis or interaction of constituent elements into stable, dynamic systems within the developmental process. George Klein, for example, has described the evolution during early childhood of an organized system of multiple, cognitive controls which together constitute a lifelong, cognitive style that is unique in each individual. He concluded that in the course of progressive restructuring of psychic mechanisms there evolves a stable, regulating organization which represents an equilibrial balance among individual variations in intrinsic ego equipment, response to the pressure of drive demands, and the necessity of accommodating to environmental restrictions (Klein, 1954), (1958); (Santostefano, 1969).

It is our impression that the age of 3 years may be a nodal point at which a crucial, developmental reorganization reaches stability. The child's style of progressive-regressive movement usually cannot be adequately appreciated until he has gone through enough of the total range of his libidinal development at least to have entered the phallic phase. Except in extreme instances, it is also not until then that the developmental impact of prephallic fixations can be gauged. Often enough, the relative balance between libidinal and aggressive drive pressures does not reach a stable enough form for it to be identified accurately before the move forward from anal ambivalence conflicts to phallic phase interests. By the age of 3, the child's ego capacities have had time to unfold and develop, and the impact of his innate endowment has had a chance to demonstrate itself. By then, there has been enough time for him to utilize his resources in interaction with an expanding object world, with its various adaptational demands and its provision of a range of stimuli and opportunities for exercise of the child's mental and emotional machinery. Three years is also the age cited by Mahler (1968) as the time when the separation-individuation process has proceeded sufficiently for relative object constancy and relatively stable self and object representations to have been attained. These various dimensions seem gradually to become organized with one another, under the direction of the integrative function (Hartmann, 1939).

The observation that certain developmental characteristics coalesce early in life into stable, dynamic groupings exerting influence upon further development is not a new one. In addition to Spitz (1959), (1965), Sander (1962), (1970), Escalona (1963), and others have made extensive investigations into the evolution of patterned modes of functioning out of the coordination of the innate rhythms and executive tendencies of the infant with the modifying influence of the mother's responses to him.

Anna Freud (1971) has described an early "psychosomatic matrix," deriving from this interaction, which sets the scene for the development of certain aspects of the pleasure-unpleasure balance, the form and strength of object attachment, certain ego strengths and weaknesses, and the pathway to somatic compliance. These form a matrix, according to Anna Freud, out of which later id and ego structures, conflicts involving the emerging component drives, and the infantile neurosis ultimately develop.

Annemarie Weil (1970) has formulated in rich detail how the interaction between the infant's equipment and early experiences leads to the emergence of a "basic core" of fundamental trends which accompanies the infant as he enters the symbiotic phase. Since the basic core influences and intertwines with later psychological developments, it continues to be evident, according to Weil, as a more or less discrete, psychic organization within the personality as it develops further.

Our own observation of a developmentally influential central constellation in the fourth year dovetails closely with the concepts of the "psychosomatic matrix" and the "basic core." What we have described in this paper appears to be a manifestation of the tendency within the developing psychic apparatus toward periodic regrouping of central tendencies and characteristics into a new, central organization which incorporates the previous one into it as it supersedes it as a central, guiding, developmental constellation. Anna Freud's concept of multiple, converging and diverging, developmental lines (1965) is pertinent in this regard. Periodically, certain key lines of development intersect in such a way that they become mutually coordinated and organized into a relatively stable constellation of forces, which then plays a central role in the developmental process. The central constellation observable in the fourth year would seem to grow out of earlier organizational constellations as they interact with new structures and with the deformations imposed upon the psychic apparatus by new developmental requirements.

We have been tracing the fate of the central constellation itself in the course of further development. What we have seen so far has indicated that it persists with sufficient stability to stamp itself upon the organization of the personality during the oedipal and latency periods. Besides affecting the form and content of oedipal conflicts and the options available for their resolution, it influences character structure, intellectual and cognitive styles, and sublimative potential, at least during the period in which we have followed the children. To understand the degree to which the constellation itself changes in the course of development through childhood and into adulthood will require further longitudinal study, correlated with study and review of the analyses of children and adults. We are not yet in a position to assess this adequately, but we hope to continue our study until the children have reached early adulthood. We are especially interested in seeing what will be the effect of the major shifts and reorganizations that can be expected to take place during adolescence.

It is our impression that our observations fit in with a current tendency in child psychoanalysis to evolve a theoretical formulation which fits the oedipus complex into the mainstream of development at the same time that it recognizes its central role in the organization of the neuroses. We are referring to a shift in emphasis from a formulation which depicts the oedipus complex as *the cause of the neurosis* to one which would consider the oedipus complex as a *dynamically central feature* of a developmental process which may or may not predispose to neurotic solutions of developmental tasks. In this formulation, unresolved oedipal conflicts would appear as a central part of the neurotic process rather than as its source. Anna Freud (1971) stated:

There is a world of difference between ... the past and the present scene. What we are pursuing at present are not evaluations undertaken from the viewpoint of any later mental disorder but an elaborate map of infantile mental difficulties as such, or, to express it more succinctly, an enumeration, description, and explanation of any interference with optimal mental growth and development. On the basis of our knowledge of developmental phases, as established by reconstruction from adult analysis, by child analysis, by direct observation of infants and young children, we attempt to do this from birth onward, with the phallic-oedipal phase placed not at the lower but at the upper end of our investigation... It appears almost as a by-product that, while doing so, we also assemble those developmental aspects which, in due course, will lend themselves to the production of conflicts and may even determine beforehand which among the available defense mechanisms the individual's ego will choose to employ and, accordingly, which forms of compromise and symptom formation will be open to him [p. 82].

This is not to say that all neurotic manifestations arise out of processes that begin in the earliest years. A developmental process that is proceeding adequately can be altered at any point, particularly by events occurring in such critical periods as the oedipal stage. An initially adequate developmental process can be transformed in this manner into a deviant one. But even in such a case, it would seem to us that organizational predispositions must also play an important role, along with and in interaction with traumatic experiences, in determining the final outcome.

Psychoanalysis has demonstrated that neurotic disorders consist of unsuccessful attempts to obtain relief from insoluble, unconscious conflict. It has been recognized that the main conflicts underlying the infantile neurosis crystallize during the oedipal period. Advances in ego psychology, investigations into the psychoses and narcissistic disorders, and the opportunity to carry out longitudinal observations of infants and young children, however, have called our attention to the enormous importance of preoedipal development in neurosogenesis. It has even led some investigators to question whether the principal determinant of emotional health or neurosis is the oedipal conflict and its resolution or whether matters are already decided in the period before the emergence of the oedipal conflict. Our study suggests to us that the issue may not be whether the earlier period or the oedipal conflicts are more significant, but how the earlier developments contribute to the content and form of the oedipal conflicts and the means employed to resolve them.

The psychoanalytic view of the developmental process emphasizes the significance of fixation points which impede developmental progression and predispose the individual to regressive flight to escape from the tensions and anxieties created by insoluble conflict at higher levels. The regression, of course, only leads to new conflicts and anxieties at earlier levels of psychic organization. We believe the understanding of neurotic functioning would be broadened by supplementing this genetic point of view, with its emphasis upon fixation and regression, with one which looks upon the developmental process prospectively as a steadily evolving and reorganizing dynamic interplay of psychic forces.

This might help clarify the individual differences among children as they progress through the various developmental phases. Employing the concept of the early crystallization of a central constellation has provided us with an extra vantage point from which to consider a number of questions. One of these concerns the ability of some children to relinquish or modify their maternal attachments relatively easily during the course of their oedipal struggles, while others cling tenaciously to them at all costs. A second involves the factors determining the choice of fantasy or action as the preferred channel of discharge and the impact of this choice upon the oedipal outcome. Other questions which seem to be elucidated concern the choice by different children of different sets of defense mechanisms with which they struggle with their oedipal conflicts, the degree to which oedipal conflicts are object-oriented or narcissistic in orientation, the tendency to employ predominantly positive or negative oedipal solutions, and certain aspects of the structure of the ego ideal and the superego's methods of enforcing its prohibitions.

The value of coordinating the genetic point of view with a developmental one emphasizes the importance of the principles of epigenesis, synthesis, progressive organization and reorganization, and change of function. When the early stages of development are reconstructed in the course of a therapeutic analysis, they may appear to be relatively discrete, well-demarcated, and discontinuous in nature. When one follows children prospectively, however, one sees a great deal of overlap, fluctuation to and fro, and a gradual, shifting metamorphosis in which old mechanisms acquire new functions and old patterns are rearranged and more or less modified in the interest of adaptation to new tasks and new requirements.

Nunberg's emphasis upon the importance of the synthetic function has been very helpful to us. He pointed out that underlying the increasing efficiency of the evolving psychic apparatus is an inherent tendency to integration and consolidation: "The tendency to simplify and generalize, to integrate and the like, reveals that the synthetic function of the ego is subject to an economic principle, which induces the ego to economize expenditure of effort... Synthesis thus brings about not only unity of the whole personality but also simplification and economy in the ego's mode of operation" (1932p. 153). The concept of a synthetic (Nunberg, 1930) or integrative (Hartmann, 1939) function operative within the developmental process has enabled us to study the ways in which developing structures and functions are fitted together and coordinated into operational systems and subsystems in the course of development.

THE CLINICAL IMPLICATIONS OF THE CENTRAL CONSTELLATION

The data emerging from our studies are clinically relevant. The diagnostic evaluation of children is complex and arduous. Symptoms and developmental disturbances, as Anna Freud (1965), (1974) repeatedly has stressed, are significant only insofar as they reflect the existence of meaningful disturbances of overall developmental progression or of key elements within it. Assessment of the pattern of developmental progression is particularly difficult with the prelatency child, for whom the diagnostic task is largely predictive in nature.

In a previous paper (Silverman and Neubauer, 1971), we stated our opinion that with prelatency children a series of cross-sectional

Profiles was required to obtain the longitudinal dimension that would permit an assessment of *the developmental significance* of temporary disturbances, symptoms, or imbalances. It is our impression at this point, however, that delineation of the central constellation identifiable by 3½ years can be an alternative means of determining the directions in which overall development is proceeding. It describes the paths being taken by important developmental lines and the ways in which they are knitting together and becoming mutually organized. It has helped us to see the degree to which various patterns and structures are open to change and the directions in which they can be expected to steer developmental responses to the phase-specific experiences and conflicts of the oedipal and latency periods. Since the constellation contains important indications of the basic fabric of the personality organization, it is a key to understanding the way in which the child will deal with the issues which have to be resolved in the years ahead.

If it turns out that treatment is indicated, the central constellation can help the clinician decide which forms of intervention are most likely to be effective. The choice is especially wide with preschoolers, since important areas of the personality are still plastic and are highly vulnerable to outside influence. Mapping out the central constellation can help the clinician to pinpoint the precise target areas toward which therapy should be directed. It may be possible, for example, by strengthening a specific ego function to alter a child's self representation in important ways and to bring about necessary changes in his or her defensive system. Recourse to the central constellation also can help distinguish between those areas which are rigidly locked into a pattern of maldevelopment and those in which longitudinal, developmental pressures are likely to bring about sufficient, fortuitous growth and reorganization that the decision whether or not to intervene in the developmental process can be postponed to a later time. The grasp of the basic personality fabric which the central constellation provides can help the clinician to achieve precision in his choice among the various therapeutic procedures available by pinpointing the impact of each at any point in time. It can help him to decide whether the best therapeutic approach will be a specific educational program, efforts to effect changes in parental handling, the provision of new object relationships, one or another psychotherapeutic approach, or a carefully planned sequence of more than one of these modalities.

We believe that our observations are of significance to the psychoanalyst whether he is working with children or with adults. The psychoanalytic task consists in undoing fixations and facilitating the resolution of repressed conflicts. The method we have been employing for this has been principally genetic and dynamic in its approach, but these points of view have been coordinated more and more over the years with structural and developmental viewpoints. The psychoanalytic method concentrated at first upon reconstructing the emergence of insoluble unconscious conflicts between drive pressures, ego and superego attitudes, and environmental demands. This has been supplemented increasingly by an interest in studying the structural organization within which the conflicts emerge and are perpetuated and in exploring the shifts and changes which take place at successive developmental levels.

It is here that our observations become relevant. We have seen that by the age of 3½, a number of influential developmental factors have coalesced into a relatively stable balance of forces within the personality organization and that this constellation helps to regulate the way in which experiences are perceived and dealt with from that point on. It would seem to us that reconstruction of the emergence of this central psychic constellation out of its constituent components and of its developmental impact (as well as of the internal changes forced upon it by developmental progression) at each level thereafter would enhance the psychoanalyst's understanding of his analysands, whatever their age. It would add to our grasp of the interplay of forces operating within them and, therefore, to the origins of their characterological and neurotic structural formations. It would place us in a better position to define the limits within which we might expect change to take place in our patients and to map out the specific strategy by means of which we might facilitate the attainment of such changes.

SUMMARY

In this report we called attention to a central psychic constellation which is observable by the age of 3 or 3½ and which appears to play an important role as a codeterminant of the form and early outcome of the struggles and conflicts of prelatency and latency. Our findings stem from a longitudinal study of the developmental process in which data emerging from regular observations and interviews have been correlated wherever possible with therapeutic insights.

We attempted to demonstrate that the central constellation arises out of the coordination during the first three years of life of certain key, preoedipal, developmental variables into a psychic organization possessing sufficient cohesion and stability to maintain a significant impact upon the course of further development. Clinical material was adduced to illustrate the constellation and its components. We described certain variables that are particularly significant in the formation of this constellation.

We considered some of the clinical and theoretical implications of our findings. Psychoanalytic investigators have been attempting to integrate the increasingly vast body of data about the preoedipal period with the assumptions concerning the central role of the oedipus complex in human psychic functioning.

We hope that our work, which focuses upon the transition between the preoedipal and oedipal periods, will facilitate the successful completion of this complex and difficult task.

REFERENCES

ABRAHAM, K. (1925). Character-Formation on the Genital Level of the Libido. In: *Selected Papers on Psycho-Analysis.* London: Hogarth Press, 1927, pp. 407–417.

ALPERT, A., NEUBAUER, P.B., & WEIL, A.P. (1956). Unusual Variations in Drive Endowment. *Psychoanal. Study Child* 11:125–163.

ERIKSON, E.H. (1950). Growth and Crises of the Healthy Personality. In: *Identity and the Life Cycle* [Psychological Issues Monogr. 1. New York: Int. Univ. Press, 1959, pp. 50–100.

ESCALONA, S.K. (1963). Patterns of Infantile Experience and the Developmental Process *Psychoanal. Study Child* 18:197–244.

———— (1968). *The Roots of Individuality.* Chicago: Aldine Publishing.

————& HEIDER, G. (1959). *Prediction and Outcome.* New York: Basic Books.

FREUD, A. (1965). *Normality and Pathology in Childhood* New York: Int. Univ. Press.

———— (1971). The Infantile Neurosis. *Psychoanal. Study Child* 26:79–90.

———— (1974). A Psychoanalytic View of Developmental Psychopathology. *J. Philadelphia Assn. Psychoanal.* 1:7–17 (1976).

FREUD, S. (1905). Three Essays on the Theory of Sexuality *S.E.* 7:125–243.

HARTMANN, H. (1939). *Ego Psychology and the Problem of Adaptation* New York: Int. Univ. Press, 1958.

JACOBSON, E. (1964). *The Self and the Object World.* New York: Int. Univ. Press.

KLEIN, G.S. (1954). Need and Regulation In: *Nebraska Symposium on Motivation* ed. M.R. Jones. Lincoln: Univ. Nebraska Press, pp. 224–274.

———— (1958). Cognitive Control and Motivation In: *Assessment of Human Motives* ed. G. Lindzey. New York: Rinehart, pp. 87–118.

KORNER, A.F. (1964). Some Hypotheses Regarding the Significance of Individual Differences at Birth for Later Development. *Psychoanal. Study Child* 19:58–72.

MAHLER, M.S. (1968). *On Human Symbiosis and the Vicissitudes of Individuation.* New York: Int. Univ. Press.

NUNBERG, H. (1930). The Synthetic Function of the Ego In: *Practice and Theory of Psychoanalysis*, pp. 120–136 New York: Int. Univ. Press, 1955.

———— (1932). *Principles of Psychoanalysis.* New York: Int. Univ. Press, 1955.

RITVO, S., MCCOLLOM, A.T., OMWAKE, E., PROVENCE, S.A., & SOLNIT, A.J. (1963). Some Relations of Constitution, Environment, and Personality as Observed in a Longitudinal Study of Child Development. In: *Modern Perspectives in Child Development*, ed. A. J. Solnit & S.A. Provence. New York: Int. Univ. Press, pp. 107–143.

SANDER, L.W. (1962). Issues in Early Mother-Child Interaction. *J. Amer. Acad. Child Psychiat.* 1:141–166.

———— (1973). Infant and Caretaking Environment *(unpublished manuscript).*

————STECHLER, G., BURNS, P., & JULIA, H. (1970). Early Mother-Infant Interaction and 24-Hour Patterns of Activity and Sleep. J. Amer. Acad. Child Psychiat. 9:103–123.

SANTOSTEFANO, S. (1969). Cognitive Controls versus Cognitive Styles Seminars in *Psychiatry* 1 291–317.

SILVERMAN, M.A. (1971). The Growth of Logical Thinking *Psychoanal. Q.* 40:317–341.

————& NEUBAUER, P.B. (1971). Use of the Developmental Profile for the Prelatency Child. In: *The Unconscious Today*, ed. M. Kanzer. New York: Int. Univ. Press, pp. 363–380.

SPITZ, R.A. (1959). *A Genetic Field Theory of Ego Formation.* New York: Int. Univ. Press.

———— (1965). *The First Year of Life* New York: Int. Univ. Press.

THOMAS, A., CHESS, S., BIRCH, H.G., HERTZIG, M., & KORN, S. (1963). *Behavioral Individuality in Early Childhood*. New York: New York Univ. Press.

WEIL, A.P. (1956). Some Evidences of Deviational Development in Infancy and Early Childhood. *Psychoanal. Study Child* 11:292–299

——— (1970)The Basic Core. *Psychoanal. Study Child* 25:442–460.

CHAPTER 4

COGNITIVE DEVELOPMENT AND FEMALE PSYCHOLOGY[1]

[From: (1981). *Journal of the American Psychoanalytic Association* 29:581–605.]

Freud never was satisfied with the theory of female development which he pieced together from his clinical observations. In his 1933 comments on "Femininity" he called it "incomplete and fragmentary" and advised his readers "to wait until science can give you deeper and more coherent information" (p. 135).

Freud was burdened by multiple handicaps in his attempts to understand female psychology. For one thing, he did not approach it directly in its own right, but in comparison with the development of the male, which can be attributed in part to his having worked out the details of the Oedipus complex in his own analysis, i.e., in the analysis of a man. His observations of women also were influenced by his fundamentally biological orientation (see Freud, 1915), (1940) that derived from the stress on anatomicophysiological explanations which pervaded the scientific approach of his time (Friedman, 1977). Freud also centered his attention on libidinal drive theory and the Oedipus complex, de-emphasizing the relative importance of aggressive conflicts, conflictual and especially conflict-free ego development, and the role of preoedipal factors. Although it is understandable that he was impelled to defend his monumental but unwelcome discovery of the role of sexuality and

---

[1] This is a revised and expanded version of a paper presented at the Spring Meeting of the American Psychoanalytic Association, Atlanta, Georgia, May 5, 1978.

especially of oedipal conflicts in the psychology of human beings against the onslaught of persistent, virulent, resistive attacks, his need to do so contributed to inevitable distortions in his view of the developmental process. There are cogent indications, for example, that the Oedipus complex in any individual cannot be understood fully unless the developmental currents out of which it develops (and which influence it further thereafter) are themselves fully appreciated (Silverman et al., 1975). Freud's method of reconstructing backward from information provided by adults with very little prospective data to balance it also led to inevitable adultomorphisms that hindered him from adopting a truly developmental approach. Even in the case of Little Hans, the one child whom he attempted (indirectly) to subject to analysis, he was hampered by an adult-oriented point of view (Silverman, 1980). His observations of female development also were impaired by the male-dominated, phallocentric, patriarchal sociocultural *Zeitgeist* in which Freud lived.

He revised his formulations as new data became available, e.g., when his attention was called to the significance of the little girl's preoedipal wish for a child, but he did not greatly depart from his early view of female psychology.

Recent Investigations of Female Development

We have begun, finally, to follow Freud's advice that we reconsider our understanding of femininity on the basis of further information provided by science. I do not mean to slight the contributions of such early psychoanalytic investigators as Jones (1927), (1935), Muller (1932), Horney (1932), (1933), and Klein (1932), whose observations and ideas have been summarized and integrated by Chasseguet-Smirgel and her colleagues (1970) and by Calogeras and Schupper (1972). Their contributions were themselves fragmentary, however, and contained distortions emanating from investigative biases and reifications—and they have not significantly eroded Freud's conceptual framework. Attempts are being made at present to correlate early observations on female psychology with new data arising out of direct observation and clinical investigation with females throughout the life cycle, aimed at devising a theoretical formulation that is balanced, developmentally oriented, and as free as possible from distorting influences.

It has become clear, for example, that a girl's core gender identity, i.e., her perception of herself as "a girl," with a whole set of cognitive and affective details as to what that means, begins to form as soon as her parents recognize her as female. Mothers, as well as fathers, react differently to their male and female offspring, who themselves show demonstrable sensory, motor, responsive, and other sex-related differences beginning at birth (see Green, 1976); (Kleeman, 1976); (Lichtenstein, 1961); (Sander et al., 1976); (Stoller, 1968), (1976). Parents handle their infant sons and daughters differently, speak to them differently, and present them with very different sets of signals, directives, and expectations, which the infants absorb and utilize as they build up mental representations of themselves. Although the attention of newborns at first is largely directed to deep, inner sensations, to which Spitz (1965) referred as a coenesthetic sensory orientation, they show sustained and concentrated, albeit initially brief, interest in stimuli emanating from the environmental surround during states of alert inactivity (Wolff, 1966). They also demonstrate an impressive capacity for learning, expressed as rapid accommodation to externally imposed variations in meaningful stimuli (Kron, personal communication).

Infants are extremely sensitive to variations in environmental input and mold and pattern themselves to the caretakers' holding behavior, just as the latter more or less empathically read and respond to the infants' cries and rhythms. The degree to which preconceived notions, biases, and culturally determined value judgments can influence caretaker's views of the infants in their charge (and these, in part distorted, views are conveyed back to the children) is illustrated in Bennett's (1971) report of observations made in a newborn nursery. A two-way communication develops between the mother (or other caretaker) and her child in which positive and negative feeling states, reaction patterns, and attitudes toward themselves and each other are perceived and exert a mutual influence one upon the other (see Mahler, 1968); (Sander et al., 1970), (1976).

As time passes, the infants increasingly use their sensorimotor apparatuses to explore their own bodies and the world around them. There is increasing definition, clarification, and discrimination, which contribute to self-object differentiation and differentiation among significant external objects, animate and inanimate. With advance from recognition memory to evocative memory, they become able by the end of the first year to construct mental images that can be manipulated and experimented with, which marks the beginning of representational intelligence. The acquisition of symbolic mental imagery, which roughly coincides with the appearance of bipedal, upright locomotion and the beginnings of verbal communication, attains stability by the middle of the second year, after which intellectual development proceeds via symbolic thought rather than sensorimotor exploration (Piaget, 1936), (1947). This cognitive advance parallels the sequence of emergence of the little girl's core gender identity, which, according to Kleeman (1971), (1976) and Money and Ehrhardt (1972), begins to be clearly observable by the time she is walking and not only achieves stability, but may be irreversible by the middle of the second year (and certainly is so by three years of age, according to Stoller [1976]). Her view of herself as a girl, in other words, appears to be an integral, very early developing part of her self-representation (it continues to undergo considerable further elaboration, of course, after the age of eighteen months). Whether vaginal awareness is present or not in the very young girl is not crucial to the development of her awareness of her gender. According to Kleeman (1976), Kohlberg (1966), Money and Ehrhardt (1972), and Stoller (1968), it is cognitive maturation and development, i.e., what she learns about herself, that established the little girl's view of herself as female.

Through her communications, verbal and nonverbal, with her parents (and other significant people in her life), as well as via further exploration of her own body contours and sensations, the little girl fills in details of her concept of herself as an individual and as a member of society at large. As she sorts out the similarities and differences she perceives among people, including herself, she begins to classify and categorize them into groups, which include male and female. She is not capable in the preschool period, however, of constructing logical classes in which criteria of inclusion and exclusion are accurately and firmly coordinated with one another. Her cognitive level permits her only to dovetail bits and pieces of information into unstable collections which she more or less intuitively contrasts with one another. The result is a prelogical system of classification in which objects possessing similar attributes are intuitively grouped together without regard for discrepancies that mar the fit and without clearly discriminating the sets from one another on the basis of differences and similarities (see Piaget, 1947); (Inhelder and Piaget, 1959); (Silverman, 1971).

Girls and women are grouped together, for example, because they "go together" on the basis of repeated communications and experiences that point in that direction. The recognition that there is a special bond between her and her mother is augmented by the little girl's pleasure and pride in being like her mother. She wants to look like her mommy (in whose clothes she loves to dress up) and do the things her mommy does, including having and nurturing babies. This both conflicts with her efforts to differentiate from her mother and resist the dependent pull toward her at the same time that it helps her to separate off as a capable, worthwhile female in her own right (becoming a mommy with babies of her own helps her to grow beyond being her mommy's baby, i.e., to grow separate from her). The degree of success she achieves in this developmental conflict depends in part upon her mother's ability to help her negotiate the ambivalent rapprochement crisis of the separation-individuation process (Mahler, 1963), (1968), (1974); (Mahler et al., 1975). Ideally, her mother will help her to achieve a relatively separate, independent, self-reliant position in which she feels proud of her ability to function on her own.

Her father's responses to her also are important. Fathers play a much greater role in the very early development of children than commonly is credited to them (Abelin, 1971); (Burlingham, 1973). Interest in the father begins very early, certainly by between eight and eighteen months (Abelin, 1971), as the child's interest in him is stirred by the discovery of him as someone different from his mother and therefore an object of interest.

Fathers, no less than mothers, respond very differently to their sons and to their daughters. A little girl in the rapprochement period (and thereafter) receives myriad cues from both parents as to their feelings about her and about women (Blum, 1976). Her self-concept as and feelings about being a girl are greatly influenced by what her father conveys to her about the way he views her and what he expects of her. This can range from delight in her femininity to disappointment and derogation of her status as a girl(see Stoller, 1976, for a striking example of the

effect of a father's encouragement of nonfeminine, masculine behavior in a girl).

Discovery of Genital Differences

A little girl's awareness that she is a girl like her mother and her feelings about what that means develop out of what she learns in
interaction with her parents (and other significant objects). Awareness of genital differences does not necessarily play a part in her
initial perception of the divisibility of people into categories of male
and female. Sooner or later, however, this criterion of differentiation
begins to make itself known. According to Roiphe and Galenson
(Roiphe, 1968); (Galenson and Roiphe, 1971, 1974,1976), genital exploratory play during the first year and a quarter is sporadic,
nonspecific, and a part of general exploratory interest in the body and
its sensations. Some time between fifteen and nineteen months of
age, however, while they are in the midst of increasing awareness of
anal and urinary functions, girls demonstrate a "heightened and
qualitatively distinctive genital awareness along with genital derivative behavior" (Galenson and Roiphe, 1976p. 38). Both endogenous
and exogenous factors seem to be involved.

Debra, for example, at twenty-one months of age, never had
had the opportunity to observe the genitalia of anyone other than
herself and her only sibling, a sister seventeen and one half
months her senior. One day, she walked into the room in which
her father was reading and sat down cross-legged on the floor in
front of him. She watched him silently for a while and then said,
"Daddy reads." "Yes," he replied, "I read a lot of books. I learn
from them." "Daddy knows a lot?" she asked. "I guess I know a
lot of things," he said, "is there something you want to know?"
Debra looked down and pointed at her genital region. "What's
this?" she asked. "That's your vulva," said her father, "all girls and

mommies have a vulva." "Oh," she said, and started to walk out of the room. "Why did you ask?" her father questioned. "It feels funny" was her reply. When her father told Debra's mother about the incident later on, she said, "Oh! That reminds me. When I've checked her the last few nights to see if she's covered, she always has her hands down there." For the next few weeks or so, Debra engaged in frequent masturbatory genital self-stimulation, especially while in her bed and in the bath, after which she seemed to lose interest in her genitals (only to regain that interest in a more lasting fashion half a year later). There was no sign of genital inflammation or irritation during the period of genital self-stimulation that began at twenty-one months.

Sooner or later, girls become aware that there are beings who possess genital organs which they themselves do not have. Freud stated that they react by feeling cheated and deciding immediately that they want a penis of their own. Direct observation confirms that little girls are distressed by their observation of the difference between the sexes. Debra, for example, first observed male genitalia when her brother was born, when she was thirty-two months old. She was irritable around him (although fascinated at the same time) and was jealous of the attention her mother paid to him. A few days after he was brought home from the hospital, she greeted her father, when he returned home from work, by gleefully playing at snatching off his nose and swallowing it. After a while he asked if it really was his nose she wanted. "No!" she exclaimed, "I want your penis." "Are you sure it's *my* penis you want?" he asked. "No," she said, with an angry snap in her voice, "I want his!" She pointed toward her baby brother, who just had been changed and was lying on his changing board naked from the waist down. Her father asked her to show him what it was she wanted. She stepped over and pointed to his scrotum, which still was in the enlarged, swollen newborn state. When her father asked what she wanted it for, she replied irritably, "I just want it, that's all!" and walked out of the room.

The observation that there are beings who possess large genital organs which she herself does not have constitutes a painful narcissistic injury to a girl in the second and third years after birth. This is a time of intense narcissistic-exhibitionistic pride in intellectual prowess and bodily strength and skill (see Tartakoff, 1966). To find that one lacks attributes and abilities that others possess is a deflating and distressing experience, especially when an area of the body is involved that is beginning to assume very special interest to parents and other significant objects.

Galenson and Roiphe (1976) have reported that all girls in their sample "showed a definite and important reaction to the discovery of the genital difference and eight of the 35 developed intense castration reactions" (p. 47). The girls tended to express considerable curiosity about their own and their parents' genitalia and used pens, pencils, and crayons in a beginning attempt at graphic representation. Intellectual activity (to compare, examine, and define) and imaginative play seemed to be spurred by mild castration reactions, but the girls with intense reactions were constricted in this regard. A tendency to derive less pleasure from manual masturbation or to give it up altogether and to switch to indirect means of genital self-stimulation was observed, together with mood changes that ranged from reduced zestfulness and enthusiasm to "a basic depressive mood" (p. 48) in one girl. The investigators were most impressed with the apparent effect on object ties. Most of the girls "seemed to have had a relatively successful experience during their first year." This group "turned to the father in a newly erotic way" that coincided with a lessening attachment to the mother (p. 51). Girls who had had disturbed maternal relations or significant bodily trauma during the first year, or who had had a sibling born during the latter half of the second year, showed an intense castration reaction to their observance of genital differences and went through a profound increase in their hostile-dependent, ambivalent relationship with their mothers that led to a predominantly negative oedipal reaction rather than a shift to the father as their primary love object.

Parens et al. (1976), in a direct observational study, found that little girls vary in their pattern of entry into the Oedipus complex, not all of them doing so via the castration complex and penis envy that Freud posited to be the universal gate of entry. All three of the girls about whom they reported, however, were visibly disturbed, although to different degrees, by their discovery of genital differences between the sexes. When the little girl discovers the existence of the male's penis and scrotum, what strikes her is that someone else possesses something of importance of which she is deprived. She does not know that his genital endowment derives from his membership in a class of beings for whom possession of certain organs is a basic attribute and the lack of other, equally valuable organs, which she *does* possess, is also a basic attribute. Her concept of male and female is intuitive and prelogical, and she has no reason to believe she should not have what she has seen on someone else's body.

Her level of cognitive organization, however, makes it very difficult for her to appreciate anything that cannot be directly seen and felt. Unlike the boy, whose genital apparatus is discrete, well-defined, and readily accessible, her own sexual organs are complex, difficult to identify and outline, and to a significant extent hidden inside her body, so that she has no direct access to them. Girls commonly are instructed that boys have a penis and girls have a vagina. This is not only incomplete and misleading, but it deprives them of the verbal referents which they so badly need to help them define the genital portion of their self-image (see Lerner, 1976). Girls are told, furthermore, that someday they will be able to give birth to a baby. This is frequently said to them in such a way that it is clear they are being offered a bit of sympathy and a measure of solace for their phallic deprivation rather than being told of something to be prized in its own right. The message received is that what they have is indeed inferior and second-best. Our phallocentric culture favors the boy and his genital. This is transmitted to each generation of girls, beginning very early in each girl's life. How often does a little girl have an aunt who, like Little Hans's aunt, praises her little "thingummy"? Freud was one of many who underestimated the primary importance to the girl of the ability to give birth to babies, an ability that is the source of immense pleasure and pride.

Little girls are greatly in need of accurate and complete instruction as to the makeup of their genital organs, external as well as internal, sexual as well as reproductive, and they need this information to be conveyed to them by parents who truly value and cherish them and their genital functions. Even were they to be fully, clearly, and appreciatively provided with such instruction, however, their cognitive organization still would make it extremely difficult for them, before at least the age of six or seven years, to appreciate their internal genitals. A child I treated some years ago brought this to my attention in a most dramatic fashion.

Faith was six and a half years old when we first met. She had a serious developmental disturbance, with phobias, obsessions, disturbed object relations, a major learning problem, and a borderline ego organization. She had had a difficult early life. Her very talented, but disturbed parents engaged in continual sadomasochistic battles before they parted company when Faith was a little more than three years of age. They would do such things as take her to a museum and ignore her requests to use the bathroom, only to heap abuse on her when she finally wet herself. Her mother was an erratic caretaker, with insufficient empathy and periodic outbursts of anger. At the time she entered treatment with me, Faith was embroiled in a hostile dependent relationship with her mother, from whom she was inadequately differentiated. She had been too afraid at three and a half years of age to enter nursery school, but after a while found the courage to attend a school picnic. On the bus, however, she became so excited that she wet her clothes. She was too mortified ever to return to that school. A few months later, she lost her father in a tragic accident.

Faith responded very well to treatment, which gave her an opportunity to exercise her latent potential for emotional growth. One of her symptoms was a fetishistic attachment to a pair of rubber boots, which she insisted on wearing whenever she left home. After several months of hard work, we came to understand what lay behind her symptom. At home she had a cat by the name of Boots, whom her mother continually threatened to send away because periodically it went round the house spraying the furniture (because her mother had been too long in getting it spayed). Dreading that her mother might one day make good her threat (after all, she had sent her father away), and living in terror that she herself would be sent away for her own wetting incidents, Faith had contrived to keep Boots with her in one form or other at all times. When this was brought into consciousness, she gave up the fetishistic preoccupation.

As she recalled her own wetting, however, she told me that she had figured out something. She had watched her mother watering the garden and had seen that she controlled the stream with something, the nozzle, that very much resembled her brother's penis. If only she had had one of those, she told me, she would have been able to control her urinary stream and thereby would have been able to avoid all her consternation and misery. I corrected her misunderstanding and, over the next two months, helped her, via discussions, books, drawings, diagrams, and models that we constructed, to know all about her vulva, clitoris, labia, vagina, uterus, ovaries, and oviducts, anatomically and functionally, as well as to become aware of the structure and functioning of the male organs. She participated eagerly and appreciatively in this piece of work, but to my consternation, she developed a new fetish. She now insisted on wearing an old pair of her brother's denim shorts at all times, refusing even to take them off at night. It took us several weeks to clear up this new mystery. Finally, she came in for a session in a dreamy, preoccupied mood. "Why are men bald?" she asked. I reminded her that we had discussed her father's baldness in the past. "That's not what I mean!" she exclaimed angrily, "why are men balled? I saw my father once without his pants on and he had two balls under his penis." With surprise, I recalled to her that we had just spent many weeks discussing such matters. She threw me a scornful look, lay down under the table and began kicking it rhythmically from beneath as she recited over and over: "In the land of France, all the boys wear pants; in the land of France, *all* the boys wear pants," and so on. I said that now I understood: she had seen her brother Frank without his pants on and she wanted to have what he had. She came out from under the table with her eyes glaring and her teeth clenched. "That's right!" she shouted, and she pounded the table with her fist. "I don't want my overalls inside! I want my overalls *outside*, like he has! He can *see* his overalls. He can *touch* his overalls. I can't see mine. I can't touch mine. *I don't know myself!*" The fetish was given up, never to be resumed.

The little girl's ability to know and appreciate, to picture and conceptualize, her inner genital organs is severely limited by her cognitive immaturity. We take for granted our adult capacity to think representationally and abstractly, and we forget the long and arduous road we had to travel in order to acquire it. Yet it was not until the ninth century that the cipher and positional numeration were first introduced into the adult thinking of Western Europe and not until the sixteenth that symbolic algebra finally was devised to lift human minds out of the immediate and concrete into the abstract and theoretical(Dantzig, 1930).

Developmental Impact of the Little Girl's Penis Envy

The discovery of the differences between the sexes presents the little girl with an intellectual and narcissistic problem the resolution of which taxes her ingenuity. Anxiety, envy, and narcissistic strain are inevitable on a temporary basis. The intensity of these reactions and the extent to which they will be overcome or will exert an untoward influence on further development depends on a multiplicity of factors. These include the success or failure of her passage through the separation-individuation process and the kind of self-representation with which she emerges; the way in which she resolves other developmental narcissistic crises, including the necessity of resigning herself to the lack of the adult feminine equipment—breasts, pubic hair, curves, and know-how—with which to compete with her mother for her father's affections; her mother's feelings about her and her femininity; her parents' ability to provide the cognitive assistance she needs from them; the way in which sociocultural input affects her views of herself and her prospects as a girl and as a woman; her ego development during childhood.

Penis envy, narcissistic vulnerability, and masochism are neither limited to the female sex nor are they essential aspects of femininity (Blum, 1976), but Freud's observations in his female patients of prominent difficulties involving these dimensions were not inaccurate. What is questionable is his elaboration of a developmental schema that viewed them as normal aspects of femininity rather than recognizing that such manifestations in adult women represent *failures* of the developmental process. Such failures unfortunately are far from rare. Applegarth (1976), for example, states: "The consequences of penis envy in the life of women can be far-reaching. I have been impressed with relatively low self-esteem of women as a group compared to male patients. Men, of course, have troubles with their self-esteem, but in women the degree of doubt of capacities in comparison with others seems to be of a different order of magnitude. These women seem to have resigned themselves to being unable to achieve except in traditional female fields, or may react to early attempts that run into difficulties with an intense feeling of humiliation at having their defectiveness once again demonstrated" (pp. 258–259).

The "defectiveness" of which Applegarth speaks is a *fantasy* which is much more than the simple persistence into adulthood of penis envy resulting from observation of genital differences. The fantasy of being defective is associated in such underachieving women with fantasied genital inferiority, but the relation between the two is not a simple genetic continuum. A thorough analysis of the feelings of inferiority of such patients reveals that their penis envy is a metaphorical condensation (Grossman and Stewart, 1976) of disturbances of self-esteem and self-image which stem from intrapersonal and interpersonal experiences that have given seeming credence to what should have been only a *temporary* misunderstanding about the difference between the sexes.

When a little girl first becomes aware of genital differences, she lacks the cognitive equipment with which to understand and appreciate her complex and largely unobservable genital organs and to obtain an accurate understanding of male and female anatomy. It is easy for her to conclude that one either has a penis and testicles or has "nothing" (see Lewin, 1948); (Abrams and Shengold, 1974). She requires a great deal of assistance from her parents and from society at large during the years that follow in order to correct her misapprehensions and to help her appreciate herself as a worthwhile, valued, and valuable human being.

Major narcissistic injuries, including humiliating oedipal defeats and disappointments *that contain elements that convey a message to the girl that she is not good enough, not attractive enough, or even* that she is despised, can become interwoven with the early fantasy of genital inferiority. The latter then remains uncorrected and persists as an emotionally charged illusion that is embroiled in intense narcissistic and sexual conflicts thereafter. If parents and other significant adults express and live out their lives in accordance with societal attitudes that portray women as inferior, second-rate, or of secondary importance, this too will tend to reinforce and fixate the little girl's fantasy of genital inferiority. Unless her early conceptual errors are corrected and she is helped to attain adequate self-esteem as a female, the little girl who concludes that either one has a penis or has nothing will grow up into a woman who believes that in life one either is a man or is nothing (see Chasseguet-Smirgel, 1976). Her self-esteem as a woman and as a person will be impaired, and she will be hampered in her pursuit of professional goals and interpersonal satisfactions by her faulty self-image. When such a woman presents herself for analysis, she will present herself with problems that can be referred to as "penis envy."

It is not enough to trace these problems to penis envy, and to stop there as though nothing more needs to be done than to confront the patient with her wish to have a penis (Blum, 1976); (Grossman and Stewart, 1976). To obtain an accurate picture, it is necessary to analyze the specific contents and details of the neurotic process as it has evolved in the course of the patient's development.

A woman in her early forties, for example, was analyzing the meaning of her disturbed relationships with men, intermittent homosexual fantasies, and periodic episodes of compulsive eating and shoplifting. The material that emerged indicated that she disliked being female, wanted to have a penis, and harbored frightening, unconscious wishes to castrate men and turn them into effeminate weaklings. She realized that the rhinoplasty she had undergone in adolescence to correct her deviated septum and make her more beautiful had been motivated by the unconscious wish to be provided with a penis. She remembered a compulsion as a child to make repeated trips to the bathroom to empty her bladder, and recalled earlier attempts to urinate standing up like a boy.

She connected the wish for a penis with the idea that her father would have liked her more had she been a boy and with her resentment of her father's treatment of women as inferior creatures who were to be available for his sexual satisfaction and to serve as mirrors affirming his masculine superiority, but who were to stay in their place and remain unassertive and dependent on his bountifulness. She was bitter about her mother's acquiescent abandonment of her own career plans to content herself with the role of a pretty, dressed-up, painted doll. She complained both that her mother kept her away from her father and pushed her toward him when she was trying to avoid him.

Further analysis (particularly of her ambivalent warding off of closeness with the analyst at the same time that she complained that he was not doing enough for her or taking good enough care of her) traced the wish for a penis in part to unresolved separation-individuation struggles and ambivalence conflicts of the preoedipal period. She connected not liking being female with not wanting to be like her mother, and with attempts to push away from her mother in order to function independently. This was traced to an unresolved, intensely ambivalent, hostile-dependent relationship in which she yearned to be protected and cared for by her mother at the same time that she grappled with urges to flee from her or to destroy her so that she could be free and independent. This had been carried forward into her relationships with men, from whom she would flee whenever they got too close only to yearn excitedly for them to chase her, sweep her up in their arms, and carry her off to bed. Whenever her seductive overtures elicited such a response from a man, she would lose interest and push him away or become terrified lest her rape fantasies be realized. In the transference, this expressed itself in the form of erotic fantasies of the analyst being smitten by her charms and falling in love with her, whereupon she would have to institute maneuvers to exert control over and obtain distance from him or to talk about going off for a vacation or even of breaking off the analysis. She tended often to report enticing dream material or other significant matters only to flee from them after only a partial analysis into humdrum issues or obsessive doubts about the analysis. The aim was to induce the analyst to "run after" her and bring her back to the more salient issues, whereupon she would become both excited and anxious about apparently having seduced and defeated him.

She not only was unclear about the way in which her genital organs were constructed, but she was uncertain about her identity as a separate, independent, whole human being. "I want to be an entity, and separate from my mother," she said. When it was pointed out that she felt that that would have been easier to achieve had she been a boy, she replied, "If I'd been a boy I would have been less like my mother and less dependent on my mother."

She had always envied the greater security boys seemed to possess about who they were and what life had to offer them. She also envied their greater strength and physical power. If she had had such power, she felt, she would have been able to fight off her mother, who forced her to submit to defeat in an early toilet training struggle, and she would have felt less helpless and in need of her mother's powerful presence later on. It was pointed out that she also envied the boy's clearer definition of his entity and identity, since he not only is constructed differently from mother, but has a more clearly and discretely outlined genital anatomy than girls do. "Because what he has is on the outside," she replied; "also if I were a boy my father would've liked me more." She went on to express the idea that had she been a boy, it would have been safer to turn to her father in order to get away from her mother.

We went on to analyze her constant need to fight people off lest she become too dependent upon them and lose her separate identity by becoming too closely involved with them and entwined in their lives. This in turn brought us back to the analysis of her oedipal conflicts on a level less contaminated by preoedipal issues. Gradually, she became able to truly enjoy her femininity and to pursue relationships with men in which she enjoyed closeness and mutual sharing of a sexual experience without fear of loss of control or loss of identity. She became able to pursue her career goals without either fearing the loss of her femininity or feeling that she was invading the territory of men to vengefully attack, dismember, and humiliate them.

Even in cases in which preoedipal conflicts play less of a role than in the one described above, it is apparent that the wish for a penis in women is not a bedrock wish but can be analyzed further, whereupon it is found to stem from multiple underlying conflicts and developmental issues. The following example can serve to illustrate this point of view.

Mrs. W., an attractive young woman in her early twenties, came for analysis complaining of depression, frigidity, and dissatisfaction with her life. Further exploration revealed a masochistic life style and phobic-obsessive symptoms that centered about rape fantasies and fear of harm befalling her husband. Although intellectually gifted, she had left college during her freshman year to marry a brilliant but sadistic man who mistreated, humiliated, and inadequately provided for her and for their child. She was the middle child and only daughter of a cold, aloof, teasing father, and a mother who openly favored her brothers, whom she permitted to mistreat and abuse her. Her mother expressed the opinion that it is a man's world, and women must do what they can to make the best of a bad bargain.

The analysis began with a dream in which Mrs. W.'s father covered her with a newspaper, as though he were embarrassed, when he saw a spot of menstrual blood on her, after which her mother *confusedly* claimed as her own a hope chest that actually was the patient's. Six months later, Mrs. W. had a fantasy of staining my couch with her menstrual blood, to which she associated that she wanted me to know she was a woman. The latter part of the dream turned out to be connected with her mother's having had increasing focal and grand mal seizures, beginning after the patient's older brother had been born and becoming frequent after her own birth. A brain tumor was discovered when my patient was entering her teens.

After the birth of her younger brother, when she was two and a half years old, the patient was sent away to relatives, although the baby brother remained at home in the care of an uncle while her mother returned to the hospital for mysterious surgery that left her without a navel. She refused her mother's food when she returned home, which led to battles between them over eating that lasted for years. She slept in a crib in her parents' bedroom until her younger brother was born, and there were opportunities later on to overhear bits and pieces of her parents' sex life. Her mother would say in the morning, after a nocturnal seizure, that she felt as though she had been beaten with a rubber hose.

Mrs. W. had revered her older brother, who seduced and excited her only to humiliate her when she expressed love for him.

While she was exploring her feelings about her brothers (which in part screened feelings about her father), she dreamt that faces kept popping up at the window to terrify her as she sat on the toilet; her clitoris grew into a huge penis, which she used to beat up those who were trying to scare her. She recalled participating as a child in neighborhood games in which the boys and girls observed each other urinating. She remembered playing with another girl at chopping up pieces of raw meat and pretending they were penises. She interpreted this as "penis envy," one of the rare occasions on which this phrase came up during the analysis. She was unable to participate in ballet lessons as a girl or to swim at school because of inability to undress in front of others. She was so inhibited in school that some teachers considered her stupid.

Attempts to put me to sleep during sessions led to recall of her delight as a preschooler in lying down with her father and, after he had fallen asleep, lovingly combing his hair. She was delighted by his interest in her at that time and by his gift of books after he discovered that she was precociously able to read (her mother put a rapid end to the gifts), but she was crushed when he began to ignore her after she entered kindergarten. Her paternal grandmother took her to church and delivered hellfire-and-damnation sermons to her during her early years. This helped dispose her to enormous guilt and terror when rivalrous sexual interest in her father arose during the oedipal period. In the analysis, she reported terrifying transference dreams in which she was carried off by the devil, as well as dreams in which the analyst appeared as a cold, forbidding Pope.

She was shy, inhibited, and fantasy-ridden during the school-age years, and her adolescence was a misery. Her mother declined slowly but inexorably despite repeated brain surgery that depleted the family finances and necessitated a series of moves to progressively shabbier neighborhoods. She nursed her mother and cooked and cleaned in her place. She was sent periodically to stay with relatives, which provided good as well as bad experiences. She learned from an aunt to love opera—and to identify with the tragic heroines. It was in the context of finding herself increasingly sexually attracted to an uncle who treated her with kindness and appreciation that she quit college and entered her disastrous marriage.

We gradually came to see that her frigidity, depression, and masochism stemmed from multiple sources: guilt and fear of her oedipal fantasies (and sibling rivalry); guilt over the wish to be healthy and happy although her mother's illness had been incurable; fear of loss of control, on a pregenital level as well as because of equation of orgasm with her mother's nocturnal seizures; fury at her family for treating her as a second-class citizen whose feelings were unimportant; Cinderella like erotization of pain and fear. Her depression gradually lifted, and she became orgasmic. She left her sadistic husband for men who treated her with far greater kindness. Toward the end of the analysis, she was able to stand on her own for a time without a man in her life. She took a job and, after a while, with the aid of loans and scholarships, returned to college, from which she graduated with an A average. She embarked on a career which she enjoyed and at which she excelled.

Mrs. W. expressed sadness and resentment that her mother had not appreciated her either as an individual or as a female and had conveyed to her a very poor opinion of women's lot in life. She described a dream that depicted her genitals as a messy, glass- and rock-strewn, deep canyon which she could not believe a man would want to enter. She connected the dream with angry fantasies of castrating men and with her low self-esteem as a person and as a woman. She recalled that as a child her genitals had seemed mysterious and unfathomable, as well as a source of desires that would consign her to purgatory. Her mother not only had not helped her to understand and appreciate her femininity, but had told her frightening stories about pregnancy and childbirth. She came to understand that her mother had blamed her pregnancies for the onset of her seizures (although she had had one or two in adolescence), but what was the most painful to her was that her mother had let her down when she had turned to her for help in knowing and appreciating herself. During the last year of the analysis, Mrs. W.'s feelings about her mother underwent important changes. She realized that her mother had suffered also, and had been a victim of life circumstances and personal limitations. During the termination phase, she went through belated mourning for her mother, who had died a few years before the analysis began. At the end of the analysis, Mrs. W. said she always had considered herself the unluckiest person alive, but never would feel that way again. The positive change in her personality as a result of her analysis reflected her new self-image and appreciation of her femininity.

SUMMARY

Freud was an astute observer, but his understanding of female psychology was distorted by centration on biological forces, the adult neurosis, libido theory, the Oedipus complex, and male psychology. His views on the role of penis envy, narcissism, and masochism in women, and on the female superego, currently are being updated on the basis of new data emerging out of psychoanalytic investigation and direct observational studies.

It has become clear, for example, that core feminine gender identity develops very early and that it is mediated in large part by cognitive development and learning rather than by the impact of the observation of genital differences between the sexes. The little girl's level of cognitive organization does not permit her at first to construct logical, consistent categories of female and male, predicated on coordination of criteria of inclusion and exclusion. She puts girls and women into one group out of intuitive recognition that they "go together" and builds up a view of herself as female on the basis of what she feels as her mother's daughter and what she perceives of the way her parents and other significant objects see her. Her mother's feelings about her, about herself, and about females in general influence her greatly, and her father's responses to and expectations of her have an important impact on her self-image and self-esteem. Her representation of herself as female at first does not necessarily take genital differences between the sexes into account.

The discovery, some time in the second or third year, that the genitals of boys and girls are different from one another presents the girl with a number of problems, however. Her cognitive organization makes it extremely difficult for her to apprehend her complex, incompletely demarcated, and to a large extent internal, unobservable, and impalpable sexual organs. Her initial conclusion is that she lacks desirable body parts which are possessed by other beings. Because of the narcissistic-exhibitionistic libidinal organization of that period of life, this represents a painful narcissistic injury.

The intensity of the girl's castration reaction and the degree to which she will be able to overcome it in the course of further development are determined by multiple internal and external developmental factors. Masochism, narcissistic vulnerability, and penis envy are neither limited to the female sex nor normal outcomes of female development. Where they are prominent features in the psychopathology of female patients, it is insufficient to interpret them as emanating from penis envy as a bedrock, primal cause. Detailed clinical examples are presented to illustrate the thesis that thorough exploration and explication of the multiple sources of such symptomatology in a female analysand is the most effective way of relieving the symptomatology and releasing the potential for emotional growth.

REFERENCES

ABELIN, E. (1971). The role of the father in the separation-individuation process In *Separation-Individuation,* ed. J. B. McDevitt & C. F. Settlage. New York: Int. Univ. Press, pp. 229–252.

ABRAMS, S. & SHENGOLD, L. (1974). The meaning of "nothing." *Psychoanal. Q.* 43:115–119.

APPLEGARTH, A. (1976). Some observations on work inhibitions in women J. Am. Psychoanal. Assoc. 24:251–268.

BENNETT, S. L. (1971). Infant-caretaker interactions *J. Amer. Acad. Child Psychiat.* 10 321–335.

BLUM, H.P. (1976). Masochism, the ego ideal, and the psychology of women *J. Am. Psychoanal. Assoc.* 24:157–192.

BURLINGHAM, D. (1973). The preoedipal infant-father relationship *Psychoanal. Study Child* 28:23–48.

CALOGERAS, R.C. & SCHUPPER, F.X. (1972). Origins and early formulations of the Oedipus complex *J. Am. Psychoanal. Assoc.* 20:751–775.

CHASSEGUET-SMIRGEL, J. (1970). Female Sexuality. Ann Arbor, Mich.: Univ. Mich. Press.

——— (1976). Freud and female sexuality: the consideration of some blind spots in the exploration of the "Dark Continent." *Int. J. Psychoanal.* 57:275–286.

DANTZIG, T. (1930). *Number, the Language of Science* New York: Macmillan, 1933.

FREUD, S. (1915). Instincts and their vicissitudes *S.E.* 14.

——— (1933). Femininity *S.E.* 22.

——— (1940). An outline of psycho-analysis *S.E.* 23.

FRIEDMAN, L. (1977). A view of the background of Freudian theory *Psychoanal. Q.* 46:425–465.

GALENSON, E. & ROIPHE, H. (1971). The impact of early sexual discovery on mood, defensive organization, and symbolization *Psychoanal. Study Child* 26:195–216.

———— (1974). The emergence of genital awareness during the second year of life In *Sex Differences in Behavior* ed. R.C. Friedman, R.M. Richart & R.L. Van de Wiele. New York: Wiley, pp. 223–231.

———— (1976). Some suggested revisions concerning early female development. *J. Am. Psychoanal. Assoc.* 24:29–58.

GREEN, R. (1976). Human sexuality: research and treatment frontiers In *American Handbook of Psychiatry* ed. S. Arieti. New York: Basic Books, pp. 665–691.

GROSSMAN, W. I. & STEWART, W.A.Z. (1976). Penis envy: from childhood wish to developmental metaphor. *J. Am. Psychoanal. Assoc.* 24:193–212.

HORNEY, K. (1932). The dread of women *Int. J. Psychoanal.* 13:348–360.

———— (1933). The denial of the vagina *Int. J. Psychoanal.* 14:57–70.

INHELDER, B. & PIAGET, J. (1959). *The Early Growth of Logic in the Child: Classification and Seriation.* New York: Norton, 1969.

JONES, E. (1927). The early development of female sexuality. *Int. J. Psychoanal.* 8:459–472.

———— (1935). Early female sexuality. *Int. J. Psychoanal.* 16:263–273.

KLEEMAN, J.A. (1971). The establishment of core gender identity in normal girls. *Arch. Sex. Behav.* 1 103–129.

———— (1976). Freud's views on female sexuality in the light of direct child observation. *J. Am. Psychoanal. Assoc.* 24:3–28.

KLEIN, M. (1932). *The Psychoanalysis of Children.* New York: Grove Press, 1960.

KOHLBERG, L. (1966). A cognitive-developmental analysis of children's sex role concepts and attitudes In *The Development of Sex Differences* ed. E. Maccoby. Stanford, Calif: Stanford Univ. Press, pp. 82–173.

LERNER, H.E. (1976). Parental mislabeling of female genitals as a determinant of penis envy and learning inhibitions in women. *J. Am. Psychoanal. Assoc.* 24:269–284.

LEWIN, B.D. (1948). The nature of reality, the meaning of nothing, with an addendum on concentration. *Psychoanal. Q.* 17:524–526.

LICHTENSTEIN, H. (1961). Identity and sexuality: a study of their interrelationship in man. *J. Am. Psychoanal. Assoc.* 9:197–260.

MAHLER, M. (1963). Thoughts about development and individuation. *Psychoanal. Study Child* 18:307–324.

——— (1932). *On Human Symbiosis and the Vicissitudes of Individuation.* New York: Int. Univ. Press.

——— (1974). Symbiosis and individuation: the psychological birth of the human infant. *Psychoanal. Study Child* 29:89–106.

———PINE, F. & BERGMAN, A. (1975). *The Psychological Birth of the Human Infant.* New York: Basic Books.

MONEY, J. & EHRHARDT, A.A. (1972). *Man and Woman, Boy and Girl.* Baltimore: Johns Hopkins Univ. Press.

MULLER, J. (1932). The problem of the libidinal development of the genital phase in girls. *Int. J. Psychoanal.* 13:361–368.

PARENS, H., POLLACK, L., STERN, J. & KRAMER, S. (1976). On the girl's entry into the Oedipus complex *J. Am. Psychoanal. Assoc.* 24:79–108.

PIAGET, J. (1936). *The Origins of Intelligence in Children.* New York: Int. Univ. Press, 1952.

——— (1947). *The Psychology of Intelligence.* Paterson, N.J.: Littlefield, Adams, 1960.

ROIPHE, H. (1968). On an early genital phase: With an addendum on genesis. *Psychoanal. Study Child* 23:348–365.

SANDER, L.W., STECHLER, G., BURNS, P. & JULIA, H. (1970). Early mother-infant interaction and 24-hour patterns of activity and sleep. *J. Amer. Acad. Child Psychiat.* 9:103–123.

———& Burns, P. (1976). Primary prevention and some aspects of temporal organization in early infant-caretaker interaction In *Infant Psychiatry: A*

New Synthesis, ed. E. N. Rexford, L.W. Sander & T. Shapiro. New Haven: Yale Univ. Press, pp. 187–204.

SILVERMAN, M. (1971). The growth of logical thinking. Piaget's contribution to ego-psychology. *Psychoanal. Q.* 40:317–341.

———— (1980). *A Fresh Look at The Case of Little Hans in Freud and his Patients,* ed. M. Kanzer & J. Glenn. New York: Aronson, pp. 95–120.

————Rees, K. & Neubauer, P. (1975). On a central psychic constellation. *Psychoanal. Study Child* 30:127–157.

SPITZ, R.A. (1965). *The First Year of Life.* New York: Int. Univ. Press.

STOLLER, R. (1968). The sense of femaleness. *Psychoanal. Q.* 37:42–55.

———— (1976). Primary femininity. J. Am. Psychoanal. Assoc. 24:5 59–78.

TARTAKOFF, H.H. (1966). The normal personality in our culture and the Nobel Prize complex In *Psychoanalysis—a General Psychology,* ed. R. M. Loewenstein, L. M. Newman, M. Schur & A.J. Solnit. New York: Int. Univ. Press, pp. 222–252.

WOLFF, P.H. (1966). *The Causes, Controls, and Organization of Behavior in the Neonate Psychol. Issues, Monogr. 17.* New York: Int. Univ. Press.

CHAPTER 5:

THE DEVELOPMENTAL PROFILE

[From: *Child Analysis & Therapy,* Ed., Jules Glenn (1978),
pp. 109–127. Northvale, NJ: Jason Aronson]

A BRIEF HISTORY OF THE PROFILE

The Developmental Profile was proposed by Anna Freud as a guide to the organization and diagnostic consideration of clinical material. It grew out of her work with children and adults, and reflects a psychoanalytic viewpoint that pays careful heed to the developmental process. It emphasizes the value of a thorough, multifaceted approach that considers clinical data from multiple, metapsychological points of view. As such, it is both a clinical tool, and perhaps even more important, a special way of thinking about the development and functioning of human beings.

The basic elements of The Profile were contained in a series of lectures delivered by Anna Freud in New York City in 1960 with the title "Four Contributions to the Psychoanalytic Study of the Child." She subsequently introduced The Profile to the Diagnostic Research Group of the Hampstead Child Therapy Clinic in London. There it was used as a diagnostic scheme designed to yield a cross-sectional picture of a child's personality organization at any point in time. She published an outline of The Profile (A. Freud,1962) in 1962, and a year later, Nagera (1963) described its practical use in the diagnostic evaluation of an eleven-and-a-half-year-old boy. Since then, there have been a number of reports describing ongoing modifications and adaptations of The Profile. Its design makes it suitable for the diagnostic assessment not only of children at different developmental levels, but also of adolescents and adults (A. Freud, Nagera, and W.E. Freud, 1965, Laufer, 1965, Meers, 1966, Silverman and Neubauer 1971).

THE USE OF THE PROFILE IN CHILDHOOD

Diagnostic evaluation is more complex and uncertain in childhood than it is with adults. Since the child has not yet completed his course of development, signs of possible pathology/ can best be understood when they are projected upon a backdrop of the normal developmental process with its numerous variations. As Anna Freud (1965) has pointed out, it is often difficult to know whether seemingly pathological phenomena represent serious disturbances for which therapeutic intervention is indicated, temporary difficulties which the child can be expected to overcome spontaneously in the course of further development, or reactions that are normal at certain developmental stages. This is especially marked early in prelatency (Silverman and Neubauer 1971), and again in adolescence (A. Freud 1958).

The Profile seeks to solve this problem by combining a developmental approach with a thorough mapping out of the total personality organization, including both its strengths and weaknesses, at the time clinical data are collected. It's aim is to examine the data in terms of the observable trends within the structure of the developing personality,. rather than viewing them in isolation. This is accomplished by systematically approaching the data from multiple points of view. Care is taken to examine all the major components of the developing personality, and an assessment is made of those characteristics which appear to be key indicators of the degree of overall developmental success or failure.

AN OUTLINE OF THE PROFILE

Before proceeding to a detailed description of The Profile, an outline of its overall organization and the items it encompasses will be presented:

Identifying Data

Sources of Information

I.   Reasons (and circumstances) for referral

II. Description of the individual

III. Family background (past and present) and personal history

IV. Possibly significant environmental circumstances (positive as well as negative)

V.   Assessment of development

  A. Drive development

    1. Libido

      (a) With regard to phase development

      (b) With regard to. libido distribution

        (1) Cathexis of the self

        (2) Cathexis of objects

    2 Aggression

      (a) According to the quantity

      (b) According to the quality

      (c) According to the direction of expression

  B. Ego and superego development<

    1. The Ego:

      (a) Ego apparatuses

      (b) Ego functions

      (c) Ego reactions to danger situations

      (d) Defense organization

      (e) Secondary interference of defenses with ego functions

    2. Superego development and functioning

VI. Assessment of fixation points and regressions.

VII. Assessment of conflicts
  A. External conflicts
  B. Internalized conflicts
  C. Internal conflicts
VIII. Assessment .of some general characteristics, with an Appendix: development of the total personality (lines of development) or age-adequate responses
IX. Diagnosis

THE DETAILS OF THE PROFILE

The Profile starts out by inquiring about the reasons, both conscious and unconscious, for the diagnostic assessment. It then calls for a description of the individual's appearance, characteristic moods, general attitudes, behavioral qualities, etc. There is a section for family background, and personal history, and one for possibly significant, past and present, environmental in6uences, positive as well as negative.

An assessment is then made of the development of the drives, the ego, and the superego. Libidinal and aggressive drive development are considered separately. Libidinal trends are considered according to phase progression, and distribution of libidinal cathexis. As to the former, a description of the degree and quality of drive activity, and its interconnection with ego development and performance is requested. An emphasis is placed upon determining how far the individual has progressed, especially whether the phallic level has been attained, whether phase dominance has been achieved at that level, and whether the highest l vel is being maintained at the time of assessment or there has been significant regression to an earlier one. The sources of information will vary, of course, with the developmental level of the individual being profiled. In latency, for example, generally much more reliance will have to be made upon fantasies and other indirect expressions of drive activity than at other times of life, because of the suppression of direct drive expression characteristic of that period. A record of the sources of the information that was utilized in preparing The Profile is called for at the beginning of The Profile. Depending upon the age and life stage of the individual involved, this might include interviews with the patient and other family members, observations, physical examinations, psychological tests, interviews of teachers, examination of school or health records, etc.

The subsections on libido distribution are concerned with (1) the mechanisms and success of self-esteem regulation, for example, whether there is sufficient narcissistic cathexis of the self to ensure self-esteem and self-regard without leading either to over-investment in, or over-estimation of the self on the one hand, or to excessive dependence upon outside objects for an adequate sense of well-being on the other; and (2) the level and quality of object relationships, past and present, and their correspondence with the level(s) of phase development which have been attained, and at which the individual is currently functioning.

Since much less is known about the phase development of aggressive drives, aggression is considered according to its expression, rather than to the issue of developmental sequencing. The Profile calls for a description of aggressive expression quantitatively—the presence or absence of overt and covert aggression in the individual's behavior, qualitatively—the correspondence of the aggressive expression with the level of libidinal development, and directionally... whether, and the ways in which aggression is expressed toward the object world and/or toward the self. Whenever possible, the profiler is expected to distinguish between defensive and. primary expressions of aggression.

Ego development is assessed in terms of the intactness or defective- ness of ego apparatuses and ego functions, the details of defense organization, and the extent to which defense activity is interfering with ego functioning. The developmental dimension comes into play prominently with regard to the drives, but structural considerations now become equally important. An attempt is made to identify and distinguish between *primary disturbances* of ego functioning arising from congenital or acquired defects in any of the various ego apparatuses and *developmental disturbances* stemming from the environment's failure to facilitate or actual interference with the ego's intrinsic potential for growth and development. The extent of the injury, the degree to which it can be reversed, and the manner in which the disturbance contributes to the development of conflicts, and to the structure and organization of the defense system constitute important diagnostic and prognostic considerations to which The Profile specifically addresses itself. Since the psychoanalytic clinician finds himself overwhelmingly preoccupied with the effects of internalized conflict, the tendency is to seek causal explanations of psychopathology exclusively in that direction. The Pro- file insists on scrutinizing the details of ego development and functioning. This helps draw attention to the possibility of arrests or faults in the ego's development which otherwise might be overlooked. Attention is also called to the role of variations in endowment, and the effect of early structuralizing experience in shaping personality organization, choice of defenses and so on.

The ego's attitude toward danger situations and details of the defense organization are to be fully outlined. The Profile asks whether defenses are employed specifically against individual drives, or against drive activity in general, if they are age-adequate, too primitive or precocious, and whether they are well balanced or restricted to the excessive use of only a few. It also asks whether and to what extent the defenses are effective against anxiety, contribute to or mitigate overall ego strength and mobility, and are able to function without assistance from the object world. Stress is placed upon assessing whether and in what ways defense activity exacts a price for its effectiveness by interfering with significant ego achievements. Allowance also is made for the possibility that the individual's defense organization provides secondary gains to the personality. This needs to be taken into consideration in deciding whether or not treatment should be undertaken, and what the individual's response might be to the initiation of a course of treatment. Subsections on affects and on identifications have been added in The Adolescence Profile (Laufer 1965) because of the special significance of these factors during that period.

The Profile examines the superego in terms of the degree of its development; its sources, functions, effectiveness, and stability; and the degree of secondary sexualization or aggressivization that might have taken place. In each instance the age and stage of the individual being evaluated is taken into consideration. The vicissitudes of ego ideal formation are stressed in the adolescent.

One section calls for the assessment of fixation points and regressive shifts, as indicated by the individual's object relationships, manifest behavior, fantasy elaborations, and by the presence of certain characteristic symptoms and character traits. The genetic origin of fixations and regressions, and their effect upon and significance within the developmental process are to be recorded. Fixations do not impede developmental progress equally or in the same way in all individuals. Temporary regressions are so frequent in childhood that the presence of a regressive movement is meaningful only to the extent that important functions are involved. A regressive movement becomes noteworthy if internal and/or external factors prevent it from being reversed, and/or it ties up such quantities of instinctual energy that it interferers with overall developmental progression (A. Freud, 1965, Frijling-Schreuder,1966, Nagera,1963, Silverman and Neubauer, 1971). Since there are variations among different children in their style of developmental progression and regression, the developmental style becomes an additional factor in assessing regressions in children.

Libidinal regression and reaggressivization of certain functions also takes place regularly in the transition between the oedipal period and latency. Normal adolescence, too, is characterized by temporary, but often sweeping, drive and ego regressions. The developmental orientation of The Profile helps to hold these factors in perspective.

Another section seeks to assess, in structural, dynamic, and economic terms, the presence of conflicts. These might include external conflicts between id-ego agencies and external objects, internalized conflicts between ego-superego agencies and the id (as well as conflicts between different ego-ideals), and/or internal conflicts between competing, incompatible, or insufficiently fused drive representatives (for example, masculinity vs. femininity, activity vs. passivity, libido vs. aggression, etc.). The relative importance of each of these subsections will, of course, vary with the age and stage of the individual being profiled. To a certain extent, what is recorded in this section will be a summarization and synthesis of material recorded earlier in The Profile.

The eighth and last heading prior to integrating the material into a diagnostic statement is the "Assessment of Some General Characteristics." This contains items of particular significance as indicators of overall development, long term prognosis, and treatability via psychoanalytic or other methods. These indicators are frustration tolerance (in general and with respect to specific types of frustration), overall attitude and type of response to anxiety (with particular attention to whether the basic mode is avoidance and warding off, or an attempt at active mastery), sublimation potential, and the balance between progressive forces and regressive tendencies.

A subsection on "Development of the Total Personality (Lines of Development and Mastery of Tasks) or Age-Adequate Responses,"

Which was included in the section on Assessment of Development in the early days of The Profile, has been shifted to an appendix to Section 8, as The Profile is currently at The Hampstead Clinic. This was done because lines of development (A. Freud, 1963) differ greatly as a conceptual category from the remainder of The Profile. They were introduced. as a means of evaluating, on a practical basis, whether. very young children have adequately progressed along certain behavioral and interactional lines of development to be ready for such steps as entry into nursery school. Laufer (1965) has revised the content of this category to make it a useful component of The Adolescence Profile and it has been modified for The Adult Profile.

The final, diagnostic statement aims at an integration of the material into a meaningful statement that formulates the type of disturbance in broad terms. A conclusion is requested that distinguishes among nor- mal development, despite the presence of transitory behavioral disturbances or manifestations of developmental strain; more or less irreversible regressions that are leading to permanent, neurotic symptoms or, character disturbances; arrested or distorted development and structuralization causing atypical personality formation; and malignant processes of fixation, regression, and ego damage leading to disorders of a psychotic, borderline, or delinquent nature.

THE PROFILE AS A DIAGNOSTIC TOOL

The value of The Developmental Profile as a diagnostic tool is obvious when it is employed in the evaluation of children, whose development is still incomplete and for whom, therefore, the diagnostic process has to be fitted into a developmental frame of reference. A modification of The Profile making it suitable for use with adults has also been prepared. Its initial purpose was to serve in studies of children and their parents, but it soon became apparent that The Profile could offer enough advantages to the assessment of adults to make it worthwhile in its own right. Although a developmental orientation is less important for adults than it is for children, its stress on ongoing development and epigenetic reorganization provides a perspective of surging life and movement. The Profile's emphasis on a metapsychologically balanced, cross-sectional picture of the *total* personality structure helps assure diagnostic accuracy. It is a particularly good instrument for assessing and studying the analyzability of prospective patients. In this regard it is notable that Freud never abandoned any of the various metapsychological points of view as new data propelled him on to new vantage points from which to observe and comprehend the workings of the human mind. As Rapaport and Gill (1959) have pointed out, human psychology is so complex that its accurate comprehension is ensured only by approaching it from multiple points of view.

It is obvious that The Developmental Profile is no more than a conceptual tool, varying in its usefulness according to the experience and skillfulness of the diagnostician employing it. It is not to be filled out like a questionnaire. The Profile embodies a particular way of looking at psychological data. It certainly cannot be expected to solve the problems of differential diagnosis.

AN EXAMPLE OF THE DIAGNOSTIC USE
OF THE PROFILE

A condensed summary of The Profile's employment in the diagnostic process with a young child can serve to illustrate its use, as well as its usefulness.

Identifying data: Frank was three years, six months old at the time of The Initial Profile. He came from a middle-class family, with parents in their early thirties and had one brother, three years eight months older than the patient.

Sources of information: The Profile was based upon review of infant study, prenursery, and nursery school records; nursery school observations over a two-month period; interviews with each parent; and a play interview with the child. Psychological testing was not done yet because of research design.

I. Reasons for Referral:

Frank was brought at age two and one half years to a child guidance center which focused on preschoolers because his mother considered herself inadequate and in need of assistance in child-rearing. She listed her son's problems as low frustration tolerance, stubbornness, refusal to cooperate with her, and a quick temper that contributed to much fighting both with his brother and her. The•center staff noted labile mood swings and a lack of animation or sustained pleasure.

II. Description of Child:

Frank at three and one half years was tall, sturdy, masculine, handsome (but less so than his brother). Despite his almost continuous smiling, he had a sad look. He was exuberant, active, and always busy. He sought and usually attained the limelight in his nursery school group by exhibiting his strength, loud voice, and an excellent physical ability of which he clearly was very proud. Frank was socially adept and quickly became the leader among his peers. With his teachers, he varied between flexible cooperation and cranky irritability. He would pout and sulk when unable to get his way, and become angry arid defiant when "given orders." Frank was particularly intolerant of frustration of his attempts to communicate his wishes, or to demonstrate independent proficiency with educational materials. He courted the (female) teachers with gallantry and charm, and the girls in the group vied to be his favorite; Frank's affects were somewhat labile. He might cry in misery or rage, and fume when frustrated, but he would not maintain his distress for long. He preferred to snap himself out of his unhappiness and cheer up.

III. Family Background and Personal History:

Frank's mother was a very attractive, likeable woman who had had a very difficult, severely traumatized childhood. This left her. with certain immaturities, and a fear of close relationships and either being depended upon or depending upon anyone. She had fears of being aroused by her infant sons, and she tended to push them away from her by distancing maneuvers that included intermittent failure to meet their requests for need satisfaction. As infants they often had been left to cry alone in their room. From eight months on, Frank often was cared for by babysitter's. The father, a writer, was an anxious; intermittently depressed, somewhat immature man who alternated between being unavailable to the children, and devoting himself tenderly to them. He enjoyed cooking for them, and actively encouraged the development of both athletic prowess and facility with words. There was continual marital strife, and the couple was contemplating divorce. The older brother was close to Frank, but continually and mercilessly teased, bullied, and hit him.

Frank's birth was unremarkable, as was the pregnancy. He was turned over to a series of short-term maids for care, and received erratic, shifting stimulation. He was constantly rocked and held in the early months to prevent him from crying. However, after one month, the cessation of the flow of breast milk led to a period of discomfort and crying. Although Frank wanted to give up his bottle at a year, his mother encouraged him to retain it to make certain he would sleep through the night. He finally gave up his night bottle by hiding it in his mother's drawer when he was three years old. Teething was painful. Very early Frank was noted to be perceptually alert and interested in his environment. He quickly became attuned to his mother's comings and goings. Motor development was adequate except that independent observers (he was the subject of an infant study) noticed "ow frustration-tolerance, perseveration, and toeing outward"during the first year. He was very outgoing by the age of two years and was rather aggressive until he settled down at two and one half. Toilet training was "easy" and unhurried. Frank developed full control within a month after a potty seat was made available to biro at age two. Until Frank was two, his mother had to clean his penis twice a week and periodically apply salve because of an incomplete circumcision. He became fearful of having his hair and nails cut after he observed his father urinating when he was one year eight months old.. Frank became concerned about broken things after he "discovered"and began to occasionally play with his penis at two years two months. He became anxious about his penis after he was bathed with a female cousin, and his brother began to tease him by telling him that his penis would fall off.

IV. Possibly Significant Environmental Circumstances:

Frank's mother sought assistance at a time when he was approaching nursery school age, his older brother was approaching termination of analytic treatment at the child guidance center (for unhappiness and fury at his mother), and her marital problems were reaching crisis proportions. Probable deleterious environmental factors have been described in the above section. Possible favorable influences include the parents' genuine affection and concern for their children, and the influence of the child guidance center personnel while conducting .the infant study in which Frank had been included.

V. Assessment of Development: A. Drive Development:

1. Libido: (a) Regarding phase development, there was evidence of early phallic ascendancy and phallic dominance in Frank's relations with his teachers and peers, his play themes, his struggle against masturbatory urges at naptime, and his intermittent castration fears. Persistent anal-sadistic conflicts were revealed in his avoidance of the sand box, discomfort with messy materials, and occasional excessive hand washing. More prominent oral fixations were suggested by an apparent need to control and regulate people to make certain that they remained available for need satisfaction, an intensive struggle against the emergence of powerful yearnings for passive care and nurturance (in which his father seemed to be the object rather than his mother), and erratic eating patterns. Frank's strong quest for attention seemed to have roots in all libidinal phases.

(b) Regarding libido distribution, Frank seemed to depend excessively on obtaining admiration and attention from the outside to maintain adequate, positive cathexis of his self-representation. His relation- ship with objects was uneven, with oscillation between cheerfully and optimistically seeking friendship and attention, and defiantly pushing people away in favor of an insistent show of self-sufficiency. This seeming paradox became clearer when viewed in terms of the fact that Frank learned early in his life that his parents were erratically available, and often needed to be entertained or cheered up. His mother was more likely to stay With him when he fought with her, than when he wooed her, either affectionately or anaclitically.

2. Aggression: Frank was noted from the beginning to be quite aggressive, with angry impulses tending to interfere with neutralization. However there was an increasing modulation, taming, and channeling of aggressive energies into relating to others, learning, and play activities using large muscles. At the time of profiling,

these modes were well-developed, with intermittent regression into short-lived, but in• tense temper tantrums, successfully but barely controlled impulses to bite, and episodes of defiance and rebelliousness. Aggressive impulses were almost always directed outward.

B. Ego and Superego Development:

l. Ego Development:

There were indications from early on of the possibility of minor, intrinsic defects in ego apparatuses implicating motor control and cognition. Observation in infancy had led to the conclusion that there were mild neurological irregularities as evidenced by perseveration, low frustration tolerance, toeing outward, and poor manipulation of objects. His parents reported that between two and•two and one half years of age, Frank had fallen a lot, tripped over his feet, and walked into walls when tired and irritable. Neurological examination when he was two and a half revealed no abnormalities except for "excessive accessory movements to maintain balance during balancing tricks." Classroom observation during the profiling period revealed that Frank at times tended to lose his balance, fall, or trip over himself. Most o the time, however, he was a superb, unusually supple, and graceful athlete. The profiler concluded that although interference with motor control by emotional conflict might have explained the occasional lapses, the possibility of a neurological defect affecting perceptual- motor or motor coordination needed to be assessed further. Ego functions were well developed except for certain areas. Although language functions were highly developed, Frank at times tended to use words that he did not truly understand, and to reverse syntactical order. In addition to the intermittent impairment of large motor control, there was some constriction of the range of affective responses, and a tend- ency to a stubborn inflexibility in cognitive operations. Frank's inter- mittently impaired frustration tolerance and excessive aggressivity were considered to reflect defective and/or delayed drive synthesis and neutralization, and hence, a general ego weakness of an as yet undetermined severity. The ego's reaction-to danger situations was difficult to clearly identify. However, there seemed to be a combination of fear of loss of the object's love, fear of loss of the object, and castration anxiety, all perceived as emanating from the outside world. Frank's more basic fear seemed to be of ego passiv- ity. His defense organization seemed to center around complex introjective/projective mechanisms to exteriorize internal and internalized conflicts. This was followed by alloplastic mecha- nisms to control external objects to ensure their availability, and the likelihood of favorable responses, and to provide an illusion of active mastery. Only if this failed was there a tendency to give in to a regressive pull to an infantile, anaclictic state in which he might feel protected and nurtured. Otherwise regression was warded off vigorously. The major price paid for the upkeep of this defensive organization was restriction of affective experi- ence, a degree of superficiality and shallowness of object relations, and a tendency toward phobic avoidance of situations threatening him either with failure of ego mastery or with the danger of passive libidinal temptation.

2. Superego Development:

For so young a child superego development is approachable largely in a predictive fashion. Superego precursors, in the form of reaction-formations and internalized parental guidelines about be- havior, seemed to operate relatively well. There were, however, intermittent eruption of aggressive defiance or attack directed mainly against his mother and female teachers. The relative insufficiency of neutralization of aggressive drive impetus indicated the danger of eventual harsh superego functioning, and obsessive struggles for self-control. The alloplastic defensive organization, in which externalization was playing a significant role, suggested possible problems later on in moving beyond fear of external punishment to true internalization of behavioral guidelines. Precociously developed ego ideals encouraged Frank to be charming and pleasing to people. These ideals could be seen as serving to help offset the tendency to attack the objects of erupting aggressive derivatives. The need for a continual show of strength and competence to maintain adequate self-esteem, it was apparent, could present problems when the inevitable defeats of the oedipal period and beyond were encountered.

VI. Fixation Points and Regressions needed to be assessed in a somewhat fluid manner in a child only three and one half years old. As described in Section V. A. 1, and 2, there was evidence of persistent oral-dependent and oral-aggressive tendencies in Frank's behavior, fantasies, and object relations. This did not, however, prevent advance into phallic ascendancy and even dominance.

VII. Assessment of Conflicts revealed external conflicts in the form of struggles with maternal figures who threatened to take over and dominate him. Internalized conflicts existed between conflicting ego ideals and between phallic-exhibitionistic, rivalrous ambitions and castration anxiety. Internal conflicts involved active vs. passive strives (with the very beginnings of a masculinity-femininity conflict) and ambivalence in object relations.

VIII. Assessment of Some General Characteristics: All informants reported that frustration tolerance was low. Observation indicated a relative intolerance to frustration of both libidinal and aggressive drives that was much less severe than had been reported by others. Inability to communicate his wishes led to the most intense frustration: The overall attitude to anxiety seemed to center around an urge to active mastery, but with a tendency to denial and externalization that could have indicated inadequate tolerance of anxiety. Although Frank's striving for achievement and the social value of the aims and directions provided by his ideals indicated a good sublimation potential, a surprising lack of creativity and avoidance of certain classroom activities were observed. There were indications of strong progressive tendencies that seemed to counterbalance a regressive pull to oral-dependent inclinations.

IX. Diagnosis: Despite early deprivations and possible minor organic defects, Frank was showing progressive development. His current symptomatic expressions could be viewed as being partly transitory and related to current environmental stresses, and partly permanent, in the form of ego distortions which were relatively ego-syntonic. It could be expected that there might be characterological deformities in the form of persistent phallic character traits. Associated with this is a diminished range of possible affective experiences resulting from the introjective-projective and alloplastic processes. These appeared to be deeply ingrained into Frank's ego structure. The balance of progressive versus regressive forces, and the intensity of his castration anxiety were not entirely clear. Frank would need to be watched carefully as he went through the turmoil of the oedipal phase. There was the real danger, because of his intense ambivalence towards his mother, his regressive tendency, his insistent passive strives, and turning to his father as the most important love object, of the development of a latent homosexuality and an obsessive tendency. The intense reaction-formations against anal erotic impulses, indicative, perhaps, of inadequate resolution of anal erotic trends, indicated a possible weak point in any future, major, regressive shift. Sublimation of drive energies into learning seemed inadequate, and required further assessment.

As a result of the findings of this Profile, the decision was made not to intervene psychotherapeutically, but to investigate further into the indications of a possible, mild, neurological defect, and to follow Frank's ongoing progress. Intervention in the form of parent counseling did appear to be indicated, and was carried out. The expectation was that depending upon the neurological assessment, there was a strong possibility that psychoeducational intervention would be required. De- pending upon the way Frank negotiated the oedipal period, psychotherapy of one form or another might prove necessary.

A second Profile, drawn up six months later, revealed the presence of a physiologically mild, but developmentally significant neurological disorder. It consisted of a mild perceptual-motor, motor, and aphasic disorder that interdigitated with other emotional-developmental factors to produce a significant learning disturbance, and a skewing of personality development. Highly successful assistance was provided for Frank (for further details, see Silverman, 1976).

AN EVALUATION OF THE PROFILE

The Profile itself is an imperfect tool, and it has been undergoing continual modification and refinement since its introduction. As Nagera (1963) has pointed out, the various items of The Profile belong to different levels of conceptualization, and the process of integration is far from simple. The degree to which the different dimensions of the personality are investigated, and the depth to which they are explored also varies from one section of the Profile to another. For example, affects, cognitive functioning, and the role of identifications in the period prior to adolescence receive relatively little attention. The Profile and the way of thinking which it represents have been applied to more and more individuals since its introduction, and have especially been applied to the study of groups of people at different levels and with different kinds of problems. The knowledge that has been gained about various aspects of human development and functioning has been integrated back into The Profile and has furthered its development as a diagnostic and conceptual instrument. This readiness to make continual changes and improvements is reflected in its instructions for use. The Profile-Maker is advised to use the various headings to facilitate a thorough thinking. through of clinical material, rather than as a questionnaire to be filled out. He is asked to look for inconsistencies and contradictions, and to use these observations to point to areas in which further investigation and clarification are necessary, rather than expecting to come to a definitive and certain diagnostic statement.

FUNCTIONS OF THE PROFILE IN CLINICAL AND INVESTIGATIVE WORK

At the Hampstead Clinic, The Profile has been utilized not only at the beginning of treatment, but at various points in the process, as well as at the end of treatment. It is not expected that a complete or entirely accurate diagnostic picture can be attained at the initial diagnostic stage. Data gathered during an ongoing analysis can be used both to improve and enhance diagnostic understanding of a case, and to assess the accuracy of the initial diagnostic process. The Terminal Profile can be used to objectively appraise the effects of treatment.

The Profile's function as a research tool is a central aspect of its use. It is hoped that by systematically collecting and comparing data from many cases, knowledge can be gained that can be used to validate and refine many of our theoretical propositions. It is also hoped this knowledge can contribute-to the eventual elaboration of a psychoanalytic classification of childhood and adult disorders. The Profile has been employed to study the development of blind children (see A. Freud, Nagera, and E.W. Freud 1965) and to investigate the functioning of atypical and borderline children (Thomas et al., 1966). Michaels and Stiver (1965) have used it to draw up a composite picture of the personality organization of "the impulsive, psychopathic character." It also lends itself very well to use in investigations of the developmental process (Silverman, Rees, and Neubauer 1975). W.E. Freud (1967, 1968, 1971) has developed a Baby Profile for recording baseline observations with predictive value for use as an initial tool in longitudinal studies of development. Heinicke (1965) has used The Profile to com- pare the effectiveness and results of different forms of psychotherapy in childhood.

The Developmental Profile, in other words, is more than a clinical, diagnostic tool. It is an encapsulation of Anna Freud's thorough, open-minded, developmentally oriented, metapsychologically balanced, investigative approach to psychoanalysis. While its use is too time-consuming and tedious to make it suitable for general use with all patients, it is greatly useful for selected purposes, and can serve as an invaluable guide to the organization and integration of data. As a metapsychological outline it can be kept in mind and mentally filled out for all patients.

REFERENCES

FREUD, A. (1958). Adolescence. *Psychoanalytic Study of The Child* 13:255–278.

———— (1960). Four contributions to the Psychoanalytic Study of the Child, Lectures delivered in New York City.

———— (1962). Assessment of childhood DISTURBANCES. *Psychoanalytic Study of The Child* 17:149–158.

——— (1963). The concept of developmental lines. *Psychoanalytic Study of The Child* 18:245–265.

——— (1965). *Normality and Pathology in Childhood, Assessments in Development.* New York: International Universities Press.

FREUD, A., NAGERA, H., AND FREUD, W.E. (1965), Metapsychological assessment of the adult personality: the adult profile. *Psychoanalytic Study of The Child* 20:9–41.

FREUD, W.E. (1967). Assessment of early infancy: problems and considerations. *Psychoanalytic Study of The Child* 22:216–238.

——— (1968). Some general reflections on the metapsychological profile. *International Journal of Psycho-Analysis* 49:498–501.

——— (1971). The baby profile, part II. *Psychoanalytic Study of The Child* 26:172–194.

FRIJLING-SCHREUDER, E.C.M. (1966). THE adaptive use of aggression. *International Journal of Psycho-Analysis* 47:364–369.

HEINICKE, C. M. ET AL. (1965). Frequency. of psychotherapeutic session as a factor affecting the child's developmental status. *Psychoanalytic Study of The Child* 20:42–98.

LAUFER, M. (1965). Assessment of adolescent disturbances: the application of Anna Freud's diagnostic profile. *Psychoanalytic Study of The Child* 20:99–123.

MEERS, D.R. (1966). A diagnostic profile of psychopathology in a latency child. *Psychoanalytic Study of the Child* 21:483–526.

MICHAELS, J.J. & STIVER, I.P. (1965). The impulsive psychopathic character according to the diagnostic profile. *Psychoanalytic Study of The Child* 20:124–141.

NAGERA, H. (1963). The developmental profile: notes on some practical considerations regarding its use. *Psychoanalytic Study of The Child* 18:511–540.

RAPAPORT, D., & GILL, M.M. (1959). The points of view and assumptions of metapsychology. *International Journal of Psycho-Analysis* 40:153–162.

SILVERMAN, M.A., & NEUBAUER, P.B. (1971). The use of the developmental profile for the prelatency child. In *The Unconscious Today.* ed. M. Kanzer, pp. 363–380. New York: International Universities Press.

————REES, K., & NEUBAUER, P.B. (1975). On a central psychic constellation. *Psycho-analytic Study of The Child* 30:127–157. Silverman, M.A. (1976). The diagnosis of minimal brain dysfunction in the preschool child. In *Mental Health in Children.* vol. II, ed. D.V. Siva Sankar, pp. 221–301. Westbury: PJD Publications.

THOMAS, R. ET AL. (1966) Comments on some aspects of self and object representation in a group of psychotic children: an application of Anna Freud's diagnostic profile. *Psychoanalytic Study of the Child* 221:527–580.

CHAPTER 6

THE MALE SUPEREGO[1]

[From: (1986). Psychoanalytic Review, 73D(4):23-40.]

Freud's early view of the superego emphasized its preoedipal origins in the ego ideal—in the child's wish to regain the lost primary narcissism of infancy through identification with idealized parental images. The persistence of this view is reflected in his use of the terms *ego ideal* and *superego* more or less interchangeably throughout his writings, even after his introduction of the latter term in 1923.

The shift to the term *superego* in *The Ego and the Id* (1923) marked a major turning point in Freud's conceptualization of the internal psychological system that deals with matters of conscience and morality. Beginning at that point and continuing more or less consistently thereafter (Freud, 1923, 1924a, 1924b, 1925, 1926a, 1926b, 1933,1940), he emphasized the centrality of the Oedipus complex, of oedipal identifications, and of the aggressive, punitive function of the system "superego" in his approach to it as a metapsychological organization within the mind. He now described the superego as "the heir of the oedipus complex" (1923, p. 36).

---

[1] I would like to express my appreciation to my good friends and colleagues, Drs. Bertrand Cramer and Katherine Rees, Mrs. Eva Wolfson, and, especially, Dr. Peter Neubauer, for the invaluable benefits obtained from discussions with them of data gathered over many years of spending up to 15 hours each week observing children in nursery schools and day care centers in the course of two research projects carried out under the auspices of the Child Development Center of the Jewish Board of Guardians (now the Jewish Board of Child and Family Services).

His reasons for the shift in his emphasis were most probably twofold. On the one hand, it appears to reflect his realization that the events of the oedipal period, during which major emotional, affective, and cognitive shifts take place, lead to crucial psychological reintegrations in which the basic structural and functional organization of the mind crystallizes into a more or less stable form that will persist thereafter. On the other, as Jones (1955), Loewald (1979), and others have pointed out, Freud was well aware of the intense resistance his revelation would evoke not only in the world at large but also among psychoanalysts themselves. It is extremely likely that his distress over the attempts of Adler, Jung, Rank, and others to replace the Oedipus complex with more palatable explanatory constellations as "the essential etiological factor in the neuroses and elsewhere" (Loewald, 1979) contributed significantly to his repeated insistence on the central importance of the Oedipus complex and on its resolution in the formation of the superego.

The disparity between Freud's variable emphases on preoedipal, narcissistic origins and on the struggle to resolve oedipal conflicts in the formation of the superego may be more apparent than real. After all, the Oedipus complex does not suddenly arise *de novo*, without any connection to the developmental issues that have preceded it, and narcissistic tensions play a major role in generating oedipal strivings and conflicts. The Oedipus complex does not emerge merely out of the ascendancy of the genital phase of psycho-sexual development. It also arises out of the complexities of self-object differentiation and separation-individuation that mediate the transition from dyadic to triadic object relations (see Jacobson, 1964; Mahler, 1968 ; Mahler, Pine, & Bergman, 1975; Silverman, 1986). The drive for oedipal victory in the face of inevitable crushing defeat and despite the danger of the terrible, retaliatory punishment that is perceived is rooted in large measure in narcissistic aspirations that are traceable back to the very beginnings of life. Even the love that is felt during the oedipal period toward truly differentiated, genuine love objects derives from passage through the intricacies involved in overcoming infantile narcissism sufficiently to perceive drive objects as separate beings who are both lovable and to be loved in their own right. Human development is protracted, sequential and epigenetic, with each phase growing out of those that have come before it.

The attainment, through the preoedipal and early oedipal years, of sufficient ego development to carry out its directives with relative consistency (see Beres, 1958) provides the groundwork for the later consolidation of the superego as an internalized, relatively autonomous, stable agency. The acquisition of *internal* controls (see Kennedy & Yorke, 1982) to replace the need for external restraints is essential to this development. Several processes are involved: (1) the emergence of defense mechanisms through which drive energies are deflected back onto the self, namely, reversal and reaction-formation in the interest of winning the parents' approval and love; (2) identification with the parents as frustrators and as providers, as aggressors and as comforters, as hate objects and as love objects (see A. Freud, 1936; Gillman, 1982; Holder, 1982; Spitz, 1958); and (3) sufficient ego advance in the areas of memory, cognitive organization and understanding, language, self-observation, and the capacity for sublimation to permit effective implementation by the ego of superego directives (see Arlow, 1982; Hartmann & Loewenstein, 1962).

The two seemingly disparate views of the superego—as "heir to infantile narcissism" and as "heir to the oedipus complex"—can be viewed as a system of moral restraint that develops over a long period, through childhood and adolescence, in which special importance is played by the impact of oedipal conflicts and

147

attempts at resolving them. It serves to ensure narcissistic integrity by protecting the individual from dangers that threaten to do harm to the individual and, at least initially, by striving after the feeling of secondary narcissistic, blissful goodness that is obtained via attainment of an idealized self image that corresponds to that which is favored by loving, protecting, and idealized parental objects. In optimal circumstances, the latter is gradually replaced by a more realistic, relatively autonomous, more mature system of abstract, ethical restraints. The time has come, as Brenner (1982, 1983) has observed, to reexamine the superego as a psychic system in its own right, independent of and superordinate to its individual constituents, contents, components, and functions. The time has also come, as Arlow (1982) has stated, to reexamine the male and female superego separately from one another. With this latter point in mind, let us turn to an examination of the development of the superego in the boy.

Superego development begins at birth with parental communication to the child of the feelings, attitudes, hopes, and expectations they have toward him. As I have indicated in a related context (Silverman, 1981, in press), parents relate very differently to their male and female children from the very outset. They expect their male children to be rougher, tougher, and more difficult to handle. In part, this corresponds to biological differences between girls and boys, since boys do appear to be intrinsically stronger and more aggressive and to be somewhat less precocious in their rate of ego development, affecting their capacity-for self-restraint and self-control. In part, however, it reflects the parents' own fantasies and the transmission through them of different cultural expectations with regard to male and female children. They transmit these attitudinal differences in the way they handle their children, applying different sets of permissive signals facilitating responses and of opposing and restraining signals inhibiting responses. They tend to be rougher in their handling of boys, furthermore, which is likely to provoke more aggression in them than in their female offspring. The expectation that girls will be "sugar and spice and everything nice," while "boys will be boys" tends to be self-fulfilling.

The interactional, nonverbal cues that indicate to infants what their parents expect of them rapidly become coordinated with their own, intrinsic tendencies to form a basic core (Weil, 1970) of emerging id and ego characteristics that include a greater tendency to aggression and a slower rate of development of the capacity for self-restraint and self-control in boys as compared with girls. Furthermore, mothers and fathers tend to handle their children differently from the very beginning and more or less continually thereafter. Through their ongoing interaction with their parents (and older siblings), children build up impressions of them in which they tend to perceive their fathers as stronger, rougher, harder, and firmer and their mothers as gentler, softer, smoother, and easier both in their appearance and in their manner. These impressions evolve over the first few years out of cognitive processes (see Kohlberg, 1966) that are coordinated with equally powerful emotional factors (Silverman, in press). The latter at first are dominated by introjective and projective tendencies that color emerging object representations with qualities that are derived from the child's own characteristics and propensities. It is natural, therefore, for boys to perceive somewhat greater aggressivity in their objects than for girls to do so. Relationships at first dyadically involve child and mother, with father apparently perceivable as "another mother." The existence of two classes of beings, mothers and fathers, females and males, becomes recognizable only much later on.

Children's self-perceptions, likewise, are greatly influenced by and incompletely demarcated from their perceptions of their parents. The character of "I" or the "ego," as it begins to form, is very poorly differentiated from that of the "other" in interaction with which the ego begins to take shape; the "I" can only begin as part of a "We" in which the two participants are unclearly and inconsistently demarcated from another. What Freud (1926a) referred to as "primal identification" holds sway at first. Via an intricate combination of sensorimotor cognition and introjective-projective emotional mechanisms, the infant gradually becomes aware of the separateness between itself and its mother. Since the functions served by the mother and her intimate and essential participation in most waking experience are integral elements in the basic feelings of unpleasure and pleasure and of helplessness s24 and the illusion of infantile omnipotence, the recognition of her separateness creates a serious tear in the configuration of the infant's primary narcissism. This apparently is repaired via reincorporative, defensive, psychological mechanisms to restore the illusion of internal oneness. Secondary or true identifications (modeled after the incorporative mode that is associated with feeding and drifting into the postprandial sleep that "knits up the raveled sleeve of care") serve developmental progression by simultaneously or alternately "identifying" the mother as separate and "identifying with" her as a lost part of the idealized, omnipotent, global self that must be reincorporated. A powerful tendency to be like the mother coincides, therefore, with the beginnings of differentiation from her.

The pull toward identificatory union with the mother presents a problem to the child, however, as the child begins to develop a capacity for genuine, self-assertive independence in the latter part of his first year and the early part of his second year. Symbolic mental imagery, including representational thought and the beginnings of language, combines with multimodal perceptual-motor coordination, crawling, and then walking to give the child enormous powers that had been lacking. As a toddler becomes intoxicated with his new abilities in the practicing subphase of separation-individuation, he undergoes a crisis of ambivalence. He finds himself torn between aggressive self-assertion and anger at any one who interferes with it, including his mother, and experiences anxiety when he realizes that absorption in the solitary, independent exercise of his motor, sensory, and intellectual capacities takes him away from the very person who is an indispensable part of himself at a time when mother is so important to him emotionally.

The ambivalent, dependent-independent conflict taking place in the child, marked by alternatively pushing away from the mother and insistently demanding the mother's presence, is matched by a complementary crisis of ambivalence on the mother's part. She too finds herself both pleased and grateful for her child's newly acquired ability to do things without her and yet hurt and angry that her "baby," who once was part of her and for whom she has lovingly and self-sacrificingly devoted herself, is now "rejecting" her care and her ministrations to move off on his own away from her. Her anger is only increased when she has to set limits for her child and curb his exploratory activities, which provokes even more negativity, anger, and rage on the child's part. The mounting conflict within each of them and between the two of them leads to an intense, bidirectional rapprochement crisis between mother and child in which they must struggle with intense feelings about their separateness and togetherness, their mutual dependence and independence, their love and hate toward one another, their excitement with and anger at one another, and so on. Although certain aspects of this conflict obtain for both girls and boys, the differences are, needless to say, quite great. For one thing, in the midst of all this tumultuous internal and external struggle, the difference between the sexes begins to make itself apparent to the child and the beginnings of gender-related attitudes and expectations that will form the core of the child's gender-role identity begin to develop.

When the boy discovers that there are beings who do not possess the genital organs he has come to prize as an integral part of his personal and sexual identity, in the course of movement from narcissistic-exhibitionistic to phallic-exhibitionistic modes, he tends to react with shock and fear that he can lose them. At first, he cannot imagine that his preoedipally perceived, all-powerful mother does not possess a penis and testicles. Even direct observation of her lack of external male genitalia is greeted at first by denial. His belief that somewhere within her she does possess these prized genital organs reinforces the interest in the insides of her body that had begun independently, in response to the boy's fascination with her ability to give birth to babies from within herself. His heightened interest in the insides of the mother's body combines with his interest in the pleasurable sensations derived from pushing his excited, tumescent penis against objects to lead him toward a dawning perception of heterosexual genital activity that intersects with his increasingly focused interest in his genitals as an essential aspect of his self-identity.

When he does finally become aware that his mother does not possess a penis or testicles (and his preoperational cognitive organization does not allow him to appreciate the value of the largely internal, unobservable and impalpable genital and reproductive organs of the female), he inevitably finds himself on the horns of a dilemma. On the one hand, his core, preoedipal self-perception is an epicene one in which identification with his idealized, all-powerful mother, in order to recapture the illusion of oneness with her and her powers, is extremely important. On the other hand, he is forced to disavow his identification with his mother in order to preserve the integrity of the masculine self-image that is emerging within him but is threatened by the castration anxiety that accompanies his initiation into awareness of the existence of two sexes in the world.

At this point, the boy's father becomes a necessary, invaluable ally. Fathers appear to play an essential role from very early on in modulating the intensity of interaction between mothers and their children. They play an important part as early as the differentiation subphase of separation-individuation, and they do so in two ways. One is by providing a buffer between the mother and the baby by competitively pulling the mother's interest and attention away from her baby. The second function they serve is that of "another" interesting parent, similar to the all-important mother but at the same time different enough to attract attention in his own right. Self-object differentiation, as Jacobson (1964) emphasized, is facilitated by object-object differentiation. Infants are aided in their cognitive differentiation of themselves from their mothers by studying the similarities and differences between their parents.

This is illustrated in the observation of a five-month-old boy who was perched in his mother's lap after a feeding, cradled by her hands and arms, facing her and keenly peering at her face, as his father arrived on the scene. The little boy appeared to be intently studying her features as he swept his eyes over them and to be attending closely to the shifts in the cadence, tone, and inflection of her voice. He smiled and gurgled whenever she spoke to him in an especially inviting way and waggled her face in front of him to invite him to respond to her. He threw an arm out periodically to grab hold of her glasses or clutch onto her hair. Mother and child clearly were having a good time together.

Suddenly, he seemed to notice his father's voice coming from above and a little beyond her left shoulder. The chortling sounds, the smiling, and the glowing look on his face instantly disappeared. With a sober, stolid look, he shifted his gaze back and forth, making 11 passes back and forth altogether, between the two faces of his parents. The studying activity then ended as suddenly as it had begun, and he returned to the glowing, smiling, chortling, pleasurable interest he had been taking in his mother's face before being interrupted by the distraction of the similarities and differences between the two parents. *From then on he paid no further heed to his father.* Clearly, although his mother was by far the primary object of his interest and of his affections, his father could attract enough of his attention to interrupt his interaction with his mother for some "scientific" study of gender differences.

Beginning in the early practicing period, as Abelin (1971) has pointed out, the father evokes the toddler's attention as someone who is an "other" like his mother, yet is somewhat different from her, which makes him very interesting. As Abelin puts it, "The father comes to stand for distant, 'nonmother' space —for the elated exploration of reality. A special quality of exuberance is linked with him" (p. 246). By the end of the practicing subphase, "The father is not consistently experienced as a rival for mother's loving attention; rather he remains an 'uncontaminated' parental love object, while the relationship with the mother tends to become fraught with ambivalence during the rapprochement crisis" (p. 247). The beginnings of some rivalry with the father (which tends to be much more pronounced in relation to siblings and peers at this age) are discernible at this time, especially in first-born boys, according to Abelin, but they play a minor role.

The difference which the boy perceives between his mother and his father becomes extremely important to him as he finds himself embroiled in the intense separation-individuation conflicts of the rapprochement period. In his desperate need to extricate himself from the pull toward oneness with his mother that opposes his narcissistic- and phallic-exhibitionistic wish to be a separate, autonomous being with pride in his own attributes and capacities and to escape from the castration anxiety evoked by his mother's lack of a penis, he finds his father a haven of safety. It is not only the possession of a penis and testicles (the testicles appear to constitute an important part of the boy's image of himself and his masculinity even if he is not yet able to clearly understand their functions) that makes the father so attractive to the boy as a love object and an object of identification at this point. The boy has been building up an image of his father as an interesting, exciting, big and booming, rough and tough tower of strength for some time. As observations and analyses of young boys repeatedly indicate, the opportunity to unite with father, to become like him offers an extremely desirable course to take; one that presents a welcome solution to the dilemma of oneness with and identification with his idealized, all-powerful, preoedipal mother. Little boys at this juncture tend to love their fathers dearly, often appearing to prefer them to their mothers.

But the rapidly expanding conceptualization of the world that the boy obtains at this time contains some disquieting elements. For one thing, a little boy and his father may be "the same," but as a five-year-old boy and a thirty-year-old man recently called once again to my attention, they are not *quite* the same. The boy may look like his father and have the same kind of external genitalia as his father, but he finds himself with a greatly miniaturized and inferior version of each. Not only is he small and weak in comparison to his father, but he possesses the soft, smooth, hairless skin, and high-pitched voice of his mother. And he has tiny genitals in contrast to his father's larger ones. Furthermore, he rapidly realizes that he does not possess any of the special prerogatives by which his father obtains access to his mother as someone very special to her. He can compete more or less with his siblings for hislain mother's attention, but as a five-year-old boy dramatized it for me recently, how is he to compete with someone who can provide money, take his mother out for dinner and a show, "wow" her with his superior genital "equipment," and give her a baby? The small boy can woo his mother with all the wiles at his disposal, and he can scream and barge into his parents' bed repeatedly, complaining of bad dreams, but he cannot dislodge his bigger, better endowed father from it and take his place. The flight from dyadic dilemmas involving his mother and later his father as an erstwhile ally and rescuer from mother only leads him to new dyadic dilemmas involving his father and, immediately thereafter, pell-mell into triadic ones that are even more complex, dazzling, and difficult to resolve.

In the course of his passage through the process of separation-individuation, the little boy has come to recognize that his mother is a separate being who exists outside his own narcissistic orbit. He has repaired the damage to the illusional self-importance that was the original source of his self-esteem by investing her with a portion of the self-love that at first had prevailed exclusively in his libidinal organization. This reparative libidinal recycling has been threatened, however, by his wish for autonomous independence from his mother, his ambivalence toward her, her own ambivalence toward him, and his need to withdraw from her to ward off the castration anxiety she evokes in him. He turns to his father, therefore, as a source of the masculine strength that he needs to pursue his mother \pard sa0 anew, only to find that his well-endowed father stands in the way of the fulfillment of that aim.

The little boy is now impelled in multiple directions all at once. He is drawn toward his father as a new love object, although this means feminine identification and the threat of psychological castration. He is impelled by narcissistic self-interest and libidinal considerations toward battling with his father to obtain the masculine power he needs to win out over him as his mother's favorite, to trick and outwit him, despite his father's greater experience and his vastly superior strength and weaponry, in order to achieve a victory over him. The story of Jack and the beanstalk aptly epitomizes this exciting fantasy. I am also reminded of a not quite three-year-old boy who hurried his father through dinner every night so they could put on their inflatable, "socker-bopper" boxing gloves and go a few rounds on the area rug in their front hall. When the father finally asked why their boxing match was so important that it couldn't even wait for dinner to be over, the little boy replied, "Well, you're big and I'm little. I want you to help *me* get big and strong so I can knock you down!" But unlike the outcome of the fairy tale, the little boy's quest can only end in defeat.

The inclination to identify with his mother, on a preoedipal level as an idealized, powerful, narcissistic love object, and on a more oedipal level as an "anaclitic" love object for whom he has fought a brave but inevitably unsuccessful fight and who therefore is lost to him, pushes him toward submitting sexually to his father as a new love object. The inclination to identify with his father, which from the first has served the interest of strengthening and preserving the boy's masculinity, now becomes much more ambivalent (see Freud, 1921, p. 105). He wants to be like his father, out of love and admiration for him, at the same time that he wants to replace his father as his mother's principal love object. His identification with his father becomes much more hostile, as his fantasy becomes regressively transformed into that of orally and anally introjecting his father into himself not only out of love for him but also in order to take over his father's power and his superior masculine attributes. The boy is intensely conflicted at the height of the phallic-oedipal phase between love for his mother and fear of his attraction to her and between love for his father and fear of him. He wants to be like his mother but

157

needs to be very different from her. He wants to be like his father but is terrified of conflicting fantasies: on the one hand, of submitting to his father sexually so as to win his love and to identify with his strength; and, on the other hand, of doing battle with his father either to defeat and castrate him or, as his cognitive awareness informs him is much more likely, to be defeated and destroyed (i.e., humiliated, castrated, killed) by his father.

The relative strength of the various components of these fantasies is determined, of course, by multiple factors. Individual variations in the strength of the child's drives (see Alpert, Neubauer, & Weil, 1956) and in his ego characteristics are of primary importance, as are his parents' capacities for empathy, tact, and understanding (see Kohut, 1971) and the qualities and contents of their residual oedipal fantasies and of their superego systems. The way in which the boy's fantasies dovetail and intersect with his parents' residual preoedipal and oedipal fantasies is equally important. Chance events and actual experiences play a major part as well.[2]

The various factors that influence the strength of the internal components of oedipal fantasies also play a major role in determining their outcome. The surge in ego development typical of the latency years makes available to boys in modern Western societies four defense mechanisms that enable them to gain temporary escape from insoluble oedipal conflicts. The first is a product of the tremendous growth in cognitive capacity between four and seven years of age, particularly the sweeping exclusion from consciousness of preoperational paleologic that accompanies the advance into operational thinking (see Greenspan, 1979; Sarnoff, 1976; Silverman, 1971). As a result of this process, the

---

[2] I once heard Lili Peller state that, "children do not fall ill because of their fantasies. All children have pretty much the same fantasies; it is when real events seem to corroborate those fantasies that children fall ill."

oedipal conflicts of the latency-age child aresubject to vigorous suppression and repression and are maintained in that state via the obsessional defenses characteristic of the juvenile period. The second defense for the boy is to regress to preoedipal sado-masochistic fantasy expressions; a third is to get away from problem parents by focusing attention on the world of peer interactions and intellectual pursuits outside the home (see Silverman, 1982).

The fourth defense mechanism is the central focus of this paper. Via identification with the parents as observing, supervising, and controlling agents of civilization, the child sets them up within himself as a "super" ego, partly within the ego (i.e., within the "I" that has been emerging out of the initial "We" that represented the executive psychological self and that now has need for union with a strong other to reinforce the I into a We) and partly outside of and apart from it as a semi-new, semi-autonomous psychological agency. As indicated at the beginning of this paper, the superego does not appear *de novo* at this time, but grows out of trends that have been present throughout the course of development to date. The intense need for self-control associated with the struggles of the oedipal period, however, presents an enormous impetus that impels the superego system toward crystallization as an identifiable, powerful psychological \pard softlineentity in its own right as the child moves out of the oedipal period into latency.

From the beginning the child has been molded in part by outside forces that approve of and facilitate some action patterns while disapproving and inhibiting others. Initially weak and helpless and then increasingly cognizant of his dependence on his powerful parents, the child has had to accept outside limitations, directions, and prohibitions so as to maintain their love. Since the child has been immersed in projective-introjective identification processes that have been playing a major role in his development since birth, it is but a natural step to install parental images within the child's psyche. In this way the introjected parents, like policemen, help them avoid fantasied danger through inner control at a time when the child's intrinsic capacity for self-control is still immature and unreliable.

The problems entailed in this process in the boy have been foreshadowed in what has already been said. The boy's self-image from birth has been influenced by parental expectations that he will be wilder, rougher, and more difficult to control than a girl child. Indeed, he has been more aggressive on the average, perhaps in part because of innate biological differences between the sexes, although this remains to be proven, and in part perhaps because of a less precocious, less rapid advance in the development of ego controls as compared with girls (again, it is difficult to know to what extent this difference is innate and to what extent it results from a difference in environmental expectation). When demands for self-control are applied during the sadistic-anal period of toddlers and younger children, greater compliance is expected from girls than from boys. Girls tend to become toilet trained significantly earlier than boys, probably not only because of intrinsic factors but also because of mothers' tendency to be more stringent in their expectation that their daughters be neater and cleaner than their sons. The latter, as Dr. Sara Vogel has called to my attention in a personal communication, can be related to the unconscious residue of the mother's need to master her own cloacal confusion over her vaginal and excretory body orifices. This tends to carry over to the expectation that the girl carefully contain her excitement and her aggression.

The boy also is spurred toward greater aggressivity than the girl during the early genital phase that follows. This is because he experiences an increase in propulsive, phallic aggression, while the girl is directed toward quiet, reflective exploration of her complex and subtly defined female genitalia. During the oedipal period, unlike the girl, who is inclined to identify with her mother's soft gentleness and quieter, more restrained temperament, the boy is inclined to be the opposite of his mother and to reassure himself about his masculinity by joining a rough and tough, aggressively macho, masculine world in identification with his father and older brothers.

When the boy arrives at the point of superego organization and consolidation in the latter part of the oedipal period, he is more physical, more aggressive, and less well controlled than is the girl at the same point in her development. This inevitably affects the kind of superego transformations that take place. For one thing, this inclines the boy to projectively perceive the critical, disapproving, punitive parental images he is introjecting into himself as harsher than they actually are likely to be (although in individual instances they may indeed be extremely harsh). The boy in general tends to be less able than the girl to obey the dictates of conscience because of his greater excitability and aggressivity and his lesser capacity for self-control.

As a result, the male superego tends to develop in directions that are harsher, more absolute, and more punitive than are characteristic of the female superego, without necessarily including a greater tendency for its dictates to be followed. Male superego activity tends toward the formal, vigorous application of rigidly codified rules and regulations that tend to become staunchly prized, protected, and promulgated for their own sake rather than applied in an individualized, personalized manner that seeks to minimize individual hurt and suffering.

As Gilligan (1977, 1982) and Oakes (see Simmel, 1984) have put it recently, there are significant differences between the typically male ethic of *justice* and the typical female ethic of *responsibility.* They correlate these putative differences between masculine and feminine moral judgmental attitudes with differences in the way the two sexes experience the world in which they live. Males, they indicate, tend to abstract from specific contingencies to seemingly hardheaded, impartial, objective decisions that accord with emotionally detached legal precedents, laws, rules, and principles of "justice." They tend to depersonalize their decisions away from the human details involved in the specific matters they are considering, the characteristics and circumstances of the people involved, and the impact on them of the decisions that are rendered. They are capable of harshly legitimizing oppression, exploitation, and human suffering, therefore, in the interest of justice and of the strict, formal application of moral codes that are abstracted away from the down-to-earth complexities of daily life lived by imperfect human beings vulnerable to their own limitations and those of others. They are quite capable of putting legality ahead of fairness, compassion, and mercy.

In contrast, Gilligan (1977, 1982) and Oakes (see Simmel, 1984) assert that female ethicality tends to subordinate principles to the practical needs and interests of human life and to uphold and preserve human values in the exercise of moral judgment. Females, they say, tend to be empathetic and compassionate, and to attend to the concrete realities and the practical, real life, complex moral conflicts of the people involved in the deeds they take under consideration rather than immersing themselves in abstract, hypothetical moral and judicial dilemmas. They tend to be sensitive to human suffering and to act in a way that minimizes personal harm instead of sacrificing the individual to presumably "larger" moral issues and legal principles as males tend to do.[3]

---

[3] The tendency for male judicial attitudes to focus upon abstract legal principles without always considering the effect upon the individual victim is illustrated in a recent book by a judge about his participation in a dramatic international court case (Stern, 1984).

It certainly is highly questionable, as Schafer (1974) and others have pointed out, that the "male superego" is a superior and socially more valuable commodity than the female version. The argument that the "female superego" is weaker and less morally reliable than that of the male, because of differences in male and female castration anxiety, is likewise untenable (Schafer, 1974; Silverman, 1981, 1986). History, as has been pointed out by historians, is a record of human events as described by the winners. Religion, philosophy, history, and economic and judicial systems have been in the hands of male leadership for millennia. It would indeed be interesting, as Simmel (1984) has posited, to see what kind of moral, ethical, and legal-judicial social structures might have developed if female leadership had prevailed instead. Male and female superegos are different in certain ways, but one is not necessarily superior to the other. From a social psychological as well as an individual point of view, each has something useful to offer and each has certain drawbacks.

At the beginning of the latency period, the boy's superego tends to be harsh, merciless, and cruelly sadistic and masochistic without, however, being greatly effective in its function of restraining and regulating the child's behavior, let alone his fantasies. It is striking to watch five- to six-year-old boys moralistically castigating others or turning them in to be punished by authorities for doing what they themselves have just done with relative impunity (girls tend to do this too at this age, but to a lesser degree). A not inconsiderable number of boys do not advance far beyond this en route to adulthood, but superego development does not end at the age of six or seven. There is room for a great deal of growth and revision during the balance of childhood and adolescence, as well as during adulthood. The introjection, during the late oedipal, early latencyin phases, of the parents, especially the father, who are then lodged like indigestible, somewhat discomfiting foreign bodies within the boy's psyche, can be subjected to the reflective reworking that progressive ego development makes possible.

The individual can revise the superego contents and organization so that greater selectivity and modulation can take place. The superego system can be transformed, through this process of true internalization and intrapsychic structuralization and restructuralization into one that is the individual's own possession (see Meissner, 1970, 1971, 1972). As such it can be designed and redesigned to the individual's own specifications rather than to those dictated by his problems in dealing with the urgency of his impulses and unreflectively shaped by the impingement of his parents and their superegos.

One important contribution is the further ego development that takes place during latency, adolescence, and adulthood. This renders the individual more able to contend with his drives and with societal demands, more able to control himself, and less in need of a powerful policeman to keep him in check. As his own inner turmoil decreases, as it should in optimal circumstances, the boy sees his father more realistically and becomes less troubled by his libidinal inclinations toward him. His fear of femininity, of being drawn to and being like his mother, decreases and results in the enrichment of his superego with the sensitivity, empathy, and compassion his mother offers him (qualities that will later make him a good husband and father). The opportunity both for ongoing contact with his parents and for interaction with new, surrogate parental figures and others is invaluable in this regard, as is the chance afforded by education and contacts within the wider community to infuse communal values and abstract ethical principles. Human development is greatly facilitated by its protracted nature, which affords repeated opportunities for cultural enhancement, expansion, and improvement of that which already has emerged. Periodic reconsiderations of established clinical and theoretical propositions, of which this paper is an example, can be considered as an illustrative aspect of that human developmental phenomenon.

REFERENCES

ABELIN, EL. (1971) The role of the father in the separation-individuation process. In *Separation-individuation: Essays in Honor of Margaret Mahler*, J. B. McDevitt & C.F. Settlage (Eds.) New York: International Universities Press, 229–250.

ALPERT, A., NEUBAUER, P.B., & WEIL, A.P.M. (1956) Unusual Variations in Drive Endowment. *Psychoanal. St. Child*, 11:125–163.

ARLOW, J.A. (1982) Problems of the Superego Concept. *Psychoanal. St. Child*, 37:229–244.

BERES, D. (1958) Vicissitudes of Superego Functions and Superego Precursors in Childhood. *Psychoanal. St. Child*, 13: 324–351.

BRENNER, C. (1982) The Concept of the Superego: A Reformulation. *Psychoanal. Q.* 51:506–525.

——— (1983) The Mind in Conflict. New York: International Universities Press.

CAPLAN, P.J. (1981) Barriers between Women. New York/London: SP Medical Scientific Press.

FREUD, A. (1936) The Ego and the Mechanisms of Defense. Reprinted in *The Writings of Anna Freud* (Vol. 2). New York: International Universities Press, 1968.

FREUD, S. (1921) Group Psychology and the Analysis of the Ego. *Standard Edition*, 18: 67-143.

——— (1923) The Ego and the Id. *Standard Edition*, 19:3–66.

——— (1924a) The Economic Problem of Masochism. *Standard Edition*, 19:157–170.

——— (1924b) The Dissolution of the Oedipus Complex. *Standard Edition*, 19:173–179.

——— (1925) An Autobiographical Study. *Standard Edition*, 20:3–74.

——— (1926a) Inhibitions, Symptoms and Anxiety. *Standard Edition*, 20:77–175.

——— (1926b) The Question of Lay Analysis. *Standard Edition*, 20:179–258.

——— (1933) New Introductory Lectures on Psycho-Analysis. *Standard Edition*, 23:141–207.

——— (1940) An Outline of Psycho-Analysis. *Standard Edition*, 23:141–207.

GILLIGAN, C. (1977) In a Different Voice: Women's Conceptions of Self and Morality. *Harvard Educational Review*, 47:52–88.

——— (1982) In a Different Voice: Psychological Theory and Women's Development. Cambridge, MA: Harvard University Press.

GILLMAN, R.D. (1982) Preoedipal and Early Oedipal Components of the Superego. *Psychoanal. St. Child*, 37:273–281.

GREENSPAN, S.I. (1979) Intelligence and Adaptation. Psychological Issues, Monograph Nos. 47/48. New York: International Universities Press.

HARTMANN, H., & LOEWENSTEIN, R.M. (1962) Notes on the Superego. *Psychoanal. St. Child* 17:42–81.

HOLDER, A. (1982) Preoedipal Contributions to the Formation of the Superego. *Psychoanal. St. Child*, 37: 245–272.

JACOBSON, E. (1964) The Self and the Other World. New York: International Universities Press.

JONES, E. (1955) The Life and Work of Sigmund Freud (Vols. 2 & 3). New York: Basic Books.

KENNEDY, H., & YORKE, C. (1982) Steps from Outer to Inner Conflict Viewed as Superego Precursors. *Psychoanal. St. Child*, 37:221–228.

KOHLBERG, L. (1966) A cognitive-developmental analysis of children's sex-role concepts and attitudes. In *The Development of Sex Differences*. E. E. Maccoby (Ed.). Stanford: Stanford University Press, 82–173.

KOHUT, H. (1971) The Analysis of the Self. New York: International Universities Press.

LOEWALD, H.W. (1979) The Waning of the Oedipus Complex. *J. Amer. Psychoanal. Assn.* 27:751–776.

MAHLER, M.S. (1968) On Human Symbiosis and the Vicissitudes of Individuation. New York: International Universities Press.

———Pine, F., & Bergman, A. (1975) The Psychological Birth of the Human Infant. New York: Basic Books.

MEISSNER, W.W. (1970) Notes on Identification: I. Origins in Freud. *Psychoanal.* Q. 39:563–589.

——— (1971) Notes on Identification: II. Clarification of Related Concepts. *Psychoanal.* Q. 40:277–302.

——— (1972) Notes on Identification: III. The concept of identification. *Psychoanal.* Q. 41:224–260.

SARNOFF, C. (1976) Latency. New York: Aronson.

SCHAFER, R. (1974) Problems in Freud's Psychology of Women. *J. Amer. Psychoanal. Assn.* 22:459–485.

SILVERMAN, M.A. (1971) The Growth of Logical Thinking: Piaget's Contribution to Ego Psycholgy. *Psychoanal.* Q. 40:317-341.

——— (1981) Cognitive Development And Female Psychology. *J. Amer. Psychoanal. Assn.* 29:581–605.

——— (1982) The latency period. In D. Mendell (Ed.), *Early Female Development: Current Psychoanalytic Views.* New York & London: SP Medical & Scientific Books.

——— (1986) Identification in healthy and pathological character formation. *Int. J. Psycho-Anal.* 67:181–191.

——— (in press) Gender Identity, Cognitive Development, and Emotional Conflict.

SIMMEL, G. (1984) *Georg Simmel: On Women, Sexuality and Love.* Translated and with an Introduction by Guy Oakes. New Haven & London: Yale University Press.

SPITZ, R.A. (1958) On the Genesis of Superego Components. *Psychoanal. St. Child,* 13:375–404.

STERN, H.J. (1984) Judgment in Berlin. New York: Universe Books.

WEIL, A. (1970) The Basic Core. *Psychoanal. St. Child,* 25: 442–460.

CHAPTER 7

GENDER IDENTITY DISORDER IN BOYS

[(Panel Report, 1993). *Journal of the American Psychoanalytic Association* 41:729–742]

Silverman opened the panel with a history of the psychoanalytic study of early male gender disturbances. Research began in the 1960's as part of an effort to understand the origins of homosexuality. Investigators such as Bieber et al. (1962) and Socarides (1968), (1970) expanded on Freud's observations of bisexuality and his hypotheses about the role of early childhood experiences in shaping the final form of sexual interests, attitudes, and preferences. The early studies described a particular constellation of factors (the seductive and dangerous mother, the unavailable father, the overly timid boy), but we now know that many constellations may be antecedent to homosexuality in adulthood. While about two-thirds of the youngsters with gender identity disorders (GID) do grow up to be homosexual adults, not all gay men suffer in childhood from GID. Young children who are brought to treatment for GID tend to be extremely unhappy and anxious, and often have serious ego disturbances. Their problems go well beyond the cross-dressing and wishes to be a girl that bring them to treatment.

Gender identity is complex, appearing to derive from the confluence of innate biological factors and the shaping effect of psychosocial influences. Money and the Hampsons (1955a), (1955b), and Money and Ehrhardt (1972) pointed to the possibility that hormonal influences beginning in utero may contribute to "masculine" and "feminine" attitudes and self-perceptions, though it is hard to demonstrate this objectively. Studies by Stoller integrated their findings into psychoanalysis (1966), (1968),(1975), (1976). The effects of environmental influences are easier to observe. From pregnancy forward, parents impose their own attitudes and expectations, conscious and unconscious wishes, demands, and conflict derivatives on their children.

Gender self-perceptions are consolidated from approximately eighteen months to between three and four years of age. During this time the child is passing through the ambivalent storms of separation-individuation and through oedipal conflicts that are colored by earlier difficulties. The complex gender identifications that result become increasingly coordinated with (as opposed to deriving directly from) awareness of genital differences between the sexes. Before the advent of operational thinking at about seven years, children are aware that they possess male or female genitalia, but may believe they could change (Kohlberg, 1966).

Silverman reviewed several theories that have been proposed to explain GID in boys. He wondered whether they could all be correct in some respect and whether we are actually dealing with multiple syndromes. Studies of intersexed children by Money and his associates stressed biological factors and also the effects of very early deleterious experiential influences. Stoller, who studied transexuals, hypothesized that boy and mother had been locked into a state of "blissful symbiosis," a state that bypassed separation-individuation conflicts and castration anxiety. Current investigators who work with children see the little boy's gender identity disturbance as a defensive compromise formation forged under the stress of terrifying separation and castration anxieties, experienced in reaction to the mother's depression and ambivalence. The small child sacrifices his reality testing sufficiently to create a rigidly held fantasy of being one with his mother, so that he can possess her awesome magical powers and control her rageful aggressive capacities, while fulfilling her need for him to remain an extension of her.

Isenstadt presented the analysis of a four-year-old boy, Donald, a healthy adopted baby whose confident, active, masculine development was suddenly reversed at nineteen months. When he was thirteen months old, his father's job had taken him abroad for six months. One week prior to father's anticipated return, Donald displayed his first interest in wearing his mother's clothes. At twenty-three months, mother filled in at her old job for two weeks. Donald's baby-sitter's daughter was a cheerleader. Her pom-pom fascinated Donald, and he reproduced it at home in the form of a girl's face with streamers of toilet-paper hair. After that, he played with "pom-pom" and wrapped towels around his waist to look like a dress whenever his parents were away. Between the ages of three and four Donald openly expressed the wish to be a girl. He dressed up in his mother's clothes, played with dolls more often than with boy's toys, and interacted with girls more than with boys his age.

Isenstadt never observed in Donald's mother any signs of the aggressive demasculinizing wishes that are said to characterize the mothers of boys with gender identity disorders. She had, however, a major unfulfilled personal goal: conceiving and giving birth. Her infertility profoundly affected her sense of femininity and self-worth. Donald's pediatrician had instructed mother to share the fact of his adoption from the beginning "in a natural loving way." As analysis showed, Donald's knowledge of his adoption gave traumatic intensity to the affects aroused by separation. He was afraid he could be given away again.

Donald's fear and rage about the adoption were expressed in play from the very start of his analysis. Mean men stole babies and took away mommies. When Isenstadt interpreted his fear of his new analyst, Donald ventured to reveal a bit more. He played "two mothers." One mother once had a baby in her stomach, but she was poor and didn't have enough food for him, so she gave him away to the other mother. Despite his efforts to keep this story loving and happy, aggression erupted. Both mothers were put in hot lava and tortured with the tips of sharp pencils. Hastily, he found two girl dolls and identified himself as one of them. Isenstadt interpreted his wish to make himself feel as if he had only "pretty feelings" when his anger at Mommy scared him. Six months into the analysis, his parents adopted an infant boy. Donald's "biting feelings," sorrow, and fear were acute. Isenstadt interpreted his belief that never again would he be loved and safe.

Donald used feminine identifications to defend against the rage, sadness, and jealousy he felt whenever he was separated from his mother. As the analytic work progressed and masculinity became more valued, he would defend against his oedipal conflicts by dressing in his mother's clothes, clinging to his pompom, and using effeminate gestures. The specific version of his Oedipus complex and his fantasies about pregnancy and impregnation were affected by his persistent wish to recapture the dyadic closeness they once enjoyed while father was away. A year and one-half into the analysis, mother finally did become pregnant. Donald perceived her pregnancy as a symbiotic love affair come true. In his play he revealed an uncanny attunement to the unconscious meaning to his mother of her infertility: He made an older motherin doll tell her pregnant daughter that she would put her love into the baby growing in her daughter. She would come alive in her daughter's baby—and then her daughter would always feel loved and alive. The pregnant mother doll replied: "My mother is my baby inside of me." Finally Donald's rage broke through. He bit his analyst on the leg and, at home, bloodied his little brother's lip. Isenstadt interpreted that when a boy is adopted he may not trust a mommy enough to have angry feelings about her.

Donald's respect for his father and burgeoning interest in his parents' sex life was enhanced by the successful impregnation. He put the boy doll in place of the father doll in bed with the mother— leading to play disruption and the expression of castration fantasies. The father doll was sent to "the wiener shop" to have his wiener chopped off. The case report covered only the first 18 months of work in progress. At that point, Isenstadt considered Donald's castration wishes to be insufficiently conflictual. To love mother like a separate masculine boy was still too much of a departure from the greater pleasure and safety of a "heavenly closeness," one which removes all emotional pain.

In his discussion, Pacella hypothesized that Donald was responding to his mother's unconscious hostility toward men, derived from fear of her alcoholic father, identification with her mother's victimized position, and sibling rivalry (mother was one of eight). Her hidden and denied hostility toward the masculinity of her child was overcompensated for by her indulgence of him. Both mother and child were defensively organized against the hostile side of their ambivalent feelings toward one another. Donald's father colluded, leaving child and mother locked together in a powerful, exclusive, shared system, and permitting the feminization of the boy.

In "Boyhood Gender Identity Disorder: An Overview," Coates presented findings from 10 years of systematic clinical research, based on over 140 cases seen at the St. Lukes-Roosevelt Childhood Gender Identity Center in New York, and a review of findings from the Clark Childhood Gender Identity Clinic in Toronto. Not one of the cases fit the "blissful symbiosis" pattern Stoller described. Boyhood GID generally occurs in the context of a disturbance in the child's relational experience and experience of the self. Chronic depression, anxiety, and borderline and narcissistic personality disorders are widespread among the parents. GID serves as a rigid defense against separation anxiety and rage, involving a self-fusion fantasy with the mother that becomes compulsively enacted. It is a kind of attachment disorder.

Coates and her collaborators (1991) have been studying the contribution of cumulative risk factors. Biological factors, trauma, disturbed family dynamics, and individual psychodynamics all play a role in the etiology of the disorder. Prenatal hormones exert an effect on aspects of temperament (not on gender identity directly). For example, growing evidence suggests that prenatal androgens influence aspects of temperament such as energy expenditure and rough-and-tumble play. Most boys with GID demonstrate an aversion to rough-and-tumble activities. They are timid where other boys are bold, particularly in new situations. They have strong affiliative needs, show extreme sensitivity to affect, vulnerability to separation and loss, remarkable ability to imitate that predates the disorder, and hypersensitivities in the entire range of sensory modalities.

Traumatic experiences in the family during the child's first three years were widespread in the cases studied, including death of a sibling, especially a female sibling, miscarriages and abortions, severe illness in the boy or in a sibling, and severe threats to the safety or life of the mother or the father. These specific events were particularly traumatic for the mother because of their meaning to her in the light of her own early history. Her depression, rage, and withdrawal induced severe separation anxiety in the boy. Often the degree of psychological suffering in the boy, the history of massive stress in the family or of traumatic maternal rage, emerged only after the family and child had been in treatment long enough to disclose painful realities or even to recover dissociated memories.

Mothers of boys with GID often used their sons to repair their own narcissistic vulnerabilities or to restore an internal tie with their own mothers. The majority had child-rearing attitudes and practices that interfered with the development of their sons' autonomy. They had trouble separating from their sons and were intrusive. They expected compliant behavior and were particularly anxious about rough-and-tumble play, which they equated with violence. Many responded to aggression with fierce counteraggression. Fathers of boys with GID felt excluded from the mother-son bond. Many withdrew when their sons did not respond to them at once, for they, too, had significant difficulties with self-esteem and problems managing their own assertiveness and aggression. Not one had developed a secure, tender relationship with his son at the time of the initial evaluation. Many of these mothers and fathers gave Rorschach responses indicative of subclinical gender confusions.

One of the hallmarks of GID is that it emerges during a relatively narrow time frame in development. Although an early interest in the mother's clothes is often reported before the age of eighteen months, in most boys the disorder consolidates between the ages of two and three, during the height of the rapprochement crisis when the boy is extremely vulnerable to issues of separation and loss. A child's verbal categorization of the self in gender terms first emerges at about age two. By two-and-a-half most children assign themselves to the correct gender, but they are still confused about its stability. Not until about five or six does the child come to realize that type of genitals overrules all the other cultural differences, and that this attribute will remain stable for life. Coates stressed that this stage of development—where *object constancy* and *gender constancy* have not yet been established—creates a fertile ground for the child to develop a gender identity disturbance, particularly if he experiences a trauma.

Coates presented the case of three-year-old Colin, whose GID appeared to have emerged in the context of a blissful symbiosis. However, as the treatment unfolded, it became clear that Colin's disorder had developed in response to his mother's pathological bereavement reaction, following the abortion of a female Down Syndrome fetus. Colin was preoccupied with "ladies with angry eyes." He would cross-dress in front of a mirror, making "angry eyes." Whenever issues of separation or anger arose, fantasies of aggression and threatened bodily intactness would follow, and then Colin would begin to talk about spinning ballerinas, or he would mold a girl out of play dough or begin stroking a Barbie doll's hair. At six, Colin drew an extraordinary series of pictures called "My Story." These were shown as slides, and they vividly portrayed the little boy's suffering. Gradually a cat was being turned into a lady. "She doesn't know why. She is screaming, she's so angry. She is crying and sad because she is turning into a lady. She still has her tail. She almost lost her tail! She is eating her mother and looks like a weirdo. She ate her mother because she was so mad." In the final picture, she is shown defecating. "She got her mother out and her mother is dead—and she's not sad" (Coates et al., 1991, pp. 508–510). Only after years of intensive treatment could Colin become conscious of his fear of his mother and, finally, of the intensity of his own rage. He drew a picture of a woman looking at herself in the mirror and seeing a hand reach out to choke her. In her own therapy, his mother recalled becoming enraged when Colin made demands on her after her abortion. With great pain, she remembered putting her hands around his neck and screaming at him and shaking him.

Coates hypothesized that Colin's cross-gender behavior was an attempt to regain a psychological connection to his inaccessible mother. Standing before the mirror cross-dressed with angry eyes represented an attempt to understand his mother's rage through "identification-knowing" (Emch, 1944). He was not playing at being mommy, but rather in the moment of the enactment, *experiencing* himself as mommy, a *self-fusion fantasy*.

Hypervigilant of his mother's needs, he tuned into her reparative wish for a female child and tried to give her the girl she wanted. In his drawings, Colin showed how he experienced himself as being annihilated by being transformed into a girl, representing this in part as a castration experience. He then transformed the passive experience into an active process by defensively incorporating the mother. The defense was effective, but at a terrible cost: he obliterated his rage, his sadness, and his experience of himself and his mother as separate persons, but he was left psychologically deadened, with a false self. Coates noted that phallic strivings do not develop in these boys or, in cases where they have been lost, do not return until the underlying conflicts over separation and aggression are significantly resolved.

Coates concluded by stressing that the second year of life is a critical period within which the genitally experienced self, the cognitively gendered self, and object constancy are all developing. All must be impacted within a narrow developmental time frame to bring about a gender identity disorder. Because no one causal factor is sufficient, GID is relatively rare.

In his discussion, Meyer took a retrospective look at two previous panels. In 1969, the children were looked upon as being unconflicted in their cross-gender identifications. By 1981, the idea of conflict emerged as a factor. Today we have an abundance of new data. Meyer called attention to the fact that the issues for a child with GID are different at two years of age and at five. GID is, in that sense, a "moving target." As the child develops, issues of eroticism and object choice are added to the problems with separation and aggression. Meyer expressed appreciation for Coates' three-generational emphasis. He cited data of his own (Meyer and Dupkin, 1985)showing how fantasies of the grandparents of GID children remained latent in their children and were manifested in their grandchildren. Since Coates had emphasized factors to do with object relations, Meyer called attention to drive-related aspects of genital body schematization and object-directed eroticism. The second year of life is also the anal phase, a time of heightened aggression and of early, severe superego precursors. McDevitt next presented the analysis of a four-year-old boy who wanted to be a girl. Billy had always been quiet, passive, and compliant. He avoided all boyish activity since he was two. By two-and-a-half, he had shown an interest in jewelry and girls' clothes. From the age of three, he liked to dress up as a girl. Billy's mother was a likeable, well-meaning woman who depreciated her own femininity.

She had tried to please her father by being a tomboy, but could not compete with the sadomasochistic attachment she observed between him and her much older sister. During latency and adolescence, she idealized her beautiful sister, particularly her breasts. During the first four or five years of his life Billy's father was little involved with him, but at six, he began taking the child to pornographic movies. On a number of occasions, Billy saw his parents having intercourse.

When Billy was an infant, his mother never thought of him as a boy or girl, just "baby." From 18 to 36 months, she could not understand or tolerate his anger any more than she could tolerate her own. She ignored and devalued his phallic urges, but let him play with her old handbag, thinking it was cute. Billy's father colluded. When Billy wanted a pink bracelet he saw in a store, his father "saw nothing wrong with" buying it for him. Billy was hospitalized for an adenoidectomy when he was 43 months old. Shortly thereafter, his hair was cut in a barber shop for the first time. Before this, people often mistook him for a girl. At 49 months he underwent a myringotomy. In the hospital he played that the gown was a dress, and adopted "swishy" movements.

Billy had less trouble than most children in separating from his mother. In fact, during his treatment he looked forward to becoming more grown-up and independent of her. His play fantasies revolved around sexualized sadomasochistic themes. Barbie was portrayed as an all-powerful female who humiliated Ken, while Ken experienced Barbie as captivating. He envied her clothes, her breasts, the attention she got, and the fact that she was superior. Initially, Billy dealt with separation anxiety by becoming Barbie. However, as the analysis proceeded, Billy managed separation differently, making Ken engage in excited sexual play with Barbie on several occasions when his parents went on trips.

During the second year of treatment, Billy began to touch his penis and to have erections in the office and at home. Experiencing pleasurable sensations in his penis and beginning to value it narcissistically made him view the male role more favorably. He dreamed that a monster pulled his penis and bit it off, replacing it with a plastic tube so Billy could urinate. The tube resembled the one used in his eustachian canal during the myringotomy. Billy endowed witches and the Barbie doll with penises. He was half boy, half girl, with both a penis and a vagina. He introduced competition between the Ken doll and the Bionic Man for Barbie's hand in marriage. The question now was whether to *be* Barbie or to marry her. It was not just a question of whether, but also of how to be a man. If he chose to be a man, how was he to resolve the competition with his father? Sadomasochistic themes became prominent once more, now accompanied by sexual excitement and erections.

Billy told his analyst that even though he still wanted to be a girl, he would not like to lose his penis. He could not understand why, despite his best efforts at learning how to be a boy, he still made movements like a girl. He wanted to learn how to love and marry a woman.

Whenever aggression or castration anxiety increased, Billy played that he was a girl. He wrapped himself in a blanket and danced like a girl in a nightclub, quickly removing the blanket to exhibit an erect penis beneath his underwear. He planted a kiss on his analyst's cheek. He insisted his behavior did not refer to feelings about the analyst, but acknowledged his love for his friend Michael. He said he preferred to show his penis to a man than to a woman.

Billy entered latency toward the end of his four-year treatment. He began to play the male role exclusively. Feminine mannerisms disappeared. He told his analyst he wanted to be a boy *but often thought of being a girl*. By the time he was eight, he said he no longer wished to be *or* thought of being a girl. The only thing that bothered him were occasional dreams of being short at or stabbed by bad guys.

McDevitt considered Billy's fantasy of being a girl to be a compromise formation. In the second year of the analysis, a shifting bisexual compromise formation appeared. Throughout the analysis, castration anxiety was prominent. Part of the rage toward his mother, against which he had to defend by identifying with her, stemmed from the feeling that he had already been turned into a girl by operative procedures. Billy's GID was determined in part by the events and conflicts of the oedipal phase, but its roots were preoedipal. The first preoedipal and predisposing factor was constitutional; second was his mother's unconscious need to "shape" him in a feminine manner. Billy may have had to choose a feminine identity to assure himself of her love. The third predisposing factor was traumatic overstimulation. Billy's mother exposed him to her genitals and to the primal scene long before father began taking him to pornographic movies. Finally, Billy and his mother shared a unique sensitivity to one another's fantasies. This sensitivity, combined with Billy's capacity for imitation, fostered the early use of identification to cope with the threat of object loss. All of these predisposing factors favored a negative oedipal solution. Billy identified with his mother's unconscious sexual fantasies, some of which had been stimulated by her observations of her older sister.

In her discussion, Tyson wondered whether the use of the term compromise formation to refer to Billy's bisexual identity might underemphasize nonconflictual elements that contribute to the sense of identity. Gender identity accrues gradually over years from a foundation of core gender identity, integrating personal identity and biological sex. Sexual and aggressive drives make their contribution, but so do object relations and the resulting identifications the child makes with *both* parents, some of which take the form of superego ideals. Gender identity, gender role identity, and sexual partner orientation are intertwining yet separate strands of development (Tyson, 1982). Gender role, which is the public manifestation of gender identity, expresses an intrapsychic, interactional mental representation which begins to form very early. The child picks up from very subtle cues the behavior mother and father wish for and expect from him—consciously and unconsciously. Socially learned roles make later contributions. Sexual partner orientation is not usually manifested until adolescence, but its foundations can be discerned at least as early as the oedipal phase. Tyson traced the course of Billy's development along these developmental lines, showing the places where he ran into difficulty.

Tyson reworded Billy's dilemma about being Barbie or marrying her: How could he *be* a man and also be *with* a man? She showed how flaunting his femininity was one of the few ways he had to express his anger. His version of femininity, then, was both an angry attack on the mother and an attempt to seduce the man. His sexual orientation appeared to be homosexual, so far as we can determine in such a young child. His wish to be a girl was but one aspect of a much larger picture of character pathology in which constant overstimulation played an important etiological role. The endless played-out sadomasochistic sexual encounters between Barbie, Ken, and the Bionic Man gave him much pleasure, with little evidence of conflict or guilt. Tyson felt that the play sequences represented an enactment of Billy's view of his relationship with his father—two males together at the pornographic movies, sharing the exciting observations of sadistic abuse of women. This kind of sexual behavior, Tyson emphasized, is not intrinsic to homosexuality, but rather indicative of a profound character disorder, with fundamental disturbances in object relations and in ego and superego functioning.

Friedman stressed the importance of a biopsychosocial systems model for understanding the syndrome of GID. The psychodynamics and psychopathology of each parent must be conceptualized, and the messages transmitted among all the family members, clarified. He noted that the child normally establishes gender identity by identifying with one parent and "complementing with" the other.

Rough-and-tumble play (RTP) is a predilection for moving the body through space, for bumping into one another's bodies, for throwing and catching, etc. It is characteristic of human males across all cultures. Juvenile males rank themselves socially according to their competence in RTP, with lifelong effects on masculine self-regard. Mothers usually value and idealize this behavior, but those who project their own unacceptable aggressive impulses onto their sons may try to extinguish their RTP. He likened RTP to a whitewater stream that cannot be dammed in some boys. These boys may become the bane of their mother's existence, but they do not develop GID. Others, on the more gentle, timid side of a hypothetical spectrum, avoid RTP and act as if their bodies were fragile. Remedial father-son athletic activities are often recommended by well-intentioned therapists for purposes of "male bonding." However, to a small boy the playful father can look like a lumbering rhinoceros. Any roughness or criticism is felt keenly. Finding common ground between macho fathers and gentle sons may require specialized counseling. From the therapeutic standpoint, it is much more important that father and son relate to each other in a mutually caring way than that they participate in sex-stereotyped activities. Father's acceptance and approval is critical in helping a gentle boy to develop adequate masculine self-regard.

Friedman presented the case of Tim, a twelve-and-a-half-year-old who had been treated with analysis by another therapist for childhood GID between the ages of four and eight. Tim did not appear gender-disturbed at twelve, but psychological testing uncovered marked gender confusion. Tim's GID emerged in a familial context that included severe gender identity and character pathology in both parents. Tim as the symptomatic child served multiple maladaptive functions in this pathological family situation. Treatment of Tim during adolescence required concurrent treatment of his parents and realignment of the family system.

Friedman went on to comment that Billy's internal gender confusion probably persisted, as did Tim's, long after its expression in overt behavior had been suppressed. He speculated that this might occur frequently following termination of psychotherapy in children with GID.

Friedman discussed the relation between GID and sexual orientation. Most homosexual men have not experienced boyhood GID, which is relatively rare. Gender "nonconformity" does occur more frequently in the backgrounds of homosexual men, but not all gender role nonconformity should be thought of as falling into the clinical domain. Homosexuality is a construct including four major dimensions: consciously perceived erotic fantasy, sexual activity, sense of identity as gay or heterosexual, and social role as gay or heterosexual (Friedman, 1988). Parents often bring GID boys to treatment to prevent them from becoming homosexual. Appropriate therapeutic neutrality should be applied to parental attitudes about this, as to other demands that the clinician behave as a narcissistic extension of parental authority. Friedman emphasized how little we know about the behavioral determinants of all forms of sexuality, including heterosexuality, bisexuality, and homosexuality. The relation between the creation of the representational world and the unfolding of erotic experience during childhood (and the rest of life) is still not well understood.

Howard H. Schlossman (Englewood, NJ) asked whether there were data to confirm or dispel the belief that there is a greater incidence of homosexuality in boys raised by single mothers. Coates replied that while there seems to be more gender-atypical behavior in that group, she knew of no data on homosexuality.

Martin S. Willick (Tenafly, NJ) commented that problems with aggression and with separation-individuation lead to character disorders of many sorts. Can we specify which of the many variables discussed by the panelists are critical for GID? Coates stressed the impact of trauma on these children, but *only* in the context of *multiple* risk factors. Traumatized children become hypervigilant and extraordinarily hypersensitive to maternal projective identifications. Identifying and working through the trauma is a critical part of the therapy. Meyer considered temperamental predisposition to be very important, but agreed that the issue of symptom choice is something about which we still have too little information.

Marvin P. Osman (Beverly Hills, CA) spoke of an adult patient who thought of himself as fused with his mother. Any independent activity on his part could hurt or even maim her, like tearing a part of her body away. He feared her massive retaliation against him in the form of castration or even death. Coates replied that some of the children treated in her unit are so symbiotically united with their mothers that treatment cannot go on unless the two are in the room together. When the child finally becomes able to let the mother leave the room, mothers describe feeling as though a part of their bodies were being cut away.

Loretta R. Loeb (Portland, OR) commented on the traumatic effect on children she treated for GID of being exposed to their mother's nude bodies. In the words of one of her patients, the woman's body is "yucky"! You have to cover it with pretty clothes. This boy wore a dress so the woman would not know about his penis, fearing her envy. "You have twenty-four penises," he assured his analyst. "I have only one. You have two boobies, two high heels, and fingers and toes with long nails." Colin's pictures of women featured the same long red talons. Billy could expose his penis to a man partly because he did not think the man would need to steal it.

Charles W. Socarides (New York) stressed the difficulties his adult homosexual patients have experienced in achieving intrapsychic separation from their mothers.

Silverman thanked all the panelists for their rich presentations. He closed the meeting by commenting on the tentative nature of our understanding of GID and encouraged further clinical investigation.

REFERENCES

BIEBER, I.; RIFKIN, A.H.; WILBUR, C.B.; BIEBER, T.B.; DAIN, H.G.; DINCE, P.R.; DRELLICH, M. G.; GRAND, H.G.; GUNDLACH, R.W. & KREMER, M.W. (1962). *Homosexuality: A Psychoanalytic Study of Male Homosexuals*. New York: Basic Books.

COATES, S., FRIEDMAN, R.C. & WOLFE, S. (1991). The etiology of boyhood gender identity disorder: a model for integrating temperament, development, and psychodynamics *Psychoanal. Dial.* 1:481-523.

EMCH, M. (1944). On the 'need to know' as related to identification and acting out *Int. J. Psychoanal.* 25:13–19. Friedman, R.C. (1988). *Male Homosexuality: A Contemporary Psychoanalytic Perspective.* New Haven, CT: Yale Univ. Press.

KOHLBERG, LA. (1966). A cognitive-developmental analysis of children's sex-role concepts and attitudes In *The Development of Sex Differences* ed. E.E. Maccoby. Stanford, CA: Stanford Univ. Press, pp. 82–173.

MEYER, J. & DUPKIN, C. (1985). Gender disturbance in children *Bull. Menninger Clin.* 49 236–269.

MONEY, J. & EHRHARDT, A.A. (1972). *Man and Woman, Boy and Girl: The Differentiation and Dimorphism of Gender Identity from Conception to Maturity.* Baltimore, MD: Johns Hopkins Univ. Press.

————Hampson, J.G. & Hampson, J.L. (1955a). An examination of some basic sexual concepts: the evidence of human hermaphroditism *Bull. Johns Hopkins Hosp.* 97 301–310.

———— (1955b). Hermaphroditism: recommendations concerning assignment of sex, change of sex, and psychological management *Bull. Johns Hopkins Hosp.* 97 284–300.

SOCARIDES, C.W. (1968). The Overt Homosexual New York: Grune & Stratton.

———— (1970). Sexual transformation: the plaster-of-paris man *Int. J. Psychoanal.* 51:341–349.

STOLLER, R.J. (1966). The mother's contribution to infantile transvestic behavior *Int. J. Psychoanal.* 47:384–394.

———— (1968). *Sex and Gender,* Vol. 1. New York: Science House.

———— (1975). *Sex and Gender,* Vol. 2. London: Hogarth Press.

———— (1976). Primary femininity *J. Am. Psychoanal. Assoc.* 24:559–578.

TYSON, P. (1982). A developmental line of gender identity, gender role, and choice of love object *J. Am. Psychoanal. Assoc.* 30:61–86.

Section III:

---

*Child Psychotherapy
and Psychoanalysis*

CHAPTER 8:

THE VOICE OF CONSCIENCE AND
THE SOUNDS OF THE ANALYTIC HOUR'[1]

[(1982). Psychoanalytic Quarterly 51:196–217]

Two patients reacted to sudden, unexpected, adventitious sounds during an analytic session as though they had been warned that they would be punished for their misdeeds. One promptly confessed to wrongdoings which she had been denying or keeping secret. It was as though a "voice of" conscience" had spoken to them to remind them of their obligations, demand compliance with the rules, and threaten them with dire punishments should they fail to obey. The sounds seemed to be experienced as a re-externalized admonishing parental voice that had been incompletely internalized in the course of superego development. Conflicts involving guilt over objectionable fantasies and acts, in part connected with primal-scene experiences, appeared to be involved.

INTRODUCTION

The role of conscience in regulating behavior is carried out by a specialized portion of the ego to which Freud applied the term "superego." In this metapsychological construct, the superego is conceived of as an internal psychological agency that watches

---

[1] I wish to express my deep gratitude to Dr. Jacob A. Arlow for encouraging me to prepare this communication and for his invaluable assistance in shaping its form and contents. This is a revised version of a paper presented to the New Jersey Psychoanalytic Society, February 1979.

over the individual's thoughts and deeds, passes judgment as to their acceptability in terms of parental and societal rules which have been internalized in the course of development, and directs behavior in a more or less realistic, rational, and reasonable fashion. Control over behavior is mediated at first largely by the imposition of external restraints. During childhood and adolescence an individual develops true self-control only to the extent that the person transcends his or her reliance upon external rules and values by accepting, internalizing, and identifying with societal directives and prohibitions so that a system of stable internal guidelines is established that is relatively independent of the actual presence" of authoritative external objects (Hartmann and Loewenstein, 1962).

The auditory sphere plays an especially important role in the process of internalization of the values, ideals, and behavioral guidelines that contribute to the formation of the superego (Fenichel, 1945); (Freud, 1923); (Isakower, 1939), (1954). The significance of vocal-auditory interaction between children and parents resides not only in its particular suitability for mediating transmission of societal attitudes, but also in its essential role in the child's acquisition of linguistically organized thought as a tool of independent strength and mastery. Children's introduction to parental prohibitions, to put it somewhat simplistically, centers largely on the experience of sudden changes in the inflection, tone, and loudness of the parental voice that signal loss of soothing, pleasurable vocal-auditory congruence between child and object and its replacement instead by harsh, disturbing sounds that are unpleasurable and even frightening (see Edelheit, 1969); (Kohut, 1957); (and Kohut and Levarie, 1950). With the advent of language, the child comes to recognize these sounds as signals of parental displeasure and, as linguistic organization proceeds, as directives indicating which behavior is acceptable and which is not acceptable. As personality integration takes place, the directives which have been introjected from outside are modified and taken over as one's own personal, independent behavioral guidelines within a more or less mature 'superego organization.

In patients whose superego development has been faulty, the analytic situation can constitute what Hartmann and Loewenstein (1962) have referred to as a "critical situation" that reveals "the degree to which the results of identification have become part of 'one's own'" (pp. 52–53). Such individuals intermittently are unable to regulate and control themselves without outside help, at which times they may turn to the analyst as an external, auxiliary superego. The form which this takes will vary from one patient to another. Knapp (1953), for example, has commented upon certain individuals who introject the analyst as an inner voice speaking within them and who carry on conversations or arguments with this inner voice of conscience between sessions. In the kind of patient he has described, the content of the fantasied interchange with the analyst is what is most important, rather than the actual sound of the analyst's voice.

In other patients, the sound of the analyst's voice and even voiceless sound itself, rather than words, can play an extremely important role in the analytic situation. In what follows I shall present two clinical vignettes in which patients whose problems stemmed in part from faulty superego development reacted to sudden, unexpected, adventitious noises during an analytic session as though they had been surprised while carrying out illicit activities and had been issued a stern warning to confess to their crimes and correct their behavior if they were to avoid terrible punishments. The first case involved a young research scientist who carried a remote paging device with him so that he could be reached at any time during a critical phase of an experiment. When the device went off during an analytic session, he reacted to this reminder of his responsibilities and of his answerability to higher authorities with intense anxiety. His associations reflected terror of being discovered and violently punished while he was acting out the reversal of primal scene experiences that had left him feeling humiliated, castrated, enraged, and eager for revenge.

In the second case, a young woman experienced intolerable distress in response to the noise of an air conditioner that had been turned on for the first time in six or seven months and then to the roaring sound of lawn mowers operated by gardeners who had arrived at the wrong time. She promptly confessed to having planned a trip in a way that she had known would be hyperstimulating to her son, and she revealed erotic and aggressive fantasies about the analyst which she had been attempting for some time to keep hidden. In her associations, she referred to dishonest acts, distrust of her ability to control forbidden sexual and aggressive urges, and reliance upon parental supervision in order to maintain control of herself. As we explored these matters, we came to see that the sound of the analyst's voice had special meaning to her, related in part to early primal scene experiences and in part to relying, during adolescence, on her mother's voice on the telephone as a form of external restraint without which she had felt unable to maintain control of herself.

CASE I

A., a man in his late twenties, entered analysis because of anxiety attacks beginning after his father's death, problems with women and with men in authority, and professional and social inhibitions. It quickly became apparent that he was a "claustrophobic character" in perpetual flight from fantasied attackers whom he unconsciously expected to castrate and kill him for besting his unsuccessful father as his mother's favorite. Connected with this was unconscious guilt as an only child (see Arlow, 1972), as a survivor of the Nazi Holocaust, and for harboring murderous fantasies connected with his mother's seductiveness and with repeated auditory and visual primal scene experiences while growing up.

During the first year of the analysis, A. became concerned when his mother took a trip north with a man who wanted to marry her. He dreamed that he was a spy following someone to the North Pole. He reported in by telephone with his assigned code words, only to be told by the operator in an unfamiliar and coldly menacing voice that his call could not be put through. He awoke in terror. His associations involved his fear of losing his mother, his father's discomfort with the telephone because of difficulty mastering the English language after coming to this country, and his own delayed language development because of repeated language changes and his parents anxious preoccupation as his family fled from country to country during the first three years of his life.

During the third year of the analysis, A. was caught up in an intense transference neurosis from which he attempted to escape by acting out his oedipal conflicts via involvement with a woman he wanted to marry, though she reminded him of his mother. He was terrified by thoughts of terrible harm befalling him. He reported a series of dreams that reflected the wish to complete his victory over his father by marrying his mother. They were followed by a nightmare (from which he awoke thrashing wildly) in which he picked up a light-weight telephone, put it to his ear, and was terrified when he heard a buzz from the receiver. In association, he reported that before the dream someone had broken into his car and stolen some valuables. He was afraid that the thief would return. When he was confronted with the wish behind the fear, he confessed that he wanted to get hold of the thief, tear him limb from limb, and kill him. He remembered that while looking at an apartment into which he might move after his marriage, he had misinterpreted a friendly comment from the current occupant as a snarling admonition for him to go away. He was confronted with the fantasythat if he married his fiancée he would be destroyed for taking away someone else's property. He became anxious and thought of his father, whom he wished to be present at the wedding. The telephone in the dream reminded him of a child's toy phone. He suddenly realized that alongside his wish for his father to attend the wedding "maybe I'm also *afraid* he'll come back and be there."

He tried to find out whether his marriage plans met with my approval or not, for example by asking if he would be charged for sessions he missed to go on his honeymoon. He struggled at length with his oedipal conflicts in his dreams, in the transference, and via excited urges toward women. He reported a disturbing dream of his father interrupting him and his fiancée in bed together, to which he associated his early prima'l scene experiences.

One day, while he was struggling to understand a dream with (according to his associations) a clearly oedipal latent content, there was a sudden, unexpected noise. The remote paging device, his "beeper," which he had been carrying since shortly before the dream of the buzzing telephone, suddenly had gone off. Following this "untimely interruption," he was unable to speak. I could not elicit associations to the noise. His anxiety over whether to marry a woman who in some ways reminded him of his mother and his excited interest in women at a time when his "beeper" subjected him to "untimely interruption" of his analytic sessions were interpreted to him as expressions of the fear of punishment for wishing to transferentially defeat and destroy his analyst-'father to revenge himself for his humiliating and infuriating childhood experiences as the excluded witness of the primal scene. This led to a period of prolonged, productive analytic work.

A few weeks later, he began a session with a long silence, after which he reported that a married former girl friend had expressed interest in having an affair with him, but that after an internal struggle he had declined. Afterward, while riding his bicycle in the park, he met an attractive woman who had just separated from her husband. She excited him, and he had to fight against his longing for her.

At this point in the session, his beeper went off again. He called in, but was told that he had not been paged. As he lay down on the couch again he stated that that happened sometimes; sometimes it just went off without his being called, probably because of a frequency close to that of his beeper setting it off. His next thoughts were very different from those that had preceded the sound of his beeper: "I feel so vulnerable, a sense of danger; that diarrhea I had; there could be some physical danger. I noticed when I came in that you looked over at something and frowned. Actually, what I noticed is that you're graying at the temples. I never noticed that before. You're getting old. The girl I met remarked on how young I look, much younger than my age. She couldn't get over it. I heard a noise outside just now and thought of my bicycle, that maybe some thief would try to take it. I get furious about something like that, that someone would take away what belongs to me, my property. I don't know why I thought of that. I was talking about all that other stuff, and I heard that noise and thought that."

He paused and seemed reluctant to continue. When I noted the sequence of his speaking about his excited interest in attractive women, the paging device going off, and his thoughts shifting to his feeling vulnerable, in danger, his bicycle taken away, his life over, he replied: "Whenever that beeper goes off,

I'm always very aware of it. It's an '*intrusion*—like someone crashing through the door, bent on retribution, like someone telling me 'Stop what you're doing! I feel an angry, anxious, sick feeling inside, like someone telling me 'You're doing wrong!'"

He paused. I said, "You feel guilty about what you were doing in the park; when your beeper went off, it was like your conscience calling you." He replied, "If you believe in such a thing as conscience. You know, sure, I feel a little guilty. But when you say things like that, I feel *you object* to what I'm doing; *you* don't want me to do it." I said, "You want to make me your conscience." "I don't want you to be my conscience," he replied. "I don't want you to disapprove of things I do. In fact, I want you to tell me you do approve, that what I do isn't bad; it's okay." To this I said, "You want me to be an approving conscience." He said, "What I want is that when I do things that maybe aren't right, to be told 'It's okay; don't worry about it; it's all right, and when I do things that are good, to get approbation then too." A.'s thoughts then went to his introduction to the word "'conscience" through the Disney movie, *Pinocchio*. Pinocchio was given Jiminy Cricket to tell him when he did wrong and when he did right. But Pinocchio didn't listen to Jiminy Cricket and went to Pleasure Island, where he enjoyed all the sensual pleasures a boy could want and got turned into a mule.

A. remembered how frightened he had been at that point in the movie and said, "You shouldn't accept the ice cream cone offered at Pleasure Island." He paused, after which his thoughts returned to his cramps and diarrhea. The cramps had begun a few hours after his return from the unveiling of a cousin's tombstone. He did feel guilty about her, he said. He hadn't spent time with her in the hospital after he had found out that she had cancer. He just couldn't stand to be with her after he had found out that she was going to die.

DISCUSSION

A. experienced two telephone dreams early in the analysis. The first was when he felt threatened by the loss of his mother to a man who was interested in marrying her. The second was when he was terrified by the twin dangers of daring to contemplate the oedipal victory involved in marrying a woman who unconsciously was a proxy for his mother, and risking his mother's withdrawal of her love and attention to punish him for leaving her to marry someone else. Fearful of being left alone to fend off his dangerous instinctual urges despite his insufficient capacity to control himself on his own, he yearned to hear a friendly parental voice that would offer comfort, protection, and the promise of the surrogate ego and superego strength of which he felt himself in need. In a recapitulation of his early life experiences, however, he found himself unable to "get through." The voice at the other end of the line in the first dream was strange, unresponsive, and unempathic. In the second dream it deteriorated even further to an uncommunicative, raucous, terrifying noise to which he associated his defeated, emasculated father's inability to cope with the new language and culture into which he had been forcibly transplanted by the implacable Nazi powers that had evicted him from his homeland.

Eventually, A. progressed to the point that he began to move beyond his preoedipal and oedipal yearning for his mother and to consider settling down and marrying a woman of his own. Since his woman friend was in part equated unconsciously with his mother, and since the thought of marrying her was associated with the excited, vengeful wish to reverse primal scene roles with his father, he was agitated by disquieting pangs of conscience. These, characteristically, were experienced in an externalized fashion. He wanted to hear the analyst tell him whether his marriage plans were looked upon favorably or not. The remote paging device that could intrude at any moment to remind him of his responsibilities and require him to call in over the telephone for instructions as to what he should do was perceived as a representation 'of the vocal-auditory superego precursors upon which he relied for the regulation of his behavior. He felt the need for an external voice to tell him whether he was being good or bad and, therefore, whether he was safe or not.

In this context, he came for a session immediately after struggling against the temptation to act out his oedipal, primal scene fantasies in a way that would entail infidelity to his fiancée and a defiant, transferential victory over his analyst-'father, whom he wished to place in the position of an excluded, frustrated, impotent auditor and observer of his primal scene activity in a reversal of his childhood experiences with his parents. When his beeper suddenly went off as he was secretly exulting in his victory over the analyst, without even a worded message to go with it, he regressively interpreted it as an angry warning that he would be violently attacked and castrated in punishment for the crime that he was contemplating.

In a brief paper, Harris (1957) described several young men who experienced anxiety when using the telephone, which he interpreted as castration anxiety stemming from intense oedipal conflicts. This was epitomized by a patient who was reluctant to use the telephone out of fear that the man at the other end would "cut him off" (p. 344). We can extend Harris's observations and recognize that there is an element in this symptom complex of insufficient internalization of the admonishing, instruction-giving, parental voice of conscience into a stable, dependable, maturely reasonable *inner* voice of one's own that can be relied upon for sensible guidance and help in keeping one's behavior safely under control.

The tendency in such individuals is to look to the outside world for signs of approval or disapproval of their actions. Their ego and superego development has not proceeded to the point where urges and impulses are securely under control and harnessed to power effective action in accordance with a realistic outlook that would recognize the value of giving up anachronistic yearnings and sacrificing immediate pleasures for more lasting, adult satisfactions in the future. The voice of conscience is heard, therefore, as an external one. In keeping with the intense ambivalence and emotional immaturity that are integral parts of the picture, its tone is unstable and shifting. When one has been good, the voice is heard as mellifluous and lovingly reassuring, but when one has transgressed the rules, it is heard as an angry shriek or growl that signals the danger of terrible punishments to be meted out.

The analysis provided data that permit speculations about A.'s superego development. A. was born while his parents were moving from country to country in flight from the Nazi armies that were advancing through Europe. There were frequent disruptions in their lives, parental anxiety that at times was intense, and intermittent preoccupation with various troubles that made his parents relatively unavailable to him during his formative early years. All this took place as he was beginning to develop tension tolerance, anxiety tolerance, the beginning of object relations leading to object constancy, core self and object representations, initial patterns of narcissistic regulation and of defense organization, and the multiple primary 'and secondary autonomous ego functions that emerge as a part of the early structuralization of the ego and of superego precursors. Delayed language development and a pattern of impulsiveness, intermittent aggressivity, and impaired self-control throughout his childhood resulted from the disturbances affecting these crucial early developments.

During the oedipal period (and beyond), there were additional interferences with the internalization of stable, autonomously functioning superego elements to guide him and help him control himself. These included maternal seductiveness and encouragement by his mother for him to be dependent upon and attached to her rather than to be self-responsible and independent. There were repeated exciting and frightening primal-scene "experiences. His father never recovered from the multiple defeats and the feelings of weakness and inadequacy involved in the loss of his status, his possessions, and his sense of masculine pride when he was driven by the Nazis from his native Europe to a new country whose language and ways he never quite mastered. This interfered with A.'s ability to internalize and identify with a strong, respected, paternal imago as an essential superego component. Intense, unresolved survivor guilt (reinforced by his status as an only child) became interwoven with his oedipal guilts, leading to masochistic fantasies of horrible retaliation against him for his mental and emotional crimes. At the same time, he had an image of himself as a special being who had been chosen to be the only one of his mother's babies to survive and who had received supernal protection (the continuing availability of which he had to test repeatedly) from Nazi pursuers. We found that because of the suffering he and his people had gone through, he considered himself relatively exempt from the rules that applied to ordinary people. This was combined with a tendency to derogate the societal rules of conduct which the Nazis had shown to be so fragile and easily set aside. He also was aware of moral struggles and lacunae in his parents, with the effect that his ability to take in societal and parental rules of behavior and adopt them as guiding principles of his own was compromised.

There apparently was partial arrest at a superego precursor or early superego level of organization in which there was incomplete internalization of parental and societal behavioral guidelines. Although his superego tended to be harshly punitive, in keeping with the insufficiency of neutralization and taming of aggressive urges that he had attained, it was unstable and unreliable as an internal monitor and regulator of his behavior. Accordingly, A. oscillated between uncontrollable acting out of his preoedipal and oedipal urges and dread that vicious punishments would be meted out against him from punitive forces which were viewed as outside of him. The latter was consonant with his dependence upon outside agencies to control his behavior and with the powerful, partially mythopoetic impact of the stories he had heard repeatedly while growing up about the barbarian Nazi hordes from which his family had fled.

CASE II

B., a woman in her early thirties, entered analysis because of multiple phobias. She became preoccupied early in our work together with the mysterious sound made by the noise machine placed unobtrusively under a table in the waiting room. In response to hearing a child outside call someone who shared her first name, she recalled a screen memory of often lying down in the sunporch of her parents home and blissfully listening to music. Associations led to the reconstruction of auditory primal scene experiences and of early genital masturbation that had been partly repressed and partly disguised.

For several months, during the third year of the analysis, we focused on the expression, in the transference and in her relationship with her son, of persistent unconscious wishes, partly oedipal and partly narcissistic in nature, to receive a phallus and a baby from her father. When she came in for a session which was marked for the first time that spring by the loud noise of a lawn mower outside the window, she suddenly developed a headache.

She proceeded in this session to relate that her son's psychiatrist had advised her and her husband to cancel a planned trip that would have been extremely stimulating for him. She castigated her husband at length for his dishonesty and irresponsibility, a prominent theme in recent sessions, but eventually admitted that she herself was not entirely innocent of deception and evasion of responsibility. For example, she had understood that the projected trip would be too stimulating for her son, but had chosen for "selfish" reasons not to cancel it. She wondered if she had not been attracted to her husband partly because they shared common defects of conscience. Lately he had begun complaining that since entering analysis, she had begun to criticize various things she used to condone in his behavior and had become so scrupulous with regard to matters previously acceptable to her that she was becoming difficult to live with.

At this point the sound of the lawn mower ceased to be heard. She paused for a moment and announced that her headache had disappeared. She said that until then she hadn't realized that it had been the lawn mower noise that was giving her the headache. She proceeded to take back her admission of culpability for not having canceled the trip that would have been harmful to her son and reverted to blaming her husband for it. A simple confrontation (the first sound of my voice that day) brought about an immediate withdrawal of her denial of complicity in the matter. She began to wonder what this might have to do with her phobias, especially the one that we had come to see had included an element of fearfulness about going off on her own without a parent to check on her and see that she stayed out of trouble. Her mother repeatedly had told her not to do things that were difficult, which she connected with her tendency "to take the easy way." Recently her mother had made a suggestion 'that they collaborate in a venture that would have been lucrative but dishonest. B. thought of an interaction while she was growing up in which her phobic mother had required that she call in repeatedly to tell her where she was and what she was doing. One aspect of this, she felt, was that her mother watched over her as an external conscience rather than encouraging her to regulate her own conduct. When she went out on dates with boys as a teenager and was tempted to engage in sexual behavior with them, she would call her mother on the telephone, after which she would no longer feel anxious or tempted.

In the next session, she reported having thought of me during sex with her husband and went on to reveal that she had been having sexual fantasies about me for some time. She struggled all through that week's sessions over whether to explore this or not and stated that she felt uncomfortable about my having said almost nothing to her all week. At the end of the week, she again reported having thought of me during sex with her husband. This time it had been followed by a dream in which someone had stolen all the shrubs from around her home until it looked barren and dismal; her husband had left with other people to search for the thief; a woman was there spraying water through a hose; she was terrified that the woman would spray water at her, and she woke up. Her associations led her to conclude that the dreams expressed a wish for the analyst to have sex with her and impregnate her. Since the previous week she had related having had a frightening fantasy of biting off her husband's penis while engaged in an activity that previously had been phobically impossible for her to do, I suggested that the dream also contained an idea of castrating me. "That would make you into a woman," she replied. In subsequent sessions, she confessed that for some time she had been having not only intense sexual feelings and fantasies about me but murderous fantasies as well and had been keeping herself as busy as possible to avoid them. One method she had employed was to spend hours on the telephone with various people.

She stated that she liked to imagine my voice speaking to her, especially with a certain soft tone to it that she found very exciting. That must be why she tries to get me to talk to her, she said. She went on to speak about her intense pleasure while listening to her father play the piano the previous week. She liked to think, she said, about his "'playing his instrument." She said that her father's playing sounded rusty now. Her mother had said that she had a good ear, but she could not play the piano as well as her parents. She said that she was overwhelmed by movies, so she avoided them by being "entranced by sound"; i.e., she loved to listen to music or stories that evoked pictures in her mind—of mountains and valleys and waves. She tried to get me to talk to her at this point, and when she was unsuccessful, her thoughts returned to her sexual feelings about me. She wondered why she didn't have sexual feelings and thoughts about me while on the couch, when she actually was with me and heard my voice. She must have been pushing them away, she concluded, since she had them while in the car alone or while in bed at home "just thinking about your voice." Further associations led to early primal scene experiences which included an extended period at age four when she shared a bedroom with her father and he put her to sleep by reading her bedtime stories.

During the next two months, she focused alternately upon her fantasies about the analyst and her anxiety as she was interviewed for a job and then kept on provisional status while it was determined whether she would be offered a permanent position. During the provisional period she complained of an intermittent, disturbing clicking in her ears. She was unable to associate directly to it. At the end of this time she came for a session and found the air conditioner on for the first time since the previous fall. She begged for it to be turned off as the noise bothered her so much. She could not speak with that noise. After I turned it off (rather than colluding with her in acting out a sadomasochistic fantasy) her thoughts turned to a group of erotic transference dreams she had been considering in recent weeks (e.g., one in which, while driving with her husband on a highway, she had seen a long, glowing, pulsating, silver airplane plummet down onto the road ahead, starting a fire that spread rapidly toward them, but from which they fled to safety on a nearby hill where she caught a glimpse of the analyst). Although she had been strenuously denying that these dreams had a sexual meaning, she now stated that it clearly was so and that she had withheld the information that she had awakened from the silver airplane dream thinking that it meant that she wanted to have sex with her analyst and that perhaps she should break off the analysis. It was not right to have such feelings toward anyone other than her husband. It had been a relief to find herself aroused by her husband since then.

The next day, she permitted the air conditioner to remain on, explaining that she had not heard the noise for a long time and that she had needed time to get used to it. She reported that she had been "claustrophobically" anxious since signing the contract for the permanent position when it was finally offered to her. She reported that she had done something very unusual for her toward the end of the provisional period. Contrary to her usual meticulous attention to the rules in such circumstances, she had failed to keep track of the time so that she had been a few minutes late for a conference with the boss. Expecting him to be extremely angry, she hastened to apologize and was terrified when he opened his mouth to speak to her. It took several minutes before she realized that he wasn't scolding her but was joking fondly with her. She realized, she said, that it hadn't been her boss but her conscience that had been berating her.

In the next session, again with the air conditioner noise in the background, she confessed that for several weeks she had been withholding the information that her husband had become involved in a business deal that might make them rich. Even now, she was reluctant to discuss the details, but spoke instead about a matter which had been intimately connected with our past discussions of her "temporarily" reduced analytic fee.

Over the next three sessions, she gradually became aware that she characteristically permitted herself to be dishonest with herself and with me and to simultaneously punish herself excessively for it. "We're seeing my conscience at work," she said. In the first session of the following week, on a cool, slightly rainy day, the air conditioner was off for the first time since it had come on ten days earlier. She began by reporting that after her last session of the previous week she somehow had left a hundred dollars on the counter of a store (it later had been returned to her). She began to analyze this neurotic act, but intense resistance prevented her from getting anywhere, and she drifted farther and farther away, with many pauses.

Then, a half hour into the session, the sound of loud power mowers suddenly was heard through the windows. She immediately responded by talking about her father-in-law's tendency to show favoritism to her husband by yelling at him for misdeeds while he ignored the behavior of his other sons. It was clear to her that this was his way of showing his favor, but her brother-in-law misinterpreted it as excessive chastisement of her husband. Her next group of thoughts centered on the realization that her mother's repeated complaint about the lack of conversation whenever they ate together stemmed from the fact that her mother never had anything to say. "I don't know why that makes me think of this," she said, "but I thought I'd get to understand something more about my feelings about money today. But I haven't worked at it, though I'd intended to. I've kept jumping away from it."

She now returned to the attempt to understand her feelings about money. What she focused upon was that she had felt poor as a child, so that it was understandable that she did not like to spend money now. She suspected that she was emulating her mother, who never liked to spend money. At first, she asserted that necessity had been responsible for her mother's attitudes about money, but as she went on she thought increasingly of incidents that illustrated not prudence but miserliness on her mother's part. She realized that her game with the hundred dollars had reflected guilt" about not wanting to pay me the full fee, though she knew that soon she would have to do so.

At this point, just before the session ended, she said: "That noise that I was complaining about has disappeared. I don't know why, but that noisy clicking in my ears stopped about ten days ago—or at most two weeks ago. I wonder what makes something like that appear and disappear."

DISCUSSION

B. entered analysis because of acute phobias and phobic obsessive preoccupations, behind which lay the fear of losing control of sexual and aggressive impulses. This was associated with intense competitive anxiety emanating from oedipal conflicts that had been shaped in part by antecedent, preoedipal, ambivalent, hostile-dependent struggles with her mother. She did not trust herself to regulate her urges on her own, but relied upon outside forces to help her to do so. In the early part of the analysis she worried repeatedly about irresponsible or shady acts carried out by various people in her life and was very attentive to the analyst's reactions to what she was saying. She was unaware that she received vicarious satisfaction from the acts she was describing, and she hid from herself the fact that at times she did things of which she disapproved when she saw others doing them.

Her parents, whose deficiencies of conscience attracted her

attention periodically, had contributed to and reinforced her tendency to rely upon external controls by drawing her into a mutual assistance pact by which they held each other in check through a "protector protected" mechanism, so that none of them would be able to stray too far off the path. An important dimension of this was the use of the telephone to keep track of each other's activities and whereabouts.

B. was very concerned about what the analyst thought of her. As long as she could hear his friendly voice commenting upon what she was reporting to him, she felt watched over and safe. She transferentially made him over into a parent upon whom she could rely to supervise her activity and to admonish her when she was tempted to give in to forbidden feelings and desires. Her actual parents had been inconsistent and unreliable in this regard. At times they encouraged her to "take the easy way," and they intermittently had been very seductive with her. Although she sought to use the analyst's comments as an external voice of conscience that would help her maintain control over her impulses, she found herself increasingly aroused by the sound of his voice. She was stirred by it to exciting but disturbing sexual and aggressive fantasies that we eventually came to understand as derived from early primal scene experiences. She withheld from me that the probability had arisen that she soon would be able to pay a full fee and thereby bring an end to her enjoyment of a special status that connoted evasion of responsibility, "getting away with something," and breaking the rules. As her guilt mounted, she longed to hear my soothing, comforting voice to indicate to her that I was not angry, would not withdraw the loving, parental attention she wished to receive from me, and would provide her with the external controls she felt she needed.

She became frightened, however, when there was a sudden intrusion into the sessions of loud, harsh sounds that hurt her head and were unbearable to hear. She responded to these noises by confessing to the wrongdoings she had been hiding and, equally dramatically, she recanted her confessions when the sounds ceased to be heard. It seemed that as she had been straining to hear the analyst's comforting, but also exciting voice, she had perceived the sudden outburst of harsh, wordless sound as an angry parental voice screaming at her and threatening dire punishments if she did not own up to her bad deeds. There had been regression to an early superego precursor level in which behavior was regulated not by stable internal guidelines, but by external, punitive forces that at times could be evaded, but that had to be obeyed when they discovered her sins. In her regressed state, I would speculate, she felt that she needed her analytic voice of conscience with her at all times, so she carried it about with her between sessions in the form of a clicking in her ears.

CONCLUSIONS

All patients who come to analysis exhibit problems of one kind or another involving self-control. In this communication, I have described two neurotic individuals who had difficulty controlling their behavior and who had not developed a stable, reliable inner "voice of conscience." They therefore looked to external agents, including the analyst, to provide assistance with behavior regulation. They both felt protected, safe, and relatively comfortable as long as they received vocal assurance that their behavior was acceptable enough for them to continue to be loved and protected from harm. They struggled continually with impulses to carry out forbidden and therefore dangerous acts, and when they had given in to their urges or felt themselves in imminent danger of doing so, they tended to regress to the early attitude they had had as little children: they looked anxiously for signs indicating that the external powers that ruled were growing angry. They listened for the rumblings and growls which to them conveyed the message that those powerful giants were withdrawing their beneficent, encouraging support, and were about to visit terrible punishments upon them. The voices they heard emanating from them began to lose the friendly, helpful, pleasant quality that was so reassuring and to shift from verbally organized, instructive, and educating speech to wordless shrieks warning them of the dire consequences of what they had done or were about to do. This appeared clinically in the form of terror of wordless sounds—the ringing of the telephone, the buzzing of a remote paging device, or the sound of an air conditioner or of loud lawn mowers.

Cases such as the ones I have described in this paper illustrate a particular form of failure of optimal superego development. As such, they help to illuminate the process of developmental progression from uncontrolled, unrestrained discharge of impulses according to the pleasure-'unpleasure principle, to the beginnings of acceptance of externally imposed rules of behavior as long as the parent who yells "no" is present, to gradual internalization "of externally imposed rules of behavior along with taking in of the words that give form and meaning and value to those rules, to the crystallization of an internal, coherent structural organization in which one can guide and control his or her behavior without having to depend upon external agencies to tell one what to do and what not to do.

A central role in this developmental sequence is played by vocal-auditory input. Such input not only provides instructions about behavior that is acceptable or not, but, equally important, it provides linguistic tools by means of which feelings, needs, impulses, relationships, attitudes, and values can be identified and represented, cognitively and emotionally, in a derived form that can be manipulated and experimented upon with a minimal expenditure of energy. This enables them to be understood, mastered, and controlled in the interest of realistic, effective, satisfying, and harmonious interaction with other beings at the same time that the individual is capable of managing his or her life relatively independently. Parents assist their children in this direction in part by providing models of effective, controlled behavior that can be imitated and eventually taken in and integrated into the developing child's psychic organization in a fashion that is consonant with the evolution of the unique personality pattern that characterizes each person. They assist them partly by lending them surrogate ego and superego strength via the imposition of external restraints and behavioral guidelines as they expect their children to develop increasing ability to control and regulate their own behavior. An important part of helping children achieve self-control is the provision of words and the cognitive grasp which they impart (Greenacre, 1950; (Katan, 1961). The importance of vocal-auditory input in the acquisition of self-control is exemplified in the extent to which superego functions are expressed clinically in the form of a "voice" of conscience.

The spoken word, the divine voice, in a related manner, is a very important theme in the psychology of the development of religion. I hope to examine this in detail in a further contribution to this subject.

REFERENCES

ARLOW, J.A. (1972). The only child. *Psychoanal. Q.* 41:507–536.

EDELHEIT, H. (1969). Speech and the psychic structure: the vocal-auditory organization of the ego. *J. Am. Psychoanal. Assoc.* 17:381–412.

FENICHEL, O. (1945). *The Psychoanalytic Theory of Neurosis* New York: Norton.

FREUD, S. (1923). The ego and the id. *S.E.* 19.

GREENACRE, P. (1950). General problems of acting out .*Psychoanal. Q.* 20:455–467.

HARRIS, H.I. (1957). Telephone anxiety. *J. Am. Psychoanal. Assoc.* 5:342–347.

HARTMANN, H. & LOEWENSTEIN, R.M. (1962). Notes on the superego. *Psychoanal. Study Child* 17:42–81.

ISAKOWER, O. (1939). On the exceptional position of the auditory sphere. *Int. J. Psychoanal.* 20:340–348.

——— (1954). Spoken words in dreams. A preliminary communication *Psychoanal. Q.* 23:1–6.

KATAN, A. (1961). Some thoughts about the role of verbalization in early childhood'. *Psychoanal. Study Child* 16:184–188.

KANPP, P.H. (1953). The ear, listening and hearing. *J. Am. Psychoanal. Assoc.* 1:672–689.

KOHUT, H. (1957). Observations on the psychological functions of music. *J. Am. Psychoanal. Assoc.* 5:389–407.

———& LEVARIE, S. (1950). On the enjoyment of listening to music. *Psychoanal. Q.* 19:64–87.

CHAPTER 9:

A NINE-YEAR-OLD'S USE OF THE TELEPHONE: SYMBOLISM IN *STATU NASCENDI*

[(1982). Psychoanalytic Quarterly, 51:598–611.]

ABSTRACT:

A nine-year-old boy in analysis for behavior and learning problems developed an intense transference reaction marked by increasing excitement and competitive anxiety. These were traceable to scopophilic interests, primal scene excitement, and oedipal rivalries. When his father underwent surgery close to the genitals, the child's conflicts surfaced with such intensity that he no longer was able to effectively master them through play and verbal expression alone. He solved his dilemma by making symbolic use of the telephone as a means of representing his masturbatory fantasies and the guilts and fears associated with them. Not only could his symbolic use of the telephone be observed as it came into being, but its utilization for the purposes of defense, mastery, conflict resolution, and the facilitation of developmental progression could be explored and understood.

It is only infrequently that the opportunity presents itself to observe the process of symbol-formation as it is taking place. It is even less often that one can participate in the analytic investigation and elucidation of a symbol when it is in a fresh, pristine state, uncomplicated by later elaboration, revision, and reorganization.

In this paper, I shall describe the emergence, in the course of an analysis, of the symbolic use of a common household article, the telephone, by a youngster whose intense neurotic conflicts had been suddenly and acutely exacerbated by an unexpected event in his life. I shall consider the symbol's significance to the youngster as a displaced, inanimate representation of certain real and fantasied animate objects of vital importance to him at that point in his development. I will also discuss the use the child made of the symbol for ego control and mastery at a time when he was embroiled in intense conflicts and emotions which threatened to overwhelm him.

A nine-year-old boy had been in analysis for about four months because of a learning and behavior disorder of long standing. During this time, it had become increasingly clear that Johnny's problems in school were emotional in origin and that his "hyperactivity" derived from impulsivity, anxiety, and depression rather than expressing intrinsic, organic drivenness. Although intellectually capable of doing well in school, he performed poorly because of anxiety and guilt over powerful competitive urges to outdo his "brilliant" father and displace him as his teacher mother's primary love object. In addition to this positive oedipal theme, one could discern a largely compensatory negative oedipal conflict in which Johnny unconsciously wished and feared that academic success might excite his father to turn to him as a love object.

Johnny had developed a pattern of continual negative behavior through which he unconsciously sought both attention and assistance in controlling himself. He was forever agitating and provoking his mother and his teachers and older sisters (to whom he tended to displace his erotic feelings for his mother) into chastising him, supervising him closely, and keeping him near them "for disciplinary reasons." He repeatedly provoked his father into applying physical punishments that temporarily relieved his guilt feelings at the same time that they brought the two of them into

214

exciting physical contact. (There were certain factors that contributed to Johnny's oedipal excitement and feelings of guilt, but they are not directly pertinent to the subject of this communication, and they will be omitted for reasons involving confidentiality.)

For several weeks, Johnny had been playing games with me in which he was intensely competitive, but extremely conflicted about winning and losing. One game involved our taking turns hiding little items from the playroom for the other to find. It was noteworthy that Johnny repeatedly managed to break or lose them, one after another, usually by pushing them into or under something or down a hole at one edge of the radiator, from which they were irretrievable. As he began to use the game as a vehicle for getting into my pockets or exploring my person, he became quite excited. He hid items in his new leather jacket, which he pointedly asked me to admire.

Another game involved our competitively tossing a soft, spongy Nerf ball into the wastebasket. He would either lose interest in the game or change the rules if one of us got too far ahead. When he won, his joyful exultation was marred by anxiety lest I become angry at him. When he lost, he was furious and attacked me with the ball. The latter behavior greatly diminished when I pointed out to him that he was reacting as though he had lost not merely a ball game but something vital to him.

He told me that he had been having a problem in school. Two sixth-grade boys were after him to beat him up. They were jealous that he, a fourth grader, was favored by several sixth-grade girls, especially one rather pretty one, who liked him because he was big and strong and good-looking. At the same time, he complained that his mother did not love him and that his father beat him up regularly, both of which I knew to be untrue.

Around this time he came in for a session with a black eye, next to which was a small cut. He stated that he had stood and let a boy hit him over and over while he made no effort whatever to defend himself. He explained that his father had forbidden him to hit boys who were smaller than he was. When I ascertained that the boy was just "a quarter of an inch" smaller (though seven pounds heavier), I told Johnny that something else must have been involved in his letting the boy beat him like that. Actually, he said, there had been something else on his mind—his father had been in the hospital undergoing a herniorrhaphy at that very time.

Johnny expressed concern and worry about his father. He also expressed confusion over just what kind of operation his father had undergone. He thought it must have had something to do with his father's testicles, but was unable to spell this out further. I said that it seemed that he had let himself be attacked, cut, and injured near his eyeball because of his feelings about what he thought might have been happening to his father's "testicle-balls." This idea startled him, and he became contemplative, though wary. In the discussion that followed, he could acknowledge that he was worried about something happening to his father's testicles. But when I suggested that perhaps he had provoked a boy to attack and injure him and had made no effort to defend himself because somehow he felt responsible for what was happening to his father's genitals, he protested vigorously. He could not imagine where I had gotten such an idea. I reminded him that he had once told me about his father getting angry when he "accidentally" hit his father's genitals while horsing around. Johnny again was startled. He had forgotten about that.

We continued to play the competitive Nerf ball game during subsequent sessions. As we did so, Johnny made a number of references to his interest in observing his sisters' activities with boy friends and to catching glimpses of his sisters partly undressed and now and then without any clothes on at all. He also expressed pride in his ability to best sixth-grade boys for the favors of sixth-grade girls, despite his anxiety about getting attacked and beaten up ("and getting your balls cut off the way you were afraid your father's were being cut off," I said).

Johnny returned to the game of our hiding an item for the other to find. When I connected it with his anxiety about his genitals, he introduced a new variation into the game. Instead of our hiding a small toy, Johnny would turn out the lights and have *one of us* hide for the other one to find. He cleverly made use of the small size of the playroom to rationalize our moving into the larger consulting room where he knew I met with grown-ups. We went there at first to play the hiding-in-the-dark game and then to sit and talk like grown-ups instead of playing games.

He spoke about his attractive seventeen-year-old sister, Janey, who he said was very pleased with herself, liked to "wiggle her butt" in tight jeans, and excited him by giving him fast rides in cars. He expressed envy of and admiration for her muscular boy friend, who lifted weights and was on the wrestling team. (Johnny's parents also informed me that Johnny wore his hair in the same style that Janey's boy friend did and had insisted on their buying him a leather jacket just like the one the boy friend wore.) He alluded to uncertainty about his sister's faithfulness to her boy friend.

Johnny went home after a session one day and told Janey that I had said that she was a flirt and wiggled her butt and shouldn't do it any more. (Needless to say, she was quite displeased and expressed some less than appreciative remarks about psychoanalysis.) At this point, he developed a new interest during the sessions. He found that he had a pressing need to make telephone calls—to a friend to tell him he would meet him later than he had thought, to his mother to ask her to bring something he needed when she picked him up, to his sister who was home ill, once to his father, and so on. Of course, since my chair was next to the telephone, this involved an element of interest in temporarily dislodging me from it and taking my place. He became very excited as he used the telephone, pushing the buttons over and over, wiggling in his seat, diving into my telephone index and card file, etc. Reversion to the game of hiding something to be found by the other person did not succeed in controlling his excitement. He fled from the consulting room to the waiting room. We played the game there, and when he was unable to find the item I had hidden (although it was almost in plain sight), he got very excited and turned off the lights for us to hide in the dark from one another. I suggested that we analyze what he was experiencing with me. Johnny said that at times he became very frightened at night and had thoughts about robbers getting in and either killing him or stealing him away for ransom. He also had scary dreams about ghosts, monsters, and robbers coming after him.

He left the waiting room and entered the playroom, where he repeatedly and excitedly dialed one of the toy telephones. He denigrated the toy phone as silly and worthless because it was not real. When I noted his excited handling of the telephone, he playfully threatened to hit me with it. He excitedly blew bubbles with his bubble gum and asked me to admire how big they were. He tore out a "hard" section in the Nerf ball which we had glued back in after it had broken off during a game of tossing it into the basket. He became more and more excited about the bubbles he was blowing and said that he could make the gum give bigger bubbles by cooling it with water (which, of course, turned out to be untrue) because "when it's hard it gets bigger." When I told him that it was his penis that gets bigger when it is hard, he grinned with embarrassment.

The next day, he flexed his muscles to show me how strong he was and returned to the consulting room, where he sat in my chair and excitedly used the telephone. He hit the buttons rapidly and at random. He took care not to dial actual telephone numbers, but then got the idea of calling people up and playing pranks on them. He dialed the operator, blew a "raspberry" at her, and quickly hung up. This was interpreted to him as a maneuver involving a macho display of fearlessness to ward off his terror at being operated upon like his father. He twice dialed a number at random (although he was careful to use a local number so that it would not be too expensive), and when a woman answered, he "cut her off." He agreed to analyze this new interest of his, and his first thought was that his sisters were on the phone a lot, with girl friends and with boy friends. He tried calling home, but there was no answer. Abandoning all logic, he excitedly concluded that one of his sisters must have been on the telephone, though she wasn't supposed to be. He would tell his mother on her, he said angrily, but he gave up the idea when I linked his excited reaction to thinking about his sister talking on the telephone with his recent efforts to get her to stop exciting him by wiggling her butt at him. He acknowledged that listening in on his sisters' conversations with boy friends excited him (a derivative primal scene experience), and he tried to call up girls he liked—especially a "beautiful" sixth grader.

When I began to integrate what he had been communicating to me about the connection between his sexual excitement and his fear of punishment, including genital injury, he became excited, came up to me, pulled a small penknife out of his pocket, and playfully menaced me with it. He would cut off my face, he said, cut off my hand, cut off my nose. "Which sticks out in the middle like a penis," I replied. He jokingly said that he would cut off my penis and made a slight motion toward my genitals. At this point, I was able to frame an integrative interpretation in which I informed Johnny that he became excited in bed at night, thought about pretty girls and about his sisters, handled his penis the way he had been excitedly handling the telephone, and became frightened that something terrible would happen to him for doing what he felt he was not supposed to do—that his hand would be cut off, or his penis, or his face that girls found good-looking. He listened attentively and thoughtfully.

When Johnny came in the following week, he was preoccupied with thoughts about things he had seen and heard. A television program had included a reference to a girl born with unclear genitalia—"like half a vagina and half a penis; how can that be?" He also had heard something about a theory that everyone is a girl inside their mother's tummy before becoming a boy. He wondered about the doctor-tennis player (Johnny's father played tennis and had a doctorate) who had undergone surgery to be made female. He had seen something on television about a man who dived handcuffed into a pool of rattlesnakes. When I connected these preoccupations with his own phobic and counterphobic anxieties about his sexual interests and excitement, he reacted by grabbing up the telephone and pushing the buttons frantically. He attempted first to call his mother. When there was no answer, he repeatedly called the operator and then decided to make "phoney phone calls." He telephoned a few people to give them the raspberry, but hung up instead whenever someone answered. He said that he was doing it to get even with someone who had called his house at 9:00 a.m., waking everyone up, and he outlined a plan to catch the criminal with the help of the operator. He called some friends and a girl he liked because she was soft-spoken and pretty. His sequence of thoughts and actions was interpreted to him as (counterphobic) proving that he could handle and play with the phone and with his genitals, with excited interest in girls, without having his genitals injured or removed to diminish his masculinity or turn him into a girl.

He excitedly used the telephone the next day to call his sister and some friends (male and female), and he fiddled with my telephone index and the telephone answering machine. At the end of the session, he excitedly jumped around and grabbed up some replicas of African statues with "ladies' breasts and penises and vaginas." With this, I could connect his anxieties of the previous day (which he had attempted to ward off via his actions with the telephone) with the castration anxiety mobilized by his observation of his sisters without clothes on and by the excited fantasies to which he had been stimulated.

He brought his knife with him and whittled the ends of two wooden sticks for most of the following session, managing to hit himself a couple of times along the way. He also made some phoney phone calls. He told me that his father had four, no, three knives and carried one with him at all times. I recalled his menacing me with the knife and interpreted his whittling and hurting himself as warding off his terror by doing to the sticks and to himself what he feared would be done to him (i.e., reversal and turning passive into active). I was able to point out to him that his interest in knives was in part a reaction to fear of being attacked with a knife.

For several sessions thereafter, Johnny either brought in or talked about his knife collection, one of which (an Exacto knife) resembled a scalpel. After he spoke about a boy stealing one of his knives, about his inability to find the Swiss Army knife his father had given him, and about his wish to have a big knife like a man, he excitedly leaped to the telephone, played with the buttons, called a sister who was ill, and made phoney phone calls. He was triumphant and gleeful when he succeeded in impersonating a young man who a girl thought was calling her, and he carried out a brief, low key conversation with her.

In this session and over many months thereafter, I was able to connect his interest in the telephone with his interest in knives and to help him see that he used them to express his excited but conflicted wish to compete with his sisters' boy friends and with his father, remove their genitals to wrest their superior masculine power from them, and take over as the preferred male. He came to understand that he feared castration as a punishment for these masturbatory fantasies and that his failure in school represented the enactment of a fantasy of auto-castration in order to turn himself into a girl so that he could escape punishment, gain love from his father instead of enmity, and capture his father's superior masculine strength by submitting sexually to him. As we analyzed the conflicts that were associated with his symbolic, defensive use of the telephone, the latter gradually was replaced by more appropriate, relaxed, unpressured use of the telephone to communicate with friends and occasionally to call up a girl his own age. The analysis eventually came to a successful conclusion that permitted him to do well in school and to have better relationships with the other members of his family and with his teachers and peers.

DISCUSSION

A case has been presented in which a nine-year-old boy in analysis was frightened by the emergence of transference derivatives of intense positive and negative oedipal conflicts. He invented games which indirectly expressed both the wish to attack, castrate, and take away his analyst's source of masculine power and the wish to be castrated and loved as a woman is loved. He was able to remain relatively calm and controlled until his father, the original object of central transference feelings and attitudes, underwent surgery near the genital region. At this point, Johnny was propelled by terror and guilt into submitting masochistically to a beating near his own eyeball, followed by a series of maneuvers, in the analysis and outside of it, through which he sought to stem the instinctual desire, the anxiety, and the guilt that were being stirred up. The transference intensified and broadened, but Johnny felt himself increasingly unable to contain the forces that raged within him. The displacements from his parents and sisters to teacher and peers which he had been employing for that purpose were becoming regressively undone, and he found himself moving backward to an intense, conflicted, anxiety-producing interest in his sisters, just one way-station away from his parents, the primary objects of his conflicted desires.

At this point, Johnny seized upon a readily available, inanimate object, the telephone, as a symbolic means of obtaining control over a situation which he felt was dangerously deteriorating. The telephone was aptly suited as an instrument for distancing himself from his excitement, anxieties, and guilts and from the overheated analytic transference so as to render them more manageable. It came to represent both a symbolic, bisexual representation of the male and female genitals (to which I shall return later) and a means of relating to the people who excited him *from a distance* instead of at close range.

In his use of an inanimate object to stand for the human body and its parts, he was in effect employing a special kind of mastery through thought. Earlier in his life he had established mental representations of inanimate objects in the external world by acting upon them with his body during the sensorimotor and preoperational phases of his cognitive development (Piaget, 1924); (Silverman, 1971). Now he was taking the reverse route by transforming mental representations of body parts into a representatoin of an inanimate, external object which thus came to stand for them. In doing so, he was establishing a new symbol for himself via the creative use of something akin to what Greenacre (1957) has referred to as the "collective alternates" employed by unusually gifted youngsters who are destined to become talented artists.

The telephone was well suited to his purposes for a number of reasons. As a device to be touched, handled, and manipulated, it presented itself as a ready replacement for his genitals in the discharge of masturbatory impulses. Unlike his genitals, which became excited and tumescent at inopportune times and which he carried with him inescapably, the telephone was both inert and avoidable. Listening in to his sisters' conversations with boy friends gave him an opportunity to indulge his primal scene interests in a safer and more diluted way than if he were to intrude directly into his parents' bedroom at night, with all the ghosts and monsters he perceived as lurking there.

The communicational function of the telephone permitted him to recapitulate an important aspect of his emotional development and to work at his past and present problems in relating to the objects of his loves and hates. (An element of separation anxiety, derived from certain experiences in the past, in part underlay his current intense castration anxiety.) By calling people, he could establish affectionate, sensual, and aggressive contact with them, at a safe distance, on multiple developmental levels. Speaking to them, listening to their responsive voices, visualizing them "in his head," making and breaking contact, being one with them and then returning to being separate, and so on, afforded him an opportunity to reach back to an oral phase level of interaction with his objects, through his mouth and senses. This facilitated growth of a well-defined, inner world of self- and object representations to serve as basic tools of ego mastery.

On an anal-sadistic, separation-individuation level, he could regulate closeness and distance, control the establishment and breaking off of contact, and ambivalently alternate between extending himself lovingly and mounting an aggressive, provocative, biting, pinching, soiling attack in which he could hurl insults, dirty words (although he did that only outside my office), or flatulent raspberries. By demonstrating that he could reestablish contact through repetitive phone calls, he reassured himself that his attacks did not drive away his libidinal objects, thus reinforcing his sense of object constancy. By calling up women, including the female operators who seemed to wield such formidable power, provoking them, and listening either to their angry voices or to their charmed, tamed benevolent responses, he could work through and master his excited but terrifying wish to submit to the strength and power of his preoedipal "phallic mother" (cf., Brunswick, 1940). Bunker (1934) called attention to the fantasy of the woman's voice as a "female phallus." Abraham (1913) and Jones (1914) even earlier had written about the ear as a genital symbol and the voice as a fantasied phallus entering it. It was not until Johnny began to make use of the telephone that I understood the full significance of his having run out to the waiting room during an early session to provoke his mother, who turned on him with a shrill, penetrating, angry shriek, the unexpected harshness of which had startled me.

On a phallic-oedipal level, telephoning was well suited as a symbol for masturbation, as Fliess (1973), Almansi (1979), and Shengold (1980) have noted (see, also, Harris [1957] on the telephone and castration anxiety). Johnny's excitement as he used my telephone to penetrate into the private space of desirable, mysterious, forbidden girls and women was impressive. In his associations, he clearly identified the telephone apparatus as a bisexual genital symbol. On one level, it represented his own penis and testicles, which he excitedly handled as he acted out fantasies of pursuing, penetrating, and pleasing desirable females. He counterphobically violated the rules about how he was permitted to use the telephone and demonstrated that he would not be cut off or lose his ability to make use of it; i.e., that he would not be castrated. On another level, the telephone clearly represented the paternal phallus, which he wanted to appropriate for his own aggrandizement and use. He took over both my telephone and my chair—my seat of power—and as I began to speak of his wish to participate in the adult sexual activities from which he was excluded, he produced a knife and threatened to cut off my genitals.

On still another level, the telephone appeared to represent the female genital. Johnny spoke about the excitement engendered by the sight of his sisters without clothes on, excitedly twirled the dial of the toy telephone and pushed the buttons of the real one, rummaged in the telephone index and card file, and fiddled with the dials of the telephone answering machine. He could not stay away from the telephone any more than he could resist the allure of attractive females. He made use of the telephone's function as a simultaneous sender and receiver of messages to ward off the castration anxiety mobilized by the sight of the female genital via a bisexual representation of human genitalia—"half a vagina and half a penis."

The superego part of Johnny's use of the telephone is clearly evident in the clinical material. One aspect of this, the use of the telephone to elicit a pleasant, reassuring, approving response from the person called or from the operator, rather than a harsh, disapproving, angry one, has been examined in another paper (Silverman, 1982).

REFERENCES

ABRAHAM, K. (1913). The ear and auditory passage as erotogenic zones. In *Selected Papers of Karl Abraham*, M.D. New York: Basic Books, 1953 pp. 244–247.

ALMANSI, R.J. (1979). Scopophilia and object loss. *Psychoanal. Q.* 48:601–619.

BUNKER, H.A. (1934). The voice as (female) phallus. *Psychoanal. Q.* 3:391–429 .

BRUNSWICK, R.M. (1940). The preoedipal phase of the libido development. In *The Psychoanalytic Reader* ed. R. Fliess. New York: Int. Univ. Press, 1948 pp. 261–284.

FLIESS, R. (1973). *Symbol, Dream, and Psychosis.* New York: Int. Univ. Press.

GREENACRE, P. (1957). The childhood of the artist. Libidinal phase development and giftedness. *Psychoanal. Study Child* 12:47–72.

HARRIS, H.I. (1957). Telephone anxiety. J. Am. Psychoanal. Assoc. 5:342–347.

JONES, E. (1914). The Madonna's conception through the ear: A contribution to the relation between aesthetics and religion. In *Essays in Applied Psychoanalysis* London: Int. Psychoanal. Press, 1923 pp. 261–359.

PIAGET, J. (1924). *The Construction of Reality in the Child.* New York: Basic Books, 1954.

SHENGOLD, L. (1980). The symbol of telephoning. *Presented to the American Psychoanalytic Association,* May.

SILVERMAN, M.A. (1971). The growth of logical thinking: Piaget's contribution to ego psychology. *Psychoanal. Q.* 40:317–341.

——— (1982). The voice of conscience and the sounds of the analytic hour. *Psychoanal. Q.* 51:196–217.

CHAPTER 10

PROGRESSION, REGRESSION, AND CHILD ANALYTIC TECHNIQUE

[(1985). *Psychoanalytic Quarterly,* 54:1–19.]

ABSTRACT:

A detailed example is presented of analytic work with a latency age youngster. The technical problems encountered in the analysis of such a child are discussed in order to consider how child analysis can help to elucidate what is involved in the psychoanalytic process.

A seven-year-old boy entered analysis because of chronic unhappiness, enuresis, and a serious learning inhibition. During our first session together, he sat hunched over on the edge of the couch and gazed unseeingly at the empty chair opposite him as tears dripped slowly down his face. He told a tale of unremitting sadness and woe. He did not know what to do. He tried to pay attention at school, he said, but his mind just wouldn't do the work. His teacher had all but given up on him, and the principal had told his parents that if he didn't see a doctor and straighten out, he would not be invited back the next year. He politely accepted my offer to help him find out what was getting in the way at school, but said that he doubted I could do much for him. How could he concentrate on schoolwork when he had so many awful things on his mind? His older sister was always teasing and tormenting him. His baby sister kept getting into his things and ruining them, and every time he tried to push her out of his room she would cry and his mother would yell at him. His parents were always fighting with each other, too. In addition to all that, his mother kept rushing to the hospital for one miscarriage after another. When I noted that his parents had told me that he had had some very distressing hospitalizations himself a couple of years back, he replied grimly that he did not want to talk about that.

Billy readily agreed to our meeting four times a week to try to get a better understanding of his troubles and figure out what he might be able to do to deal with them more effectively. He was glad that I could see him right after school. That way he could walk to my office by himself, without having to depend on his mother to get him to me. She had a lot of trouble getting places on time. He never knew when she would get home from her volunteer work, which involved taking care of *other* children! And when she *was* home, she was always on the telephone, he said; and he warned me that I better not answer it if my telephone rang while we were meeting. He had some other complaints about his mother as well. She favored his sisters and she didn't know how to cook. She couldn't even boil an egg. The housekeeper had to prepare all the family meals. His father kept complaining about it, but that didn't help. His father was always storming about and railing about something, in fact, but nothing ever changed. His mother kept telling him not to pay attention to his father's yelling, saying that he was just nervous about business. *She* certainly didn't pay any attention to what he said, which only got him madder. They would argue and argue until the two of them were screaming at each other, and then he and his sister would stay away from both of them. It was a lot more peaceful when his father was away on one of his frequent business trips, though he missed his father when he was away.

During the next few months, Billy gave a good deal of thought to his parents' arguing and its effects upon him. His inclination was to go into his room, shut the door, and drown out his parents by turning on the radio, but he couldn't keep his mind off what was going on between them and he had to listen in from time to time. He was afraid at times that things might get totally out of control and the threats of separation and divorce might actually get carried out. Sometimes his mother would begin to cry, and then his father would stop yelling, begin to apologize, and speak softly and accommodatingly to soothe her hurt feelings and calm her down. Then it would become very quiet in the house, and oddly enough, *that* would make Billy uncomfortable too. He would listen intently, troubled that he didn't know what was happening. It gradually became clear to us that his disquietude had something to do with Billy's anxious concern about his mother's repeated pregnancies. Not only was he saddened and troubled by the thought that his parents wanted to have other children to take their time, attention, and love away from him, but his mother's repeated miscarriages were a great source of worry to him. She was very unhappy, withdrawn, and unavailable to him for a while each time. He also worried, when she was rushed to the hospital bleeding, that she might die. To complicate things, this reminded him of the time he had been hospitalized for treatment of an acute kidney ailment. What had seemed like quarts of blood had been drawn from him several times a day and he had been very much afraid that he would die. Billy had astonished me toward the end of his first visit by saying that he had noticed a hole high up on a wall in the waiting room and asking if I kept a pet bat. What had seemed like such a peculiar idea was now comprehensible. We were ultimately able to analyze it together (along with his fascination with vampire stories of which he eventually informed me), in terms of his anxieties about his health and his guilt over his mother's miscarriages.

I raised the possibility at one point that Billy's difficulty concentrating in class was connected with his anxious listening to find out what his parents were doing together while they were making up after a fight. "I'm worried that they might be doing something to make another baby," he said. "When I'm at school, I can't see what my parents are doing at home." We began to understand at this point why he wet his bed and periodically "sleepwalked" at night: he was worried about what his parents were doing and felt a need to go and check on them. He was still very worried about his kidneys (and afraid, therefore, to let urine accumulate within his body at night) and couldn't take a chance on losing his parents' undivided, attentive care and protection. As Billy explored the meanings of his excited interest in what his parents were doing together when he was not around, his school performance gradually improved.

He discovered, however, that his school problems involved more than trouble concentrating. The metaphorical significance of some of the things he was studying in school also played a part. He could not deal with any aspect of arithmetic, for example. He eventually summed it up as follows: "I couldn't do anything in math. Everything in it reminded me of stuff I was worried about. I couldn't do addition because it reminded me of additions to the family, of my mother having babies. Subtraction made me think of my mother's miscarriages. I blamed myself for them because I didn't want another baby in the house. We used to call it 'takeaway' and it reminded me of my operation. It scared me when the teacher said we would learn multiplication and division. Everyone knows what rabbits do, and when I thought about division it reminded me how afraid I was that my parents would get a divorce. I couldn't do any math!"

Billy gained this kind of understanding of his learning blocks through our joint efforts to comprehend what he communicated to us via the combination of verbalization, drawing, and thematic play that is typical of early latency age children in analysis. In the course of it, the degree to which his learning was invaded and compromised by neurotic defensive activity *decreased*, and his ability to make efficient use of his emotional and intellectual resources to solve problems *increased*. His performance in school improved sufficiently for him to be invited back for the following year. His self-image, self-esteem and confidence all perked up noticeably. He even began to defend himself against some bullies at school who had been tormenting him.

Whereas at first he had insisted that he was too outnumbered, outgunned, and helpless to deal effectively with his parents and siblings and had pleaded with me to intervene with them on his behalf, which I had steadfastly declined to do, he now began to wonder with me what *he* could do about the problems he was having at home. He mustered up the courage to stand up to his older sister and, to his surprise, he found that it worked. When she saw that he would no longer submit to her cruelties without a struggle, she backed off considerably. He also found ways to more effectively protect his possessions against his little sister's invasive onslaughts. He even achieved some limited success in his attempt to get his mother to recognize that his rights needed to be protected as well as those of his sisters. His efforts to convince her that he needed her to be available to him in a more consistent and reliable way were less successful, however, and, for reasons that were not yet clear to him, he could not bring himself to speak with his parents about the deleterious effects upon him of their frequent battles.

Billy turned his newly found assertiveness upon me at this point. He insisted that I provide something for him to eat during his sessions. His argument was a convincing one. He had done his utmost to call his mother's attention to his need for an after-school snack to bring with him to his sessions with me, but in the turmoil and confusion that prevailed at his home in the mornings most often it was forgotten. Perhaps some day, Billy said, he would be able to work that out, but at present it simply was not realistic for us to expect him to get the snack he needed by seeking it at home. The only way he could get it would be for me to provide it for him. My attempts to analyze his request instead of granting it were altogether unsuccessful. He conceded that I might be right that there was more to his looking to me to provide what he wanted but did not receive from his parents than was evident in the immediate realities of the situation, but he insisted that that was irrelevant. We could talk about it and try to understand what else was involved, but he still needed the snack. Besides which, he argued, we had seen how his difficulty concentrating in school had interfered with his ability to learn. How could he concentrate on learning about himself with me if he was so hungry and empty inside that he couldn't concentrate on his work with me? How would we ever find out what else might be involved in his request for food from me if he couldn't participate with me in thinking about it? Maybe we would decide later on that I should no longer provide a snack for him, but right now he needed it and that was all there was to it. He was so adamant and so persuasively logical that I could find no flaw in his argument. I could not see how it would further his analysis, furthermore, for me to thwart him as he exercised his newly won capacity to assert himself. I agreed with his request for the time being, the agreement subject to reconsideration if indicated in the future, and began, with his parents' permission, to provide an item or two (pie or cookies and milk, pretzels, crackers, etc., as per his shifting request) for him to eat each time he came.

Billy's assertion that providing something for him to eat during his sessions with me after school would not interfere with our analytic work together proved to be well founded. He continued, for example, to puzzle out the problems he was having at school so that he could understand and resolve them. He had gone a long way toward working out the block against arithmetic by then, but he also was having trouble with reading. It was difficult for him to maintain control over the process of scanning the words and lines on the printed page, extracting their meaning, retaining what he had read, and conveying the message he had derived from it to his teacher, as she requested him to do.

One day, as he was describing the details of the reading problem to me, he played a little game with the contents of the small bag of M & M candies I had provided for him. Instead of simply eating them from the bag, he poured them out on the table at which he sat and arranged them into letters and words, which he had to keep revising, since their number steadily diminished as he ate them one by one. He stated that this was a game he often played when he had M & M's to eat. As he went on, I noticed that he consumed the candies color by color until none were left except the light and dark brown ones, at which point he stopped eating them. When I commented on this, he said, "I hate the brown ones. They're awful. I don't know why anybody eats them. I always give them to my little sister. She'll eat anything." I expressed puzzlement about what he had said, stating that I had known people to whom the brown ones had been their favorites. I added that perhaps he just didn't like the idea of putting something brown in his mouth. The vehemence of his reply surprised me: "That's stupid! Nobody likes the brown ones! None of my friends eat the brown ones! Only my baby sister! And she doesn't know any better!" He apologized for snapping at me, but he was astonished that I could say something so stupid. The session was just about at an end. As he gathered up the remaining, brown M & M's to take home to his sister, he said, "Oh, by the way, I didn't tell you what I call the word game I like to play with the M & M's. I call it 'vowel movement.'" With this, he left.

Over the subsequent weeks and months, we analyzed Billy's reading difficulties, discovering together that multiple conflicts were involved. There were conflicts about looking, related in part to feelings about his observations of his parents' quarrels and his interest in seeing his mother and sisters semi-clad or unclad. There were conflicts about knowing, related to his hospitalizations and his uncertainties about his health (with wishes to know and not to know and related tendencies to repress or deny what he knew). Masturbation conflicts, regressively displaced and revised, were involved. Problems related to his self-regard and self-esteem (feeling helpless, lacking in value, like "shit") and to conflicts about male-female identity proved to be playing a part. Ambivalence conflicts were prominent, as had been indicated by his initial, angry outburst at me. These were expressed at home via passive-aggressive dawdling and failure to get things done, picky eating, enuresis, and temper tantrums. We eventually discovered that they had been revived and perpetuated by his experiences of serious illness and hospitalizations, which had contained elements of being rendered weak and helpless while he was bodily assaulted and his very life was threatened. Of course, conflicts about control and relinquishing control to others (mother, father, older sister, doctors, nurses, teachers, etc.) were prominently involved. These were related in part to domination-submission conflicts, dependence-independence issues, and difficulty in trusting and relying upon adults to protect him against harm and to provide for his needs.

Billy's eighth birthday approached. He excitedly looked forward to receiving a present from me as an indication that I was a giving friend who valued his importance and would provide what he needed from me. He was deeply impressed when I did not give him any of the toys he mentioned as possible presents, but remembered that some time earlier he had expressed a fleeting interest in having a chemistry set.[1] The latter had come up in association with a sustained interest in water play during his sessions and vigorous, tight-lipped denials that he was worried about his doctor's requiring him to test his urine for protein each day, as a precaution, even though it has been consistently negative for some time. He was delighted with the simple chemistry set I gave him. He talked with me about the experiments he carried out with it and then began to speak for the first time (after first making some drawings that reflected anxieties about his testicles and fear of monsters) about his hospitalizations.

In the course of this, he suddenly realized that the letters "M.D." after my name stood for "medical doctor." This ushered in an intense, negative transference reaction in which he became increasingly annoyed with me, accused me of not helping him, and began to say that analysis took up all his time after school and he did not want to come any more. Despite his protestations, however, he appeared for nearly all his sessions and he heard everything I said to him about the possible unconscious reasons for his intensely negative feelings about me. At times, his responses, hostile as they were, contained comments that either extended the interpretations I made or gave me an opportunity to do so. It gradually became clear that he was perceiving me as coldly, callously attempting to get inside of him so that I could "learn" from him and "change" him for my own selfish purposes rather than being truly interested in helping him, relieving his pain and suffering, and making him well. Exploration of this connected it with his experiences in the hospital for treatment of a nephrotic syndrome and for surgical removal of a hydrocele that had appeared in the midst of it.

---

[1] The giving of gifts and of food to child analytic patients, while once an accepted part of child analytic practice, is unusual now, as experience has indicated that child patients in general can tolerate abstinence by and large as adults can.

His transference reaction rapidly developed into a terrifying fantasy that I was a "mad scientist" who would transform him into a "monster." Interpretation of the fantasies a reliving of the medical and surgical experiences for the purpose of mastery led to its dissolution and a return to the primarily positive attitude toward me that had prevailed most of the time before that and was to prevail thereafter, except for occasional recurrences of intensely negative transference reactions. Interestingly, about a year later, in mid-February, he brought me a Valentine's Day card he had made for me, with a large red heart on it and inscribed "To My Friendly Enemy." When I inquired about the inscription he replied, "You're my friend because you're the enemy of what's inside me that makes trouble for me."

Over several prolonged periods that were separated from one another by attention to other matters, Billy analyzed his violently negative "doctor-transference" to me and its connection with his terrifying experiences in the hospital. The meaning of it was quite complex and deserves to be described in a separate paper. The issues involved became clear in the course of analysis of his verbal communications, resistive defensive operations, drawings (including a comic book he created during two weeks of sessions), and his play. In capsule, his reaction became intelligible in terms of conflicted, repressed, preoedipal and especially oedipal wishes, for which he was laden with guilt and fears of punishment, and sexual identity confusion related to identification with his mother (and sisters) both as a lost love object and as an aggressor. Confusion over the relationship between his hospitalizations (for body swelling and for removal of something from his body) and his mother's hospitalizations (for childbirth and for miscarriages) played an important part. The need for food from me eventually faded, as we analyzed these matters. His intense need for feedings during his sessions became clear in terms of the terror for his life with which he had had to contend. Once we came to understand that his requirement that I feed and take care of him derived in large part from his anxiety that he would die if I did not do so, he no longer needed this from me. All the attention the doctors and his parents had been paying to the importance of nutrition in the treatment of his nephrotic syndrome and the symbolic connection between M & M's and the pills he had received turned out to have played a part.

Whenever his father went away on one of his business trips overseas, Billy was exhilarated at being named "man of the house" but was very nervous about it. It gradually emerged that there was a connection between his anxieties about water buildup in his body and an ongoing fantasy that his father's plane might crash into the ocean and he might drown. He warded off this fantasy with the idea that even if his father's plane were to go down, there probably would be an island to which he could swim, but his ambivalence cut his relief short by populating the island with hostile pirates. Billy's mixed feelings also were re-vealed in his fascination with piranhas and man-eating sharks. Slow, persistent analytic work uncovered the oedipal conflicts that were connected with all of this.

Suddenly, the picture in the analytic sessions appeared to shift. Billy's whole demeanor changed and he began to appear harried, slowed up, sad, and preoccupied with thoughts of food. He alternated between telling me about various dishes he claimed to be able to cook or bake and alluding to fears of starv-ing. He indicated that it was important for him to grow up and look out for himself, and he began to bring in food himself rather than looking for me to provide it for him. I received no clues ei-ther from Billy or from his parents as to what might have been stirring these concerns about feeding. I knew that Billy had been kept on the bottle until three years of age, but also that he had been bathed with his twenty-months-older sister during that period of time and had been exposed to a good deal of sexual stimulation throughout his life. Of course, his medical and surgical experiences had intensified the fear of dying that had plagued him, and his oedipal, rivalrous anxieties about his father's safety during his trips away from home included oral-regressive elements of fear that his father might be eaten by piranhas or sharks. I could not figure out what was taking place until I learned that Billy's parents had made plans to travel together to Europe for two weeks, the first time that they would be away alone together since he had been born.

To ease his concerns and perk himself up, Billy devised a game for us to play during our sessions. He divided the plastic animals and soldiers that were in the office between the two of us. He set his up on the toy cabinet, on one side of the room, and had me set mine up on my desk, on the other side of the room. He made a paper airplane, which we were to alternate throwing at the other one's soldiers and animals. The rule was that if the one throwing the plane hit one of the items belonging to the other person, he would take it and add it to his own collection, but, if the other person caught the plane instead, he would take one of the items belonging to the thrower of the plane. To win, one of us would have to end up with all the animals and soldiers. Billy anxiously made certain that he was always well ahead, but he would not permit me to be defeated and wiped out.

As we played the game, day after day, we talked to one another. Billy expressed considerable interest in the approach of Thanksgiving. It gradually dawned on him that the holiday would interfere with our schedule of meetings. He was relieved that we would have our session on Friday of that week, but he grew increasingly distressed, then annoyed, and then incensed that he would be done out of his Thursday session. What right did I have to deprive him of his session just because it was Thanksgiving, he asked. He was not permitted to simply take a day off if he felt like doing something else instead, so why should I be able to do so? It was not fair. He was entitled to his session and he wanted it.

Suddenly, an idea occurred to him. Why couldn't I come to his house for Thanksgiving dinner? His mother was a wonderful cook, he told me with enthusiasm (temporarily setting aside all his complaints about her inability even to boil water). I would enjoy the meal thoroughly. We could eat our turkey dinner and then excuse ourselves, go to his room, and have our session. That way everything would work out perfectly. He grew increasingly angry as I declined to accede to his plan for our spending Thanksgiving together and stood firm about my preference that we analyze the wish instead. He finally lost his patience, bared his teeth, made a motion toward me as though to strangle me, and advanced toward me menacingly.

"Are you sure it's turkey you want to eat on Thanksgiving?" I asked. "No," he replied, "it's *you* I want to eat," and he lunged toward me. "Are you sure *I'm* the one you want to eat?" I asked. "No," he said, "it's my *parents* I want to eat! They're going away to Europe and are leaving me and my sisters alone with the housekeeper. Sometimes she doesn't show up. What if my parents are away and she doesn't show up? I'll starve! If I eat up my parents, they'll be inside of me and can never get away from me." Suddenly, Billy recoiled in horror. "Oh no," he cried, "if I ate them, that would destroy them!"

We talked together about Billy's fear and anxiety about his parents' projected trip. He didn't like his father taking his mother away on a trip with him, much preferring the usual practice of his father going off alone and leaving him to take charge as "the man of the house." Ever since his kidney ailment, as I reminded him, which as a little boy he had interpreted as a punishment and a warning for his ideas of getting rid of his father and taking his place with his mother, he also had been very much afraid that without his parents' constant protective presence he could die.

"There's something I haven't told you," he said, as he caught the paper plane I threw in his direction as part of the game we were playing. "I didn't tell you because I was afraid you'd think I was being childish. Every night for the past couple of weeks I've been putting myself to sleep by imagining that I'm a giant standing in New York Harbor, and every time an airplane takes off from Kennedy Airport I catch it." A look of sudden comprehension spread over his face. "I don't want to let my parents fly away to Europe!" "And that's why you're playing this game with me," I said. He dropped his insistence that I have Thanksgiving dinner with him and launched instead into an ongoing exploration with me of his oedipal guilts and anxieties.

Billy's analysis eventually came to a highly successful analytic conclusion, with an excellent clinical result. I heard from him once, about a year after it ended, when his mother developed a serious life-threatening illness and he wanted to talk to me about it, but, after that single session, I had no more contact with him. About six years after the end of the analysis, however, I received a note from his mother informing me that she was fine, thanking me for what I had done for Billy, and stating that I would be pleased to know that he had sustained all the gains he had made in the analysis and was doing extremely well in all respects.

DISCUSSION

This case illustrates the way in which psychoanalysis can be used to effectively motivate a latency age child to explore the unconscious conflicts that generate the neurotic problems making him suffer. Early latency age children tend to be open enough to accepting outside help in struggling with their conflicts to join in an analytic venture relatively readily. They are very different in this respect from late latency children, who have achieved greater defensive stability and tend to resist an approach that aims at undoing their defensive operations in order to examine the conflicts hidden behind them (Becker, 1974); (Bornstein, 1951). Not only was Billy a typical early latency child in this regard, but he was in so much conscious emotional distress, so frightened about his health, and felt so unable to rely on his parents to help him out of his plight that he was more than commonly willing to do whatever might be necessary to obtain relief from his sufferings.

He was able to set aside his wish for immediate relief sufficiently to accept the analyst as someone who might help him to look into his problems and eventually find ways to deal with them more effectively. He was aided in this by experiences during his first three or four years that had contributed to good feelings about what came to him from the adult world before a series of events shattered his sense of security and contributed to a set of neurotic conflicts, guilts, and anxieties from which he could not get free.

He initially turned to the analyst as a supposedly powerful adult who might be able to do something to eliminate the sources of his difficulties and offer him the outside strength and protection for which he hoped. Later he was buoyed by the discovery that he could by his own efforts, merely aided by the analyst, do things that would ameliorate his problems, first at school and then at home. Encouraged by these gains and by the increased confidence in his strength and abilities that they afforded him, he began to make use of the analyst as a knowledgeable ally who might help him to tackle the sources within his own being that contributed to his unhappiness. As he did so, some of the differences between children and adults that affect the way they participate in the analytic process came into focus. For one thing, Billy was not able to communicate through words alone but also resorted to drawings and to the action sphere of play to express himself; this is in keeping with the level of incompletely matured cognitive and emotional development which he had reached at that point in his life. For another, a number of factors affected his ability to make use of an analyst to aid him in understanding himself better. He clearly could utilize me as an object to whom he could transfer key yearnings and attitudes as a way of actuating and obtaining access to conflicted, internalized object relations. Unlike adults, however, he still lived with his primary objects and still was engaged in interactions with them of an internalizing and externalizing nature that were continually revising his internal representations of them and his relations with these internalized representations. Even more than do adult analysands, he turned to his analyst as a new object to whom he could relate in new ways and with whom he could practice approaches which he had not been able to successfully utilize before. He could practice asserting himself, for example, in ways in which he could not, either in the past or in the present, assert himself with other adults. That he needed to be permitted to do so was very evident.

When Billy insisted that the food he needed for an after-school snack be provided for him, it was clear that his request had a very different meaning than it would have had if an adult had made such a request. Billy was still at a developmental level at which he realistically depended upon adults in significant ways to provide for many of his needs. He was still at a level at which his ability to tolerate drive tension, anxiety, frustration of basic needs, and physical and emotional helplessness was limited. To expect more than he was capable of at his stage of life would not only have been unrealistic but would also have interfered with his capacity to rely on the analyst to help him *build* the capacities we expect of adults, capacities which young children simply have not yet acquired. It was more in keeping with his level of development to accede to his request, with joint recognition that the need to do so was only temporary, awaiting the time when he would acquire the capacity to do without it.

Ego immaturity and an obligatory thrust toward developmental progression play a central role in shaping analytic technique with latency age children. One of the issues that needs to be recognized and accepted in child analysis is that children are still in the process of developing some of the ego capacities that we associate with the ability to participate in a psychoanalytic approach to solving life problems. A *prospective* attitude is required of the child analyst, in which he is willing to permit and facilitate developmental progress that will eventually lead to the ability to proceed in a more mature, advanced fashion in the analytic work. In this respect, child analysis regularly involves acceptance of and respect for the kind of temporary deviations from the optimal to which Eissler (1953) referred as "parameters" in psychoanalytic technique with some adults who exhibit ego immaturities and deficiencies of certain types.

Children are not able to restrict themselves to a verbal sphere of communication or to free associate. Nor are children, with the relative newness and instability of their developmental gains and of their acquisition of secondary process dominance (see A. Freud, 1965); (Glenn, 1978); (Kramer and Byerly, 1978); (Silverman, 1971), able to tolerate the kind of induced regression that is stimulated by the recumbent posture and lack of consensual validation involved in the use of the analytic couch. What is required in analytic work with children is to adopt an attitude in which one helps the child to grow in his or her movement *toward* the capacity to work analytically the way adults do, i.e., to assist

245

them in progressing toward adulthood rather than expecting them to participate in psychoanalysis the way adults can be expected to do.

Psychoanalytic work with latency age children is complicated further by their tendency toward the spontaneous regression to escape from oedipal conflict that plays a prominent part in the developmental process at that time of life (see Silverman, 1982). This imposes as much a requirement for the analyst to be restrained, cautious, and tolerant of natural processes as do ego immaturity and the latency age child's determined thrust toward developmental progression.

At the same time that the latency age child's push toward increasing independence, self-reliance, and ego autonomy demands the analyst's respect and forebearance, regression, paradoxically, is a regular and central feature of instinctual drive expression during latency. One way in which this can be formulated is to state that latency is characterized by simultaneous ego progression and drive regression, both of which strongly influence the way in which psychoanalysis proceeds with children in that age period. An alternative way of putting this is that, during latency, overall ego progression is facilitated by temporary regression in drive expression and in certain ego activities that are very close to the drives.

The net effect is that analysis of a child of Billy's age and developmental level by necessity proceeds in such a way that the analyst finds himself in something of a quandary. He must respect the general forward thrust of ego progression that is taking place and not interfere with the child's need for autonomy, self-determination, strengthening of defenses against the drives, and strict, even moralistic superego attitudes toward his urges and impulses (even if he is not always capable of controlling them). He can intrude only to the minimal extent that is absolutely necessary to engage the child in investigation into key conflicted areas that are impeding the success of that forward thrust. The need on the part of the analyst to respect the latency age child's use of regression as a means of containing and avoiding conflicted, oedipal urges which he is not yet able to relinquish or control contributes to a tendency to work most of the time with regressive substitutes for oedipal issues rather than directly with them. This has led Geleerd (1967) to adopt an almost apologetic tone in her introduction to the fine collection of papers, *The Child Analyst at Work*, with regard to the prominence of regressive preoedipal themes encountered in the clinical descriptions scattered throughout the book.

Billy's conflicts were expressed for a long time on a pregenital level of drive organization. This was exemplified in his fear of starving, his helpless yearning for powerful, outside help to rescue him from the dangers that faced him, his passive-aggressive and passive-resistant struggles with his parents, the ambivalence conflicts that invaded his thinking and blocked him from learning, etc. The regression was epitomized in his requests for food from me and in the "vowel movement" game he played with the M & M's. Throughout most of the analysis, derivatives of the oedipal conflicts that constituted the more primary issues generating his inhibitions and symptoms surfaced only intermittently and could be explored analytically for no more than brief moments before they were re-repressed and buried again beneath preoedipal substitutes. It was not until late in the analysis, when Billy felt more secure in his developmental advance, that we became able to analyze the core oedipal conflicts in a consistent, more or less direct fashion (and this followed a relatively prolonged period of typical, late latency preoccupation with the rules and structure of competitive games, discussion of books and stories he had read, etc.).

Analytic experience with children yields valuable understanding of the developmental process within which psychopathology is formed and transformed on the way toward its final, layered content and organization in adulthood. It also helps to shed light on the complexities of the psychoanalytic process, which, as Weinshel (1984) recently has emphasized, is still a fair distance away from being adequately understood. Children are still undergoing the development of the capacities for reflection, self-observation, tension tolerance, anxiety tolerance, controlled regression, verbalization, humor, and perspective that are essential ingredients of analytic self-scrutiny. They are still going through the natural processes involved in developmental acquisition of the abilities and strengths that an adult analysand struggles to attain in the reparative rebuilding and reorganization that is an essential part of the adult psychoanalytic process. Child analytic experience, therefore, affords a window through which we can make important observations into very basic dimensions of psychoanalytic fundamentals by highlighting the ego building and progressive-regressive ego and drive vicissitudes that lead to the capacity for gaining insights which are essential in obtaining an analytic cure.

REFERENCES

BECKER, T.E. (1974). On latency. *Psychoanal. Study Child* 29:3–11.

BORNSTEIN, B. (1951). On latency. *Psychoanal. Study Child* 6:279–285.

EISSLER, K.R. (1953). The effect of the structure of the ego on psychoanalytic technique. *J. Am. Psychoanal. Assoc.* 1:104–143.

FREUD, A. (1965). *The Writings of Anna Freud Vol. 6 Normality and Pathology in Childhood: Assessments of Development.* New York: Int. Univ. Press.

GELEERD, E.R. (1967). Introduction In *The Child Analyst at Work, ed.* E. R. Geleerd. New York: Int. Univ. Press, pp. 1–13.

GLENN, J. (1978). *General Principles of Child Analysis. In Child Analysis and Therapy,* ed. J. Glenn & M. A. Scharfman. New York: Aronson, pp. 29–66.

KRAMER, S. & BYERLY, L.J. (1978). Technique of psychoanalysis of the latency child. In *Child Analysis and Therapy,* ed. J. Glenn & M. A. Scharfman. New York: Aronson, pp. 205–236.

SILVERMAN, M.A. (1971). The growth of logical thinking. Piaget's contribution to ego psychology *Psychoanal. Q.* 40:317–341.

———— (1982). The latency period In Early Female Development: Current Psychoanalytic Views ed. D. Mendell. New York/London: SP Medical & Scientific Books, pp. 203–266.

WEINSHEL, E.M. (1984). Some observations on the psychoanalytic process *Psychoanal. Q.* 53:63–92.

CHAPTER 11:

SUDDEN ONSET OF ANTI-CHINESE PREJUDICE IN A FOUR-YEAR-OLD GIRL

[(1985). *Psychoanalytic Quarterly* 54:615–619.]

Racial and ethnic prejudice is not a simple phenomenon. It is the complex result of multiple factors—cultural, economic, group psychological, and individual psychological. The socioeconomic factors, by and large, are beyond the competence of a psychoanalyst to elucidate. Psychoanalytic investigation can provide observations, however, that can help shed light upon the psychological factors involved in generating antipathy toward a particular racial, ethnic, or religious group.

Ackerman and Jahoda (1948), Bird (1957), Zilboorg (1947), and others have addressed themselves cogently to the psychological factors involved in prejudice and bigotry. They have emphasized the importance of problems involving narcissism and narcissistic vulnerability, aggression, hatred and self-hatred, identification with the aggressor, castration anxiety, superego defects, symbolism, and the mechanisms of denial, exteriorization, projection, and displacement.

This communication is extracted from a longer, forthcoming paper on the connection between symbolic expression of unconscious emotional conflict and racial prejudice. A clinical vignette will be shared that illustrates the way in which chance dovetailing between certain attributes of a particular racial group and key aspects of highly charged, conscious and unconscious emotional conflicts can contribute to the development of racial or ethnic prejudice in a young child.

Cora was just under four years of age when she startled her parents, neighbors, and nursery school teachers by suddenly expressing intensely negative feelings about Chinese people. She could not tolerate the sight of an Oriental person, nor could she bear even to hear of anyone who was Chinese.

Everyone was flabbergasted. Nothing had occurred that to anyone's knowledge could account for Cora's strange new aversion. She had never expressed such feelings about any group of people before, and no one could imagine how she had developed such an attitude. She always had gotten along well with everyone in the highly diverse, polyglot, urban neighborhood in which the family resided. Her parents were not aware of harboring ill-will or negative attitudes toward any racial, religious, or ethnic group, and they were at a loss to understand what had come over her.

Cora was the younger of two children, two years apart in age, born to a young, middle-class couple. She adored her older brother, even though he tended to tease and at times even to torment her. When he was in the mood for it, he could be quite affectionate with her, but her own affectionate overtures to him most often were coldly rebuffed. At times, he initiated sexual play between them. For example, he would lie on top of her in bed or invite her to engage in exploration of each other's bodies. There was repeated friction and squabbling between them. It was most regularly noticeable in the bathroom when they were being bathed together. Cora's brother would tease her about her not having a penis, and she would sputter and fume in a frustrated, unsuccessful attempt to come up with a suitable retort. To complicate matters, Cora's father, whom she deeply loved, often was away from home on extended business trips, during which she was quite noticeably sad and dejected. There were serious problems in her parents' marriage, furthermore, and her father was beginning to talk about leaving for good. Her mother was intermittently preoccupied, unhappy, and irritable because of the marital discord.

What all this had to do with Cora's abhorrence of Chinese people remained quite mysterious until a chance remark by another child in her nursery school class provided an unexpected solution to the mystery. When the remark was repeated by an adult who had overheard it, this led to the realization that Cora's intense anti-Chinese feeling had begun after a boy in her class had made the following suggestion to her: "Let's play a game. I'll show you my penis, and you'll show me your china."

Cora's mother responded in several ways. She discussed the differences between the sexes with Cora, and she had a series of talks with her in which she tried to clarify Cora's anatomical and linguistic misperceptions and to help her to appreciate and value herself as a female. She stopped bathing the two children together and provided Cora with somewhat better protection against her brother's mistreatment of her. Her father arranged to spend more time with her, and he attempted to reassure her that he loved her. He indicated to her that no matter what happened in the marriage, he always would remain interested in her and would be devoted to her. Cora's anti-Chinese sentiment vanished, never to return.

It is clear that the sudden, unexpected outbreak of racial prejudice in this little girl was the product of an emotional reaction to all that was going on in her life. She was being teased, taunted, and humiliated by her brother. Her father was abandoning her for long periods of time, and she felt that she was in danger of losing him altogether. Her mother's emotional availability was inconstant, as she was prevented from tuning in consistently to Cora's needs by all the troubles she herself was experiencing. And she certainly was not giving her the protection she needed from her brother.

Cora was presented with the need to find ways to deal with a set of exquisitely painful narcissistic injuries and with intense rage at the very people whom she most loved. Unable to tolerate what she was feeling and unable to take effective action to relieve it, she seized upon the linguistic error of her nursery school classmate as a metaphorical avenue through which she could escape from her inner distress. She symbolically linked the words "china" and "vagina," which helped her to redirect her attention—away from the hurt and rage she felt inside and toward a group of substitute objects outside her whom she could disparage, denigrate, and despise in place of herself and her family members.

Instead of hating herself and her femininity in response to the rejection she felt she was receiving from her brother and father, she could, via reversal and identification with the aggressor, turn on a group of outsiders as objects of her hatred and scorn. She could reject them the way she felt she was being scorned and rejected at home. She could salvage her regard for herself and for the love objects in her family by splitting off all the negative feelings and ridding herself of them by aiming them instead toward objects outside herself and outside her family.

She connected Chinese people with the female genital her brother had derided because of his castration anxiety and his fear of his sexual excitement. Thus she was able to deflect the self-hatred she had developed as a seemingly devalued person and to project it onto others. When her mother helped her to understand that her brother's taunting derived from his own problems rather than from defectiveness in herself and when her father reassured her somewhat as to her lovability, her need for this kind of projective scapegoating greatly diminished.

Cora was able to protect her libidinal ties to her love objects within her family by xenophobically selecting a group of strangers, very different from her family members, onto whom she could displace her disappointment with and rage at her parents and brother. Zilboorg (1947) in particular has emphasized the importance of this mechanism in the dynamics of racial and ethnic prejudice. When her parents became aware of her pain and took steps to ameliorate it, her fury at them and at her brother subsided. Her need to displace her rage to people outside her FAMILY diminished, therefore, and she could give up her antipathy toward Chinese people.

One outstanding feature of the episode described in this communication is that Cora's selection of the target group for her negative feelings was based purely on accidental factors. The only link between the group of people toward whom she suddenly developed intense animosity and the emotional conflicts within her from which those feelings were derived was a remark made by a boy that contained a misunderstanding about two words that sounded similar. If this is all it takes for someone to be chosen to serve as a victim of prejudice and bigotry, without even the remotest rationale for the attitudinal shifts that are involved beyond the mere sound of a word, is anyone justified in feeling safe?

REFERENCES

ACKERMAN, N.W. & JAHODA, M. (1948). The dynamic basis of anti-Semitic attitudes Psychoanal. Q. 17:240–260.

BIRD, B. (1957). A consideration of the etiology of prejudice J. Am. Psychoanal. Assoc. 5:490–513.

ZILBOORG, G. (1947). Psychopathology of social prejudice *Psychoanal. Q.* 16:303–324.

CHAPTER 12:

IDENTIFICATION IN HEALTHY AND
PATHOLOGICAL CHARACTER FORMATION[1]

[(1986). *International Journal of Psycho–Analysis*, 67:181–190]

Character, as Freud observed in 1933, is 'a thing hard to define' (p. 91). Like the concepts of personality, identity, and self, to which it is related, it is best understood as a complex, superordinate, psychological epiphenomenon that involves all dimensions of the psyche, cross-sectionally and longitudinally. It involves the characteristic ways in which a person views him or herself and others, including the basic attitudes and value systems which guide one's general behavior; one's predominant ways of negotiating inner requirements and external demands so as to obtain relative harmony and consistency in the way one lives out one's life; and the overall pattern of fundamental preferences, antipathies, styles, modes, tendencies, quirks, and idiosyncrasies that make a person recognizable as an individual to those who observe him or her frequently or regularly. It is the more or less jelled result of all the formative experiences through which one has passed on the way to adulthood. It is the net effect of all the multiple compromise-formations (Brenner, 1983) which the individual has had to make in order to accommodate the multiple, at times conflicting, and at other times concordant or parallel, internal and external pressures and demands encountered during those formative experiences.

---

[1] Presented at the 34th International Psychoanalytical Congress, Hamburg, July 1985.

The main approach which psychoanalytic investigators have taken in their attempt to define character has centered upon the roles of conflict and defense, particularly with regard to struggles involving oedipal conflict. Freud set the tone for this in his comments, in 1908, on anal and urethral character traits and in his description, in 1916, of certain well-defined, neurotic character-types he had observed clinically. Abraham (1921), (1924), (1925) widely extended Freud's observations in his landmark researches into the characterological effects of conflicts at the various stages of early psychosexual development. Fenichel's (1945), (1953) definition of character, which followed Reich's (1933) earlier efforts, exemplifies this approach in focusing primarily upon the ego's habitual ways of effecting harmony among conflicting intrapsychic requirements.

Arlow (1964), (1966), (1971) has also emphasized the role of conflict resolution in character formation. Depending upon the way in which the ego defends against anxieties associated with the unconscious fantasy expression of psychological conflict, he points out, either neurotic symptoms, perversions, or character traits will emerge. Stein (1969) has distinguished between character traits and neurotic symptoms largely in terms of the greater stability, ego-syntonicity, and acceptability to the individual of the former as compared to the latter. Character traits are viewed as more distantly derived forms of conflict expression, with transformation into more disguised kinds of representation that are relatively smoothly integrated into the individual's perception of his or her core identity, so that they blend into it harmoniously rather than being experienced as alien and troublesome. Boesky (1983) has recently questioned the validity of this view, pointing out that different individuals tend to have very different, usually complex and fluctuating, attitudes toward both their character traits and their symptoms. Either may be experienced as more or less tolerable and consistent with consciously held attitudes and value systems. The differences between symptomatic and characterological expression are not always clear, and the two often coexist in the same person.

At times, the transformation of childhood neurotic symptoms and/or perverse inclinations into substitutive characterological expression in adulthood reflects an at least partially successful acquisition of greater self-control and improved mastery over inner conflicts. This is not always the case, however. Neurotic character traits are not always an improvement over neurotic symptoms and do not always arise out of efforts to obtain mastery over them. They also can arise in their own right, as primary psychopathological constellations. There are neurotic characters who are rendered painfully dysfunctional by their characterological problems and are utterly miserable. Surely, character formation cannot be understood entirely in terms of the variable expression of, and the struggle to overcome, neurotic conflict.

If this is so, what other approach might help us in our efforts to understand the origins and meanings of character pathology? In recent years, there has been increasing interest in studying character formation from a developmental point of view, just as there also has been increasing interest in studying the Oedipus complex hat plays such a central role in the neurotic struggles of those who present themselves to psychoanalysts from a developmental point of view. Psychoanalytic investigators have amassed a wealth of data about pre-oedipal (as well as post-oedipal) development that can shed a good deal of light upon character formation, healthy as well as pathological, as well as upon neurotic disturbances in general.

Freud had anticipated this in his assertion that 'the character of the ego is a precipitate of abandoned object-cathexes' (1923p. 92). In making this observation, he had pointed to the importance of the developing child's ongoing experiences with significant others, at first dyadically and then in more complex, multiple relationships, in determining the shape and the specific contents of the person's emerging character structure and organization. In this regard, it is useful to reflect upon the ambiguous, multiple uses Freud made of the word 'Ich', which unfortunately has been translated into the even more ambiguous and depersonalized word 'ego' in English-speaking countries.

Freud used the term 'Ich' in one sense to refer to the objective 'Ich', i.e. the person one is, the psychological entity one knows oneself to be, as opposed to one's corporeal identity. He used the term in another sense to refer to the subjective 'Ich' that interacts with others in living out one's life, i.e. one's active, experiencing, operant self. A third use Freud made of the term was with regard to the structural 'Ich', to the executive agency within one's psyche that assesses internal requirements and external constraints and demands and develops patterns of action that can meet them in ways that more or less effectively co-ordinate and mediate between them. A fourth use he made of the word 'Ich' referred to a person's self-representation, i.e. to the intrapsychic representation of the actual and preferred characteristics that set oneself apart from others as a unique, individual human being. A person's character implicates all of these various dimensions of one's 'Ich' or 'I'.

To understand the way in which it develops, it is helpful to reflect upon it not only in isolation but also in terms of its relatedness to the meaningful others with whom one interacts in the course of one's development. The 'I' in other words, begins, remains, and, in a very real sense, can only exist as part of a 'We'. Initially, the 'I' and the 'We' are indistinguishable or only fleetingly and unclearly distinguishable from one another. Definition of one, in the course of ongoing experience of the two, is established, *pari passu*, along with simultaneous definition of the other. Increasing awareness of the difference between the two is experienced positively and also negatively, with resultant pressure to effect ways both of re-establishing the undifferentiated unity between self and other, between 'I' and 'not-I', that prevailed at the beginning and of establishing oneself as a separate entity able to exist independently of the other. To effect the latter, it is necessary to come to be able to relate to the other in such a way that the originally undifferentiated 'We' of which one's 'I' was once experienced as a part and within which it developed, becomes largely replaced by a partly external, more or less realistic and objective 'We' that is recognized and accepted as consisting of two separate and independent entities, with desires, wills, powers, and capacities that dovetail fortuitously at times and clash violently at other times, in a larger world of independently and collectively operant beings. The latter is achieved via a developmental process that contains within it, as a core element of it, a series of identifications that are necessary to maintain a sufficient, ongoing inner feeling of secure oneness with the increasingly recognized other that completes the increasingly recognized 'I' within the 'We'. This permits increasing relinquishing of the illusion of oneness as the separate, individual psychological strength is built up within the 'I' that eventually largely obviates the need for such an illusion of undifferentiated oneness.

The identification mechanisms that are involved simultaneously serve the function of 'identifying' the difference between self and other and the function of psychologically uniting self and other by 'identifying' one with another. They consist in a progressive series of different types of identification mechanisms that in optimal circumstances gradually replace each other. The overall success or failure of the ongoing process depends upon the extent to which true, effective internalization and structuralization can take place within the developing individual.

The first phase can be characterized as one of 'primal identification'. Human beings are born in an extremely helpless, still embryonic state in which they require absolute external care for survival. At the beginning, the child is aware only of discontinuous, global feeling states. If it is awake and hungry, it knows hunger. If it is fed, it feels content and returns to sleep. If there is pain, it knows pain. If there is pleasure, it knows pleasure. With ongoing experience comes continuity and the beginnings of sensorimotor awareness (recognitory assimilation) of these feeling states and the experiential contexts in which they occur. Since the feeling states are mediated by motor acts (crying, thrashing, mouthing, sucking, kinaesthetic movement, smiling, touching, etc.) and are experienced primarily in the context of caretaking activities involving child and mother together, the motor behaviour and the sensory impressions of the mothering person gathered during them then inevitably become associated with one another.

Increasing wakefulness and the opportunity to study these experiences in a more or less calm state of alert inactivity allows the child gradually to distinguish its own motor acts and sensations from the mother's ministrations with which they are associated. The intense emotionality that prevails during feeding situations tends to blur the appreciation of the distinction between them being attained in these quieter times, however, so that increasing differentiation between them alternates with de-differentiation, with both being part and parcel of the ongoing relationship between child and mother. Awareness of their separateness and separability crystallizes more and more, as exemplified in the four or five month old infant reaching toward its mother and crying when she leaves the room. The realization of their separateness is problematic in several ways. It not only disrupts the feeling of primary narcissistic omnipotence that must prevail in early life, but also impinges in a critical manner upon the libidinal and aggressive drive organizations that are beginning to form during those early months after birth.

Via the apparent use of introjective and projective psychological mechanisms, modelled after the physiological activities of taking in nutriment and expelling body contents in sneezing, spitting out, urinating, and defaecating (respiratory inspiration and expiration may play a modelling role as well), the child seems to create an idealized perception of things in which all that is good and desirable is taken in and felt as inside and all that is bad and undesirable is put outside. This is exemplified perhaps in the observation of a five month old girl who, after glowingly enjoying a very pleasant feeding experience in which her father (who is experienced early in life as another mother) had smilingly fed her one of her favourite foods while speaking to her cheerfully and lovingly, reached her head and mouth toward him, with bright and shining eyes, with a motion as though to swallow him down. This contrasted sharply with her tendency, when in an irritable, fussy, unhappy mood, to arch and pull back from him with pursing mouth movements and a facial expression that were similar to those observable when she instantly spit out baby food containing liver when it was given to her for the first time.

Babies show a capacity for imitative behaviour, such as smiling or frowning in response to the sight of an adult face smiling or frowning, and opening and closing the mouth in response to observing an adult do so, as early as the very first weeks after birth. They also tend to study the human face and to reach out and explore the mother's hair and face and clothing during quiet wakeful times, for example after feedings. It can be postulated that there is a connexion between these imitative and exploratory behaviours and the taking in, the introjection, of attributes of the mothering person that are essential to the reestablishment of the illusion of oneness with all that is good and desirable and exclusion of the opposite, at the same time that it contributes to awareness of difference. There is simultaneous identification with the caring, providing mother and identification of her as separate and different.

The introjection of the mothering person into oneself, as a sense of oneself is developing, is always ambivalent, however. The mother is identified not only with the restoration of peace and contentment and with the provision of pleasurable experience, but also with the pain, distress, and sensations of hunger that at first initiate most of the contacts that are made with her. Ingestion of food, upon which the psychological mechanism of introjection appears to be largely modelled, not only makes it part of oneself but also destroys it. It makes it disappear from the external perceptual field. Whether the ongoing interactions between child and mother are experienced predominantly as pleasurable or unpleasurable, positive or negative, is crucial to the images that begin to form as the rudiments of symbolic thought emerge during the latter part of the first year (see Piaget, 1947); (Silverman, 1971).

If the interactions are experienced as having a predominantly positive tone to them, the fundamental 'inner' feeling that is likely to develop is generally positive, setting the stage for a generally positive self-feeling, associated with a feeling of basic trust (Erikson, 1959) or confident expectation (Benedek, 1938) that is an essential ingredient of a benign and necessary illusion of constant togetherness with the mother that approaches oneness with her. Such a set of positive inner feelings provides a baseline sense of security and optimism that is enormously helpful to the child in weathering the disruptive effects of the pain and anger that accompany the inevitable disappointments and frustrations that are encountered in the process of development. The latter play a central part, in fact, in initiating psychological activity by the child that promotes reality testing, self-other differentiation, and recognition of one's self and of others.

If a negative tone prevails in the infant-mother interactions or if there is too much jangling, frustrating, painful, angry experience (and 'too much' for one child can be very different from what might be 'too much' for another child), this gives rise to a basic sense of insecurity and of inability to rely confidently on reliable forces that can be counted on as sources of necessary soothing and comforting. This in turn will interfere with and limit the child's capacity for relinquishing the primary narcissistic illusion of oneness with the source of soothing and comforting that provides a sense of primary omnipotence. Negativity, of course, does not necessarily arise either from intrinsic vulnerabilities (intensities, unsoothability, etc.) in the child or from parental deficiencies (depression, lack of empathy, illness, etc.) alone, but from a variable combination of the two.

During the latter part of the first year and the first part of the second year, the child becomes increasingly unable to maintain the illusion of primary narcissistic, omnipotent unity that initially is valuable and necessary. The separateness and separability of mother and child inevitably must be recognized. For one thing, there is an innate push toward independent functioning within the child that propels it toward separation and individuation. Hendrick (1943 a), (1943 b) called attention to the important role of *Funktionslust* and *Bemächtigungstrieb*, of pleasure in functioning and mastery in human development. The same little girl who at five months of age had wanted to swallow down her father after a mutually enjoyable feeding experience became able about a month later to roll over from a prone to a supine position. She could not at first return unaided to a prone position, however, so her parents helped her to do so. One day, after her father had repeatedly helped her turn back on to her belly so that she could push herself over on to her back again, she suddenly found herself able to flip herself back over on to her belly all by herself. She looked surprised for a moment, and then flipped herself on to her back again. She immediately turned back on to her belly, and, to her father's astonishment, did not continue with the game of flipping back and forth but began to push up with her shoulders and hips as though trying to stand up (which she did not actually become able to do until several months later). Another observation comes to mind of an eight month old who suddenly refused to eat anything from then on that she could not pick up and put into her mouth with her own hands.

This movement through what Mahler (see Mahler et al., 1975) has termed the 'differentiation' and 'practising' subphases of separation-individuation coincides with the rudimentary beginnings of symbolic thought, which itself derives in part from imitation, i.e. via imitative analogy (see Piaget, 1947); (Silverman, 1971). The increasing separation awareness taking place during these subphases shatters the illusion of primary omnipotence. It is accompanied, therefore, by separation anxiety(see Spitz, 1965); (Mahler et al., 1975), that propels the child back toward a 'rapprochement' with the mother and toward the use of symbolic, 'transitional' objects and other phenomena (Winnicott, 1953) that are used by the child to regain the illusion of omnipotent unity that has been lost. This ushers in a new phase of rudimentary or transitional identification that leads to an illusion of *secondary* narcissistic, omnipotent oneness with the mother.

During the period of primary identification, the child has built up an inner feeling of strength and power that derives from the illusion of oneness with a source of relief from pain and discomfort that actually is outside of it. Ego maturation and development has led to increasing awareness of separateness from that source of power and of the limitations in the child's actual powers apart from that external source that make it highly vulnerable to pain, discomfort, and deflation of its feeling of omnipotent perfection. Although there is delight in the ability to do things that could not be done before and actively to do for oneself what used to require external assistance, the very ability to do those things propels the child outside the orbit of shared activity with the mother and away from the mother who is beginning in a rudimentary way to be invested in as a true, external love object rather than as a narcissistic extension of oneself. The intense crisis of ambivalence about being separate from, or together with, the mother that ensues is heightened by the (apparently maturationally and developmentally) sharply increased intensity of aggressive drive expression that is apparent during the toddler phase (see Peller, 1965). The toddler is not only beginning to perceive the mother as an external love object who can be lost, but also as an external hate object that can be driven away or destroyed. This contributes to intense anxiety, pressure to employ psychological defence activity to resolve the dilemma created by intensely ambivalent feelings (see Winnicott, 1958), (1971), and a need to resolve the tension between simultaneous wishes for separateness and independence, on the one hand, and the longing to return to the de-differentiated illusion of narcissistic unity with the mothering person that had prevailed at an earlier time, on the other.

The way in which the child deals with this 'rapprochement crisis' (Mahler et al., 1975) depends very much on what has taken place during the earlier phase of primary identification. (We owe a debt of gratitude to Karl Abraham for emphasizing the epigenetic nature of psychological development.) If the child has been fortunate enough to have been able to build up an inner feeling of relative internal harmony and unity, in co-ordination with the illusion of oneness with a relatively consistent, reliable mothering person, it will be possible to relinquish *some* of the internal oneness with that person in exchange for an alternative source of strength. The latter includes a combination of partial acceptance of her separateness, partial reliance on one's own resources (with pressure increasingly to accept their limitations and to build and develop more or less realistic, autonomous ego capacities organized in a secondary process fashion that increase the capacity for tension tolerance and frustration tolerance), and resort *at times of particular stress and excessive discomfort* to transitional objects and phenomena that provide a temporary, *external* illusion of oneness with the mother when it is needed. The use of a transitional object represents a major developmental advance over the earlier, *internal* illusion of oneness with her in that there is a good deal of awareness of the separateness from the mother and of the illusional, make believe, substitutive quality of the blanket or teddy bear as a comforter and provider of inner peace and harmony *from the outside*. The intense wish to take the comforter back into oneself is poignantly expressed in the vigorous thumb-sucking that accompanies the use of transitional objects and in the essential role of the mouth in the lallating, humming, or singing that can replace it as a non-corporeal transitional phenomenon.

The awareness of the separateness of the transitional object both from oneself and from the mother it symbolically represents, as well as the illusional setting aside of that awareness for the purpose of aiding the child in making the transition from primary identification to self-object differentiation and autonomous ego growth is exemplified in the following. A twenty month old girl had not developed an apparent transitional object but had stopped referring to her twenty-one month older sister by name (although her name had been her first real word) at the same time that she had begun to refuse to go to sleep unless her sister, with whom she shared a room, was already in bed. A little while before this, she had gone through a period of insisting that her mother stay in the room with her at bedtime, fighting sleep to make certain that she did not leave the room. When her father pressed her one evening to tell him who it was in her sister's bed, at first she evaded his repeated question by proudly naming other objects in the room: 'window' (pointing to it), 'ceiling' (pointing up), etc. 'But who is *this* ?' he asked, pointing to her sister. 'Bed', she replied gaily. 'Yes, this is a bed, very good', he said, 'but who is in the bed?' She frowned a bit. 'Not Mommy, not Mommy, not Mommy', she said, with a sober look on her face.

The fortunate toddler, who has had a good primary identification phase and does not encounter serious problems during toddlerhood to throw him or her back into illusional or delusional, compulsive primary identification, begins to move into true object-related identification (which requires recognition of the mother as an external, separate, dyadic love and hate object) by identifying with the mother's activity and the mother's activities (see Peller, 1965). Imitation now is utilized not so much in connexion with the wish to swallow her down whole but in the service of taking in selected desired attributes of someone who is more and more accepted as a separate, independent person with a will of her own who is to be emulated for a variety of reasons. One is the wish to take in and acquire (idealized) qualities and powers for secondary narcissistic purposes. Another is the wish to model oneself after her in ways that facilitate the acquisition and building up of strengths that enable the child to fend for itself and more and more to do without her. Increasingly, there is the wish to be like her because she is admired and loved.

The more unfortunate toddler, who has not built up a sufficient inner sense of relative harmony and unity and of reliable availability of assistance when it is needed, or whose mother abandons him or her (literally or in terms of her sensitivity to his or her needs), or cannot tolerate her child's growing up and away from her, cannot afford to give up the illusion of inner, primary narcissistic oneness with the mother. This is the kind of child whose response to the rapprochement crisis is to cling to mother and/or run away from her in order to be chased and brought back, or in even more serious instances, to resort to intense, rigid defensive manoeuvres to deny the loss of primary narcissistic unity and/or *excessively* to create secondary narcissistic identificatory illusions or even delusions that impede emotional growth.

A man in his mid-thirties, for example, entered analysis because of chronic unhappiness, alcoholism, hypochondriasis, and inability to establish a meaningful ongoing relationship with a woman. He ambivalently idealized and worshipped a woman with whom he knew a lasting relationship was impossible for a number of cogent reasons, whom he strongly disliked for multiple reasons, and who teased, tantalized and repeatedly threatened to leave him. He lived at home with his mother after having tried unsuccessfully to establish himself in an apartment of his own. He spent his evenings in bars, where he often would pick up a woman and spend the night with her only to find himself disgusted and eager to get rid of her by morning. His wistful yearning was for older women. He was narcissistically preoccupied with his appearance, his clothes and his possessions, all of which had to be immaculate and the very best. He was perfectionistic and demanding to an extreme degree.

In the analytic sessions, he looked to the analyst to empathize, understand, and relieve his distress without his having actually to communicate what he was feeling and thinking to him. The analysis included long silences. When he did speak, it was mainly to complain and to express hopelessness about his situation. The analyst felt consistently that he was perceived as an agent who was expected intuitively to protect and take perfect, even magical care of him. He felt strongly and consistently during the first two years that the analysand viewed him as an idealized extension of himself rather than as a separate person. There certainly was no indication of the development of an oedipal transference. Elements of an idealizing father-transference began to appear, in which the wished for father very much appeared to possess the qualities of a 'better mother', as the patient improved clinically in response to an empathic interpretive approach that centred about the emptiness, chronic rage, and intense longing for care and nurturance that were evident.

The alcoholism was gradually overcome, and instead of spending his evenings drinking in bars he began to frequent sushi bars instead, consuming what felt to him like endless quantities of the pink raw fish, wrapped delicately and delectably in pearl white rice and served lovingly by hand by devoted, dedicated craftsmen, that he came to recognize symbolically represented to him tenderly nourishing breast material he voraciously and endlessly yearned to ingest 'cannibalistically' so that they would become an integral part of him, although he feared that once inside him it might kill him. Bits and pieces of early memories began to emerge that permitted reconstruction of an unsatisfying, unpredictable, erratic set of early life experiences in which his mother, who had had lifelong, serious emotional problems of her own, had turned him over to the care of a series of maids whom he had experienced as cold, hard, ungiving, and punitive, while his nervous, critical, and demanding father had been too preoccupied building his business and looking after his own considerable problems to have been available in a warm, empathic way more than occasionally. It was clear that he had not been able to develop the kind of fundamental foundation of reliable, inner unity with a caring, giving, nurturant, protective, tension-relieving power that he had needed within his ego core to develop either a consistent, harmonious, integrated, reliable, reasonably contented sense of self or a view of others as separate, exciting, desirable objects toward whom it would be worthwhile to direct love or safe enough to direct hate.

It is only when the latter self and object attitudes have been established, in the course of fortuitous interpersonal experiences, that it is possible for a child to turn to people as whole objects and to develop a focused, excited, optimistic yearning to be like them, to take on their attitudes, standards and values, pursue them as love objects, and compete with them as rivals in the triadic, genital oedipal way we have come to recognize as essential for even the beginnings of emotional maturity. Children who have been constitutionally unable to make effective use of parental care and/or have been abandoned, received significantly erratic, unempathic or even brutalizing treatment during the pre-oedipal period, are unprepared for the developmental demands, intense conflicts, and structural stress and strain of oedipal involvement.

Children who have had fortunate experiences during the pre-oedipal period, however, have built up enough of a feeling of primary basic ego strength (especially frustration tolerance, tension tolerance, self-control, and secondary process functioning) that they can afford progressively to relinquish the illusion of oneness with the mothering person and replace it with a more or less realistic acceptance of their separateness that permits entry into an oedipal, triadic developmental period. (This is always carried out via a series of to-and-fro, progressive and regressive movements, and probably is never done completely.) The sense of trust in oneself and in the other, who originally was perceived as part of oneself but now is allowed to be separate, requires considerable strengthening if this new phase is to be successfully negotiated.

The oedipal child is buffeted by increasing realization of his or her relative smallness and weakness, with regard both to inner drive pressures and to demands to conform to externally imposed behavioural requirements. With recognition of the other's separateness comes awareness of the other's involvement with yet others, including intimate, affectionate and sexual relationships from which the child is excluded. The narcissistic mortification (including extremely painful feelings of general and genital inadequacy) and narcissistic rage (Kohut, 1978) that are created by inevitable oedipal defeats disrupt the positive narcissistic balance that has been attained. Together with fear of loss of the other's love and of retaliatory aggression, this spurs the child to utilize a number of defence mechanisms in an effort to protect its beleaguered selfesteem and to ward off intense oedipal anxieties. Chief among these is an impulsion toward dedifferentiating regression back to the illusion of narcissistic union with the mother. This conflicts sharply with the powerful developmental thrust toward independence, self-reliance, and self-expression that plays an integral part in the child's sense of pride and integrity, however.

An apt compromise is available through which the conflict between the conflicting progressive and regressive inclinations can be resolved. Identification with aspects of the loved objects, the loved objects' preferred objects, and with the frustrating, disappointing, defeating, and punishing maternal and paternal objects is carried out in a much more controlled, selective, complex manner than the global, introjective identifications of the earlier, pre-oedipal periods. It affords a wonderful opportunity not only to defend against the anxieties and shattering defeats that are being experienced but at the same time to unite with the parents in selected ways that permit the borrowing or acquisition from them of selected strengths and internalized feelings, attitudes, and approaches to serve as scaffolding or as a skeletal framework around which the child can build true, personal, autonomous, effective, executive ego capacities that eventually can ensure the ability to move beyond dependence upon parents to truly independent, mature, adult functioning.

Freud referred to this type of identification as 'hysterical' as opposed to the earlier 'narcissistic' type of identification (1900), (1905), (1921). Imitation plays a role, as evidenced by the great interest shown by oedipal (and early latency age) children in dressing up in their parents' clothing and in engaging in adult role play activities. Introjection also is involved, as is especially evident in early superego identifications, which tend to lodge parental imagos within the ego in part as tyrannical, rule-enforcing foreign bodies or agents in their critical function, alongside the more smoothly integrated, less noisily operative approving and loving, so-called ego ideal parental imagos. It is quite dramatic to watch a 5 year old harshly chastising another child or turning him or her in for harsh punishment for breaking a rule which he has just casually and guiltlessly broken himself or is about to break.

What is distinctively characteristic about oedipal identifications is that they are not merely defensive in nature but serve a crucially essential developmental function as well. They not only are partial and selective (which becomes especially important in connexion with the need of boys and girls to be very different in their selection of certain aspects and attributes of their male and female parents with which to identify), but they are subject to ongoing, active reworking and revision that transforms their initially, incorporative, introjective nature into one that integrates them with one another and with a transcendent, superordinate, uniquely personal schema in which their roots as aspects of external agents eventually are much less recognizable. Some of what is initially introjected will ultimately be discarded, in fact, or so revamped that its original source is no longer relevant.

To the degree that these partial identifications are continually revised, reorganized, and integrated into an emerging, unique ego core or character, they promote strength-building structuralization and restructuralization, internalization of external controls into autonomous self-control, taming and neutralization of drives so that their energies can in part be transformed into ego energies; depersonification and abstraction; and the ascendancy of reasonable, reflective, thoughtful action in place of impulsive and compulsive (i.e. defensive), driven activity. The importance of the developmental advance effected by this progressive structuralization within the ego has been emphasized by Jacobson (1954), (1964), Loewald (1962), Hartmann & Loewenstein (1962), Sandler & Rosenblatt (1962), and Meissner (1970), (1971), (1972); also see Ritvo & Solnit (1958) with discussion by R. M. Loewenstein, J. A. Arlow, and R. P. Knight.

There are multiple pitfalls and potential derailments that can seriously interfere with the outcome of the process of oedipal identification, of course. One is that the processes of pre-oedipal, primary and secondary narcissistic identification may not have established a solid enough base to permit the child to weather the *Sturm und Drang* of oedipal conflict. Another is that oedipal experiences may be so stressful and difficult that they would be beyond the coping capacity of nearly any child(traumatic experiences such as serious injuries or illness, and the effects of significant psychopathology in the parents, siblings or other influential individuals that specifically affect the oedipal period are important in this regard). In either instance, there may be overwhelming pressure to regress back to pre-oedipal narcissistic modes that are structuralization-impeding and otherwise seriously impede developmental advance. Parental failure to provide optimal modeling for growth-facilitating identification is another common developmental deficiency. This may be especially important where there is use of developmentally unfortunate defense mechanisms by the child, such as extensive denial or projection, which needs to be counteracted by parental modeling that will help to offset it rather than that which parallels and reinforces it. Parents and other significant objects also impose significant details into the self-representations that are part of a child's developing set of identifications and character structure that are not always fortuitous ones.

I should like to offer a brief clinical vignette in illustration. Miss A had been a timid, shy pre-oedipal and early oedipal child whose mother permitted and encouraged her to 'hold on to her apron strings' rather than supporting her erstwhile efforts to express herself in an independent, self-reliant, demonstrative manner. Her mother also openly favored her brother, with whom she bathed her until she was 5 years of age. During her oedipal years, she found herself repeatedly rejected and humiliated by her father and brother, both of whom were angry people who continually disparaged and denigrated her. Her mother not only did not come to her aid, but herself accepted (and provoked) ongoing verbal abuse from her father and presented herself as chronically angry, dispirited, and beaten, with a low view of women's lot and little hope of its ever improving. Miss A retreated from excited oedipal pursuit of her father and brother to an angry, disgruntled, masochistic identification with her mother, to whom she clung and with whom she longed to be united in protected, blissful harmony. When she entered analysis, she was an extremely unhappy, lonely, overweight, socially isolated, phobic, masochistic, angry young woman who avoided men completely in reaction to terrifying unconscious fantasies of brutally masochistic submission to them. She lived at home with her parents and considered her mother her 'best friend'. She still held her mother's hand as they walked together in the street. In the analysis, she repeatedly developed excited, oedipal, father transference feelings and fantasies toward her analyst only to flee from them to a pre-oedipal, ambivalent attachment to the analyst as a protective, caring mother who would look after her in what she hoped would be an analysis that would never end.

One final comment is in order. The yearning for blissful, enveloping union with an all-giving, all-providing, all-powerful, maternal presence is never fully given up, as Lewin (1946) has observed in elaborating his concept of the 'oral triad' and as Kohut (1978) has emphasized in his concept of 'selfobjects'. Under the impact of an intrinsic developmental thrust toward active, assertive, self-expressive, independent, autonomous functioning, more or less supported and facilitated by parents and the world at large, the child more or less successfully transforms this yearning into the pursuit of separate, external love objects with whom there is the opportunity for intermittent recapture of the illusion of mingled union. What else are hugging, kissing, sexual relations, and orgasm?

At times of heightened or unusual stress, people experience a regressive pull back toward the illusion of narcissistic union with an all-powerful parental force that provides absolute protection and ensures that all needs will be met. Whether this pull will be resisted or not will depend upon the extent to which the character of the ego has developed along the line from the initial, undifferentiated, infantile omnipotence of primary narcissistic identification to mature, differentiated, realistic self-other perceptions, with ego structuralization and internalization of personal and societal values that include both healthy self-regard and respectful appreciation of the rights and needs of others. Implicated in this are the degree to which child-rearing views and practices, and the sociocultural attitudes from which they derive, foster the development of integrated, independent, autonomous, feeling and thinking individuals who are both self-respecting and respecting of others.

SUMMARY

The character of the ego is built up via a series of identifications carried out in the course of development. As infants are forced by experience to give up the 'internal illusion' of primal identification with the powerful mother, the sense of helplessness that ensues leads to secondary identification to create an 'external illusion' of oneness with the mother during heightened stress or tension.

Adequate experiences, leading to increasing trust and tolerance of frustration and tension, promote ego structuralization, self-object differentiation, and oedipal, triadic object relations. Inadequate experiences lead to pathological identifications that interfere with ego development. Oedipal conflicts produce new problems, which are dealt with in part by complex identifications that contribute extensively to the child's personality structure. Superego crystallization derives largely from these later identifications.

In optimal circumstances, the identifications out of which the child's character is built become reworked and modified so that it becomes increasingly unique and independent of its sources in others. Stability is never absolute, however. Under stress, reversion is possible to dependence on powerful, charismatic leaders that offers return to the illusion of identificatory union with a powerful, protective, parental 'other'. This can be exploited by potentially dangerous, destructive leaders.

REFERENCES

ABRAHAM, K. (1921). Contributions to the theory of the anal character. In *Selected Papers*. London: Hogarth Press, 1965 pp. 370–392.

——— (1924). The influence of oral erotism on character-formation. In *Selected Papers*. London: Hogarth Press, 1965 pp. 393–406.

ABRAHAM, K. 1925 Character formation on the genital level of the libido In *Selected Papers*. London: Hogarth Press, 1965 pp. 407–417.

ARLOW, J.A. (1964). Symptom formation and character formation: summary and discussion *Int. J. Psychoanal.* 45:167–176.

———— (1966). Character and conflict. *J. Hillside Hosp.* 15:139–151.

———— (1971). Character perversion. In *Currents in Psychoanalysis ed. I. Marcus.* New York: Int. Univ. Press, pp. 317–336.

BENEDEK, T. (1938). Adaptation to reality in early infancy. *Psychoanal. Q.* 7:200–214. BOESKY, D. (1983). Resistance and character theory: a reconsideration of the concept of character resistance. *J. Am. Psychoanal. Assoc.* 31(Suppl.):227–246 .

BRENNER, C. (1983). *The Mind in Conflict.* New York: Int. Univ. Press.

ERIKSON, E H. (1959). *Identity and the Life Cycle. Psychological Issues. Monograph No. 1.* New York: Int. Univ. Press.

FENICHEL, O. (1945). *The Psychoanalytic Theory of Neurosis.* New York: Norton.

———— (1953). Concerning the theory of psychoanalytic technique. In *Collected Papers Volume 1.* New York: Norton, pp. 332–348.

———— (1954) Psychoanalysis of character. In *Collected Papers Volume 2* New York: Norton.

FREUD, A. (1936). *The Ego and the Mechanisms of Defense. The Writings of Anna Freud Volume 2.* New York: Int. Univ. Press, 1966.

FREUD, S. (1900) The interpretation of dreams *S.E.* 4/5.

———— (1905). Three essays on the theory of sexuality. *S.E.* 7.

———— (1908). Character and anal erotism. *Standard Edition* 9.

———— (1916). Some character types met with in psycho-analytic work. *Standard Edition* 14.

———— (1921). Group psychology and the analysis of the ego. *Standard Edition* 18.

———— (1923).. The ego and the id. *Standard Edition* 19.

———— (1930). Civilization and its discontents. *Standard Edition* 21.

———— (1933). New introductory lectures on psycho-analysis *S.E.* 22.

HARTMANN, H. & LOEWENSTEIN, R. (1962). Notes on the superego. *Psychoanal. Study Child* 17:42–81.

HENDRICK, I. (1943a). Work and the pleasure principle. *Psychoanal. Q.* 12:311–329.

——— (1943b). The discussion of the 'instinct to master.' *Psychoanal. Q.* 12:561–565.

——— (1951). Early development of the ego: identification in infancy. *Psychoanal. Q.* 20:44–61.

JACOBSON, E. (1954). Contribution to the metapsychology of psychotic identifications *J. Am. Psychoanal. Assoc.* 2:239–262.

——— (1964). *The Self and the Object World.* New York: Int. Univ. Press..

KOHUT, H. (1978). *The Search for the Self: Selected Writings of Heinz Kohut, 1950-1978,* ed. P. Ornstein. New York: Int. Univ. Press..

LEWIN, B D. (1946). Sleep, the mouth and the dream screen. *Psychoanal. Q.* 15:419–434.

LOEWALD, H. (1962). Internalization, separation, mourning and the superego. *Psychoanal. Q.* 31:483–504.

MAHLER, M.S., PINE, F. & BERGMAN, A. (1975). *The Psychological Birth of the Human Infant.* New York: Basic Books.

MEISSNER, W. (1970). Notes on identification. I: Origins in Freud. *Psychoanal. Q.* 39:563–589.

——— (1971). Notes on identification. II: Clarification of related concepts. *Psychoanal. Q.* 40:277–302.

———1972). Notes on identification. III: The concept of identification *Psychoanal. Q.* 41:224–260.

PELLER, L.E. (1965). Comments on libidinal organizations and child development. *J. Am. Psychoanal. Assoc.* 13:732–747.

PIAGET, J. (1947). *The Psychology of Intelligence.* Paterson: Littlefield, Adams, 1960.

REICH, W. (1933). *Character Analysis.* New York: Noonday Press, 1949.

RITVO, S. & SOLNIT, A.J. (1958). Influences of early mother-child interaction on identification processes. *Psychoanal. Study Child* 13:64–85.

SANDLER, J. & ROSENBLATT, B. (196).2 The concept of the representational world. *Psychoanal. Study Child* 17:128–145.

SILVERMAN, M. (1971). The Growth of Logical Thinking. Piaget's Contribution To Ego Psychology. *Psychoanal. Q.* 40:317–341.

SPITZ, R. (1965*). The First Year Of Life.* New York: Int. Univ. Press.

STEIN, M. (1969). The problem of character theory. *J. Am. Psychoanal. Assoc.* 17:675–701.

WINNICOTT, D.W. (1953). Transitional objects and transitional phenomena. *Int. J. Psychoanal.* 34:89–97

——— (1958). The capacity to be alone. *Int. J. Psychoanal.* 39:416–420.

——— (1971). *The use of an object In Playing and Reality.* New York: Basic Books, pp. 86–94.

CHAPTER 13

POWER, CONTROL, AND THE THREAT TO DIE
IN A CASE OF ASTHMA AND ANOREXIA

[From: *Psychosomatic Symptoms. Psychodynamic Treatment of the Underlying Personality Disorder*, edited by C. Philip Wilson, M.D., & Ira L. Mintz, M.D. Northvale, NJ/London: Jason Aronson, pp. 351–364.]

Laura, painfully thin, her face pinched and wizened, hunched forward in her chair and spoke laconically and almost inaudibly during her first session. With her delicate features, long blonde hair, sad eyes, and long eyelashes, she was pretty and appealing in a very fragile, plaintive, doll-like manner.

Now 10 years old, she had been asthmatic since. age 5, much more so since her older brother had gone off to camp in a flurry of hypochondriacal anxiety two years earlier. She very much wanted to stop wheezing,-she said, since it interfered with so many aspects of her life and repeatedly kept her from having fun. Her anorexia troubled her much less, however. She wished her mother would stop worrying that she would starve to death. Her mother, she said, worried about her too much altogether. Paradoxically (though Laura herself saw no inconsistency in it), she enjoyed her grandmother's fussing over her and plying her with all kinds of special food,. in an effort to put meat on her bones.

Laura's asthma had begun in a very dramatic way. She had been a breath holder between 2 and 5 years of age When thing did not go her way, she would hold her breath, turn dead white, and pass out. Her mother, who always had been very phobic and had been obsessively worried about Laura's health ever since she was born, was terrified every time it happened. Laura's breath holding ended when she reached age 5. To everyone's dismay, however, it was replaced with a relatively mild, but unnerving case of bronchial asthma.

Her father had been very ill with a protracted case of largely antibiotic-resistant staphylococcus pneumonia through the latter part of her mother's pregnancy with her older brother. Afterward, he suffered repeated episodes of pneumonia and other lung disorders. His own childhood had been powerfully influenced by his mother's single-minded devotion to his brother, who had nearly died of staphylococcus pneumonia and had remained in very delicate health thereafter, with repeated respiratory problems that occupied her attention. The anorexia went back even further, and it was much more subtle in its origin and development. When Laura was born, two years after her brother, her mother was delighted. Not only was Laura a girl, which she had wanted very much, but also, in sharp contrast to her brother, she was quiet, placid, undemanding, and easily contented. Her brother had been a fretful, restless, over-hungry baby, who never seemed to be getting enough from her. Laura was a small eater, waited patiently for her feedings, and was easily satisfied. The mother had always wanted a daughter and always kept Laura very close to her. Laura's father joked that she couldn't do without Laura and would accompany her on her honeymoon. She fondled and fussed over Laura as a baby and took her with her everywhere she went.

A phobic-obsessive worrier for as long as she could remember, Laura's mother had worried about her daughter's health and welfare from the time she began to walk. She repeatedly worried that something terrible might happen to her, so that she would lose her. Whenever she was even mildly ill, she nursed her with tenderness, lavish attention, special privileges, and little gifts. Laura's thinness frightened her and made her feel hurt and rejected. Laura's refusal to accept the nourishing foods that her mother kept offering her seemed like a rejection of her mother.

Laura's "prudish" mother took care to keep herself well covered at all times, and she could not bring herself to talk with Laura about anything involving the human body. Her father, however, had no compunctions about walking around the house in tight-fitting underwear, despite Laura's frequent objections. Laura had been bathed regularly with her brother, until her mother's own doctor had advised against it when Laura was 2 years old. Her mother had entered psychotherapy because of tension on headaches, low self-esteem, and a poor opinion of herself and of women in general. As a child, she had wished that she were a boy. She felt that this had contributed to Laura's own repeated assertion, when she was younger, that she •should have been provided with a penis like her brother.

Psychosomatic expression of emotional conflict appeared to be a family tendency. In addition to Laura's anorexia and asthma and her mother's headaches, her father suffered from repeated attacks of various gastrointestinal disorders (including frightening episodes of difficulty breathing and swallowing) and an intermittent bad back, and her brother had undergone psychotherapy for mild asthma and multiple gastrointestinal complaints.

Laura and I worked together in a long course of treatment that lasted until she graduated from high school and went off to college. We had sessions three• and then four times a week after the initial evaluative period. Although she had been rather communicative during her first visit, she retreated after that into almost total silence. She appeared to appreciate my extensive efforts to break the impasse and help her to speak by groping for explanations of her protracted silence.

My proffered explanations included her difficulty trusting herself and trusting me; discomfort about-opening up and exposing her feelings and thoughts to a man; fear of relaxing her guard against her intense rage; feelings of powerlessness and pessimism about achieving success in therapy; depression that sapped her emotional and physical energy; sputtering but helpless outrage over the consulting psychiatrist's telling her she would have to wait for my arrival in the area before she could begin her own treatment, while he took her brother, who had suddenly burst out in a rash of acute psychosomatic symptoms, into weekly treatment with him; fear of giving in to her dependent yearnings, thereby compromising her determined wish to be self-reliant; a need to test my interest, devotion, and willingness to persevere and expend effort on her behalf; a desire to not merely describe to me her feelings of frustration, helplessness, and impotence, but to get me to feel, in all its intensity, what she herself felt; and so forth.

She would hunch over and nod weakly as she labored to force air through her tightly constricted bronchial passages. Her bony rib cage rose and fell, and she struggled to raise her heavy lids to look at me. In response to me, she might even gasp a few words, in a tone of anguished sorrow and pain. For the most part, however, she remained deathly still, except for the rasping of her wheezing inspirations and expirations. When four or five months had elapsed without any essential change either in her behavior during our sessions or in her symptomatology, I found myself growing increasingly concerned (like her mother?) and beginning to wonder whether I was the wrong person to treat her. I gingerly raised this possibility to her. I said that I wanted very much to help her, but that, since she had been almost totally unable to speak to me, perhaps she might find it easier to speak with someone else, maybe with a woman rather than a man. She responded by hunching over even more from the edge of her chair, wheezing a little more laboriously, and pulling her shoulders forward so that she looked even more starved and wraithlike. A large tear rolled down one cheek and dropped to the rug. "If you send me away," she said, "I'll die!"

Things continued pretty much the same over the next three or four months, during which Laura remained all but completely silent while I put into words what she seemed to me to be feeling, and shared with her my impressions as to the dynamic conflicts that seemed to underlie her feelings. She showed hers if in general agreement with my observations, indicating this by nodding assent, but she did not hesitate to let me know when she disagreed with something I had said.

Finally, eight months after we had begun working together, she suddenly ended her silence and began to talk. The first thing she spoke about was her consultation with the psychiatrist who referred her to me.

He had said that her condition was very serious and that she needed several treatment sessions a week. Since his office was quite a distance from her home, he had told her, the best thing for her would be to enter treatment with me, since I soon would be moving, not only to her area, but very close to where she lived. She had been disappointed, she said, but could see the wisdom of his remarks. It would have been all right, she added, if he hadn't taken her brother into treatment. Her brother had come down suddenly with a number of psychophysiological symptoms that had mimicked some of her problems and some of her father's recurrent problems, and the psychiatrist who had turned her away had taken her brother into treatment instead. She could understand his treating her brother, since he knew the family pretty well by then and her brother needed to travel to him only once a week for the relatively quick recovery he made. Still, she said, "It's not fair; it's not fair; I saw him first; why should he take him and not me?" She literally shuddered and shook with rage.

The consulting psychiatrist had told her that I would be arriving in a couple of months, but he was wrong. It was eight long months before I arrived. She had had to wait eight months for me, so I had had to wait eight months for her!

At first I was stunned. When I recovered sufficiently to reflect upon what she had said, I found myself impressed not only with the primitivity of Laura's vindictive rage, but also with her obdurate adherence for eight long months to the single-minded goal of wreaking revenge upon the doctors, because they had inflicted upon her the narcissistic injury of being sent away "in favor of" her brother. And she had done this in total disregard of the cost to her in pain, suffering, and deprivation of precisely what she had wanted but which had been withheld from her in the first place. Her masochistic way of dealing with narcissistic mortification was impressive indeed.

During the months that followed, we scrutinized the dramatic beginning of her treatment with me. Not until several years had gone by, however, did we come to understand its full significance. The first topic that emerged, naturally enough, involved her relationship with her brother. She adored, admired, and envied him, but she also was furious at him for what she perceived as his teasing and tormenting of her, his failure to. appreciate and respond to her, and his getting favored treatment from her parents.

What occurred with the consulting psychiatrist, she felt, only mirrored what she had experienced within her family over the years. Her love for her brother had always been a source of problems for her. She had been loyal to him, covering up for him to their parents whenever he had needed it and had been prepared to do just about anything for him. She had openly adored him. And what had been his response? He had ignored her overture of affection; he had repeatedly gone off with his friends and rebuffed her when she had wanted to join in with. them; he had turned her in to their parents on multiple occasions.

288

What especially hurt and incensed her was her brother's practice of teasing and picking on her at the dinner table, until she would lose her temper and begin screaming or throwing things at him. Her father would invariably explode in anger, leap out of his chair, and go after her. As afraid as Laura was of her brother's temper, her father's absolutely terrified her. She would take off at top speed to her room, with her father running after her. Usually, she would barely reach her room ahead of him, just manage to slam and lock the door, and collapse on the floor, her heart pounding, panting for breath. Soon she would be wheezing heavily, far too ill to eat. Seeing him coming after her with his eyes blazing in fury, she pictured him beating her to a pulp "or worse," although she could not remember his actually ever laying a hand on her (Wilson 1980).

Most infuriating of all, according to Laura, was her mother's failure to intervene. She would roll her eyes and groan, but she did nothing either to protect Laura from her brother or to restrain her father. Her mother claimed to be helpless to stop Laura's brother from teasing her or to calm her father down once he got his dander up. Laura was convinced that her mother did not side with her because she favored the males in the family. Her mother counseled her to pay no attention to her brother's barbs. She advised that he couldn't get her goat if she were wise enough not to respond when he goaded her. Laura viewed this as being told to swallow her pride and knuckle under to him. He was always getting favored treatment, Laura felt, going back as far as she could remember. What had happened with the doctors was only another episode in an old story.

Being a girl was a disadvantage, Laura indicated, especially when it Was complicated by the debilitating effects of asthma. At home she was no match for her brother and father. At school she could not compete with the boys athletically or win the interest and devotion she wanted from the other girls, although intellectually she held her own quite well. She was too thin and scrawny and much too quiet and shy to attract the boys' attention. She huffily resented the preference shown by the other girls for involvement •with boys. Either they attempted to stir the boys' interest in them or they attached themselves to the boys' athletic activities in the auxiliary capacity of cheerleaders or boosters, rather than concentrating on their own. clubs and athletic teams, as Laura would have preferred. (Eventually, Laura grudgingly acceded to the prevailing modes. She tried out for the cheerleaders and came surprisingly close to making the squad, until a bad asthmatic attack prevented her from attending the final tryout- probably, as I noted to her, because her exhibitionistic anxieties had supervened.)

Laura seethed with resentment over her mother's failure to pay her adequate attention (i.e., to make herself totally available to her as her first and foremost priority). She ignored the effort her mother was making, in response to Laura's own request, to stop worrying about her so much and to allow her more independence. She fumed also over her female classmates' tendency to "ignore" her. Nor was I exempted from her wrath.

She put •me through a series of severe trials to test my interest, my devotion, my allegiance, my willingness to be available to her, and my readiness to sacrifice myself and my other interests for her, all of which she required to an absolute degree.

How was it, she would complain, that I did not always understand the nuances of what she was feeling? It was my job to understand. If did not, it had to be that I was not sufficiently interested in her. I was not expending all the effort she had a right to expect from me. And when she was feeling particularly awful, how was it that I did not always know what to say to comfort her and make her feel better? Even her mother used to worry more about her and used to work harder to cheer her up and take care of her and try to -make her feel better. Never mind that she used to complain about her mother babying her and worrying so much over her (and still complained when her grandmother did so, even though she obviously loved her grandmother showering attention upon her). And why was her mother paying less attention to her and backing off from trying to get her to gain weight? Was I responsible for that? Was I coming between her and her mother? Was it true that I only listened passively to her mother when she visited me, or was I advising her to pull away from Laura and stop devoting herself to her?

A series of events occurred that literally forced me to demonstrate that I was prepared to go to great lengths to be of help to her. Laura's asthma grew much worse, and her weight began to decline from its already precariously low state. She began more and more to resemble a cachectic concentration-camp victim, racked with pain and suffering, starved and starving, unable to breathe, pursued by the specter of death. Laura began to express the fear that she would die, despite my efforts to save her, or *because* of the inadequacies in my ministrations to her. I had taken away all the anxious and anxiety-provoking, but nevertheless devoted, nursing care her mother had been giving her. I had done so, if not directly, then by strengthening Laura's resolve to grow up and solve her own problems independent of her mommy's care. And I was proving to be a poor substitute for her mother indeed. Instead of helping her, I was killing her!

Not only was I finding myself increasingly anxious about the way things were going in Laura's treatment, but so were her parents and her pediatrician. Her parents began to look into alternative forms of treatment, and her pediatrician began to insist that Laura take the anti-asthmatic medications he had been prescribing. She had been using them only sparingly, out of reluctance to depend upon external, chemical means of controlling her wheezing. He started her on chromalin sprays, and he *insisted* that she begin to ingest high-calorie diet supplements, or he would put her into the hospital for tube feedings.

Laura grew more dejected and pessimistic, and she made increasing demands upon me. I was required to shift appointments for her, deferring to the increasing visits to other doctors and to her need to stay after school to make up labs and examinations she had missed because of illness. I had to agree to giving her extra appointments she insisted she needed, at times late at night, on Saturday evening, or on Sunday. She was outraged when I had to be away for a weekend. When I told her once after an extra session early on a Saturday morning that I would be in New York teaching till mid-afternoon, her eyes flashed and she said, "What do you do that for? Don't you know you're needed *here!*"

"Mixups" in communication between Laura and her parents began to occur, which left her without transportation back home after a session. I found myself faced with the choice of either forcing Laura to walk the mile or so back to her house, wheezing badly and feeling so weak she felt faint, or else driving her there myself. I felt that I had no choice but to chive her on the few occasions when this occurred-just as I felt I had no choice but to accede several times to her request that come to her house for our session when she felt physically unable to make the trip to my office.

We met in the new den her parents recently had added onto their home, although, as Laura emphasized, she hated that room. It had extended the house so that it now intruded into the flight path of birds that flew down from the woods. Periodically one would fly right into the big picture window and kill itself. What a horrible thing to happen! She felt sick every time she thought about it, and she was very angry at her parents for doing that to the birds. Sometimes, she said, she felt like she didn't have a friend in the world.

"You're talking about yourself," I replied. "You're one of those little birds. You feel little and weak and helpless and unable to deal either with the people around you, who seem so strong and powerful and uncaring about you, or with your own *inner* feelings and needs. And you've decided that the only way you can acquire power is to force people to pay attention to you and do what you want by threatening to kill yourself, by threatening to get terribly sick and die."

Laura burst into tears. Sobbing profusely, she delivered an abusive tirade against all the people, within her family and outside it, against whom she harbored a long list of accumulated grievances for not meeting her wants and needs sufficiently. It was true, too, she said, that she felt helpless not only against them but also against her own self. If she hadn't had desires and wants and needs, the satisfaction of which required the cooperation of people who refused to cooperate the way she wanted them to, she wouldn't need things from them in the first place. She didn't know if she were angrier at them or at herself, and she didn't know if she felt more helpless in dealing with them or in dealing with her own self! And then, to her astonishment (and to mine, too, I have to add), an extremely dramatic thing happened. She stopped wheezing. Also, as she informed me in a telephone call I received as soon as I returned from her home, she was ravenously hungry. She could hardly wait for our next session.

During the following months, nearly four years after we had begun, we worked very hard together at understanding the way in which she had focused her sense of helplessness and powerlessness upon her interaction with me, leading to the need to bully and blackmail me into becoming her dutiful slave by threatening to die unless I did her bidding. We found she had observantly recognized from very early on that she possessed a powerful means of reversing things so that she could obtain control over her parents. She accomplished this reversal by passive-aggressively plucking the strings. of their hurt, fear, guilt, and frustrated sense of helplessness when she didn't eat, or when she held her breath in a temper tantrum and passed out. After she gave up the breath-holding she developed mild, apparently allergic wheezing. This, abetted by the lingering impact of the serious lung problems that had plagued her father and her paternal uncle before him, terrified her parents and provided her with enormous leverage against them. Her family's shared phobic-obsessive fear of aggressive impulses and of murderous fantasies, combined with a tendency to flee from them into substitutive psychosomatic expression, contributed to the crystallization of Laura's use of asthma and anorexia. They were an effective means of acquiring a feeling of power with which to overcome the narcissistic mortification of continual failures and defeats, real and imagined, and to keep her dangerous internal impulses at bay.

As we reconstructed the development of Laura's psychosomatic constellations, preoedipal factors at first predominated extensively. We moved beyond this stage as we scrutinized its transferential expression in Laura's feelings and fantasies about me (e.g., her competition with other female patients of mine or with female acquaintances she came to believe may have been in treatment with me, and her impression periodically that I was more interested in what her mother had to tell me than in what she had to say, or that I was taking her mother's side in conflicts between them). We were then able to address the oedipal conflicts that also underlay her symptomatology. I was able to help her see, behind her rage at and fear of her brother and father, the intense, overwhelming excitement she felt at being picked on, chased, or getting her feelings hurt by them, which had unconscious sexual connotations. Behind her anger and resentment at her mother lay similar excited feelings, which she felt the need to repress, deny, cover over, and transform into opposite feelings.

Laura gradually overcame her anorexia, and by the time she went off to college, seven years after the beginning of her treatment, her asthma had decreased enormously in intensity. I eventually learned, through chance meetings with her mother, that she had a very successful and enjoyable college experience. Afterward she settled in another state, where she now is happily married and is herself a mother. She wheezes slightly on occasion, but her anorexia has not recurred.

DISCUSSION

Child development, as Freud (1905) pointed out a long time ago, is molded by the confluence of three very important factors. First, human infants are born in an extremely immature, in fact premature, state, in which they are utterly helpless and totally dependent upon outside forces for their survival. Second, the road to adulthood is an extremely protracted one. Even after they have acquired sufficient maturity to take a very active part in meeting their own needs, children and adolescents for many years still find themselves highly dependent upon the adult world for sustenance, support, and a vast amount of assistance, emotionally as well as physically, before they are able to take over their own reins and more-or-less assume independent control over their lives. En route, they are keenly aware of their relative weakness, the incomplete development of their capabilities, and their need to bow to externally imposed rules and expectations. They know very well that they depend upon the adult world to provide for their immediate needs and to train and prepare them for their future adult roles.

Third, the balance between instinctive, automatic stimulus-response patterns and the learning (i.e., cultural transmission) of the methods by which internal and external requirements can be met and life's problems can be resolved is heavily weighted in favor of the latter. Human beings are equipped with very little in the way of built-in, pre-wired, instinctive mechanisms with which to gain control over the world around them, and over the surging impulses emanating from the world within them. Children are forced to slowly and painstakingly acquire the emotional and intellectual skills with which they can obtain mastery over their environment and exercise control over themselves as they respond to their sexual and aggressive urges. Along the way, they are exquisitely (though not necessarily consciously) aware of their relative lack of power *vis-a-vis* the outside world and of the relative precariousness of their capacity for self-control.

In the best of circumstances, children chafe under the yoke of dependence upon, and domination by, their parents and other adults. They struggle mightily, but with only limited success, against. the importunate demands of their internal, instinctual drive derivatives. To assist them in dealing with both sets of issues they use a variety of autoplastic and alloplastic mechanisms. Their own emotional conflicts and their own executive and adaptive styles, which evolve from a complex, spiral interaction between innate tendencies and experiential impact, interweave, in a reciprocally influential interaction, with those of their parents, siblings, and other key persons. Out of this interaction a variety of personal problems can emerge. If their parents' problems impinge directly upon them, this complicates matters even further.

Multiple. factors can predispose to an outcome that includes somatic symptoms as an important mode of expression of emotional problems and struggles. Among these factors are an. inherent disposition to certain kinds of physical illness, owing to individual physical variations. Different people are subject to different sorts of physical illness Certain organ systems may be more susceptible to illness than others. Resistance to infection is not the same in everyone, and some individuals are more subject to intense muscular spasm affecting key structures d organs, greater tissue• friability in particular body parts, hyper- or hyposecretion of certain body substances, allergic hypersensitivity and reactivity, and so on. Influential family members can encourage or reinforce a tendency to somatic expression of emotional conflict by encouraging certain inclinations and discouraging others and by presenting themselves as models for psychosomatic identification. Chance, too, plays a part in predisposing a child to an expressive association between intense emotional conflict and somatic illness. Among others, F. Deutsch (1939), Alexander (1950), and L. Deutsch (1980) have emphasized the multiplicity of etiological factors in the generation of psychosomatic disorders.

Although a certain amount of dynamic specificity appears to exist among the various forms of psychosomatic illness, certain characteristics appear to be more or less universal. Among these are a tendency to predominance of pregenital conflicts, with an emphasis on separation problems,• intense mother-child ambivalence conflicts, a strong disposition to narcissistic vulnerability, narcissistic entitlement and narcissistic rage, and regressive flight from the complexities of triadic interactional conflict to the seemingly simpler issues involved in preoedipal, dyadic interaction (Fenichel1945, Sperling 1978). All of these were quite evident in Laura.

What was highlighted in Laura's case was the child's use of somatic illness to gain leverage and power to exert control over her parents instead of being dominated, controlled, frustrated, disappointed, or pushed around by them. Laura learned very early in her life that by not eating she could frustrate, hurt, frighten, and induce painful guilt feelings in her mother and could manipulate her parents and grandparents into ex- tending themselves on her behalf and devoting themselves to her welfare. She learned that by holding her breath and passing out she could terrify and enslave her mother and then that she could accomplish the same ends by wheezing instead. She discovered that she obtained far more attention by being sick than by being well and that if she were ill with respiratory problems, she would be showered with tender, loving care. As time went on, she made increasing use of her asthma and anorexia to serve additionally as a substitutive expression of the fantasies of aggressive, furious attack upon her parents, brother, and friends that frightened her and made her feel very guilty and of the masochistic rape fantasies that excited but terrified her. In this way her wheezing attacks and anorexia came to represent not only the means for gaining a sense of control over the bigger, more powerful people around her, but also over the sexual and aggressive impulses within her that dominated and frightened her. Understanding and analyzing these dimensions as they appeared in the transference and countertransference enactments taking place in her treatment enabled them to be accessed and to be traced to their genetic and dynamic roots within her relationships with her primary objects.

REFERENCES

FREUD, S. (1905). Three essays on the theory of sexuality. *Standard Edition* 7:125–245.

HOGAN, C.C. (1983). Object relations. In *Fear of Being Fat: The Treatment of Anorexia Nervosa and Bulimia*, rev. ed., ed. C.P. Wilson, C.C. Hogan, and I.L. Mintz, pp. 129–149. Northyale, NJ: Jason Aronson, 1985.

SOURS, J. (1969). Anorexia nervosa: nosology, diagnosis, developmental patterns, and power-control dynamics. In *Adolescence: Psychosocial Perspectives*, ed. G. Caplan and S. Lebovici, pp. 185–212. New York: Basic Books.

SPERLING, M. (1978). *Psychosomatic Disorders in Childhood.* New York: Jason Aronson.

———— (1983). A reevaluation of classification, concepts, and treatment. In. *Fear of Being Fat: The Treatment of :Anorexia Nervosa and Bulimia*) rev. ed., ed. C.P. Wilson, C.C. Hogan, and I.L. Mintz., pp. 51–82. Northgate, NJ: Jason Aronson,

WILSON, C.P. (1980). Parental overstimulation in asthma. *International Journal of Psychoanalytic Psychotherapy* 8:601–621.

CHAPTER 14:

HOMOSEXUALITY IN TWO WOMEN TREATED FROM THE AGE OF NINE YEARS

[(2002). *Psychoanalytic Inquiry* 22(2):259–277.]

Homosexuality is most probably variable in its pathway of origin. Reports of instances of when it has been possible to follow its development from childhood into adulthood are lacking in the literature. In this paper, the author describes his experience of treating two nine-year-old girls who had had serious problems in their relationships with their parents and who developed lesbian relationships when they became adults. In each instance, there were extremely traumatic experiences with the girl's father and failure of the mother to intercede on the girl's behalf. One patient was treated up into adolescence, with a follow-up later on, and the other was treated well into adulthood. Psychological factors that seem to have contributed to the eventual development of a lesbian sexual orientation are discussed in this paper.

What is the origin of homosexuality? Is it biological? Is it psychological? Does it derive from an innate, biological disposition that will express itself regardless of experience? Does it emerge out of a particular set of environmental influences impinging upon a child growing up within a certain type of family constellation? Is there just one route to homosexuality or are there multiple pathways that lead to a common outcome? Sexual orientation is not a simple matter. It is complex. It can change in some people in response to altered circumstances, but not in others who are thrust into the same, new situations. It is firmly fixed in some people but more fluid and variable in others. There are people who are securely comfortable in their sexual orientation, while others are unhappy or even miserable.

What appears to be the same on the surface might be very different underneath. Perhaps we should not speak of "homosexuality," in fact, but of "homosexualities," in the plural. Human beings are complex, biopsychosocial creatures, with an enormous range of individual differences. It is all too easy to lose sight of those differences as we look for commonalities that will enable us to group individuals into identifiable, collective units. We do not know enough yet about heterosexuality, let alone about homosexuality or about many other aspects of human sexual functioning. What we do know is that human beings are multidimensional; that the various dimensions of the human psyche form epigenetically over a protracted time period, during which, in ordinary circumstances, there is close involvement with other members of the nuclear family; and that the various dimensions within the psyche intertwine with and influence one another. All we can do is to keep on collecting data, both normative and clinical, share them with one another, and work together to improve our understanding of the complexities of human nature. That is what psychoanalysis is all about.

Most clinical reports are retrospective in nature. Reconstructions are made about the past from what is presented by adult patients. In this paper, I shall make a contribution from the opposite direction. I shall describe my experience with two little girls whom I first met when they were nine years of age. Each of them was in need of assistance because of problems within the family that impinged upon her in ways that could be expected to affect her emotional development. In neither instance, however, could it be predicted at the outset what the ultimate outcome would be.

Helen, as I shall call her, was having a very difficult time handling the separation that had just taken place between her parents.

She was angry, agitated, extremely unhappy. There were frequent temper tantrums. She had difficulty going to sleep at night, and then would find it hard to get up in the morning to go to school. She was devastated by her father's departure. How could he leave? He knew how much she loved him. He knew how hurt she felt and how painful it was for her to see him go, yet he left anyway. She was furious at him for leaving, and told him so in no uncertain terms. She screamed at him, hurled invectives at him, and told him that she hated him and never wanted to see him again, but she clung to him sobbingly each time she visited with him and begged him to return to the family. During the visits with him, she jealously guarded her time with him and measured carefully the amount of affection and the gifts he gave to her in comparison with what he gave to her older sister. She erupted in tirades of fury when she felt he had lavished more love on her sister than on her. At such times she could become worked up into destructive wildness, and on a few occasions she smashed things her father had given her sister. Once she even wrecked things of her own which her father had given her. Especially on that occasion, after she finally had calmed down, she was contrite, penitent, and frightened by the degree to which she had lost control.

When I met Helen for the first time, she presented as a slim, wiry, pretty little girl with a baseball cap on her head that was turned round to the back. Her mouth was twisted up on one side into a pugnacious half-smile that made her look like Popeye the Sailor Man of the cartoons. She matched this remarkable physiognomy with a feisty, challenging, tough-talking manner that was almost humorous coming from the baby-faced, almost cherubic little creature that tossed off that persona so theatrically. The net appearance was of a bedazzled, overwhelmed, anxious, fragile, and helpless little girl who was mustering up her resources so that she could make people believe that she was strong, confident, and a force to be reckoned with. It was clear that above all she needed to convince *herself* of that.

She insisted that she didn't need any help, that she was managing quite well on her own, thank you, and that everything was under control. Her parents were jerks, she informed me, who didn't know how to take care of themselves, let alone of their children. *They* were the ones who needed help, not she. Maybe I could talk to them, she said. Maybe I could teach them how to get along with each other. Maybe I could talk some sense into them, in fact. There was no good separating. They were like children, she said. Maybe I could help them grow up. Her sister, she said, was all right. It was just that she was so sweetsy and cutesy, and acted so helpless all the time, that she made Helen sick. And it infuriated her when her sister played up to her father to get close to him. *She* would never do that, she said, even if her father was such a sucker for a pretty face. Anyway, her sister should realize that it didn't work. She, her sister, and her mother all were as pretty or prettier than anyone else he could find, and he was leaving them anyway. Helen softened briefly as she asked if I thought I *could* do something to bring her parents back together. She looked crestfallen as she read the doubtful look on my face. She gratefully accepted my offer to do whatever I could to help in the situation. Then she put her Popeye face and manner back on again.

Things grew steadily worse rather than better between Helen's parents. Her father came in to see me, and tearfully informed me that he could not take things the way they were any longer and was preparing to go away. In the interest of his work, and in order to get away and think, he was planning to travel halfway around the world and, at least for a while, set up a new life for himself. He was aware how hard all this was being on Helen, and, sobbingly, he asked me to help her get through what she had to get through. Helen's Popeye persona became much more understandable when

I learned more about her and about her family. She had always been a highly sensitive and vulnerable child whose feelings could be easily hurt and who could be thrown into a state of anxiousness approaching panic when her ability to cope with emotional stresses was stretched to its relatively narrow limits.

Her father was a brilliant, talented, creative man who had achieved a high degree of success in his field, and of fame along with it. He was a handsome, articulate man who had a good deal of talent and was charming enough to get away with offbeat, even outrageous behavior that would not be accepted from ordinary individuals. He was so self-centered, narcissistic, demanding, and perfectionistic, however, that he also had been accumulating enemies and making problems for himself in his area of work. He loved the sea and boating, and was an expert sailor.

Helen's mother was an intelligent, attractive, capable woman who had sacrificed any ambitions she may have had for herself in order to devote herself to her husband. She aided him in his work, bailed him out to the best of her ability when he alienated influential people whose good favor he needed, and, as she eventually confided to me, even sex her children aside when she felt she had to do so in order to satisfy his need to be the center of her universe and to come first, last, and always as far as she was concerned. Even now, when he was blaming his problems on her and was leaving her and the children to go off elsewhere with someone else, she still loved him, felt sorry for him, and was prepared to do what she could for him. She hoped that he would come to his senses and return to her.

Helen's sister was a bright, strikingly attractive teenager with a gentle, mild, sweet and loving nature. She loved her father passionately. She lit up when he paid attention to her, and glowed when he took notice of how pretty she was. When he forgot about her, or when he turned upon her in an accusatory rage, as he did periodically, she suffered in weeping silence. She was intelligent, but in deference to her father's apparent inability to tolerate competition, she suppressed her intellectual interests and capacities and became the equivalent of a pretty, mindless mannequin. I eventually helped her to obtain psychotherapeutic assistance for herself when she became increasingly depressed and all but totally blocked in school.

Helen accepted my offer of assistance, despite her initial denial that she needed it. We were to know each other for a long time. About two months after we began to work together, in twice weekly psychotherapy, supplemented by additional sessions when needed, her father left. He moved thousands of miles away and moved in with a woman who had a number of children of her own. Helen was heartbroken. She alternated in her sessions with me between railing furiously at her father and trying desperately to understand why he had done what he had done, between insisting that she was better off without him and trying to get me to rouse her mother into finding a way to get him to return, and flailing in helpless desperation and deflecting her fury onto her sister and onto her mother to relieve her sense of utter and intolerable powerlessness.

Helen became flip, rude, and pseudotough with me, her mother, and her teachers at school. At home and in her sessions she talked about her father constantly. She carried around possessions he had left behind, especially his fishing gear. She repeatedly brought in pictures of him to show me. She sent him frequent letters and eagerly looked forward to the letters that came from him. Men began showing an interest in her mother, whereupon Helen and her sister began to express fear that she would remarry and forget about them. Helen became terrified that her mother too would abandon her. She expressed fear that she would be placed in a foster home. She persisted in this despite her mother's reassurances, and produced a photograph she had found of her parents standing in front of a bed and breakfast at which they had stayed on a trip together with a sign on it that read "Foster House." She had periodic rage outbursts at her mother and her sister.

Three months after her father's departure. Helen's longing for him turned into increasing anger at him for having gone away. She now refused to read his letters. She brought in an unopened letter from her father and wanted to tear it up sight unseen. She let me keep it for her in case she might one day want to read it. It became apparent as we considered this together over time that she was afraid both of it containing a message that indicated that he no longer cared for her and of the enormous, murderous rage that welled up inside her in response to the mountain of pain that she felt at his rejection of her. She also began to say that she did not want to see me any longer.

When she finally came to the point of reading the letter, many weeks after its arrival, she erupted in tears and blinding fury and started to tear it up instead of reading it. It was all I could do to rescue that letter and those that followed it so that I could save them until the time when she might indeed be able to face her feelings about her father. She eventually expressed gratitude to me for rescuing the letters from her pain and fury, so that she could know about and face whatever it was that he was communicating to her about his feelings for her. The letters expressed love for her and deep regret for the pain he was causing her, at the same time that he insisted that he had had to leave for his own reasons. Helen was relieved, crushed and deflated all at the same time. She gradually resigned herself to the certainty that she would never have the kind of relationship she once had had with her father and the real possibility that she might never even see him again.

It eventually became apparent that Helen's father had been crazy about her during her early years. He swooned over his beautiful baby after she was born, took hundreds of pictures of her, showed her off to people, and in myriad ways made her feel enormously important to him. This continued through her toddler years and into her early preschool years. After that, he seemed to lose interest in her and, as Helen came eventually to see, was so narcissistic that he probably was enamored of her to begin with as *his creative product, as his accomplishment, as a beloved part of himself.* The pain of loss, after having been elevated so high, was intense and infuriating.

To everyone's surprise, Helen's father returned three and a half months after he had gone. Things had not worked out where he had gone, and, it became clear, he had become emotionally undone. When he returned, he was in the process of undergoing a nervous breakdown that soon landed him in a hospital. A diagnosis of a schizoaffective disorder was made, with depressive, manic and grandiose-delusional elements. He underwent an up-and-down course thereafter, with a sine wave that led downward into progressive deterioration over time.

There were indications that her father's emotional turmoil had been triggered in part by Helen's older sister's entry into puberty and then adolescence. His narcissistically organized oedipal stirrings had been too much for him to handle, and he had had to leave. He had been alternating, it turned out, between showing great interest in her beauty, including taking pictures of her in partial undress, and turning viciously against her in a cruelly critical and demeaning fashion. Later on, after his return, he became involved in an affair with Helen's teenage babysitter, a girl to whom Helen had become extremely close, viewing her as a loved and loving best friend.

Helen went through a rocky course in parallel with that of her father. She became increasingly phobic, and for a while was so school phobic that she was unable to attend classes with any regularity. One of the things that helped her through was a warm, close relationship with a girl slightly older who was a lot like Helen in that she was highly intelligent, attractive, sensitive, and creative, in an almost twin-like fashion. This friend, whom Helen brought with her to some of her sessions with me, had an intelligent, attractive sister, a father who was chronically ill (although physically rather than emotionally), and a mother who devotedly stood by her father and held the family together like Helen's mother. The two families had long been very close, and Helen felt as at home in her friend's house as she felt in her own. She also found an additional source of needed self-esteem. It turned out that she was a gifted, natural athlete. When she was not yet a teenager, she became the only nonadult member of a woman's athletic team. A female coach in another sport offered to take her in hand and develop her into a professional. She spurned that offer, and turned instead to Little League baseball. When her mother threatened legal action because of her daughter's exclusion as a girl, Helen was allowed to try out for the boys' Little League team. She not only made the team, but went on to lead the team in every category and to be named Most Valuable Player in the league.

When Helen entered puberty and then adolescence, she became involved in a series of very troubled and troubling heterosexual relationships. Hungry to be loved and wanted, she was easy prey to teenage boys who exploited her needfulness, seducing her easily into sexual activities, including fellatio, only to abandon her, revealing themselves to have been insincere in their expressions of love and caring. This was extremely painful to Helen, even after she came to understand that she had been irresistibly drawn into a repetition of her experience with her father. If her effort to wrench herself away from her vulnerability to seduction by other boys who were attracted to her (she was turning into an extremely attractive young lady), she turned to a kindly, older man who presented himself to her as an avuncular if not paternal protector. He turned out, of course, to have less than honorable intentions himself.

This greatly compounded her pain, but she did not give up on her yearning for a loving relationship with a man. She entered into a close, platonic relationship with a young man from a family that had long had close ties with her own family. Eventually, however, this too turned into an exploitative sexual relationship that left her feeling used and abused. For a long time, she kept this turn of events hidden from me, even though we had explored at length together the transference meanings, with relationship to her father and to me, of the previous heterosexual involvements she had had that had ended up badly for her, and we had discussed her vulnerability to further repeats.

As her best friend began to grow away from her and toward boy friends, with an apparent component of pushing away from their twin-like closeness in an adolescent thrust toward autonomy and independence, Helen began simultaneously to express distrust of male relationships and to become enamored of first one and then another beautiful model turned television star. Although she was aware of the powerful narcissistic dimension of this—that is, her avid search for self-love and self-regard and of the need to replace the best friend who was leaving her, as well as to find a replacement for her mother, from whom she needed at that point in her life to individuate—the pull to the sex goddess, the TV stars, was irresistible. As she struggled to understand what she was swept up in, she expressed painful disappointment in her mother. Among her complaints were that her mother had failed to manage things more successfully with her father, that she had been, as she saw it, too loving and giving and not sufficiently aware of her need for help in becoming independent and self-reliant, and that she had not remarried and thereby given her a chance to give her mother up and to try to work things out with a new father. It had been helpful to have me on her side, but I could only be her doctor. Although for a number of years she ironically sent me Father's Day cards, she was painfully aware that my presence in her life was not enough to meet her need.

Two prose poems Helen wrote when she was twenty-one years old convey the emotional turmoil, the bitter anguish, the hopeless yearning, the homicidal-suicidal rage, the insufferable feelings of entrapment in an arrested state of development that she was feeling at that time.

When Helen became a young lady, in her early twenties, she met a somewhat older, unhappily married young woman who had had a horrible experience during her early adolescence in which she was raped repeatedly at knifepoint. This young woman, who was herself very intelligent and attractive, entranced her from up close and in the flesh the way the TV star-models had entranced her a few years earlier. They grew closer and closer, until they became inseparable. Then her newly found friend revealed to her that she was losing her sexual interest in men and was finding herself turning toward women. She invited Helen, by way of increasing inference and innuendo that led ultimately to a direct invitation, to enter into a lesbian affair with her. Helen at first was surprised and shocked. She broke off contact with her new friend. A little while later, she learned that her friend had separated from her husband, a young man to whom in the past Helen herself had been strongly attracted. The young woman called her, and, despite her effort to resist the pull, she met with her repeatedly and after a while entered into a sexual relationship with her.

The relationship was an extremely ambivalent one, with intense jealousy on Helen's part, frequent fights, and repeated separations followed by reunions. After a while, the friend announced to her that the relationship between them was no good for them and that she was breaking it off. Helen was crushed. She tried alternately to forget her and to patch things up between them. She could see the similarity between what had been taking place and what had taken place between her and her parents, but she could not stop herself. After a while, she resigned herself to the end of the relationship. She replaced it with a series of lesbian relationships that were every bit as ambivalent as the first had been. Some time later, as she was becoming disillusioned with the life she was leading, she developed an eating disorder that led to a temporary cessation of her menstrual periods. She recognized spontaneously that she was seeking to become asexual. She recovered from the eating disorder, menstruation returned, and Helen entered into a prolonged struggle over whether she wanted to be heterosexual or homosexual. I remained neutral in this regard. Homosexuality strongly predominated, although she attempted periodically to try herself with men. For periods of time, she found herself unable to be sexual with women or with men.

Let me turn at this point to another nine-year-old girl, whom I shall call Kim. Her father had become depressed about eight months earlier and had entered psychotherapy, in the course of which he revealed that he had been engaging in multiple sexual activities with Kim since she was an infant. He put an end to these activities, but his therapist recommended that he reveal what had been going on and arrange for psychotherapy for Kim. He told me about the intermittent sexual activities. It had been a secret between them. Most of the time, he said, Kim had not resisted. He expressed uncertainty about his ability to refrain from what he had been doing, but accepted my insistence that I would only treat his daughter if the sexual involvement between them did not recur.

Kim presented as a bright, perceptive, pretty little girl who was cautious and quiet. She said that she was glad to be able to talk to someone, but "scared" at the same time. She told me that she was unhappy much of the time but did not know why. She related rather blandly, with little affect. She told me about her interest in magic tricks and ventriloquy, and informed me that she had learned to wiggle her ears, raise one eyebrow, make a fish mouth, and so on. She said that she was not double-jointed, but added, "that doesn't mean I'm not impeculiar." When I asked what she meant she said, "I am peculiar; I'm not a lady-girl; I'm not delicate; I'm a tomboy; I'm not a girl-sex; I like to do things that boys do; they're more exciting." She added, however, "I know God made me a girl" and "I am of the girl sex."

In an early session, she toyed with some doll figures, after mumbling something about angry feelings, repeatedly pushed the mother's breasts in and out, organized a family of children around the father doll, with the mother left out, and said, "Would you believe I don't like to play with dolls?" She expressed a fear of being crazy and a fear that she was "different." At the end of the session, while we were waiting for her father, who was late picking her up, she expressed one of her main fears: "I'm not a girly-girl; I'm a tomboy; I like sports and sports books instead of Nancy Drew."

Kim's father was a rigid, angry, irascible, chronically depressed man who led a very isolated life. He worked at a solitary job and had very few friends and no close ones. He had lost his father when he was very young and had grown up essentially only with his mother. He and his mother had slept in the same bed through his childhood and adolescence.

Kim's mother eagerly participated in parent sessions. She made it clear, in fact, that she was not about to be left out again while her husband and daughter were involved in treatment. Her parents divorced when she was two and a half years old. Her mother remained very angry and "had no use for men" after that. She and her mother moved in with her maternal grandmother and her mother's two unmarried brothers. She was sent to an all-day nursery school while her mother worked. She was sent away to boarding school from five to nine years of age, and her father went into military service a few months after she went off to school. She felt "unwanted and insecure." Her father remarried several times, and each remarriage was painful to her.

The circumstances of Kim's older brother's conception and birth are significant. Kim's mother became impregnated, without even vaginal penetration, at the age of seventeen, by Kim's father, who was then in military service. This led to a hasty marriage, just before which Kim's mother's father died. She never was truly certain that he would have married her if she had not become pregnant.

Kim's mother depicted herself as an anxious, inhibited, fearful person with fragile self-esteem, a terror of being abandoned, and utter dependence on reassurance of her desirability and worth to stave off depression. She had gone into analysis at one point but had dropped out after a year. Her former analyst indicated to me that she was a borderline person, with shadowy self and object representations. I came to a similar conclusion as time went on, and eventually so did she. At one point, several years later, she told me that she had to admit that she had had much deeper problems than she had been willing to recognize in the past. She said that she had been growing as a person as a result of the reflections she was making in her meetings with me. For the first time, she said, she was picturing her husband's face while they were making love together instead of "picturing him as a stick figure with a mustache."

To begin with, Kim's mother told me that she felt jealous and hurt over what had taken place between her husband and her daughter. She also implied that it was not such a secret and that she could have stopped it. As time went on, she came to realize that, without being conscious of it, she had actually encouraged what was taking place, out of fear of abandonment should she oppose it, as an acting out of old wishes involving her father and her uncles, and in response to her own homosexual arousal vis-a-vis Kim.

I saw Kim twice a week for more than three and a half years. Kim was very reserved and cautious at first, although she wanted help in figuring herself out. She turned ten a few months after we started working together. She told me that she had liked the birthday "Spin the Bottle" game at her birthday party, but also had been scared because of fear that boys might not want to kiss her. She arrived at the next session with a charley horse. She said that exercise built muscles, but she didn't want muscles because she was a girl. She told me that because she was a girl she couldn't have things that she wanted, like the walkie-talkies and darts that her boy friend got for his birthday. She drew a picture of a girl who was angry at her pipe-smoking boy friend for reading a book called "For Men Only—I Hate Women." She provided the girl with a book titled "I Hate Men." I related this to the impact upon her burgeoning interest in girl-boy relationships of her earlier experience with her father. She intensely and angrily objected to what I said.

In an early session, she brought in a rubber ball for us to throw back and forth. She threw it hard toward my genitals and then told me about having been taken to a baseball game because a man who was a Cub Scout Master liked her. She said, however, that she did not like his buying her candy and soda. I commented on her wariness with men after what she had experienced, and connected it with the caution she had been showing with me. It could be scary for her to like me and for me to like her. She looked anxious and objected to my talking about her father, but then she seemed relieved. She related a TV story about a boy who was a "drop-in" at a college. He got into trouble and almost got operated on for impersonating the students who really belonged there. Then she told me about a book in which a boy discovered how to feel admired and worthwhile and to feel good about himself without having to star in athletics or attend a posh school. She toyed with a little wooden incense burner I had on a shelf that was in the form of a woodcutter with a pipe in his mouth carrying a small fir tree. She asked me to put a "candle" in it and then, while standing behind a chair, asked me to forget that she was a girl and to throw the ball hard to her. She listened attentively but quietly as I commented on how problematic it was for her that she was a girl and I was a man, especially after what she had gone through with her father. I said that she could not be a woman to her father but needed nevertheless to impress him and be loved by him. Perhaps it felt safer to impress him as an athlete.

A couple of sessions later, she came in sobbing, but couldn't say what was bothering her. Finally, after much hesitation, she wrote out, "*Why* am I such a tomboy? I *want to but I don't want to*." She struggled at length over her conflict between wanting to be attractive to boys and wanting to *be a boy*. I commented on her natural wish to be found attractive to and loved by men, including her father as the first man she had encountered in her life, and I empathized with her fear of being feminine and attractive.

She complained of having hurt the base of her thumb near the scar from where the doctor had removed "a wart or something." She blamed herself for it. If she hadn't scratched it when it itched, so that it opened, it wouldn't have been cut off. She said it "can itch even when there is nothing here … it's the space that itches now." She attached an elongated piece of clay in the shape of a thumb to a ball of clay. Then she pouted and complained angrily that I had not yet brought in a candle for the Woodsman nor provided candy for her during our sessions although I had spoken about doing so. Behind the anger, we discovered, was fear of having to talk about such things as masturbation and menstruation and, especially, about what had happened between her and her father.

She rolled Play-Doh into a sausage, kneaded it, and said, "I need it." She told me she'd played "Flog" (golf spelled backwards) with a girl friend, and that she wanted to play it with me. She had played it with her father, she said. She said, "I got a hole in one, but it didn't count because my father was still on another hole." Kim then told me that she had seen an accident in which cars and a motorcycle had smashed up badly; a girl got bruised and had her glasses broken but the man driving the red sports car was not hurt. She then launched into a diatribe of anger at boys. She rummaged through my desk drawers, although I had indicated that they were private, and said that she wanted to be the "only one" to play checkers with me. I related this behavior to her painful conflicts involving competition for and with males.

During the treatment, I helped Kim to "figure (her)self out." We addressed her concerns about her pubertal and early adolescent development. Breast development, the approach of menarche, her wish to be attractive to boys and her fear that she would not be, conflicts involving competition with her girl friends at the same time that she needed them to accept and like her, and so on, were prominent themes. An overriding theme was her intense conflict between welcoming and wanting my assistance and insisting that she was being forced to come to me and wanted to quit. She made it very clear that she needed and wanted a very special relationship with me in which she received very special attention. abundant care and feeding (figuratively and literally), and special gifts. At the same time, she complained continually that I was a dodo (though "dodos are cute"), that I said crazy things (though she often liked the "crazy" things I said), and so forth. It eventually became clear to both of us that she could not let herself like me or the treatment because she felt evil, like the "devil," for enjoying the sexual activities with her father and for being conflicted about whether they should stop or not. She was repeatedly flirtatious and exhibitionistic, but more often caustic, hostile, and angry.

She eventually revealed that she feared she had been damaged by what her father had done, that she had lost her virginity and was no longer "unspoiled." She expressed fear that she would be unattractive to a man and would be deprived of the opportunity to marry and become a parent. She was afraid of her anger at her father and, by extension, at *all* men When Kim was almost 13, she proudly showed me that she had had her ears pierced. This led to references to her breasts developing, but it was difficult for her to talk about that. When I noted that it was difficult for her to talk about her developing femininity, she said, "My father took out his sexophone [*sic*]. He took it out—his sexophone [*sic*]. We blew or it—and sang. He's studying the saxophone." She sang a song: "I don't look ahead to seeing it."

For a long time, Kim could not speak directly about what had taker place with her father. She even kicked me in the shin and left a scar when I said something about it relatively early in the treatment. Then she began to speak about her anger at him for using her and being "mean" to her by doing so. She still assiduously protected her mother as her only real friend and the only one who really understood her. Eventually, however, she expressed poignant hurt and anger and bewilderment at her mother's failure to protect her. En route to this, she deflected her anger onto me and my Woodsman. She brought in incense for the Woodsman and lit it. She became agitated when I failed to indicate to her that I liked it so much that I would keep it burning even after she left. Things quickly got out of control. The Woodsman's axe got burned up, ashes fell on to one of my chairs, and she burned a hole in my rug. She became very frightened, and, as I recorded in my notes, I found myself wondering if her rage would relegate her to rage at men or to incapacity for a satisfying sexual relationship later on in life if she did not somehow come to terms with it.

When Kim was thirteen and a half, she liked boys, had two boy friends, and entertained romantic and erotic fantasies about them. When she received a medal for being the best girl athlete at her school, however, she expressed puzzlement about being "different from other girls" by being an athlete and a "tomboy," although she loved boys and loved their being attracted to her. Mixed with this was expression of outrage at her parents for attacking her physically. Her father, she said, twisted her ankle and socked her in the jaw when he had gotten drunk and her mother lost control periodically and cursed her and hit her. They treated her as if she were bad, she said, a devil.

Her parents decided to move, also when Kim was thirteen and a half. She would have had to travel a very great distance to see me, and her parents were very reluctant to have her do so even at a greatly reduced frequency. Kim felt that she was ready to stop. After considering it together we decided to draw her treatment to a close within a few months, with the proviso that I would keep her time open in the fall until I heard from her that she still felt ready to stop. We talked about her ability to return to treatment in the future. Kim had been moving more and more away from tomboyishness and into interest in boys. At one point, however, she said that as soon as a boy she was interested in returned her attention she would lose interest in him. She thought that this was only because she was still young, but she did recognize that she took satisfaction at times in getting revenge on boys for having thrown her over by doing it to them instead. I connected this to her experience with her father.

Kim thought she would be able to deal with things on her own, although she did express concern at one point that she might "become a retard again" without my help. The ending of the treatment coincided with her graduation from junior high school. She thanked me for having "saved" her and said that, "the one person I want at my graduation party won't be there." She also told me that she had decided to major in psychology when she went to college. At the time we ended the treatment, Kim had just had her second menstrual period.

I heard from Kim a couple of times during the following academic year, and then from her parents during her senior year of high school. Things seemed to be going well. About ten years after I had last seen Kim, I received a telephone call from her asking to come in and visit with me. When she arrived, she was not at all friendly. She told me about having done well in college, but not well enough to gain acceptance to the graduate school program she wanted. She had had to enroll in additional schooling and to work at difficult jobs before finally gaining the acceptance she had been seeking. A number of relationships with men had been unsatisfactory, and she had finally turned away from men and had entered a series of lesbian relationships. She related in detail the delights of sexual experience with a woman. The affect that accompanied her account was not excitement, however, but vengeful bitterness. When I noted this, she expressed anger at me for having ended her treatment when I did. I should have known, she said, that she was not really finished but still needed me. She also told me that she had become estranged from her parents, toward whom she felt quite bitter, and had not seen them for a couple of years.

DISCUSSION

The path which Helen and Kim traversed en route to their adult sexual orientation would appear to exemplify the course that leads to one form of female homosexuality. Each girl started out in life feeling very important and very special to her father. Helen's father doted on her, fussed over her, took hundreds of pictures of her, and centered enormous attention upon her from the moment she was born, as he had done with her older sister, his other creation, before her. He was flamboyant, charismatic, and swept her off her feet even before she could stand up on her own. When she was still only a little girl, between eight and nine years of age, her bubble burst as it became painfully apparent that there was a self-centered, narcissistic, exploitative core to his attentions to her and to her older sister. Unable to deal with the intense sexual arousal that was evoked in him when her older sister developed into a beautiful, lithe teenager (the *Galatea* to his *Pygmalion*), he suddenly bolted from the scene and fled halfway across the world. Helen was utterly devastated.

Her father returned a few months later, in a grandiose, hypomanic state that rapidly deteriorated even further. He made a seeming recovery, but it was short-lived. He soon went steadily downhill, in the course of which he entered into an affair with Helen's teenage babysitter. Helen felt devalued, unloved, used, and abused. Seeds had been sown that would sprout into a powerful distrust of men.

When Helen became a teenager, she was encumbered by a hungry need for the interest and attention she needed from males to enable her to regain the feeling of being loved, treasured, and extremely special as she had been with her father but then had lost. Her search, however, led her to males, both boys and men, who resembled her father. She became involved with one male after another who excited her with the promise of fulfilling her hopes and dreams only to repeat what her father had done when they went on to disappoint her, misuse her, abuse her, and abandon her. She could only conclude that men are exciting but dangerous, and are to be avoided. Men have power, she realized, that exerts a magnetic attraction but which can be as destructive as the flame to which a moth is drawn.

Kim's father not only made her feel very special, his chosen love object in every sense of the word, but had a secret "love" affair with her that began soon after her birth. As with Helen, the special relationship suddenly ended when she was approaching her ninth birthday. The awareness that her father had been using her for his own narcissistic purposes rather than loving and treasuring her in her own right, as she had been led to believe, was so painful to her that she could not face it for a long time. In part he had seduced her, but in part he also had forced himself upon her. By the time the sexual activity ended, a fear of being feminine and attractive had built up within her, together with a distrust of men, whose interest in her and attentions to her had to be suspect. She also had built up a (more or less repressed and suppressed) rage at her father that extended to men in general. She envied men the power she perceived in them, but she both feared that power and resented it.

Kim's parents relocated and they removed her from treatment after she had entered her teenage years, so that it was not possible to follow her through adolescence. She was drawn toward boys as a young teenager, although with trepidation about having been "spoiled" in her capacity to appeal to them. As time went on, it subsequently was revealed that her relationships with boys suffered from the pernicious shadow of the past. In college and afterwards, she entered into a series of heterosexual relationships with young men that were increasingly disappointing and unsatisfying. She became angrier and angrier at them and then turned away from men altogether and shifted into a homosexual direction.

Problems these two women had with their fathers while growing up are only one side of the story, however, Helen and Kim both expressed enormous hurt and pain that their mothers were not there for them when they needed them. They were extremely sad that their mothers did not protect them from what their fathers had done, causing them so much pain and suffering. They felt both wounded and outraged that their mothers put their own security first, ahead of their daughters', and that they nurtured and protected their relationship with their husbands, at Helen's and Kim's expense, rather than nurturing and protecting their little girls as a primary responsibility. Helen had an opportunity to work out her feelings of disappointment in and anger at her mother in therapy, as well as being able to deflect a part of her anger at her mother onto her older sister. Kim was in the difficult position of lacking both of these avenues for dealing with her rage at her mother.

The intense disappointment and anger Helen and Kim felt toward their mothers added to their difficulty feeling good about themselves and cherishing themselves as valued and valuable human beings. If a girl does not feel that her mother has considered her valuable enough to guard and protect her from harm, how can she feel valued and valuable? Inability to value and look up to her mother as a role model with whom she can identify deprives her of an invaluable and necessary source of self-esteem and self-regard. And how can she become able to guard and protect herself from harm from men who would exploit and abuse her if her mother has not done so?

Helen tried valiantly over the years to connect with her father and to overcome her hurt and anger at him sufficiently to allow her to maintain a relationship with him. She attempted repeatedly as an adult to form relationships with men, and she was able intermittently to have a sexual relationship with a man. No relationship ever lasted a significant period of time, however. She wrestled with her ambivalent relationships with her mother and sister. She was much more successful in regard to her mother than with her sister. Kim started out by fiercely guarding her filial allegiance to her parents against her anger at them. As she gained increasing independence from them and from her financial reliance upon them, her anger more and more outweighed her loyalty to them. Their refusal to take responsibility for what they had done to her that had contributed toward her problems in life was more than she could bear. She finally broke off all relations with them.

For Helen and for Kim, movement toward homosexuality rather than heterosexuality seemed to be propelled from two directions. One was the enormous disappointment in, anger at, and fear of their fathers that became generalized to all men. The other was the need for and yearning for loved and loving, protective, and caring maternal figures to connect with and with whom to identify. The combination of these two pushed them away from men and toward women to love and with whom to identify.

The need of a girl growing up for a strong, paternal figure with whom to identify as a source of strength tends to be overlooked in psychoanalytic theory and practice. For both Helen and Kim, their fathers (and, by extension, men in general!) were perceived as misusing their masculine powers and their powerful male organ as weapons that hurt and injure women. It was clear for them that it was much better to be *like* their father and make love to a woman than to submit to being made love to by a man, with all the dangers that go with that. Unconsciously, this also would mean loving herself and her mother and being loved by her mother.

Helen spoke repeatedly of needing the shark's "dorsal fin" on herself and for years signed the poetry she wrote with a shark stamp. Kim came back to me to skewer me incisively with words, just as I had recalled her father doing with me during parent sessions when Kim was a girl. It was in marked contrast to her inability for a long time to even allow me to say something that could be construed as negative about her father and to be able only to express tempered criticism of him when she did become able to say anything herself.

When something so complex as human sexuality is concerned, we need to be cautious about the inclination to oversimplify in order to avoid being intimidated by multiplicity, variation, and complexity. We do not know enough about heterosexuality, let alone homosexuality. It is likely that there are multiple pathways to gay and lesbian sexual orientation. We have need for continual study—for ongoing gathering of data, sharing of data, examination of data, and discussion of data with openness of expectation and without preconceived notions.

CHAPTER 15

WORKING WITH PARENTS AT THE BEGINNING OF TREATMENT

Edited by M. Hossein Etezady, M.D. Northvale, NJ/ London: Jason Aronson, pp. 9–17.]

[From: *The Treatment of Neurosis in the Young: A Psychoanalytic Perspective.*]

I have frequently heard from mental health professionals who work with children in intensive psychotherapy or psychoanalysis something like the following:

Working with children is so great. It's exciting. It's fun. It's challenging. The only problem with seeing children is that they have parents. That's where all the problems come from. They don't cooperate. They make impossible demands. They do things that undo the very things you're trying to accomplish. They don't appreciate or value what you're doing for their children. They rank tutors and tennis lessons as more important than therapy. They repeatedly inconvenience you with re-quests for schedule changes. They take their children away on trips. They pull them out of treatment just when you're beginning to get somewhere. If only children didn't have parents!" But children do have parents. In fact, most of the time, if it weren't for their parents; they wouldn't get into treatment in the first place. Very few children ask for treatment on their own; usually it is their parents who bring them for treatment. Even when they have been encouraged to do so by the school authorities or by the pediatrician or by friends or -../' relatives, it is the parents who are concerned enough about their children's welfare to bring them for evaluation and to be willing to go to the trouble and the expense of placing them in treatment when that recommendation is made to them. And it is far from infrequent that we find ourselves relying on the parents to keep their children in treatment, especially at the outset, in opposition to the internal resistance being thrown up against us by the children's neurotic defense constellations.

So how can we understand the discrepancy between parents' role as the principal allies and supporters of treatment on the one hand, but also the source of so much difficulty on the other? It is not easy for parents to bring a child for treatment. Not only does it entail acknowledging that something is seriously enough wrong with the child to require professional assistance, but it also tends to imply that the parents have failed in their responsibility to foster healthy development. Parents tend to have painful feelings of shame and guilt, which, more often than not, are more latent or suppressed than they are apparent.

'Their child's public behavior exposes them as having failed in their quest to be perfect parents producing model children who will bring honor to them and, by narcissistic extension, will achieve and accomplish 'in exemplary ways that will enhance their own image and extend and enlarge upon their own accomplishments. Parents inevitably have a narcissistic investment in their children. They identify with them, feel responsible for them, feel proud of their successes, feel ashamed and embarrassed by their failures.

When parents bring a child for assessment and then for treatment, they feel conscious and unconscious guilt for having contributed to his or her problems, or at least for not having been wise and powerful enough to prevent them from having arisen. They expect to be blamed for the child's problems, an expectation to which the mental health community has intermittently contributed. When I was a resident in psychiatry, for example, the inpatient children's unit had a sign on the door that read: "Save a boy and you save a man. Save a girl and you. save a family." I was pleased to see that this bit of mother-bashing was eliminated by the time I started my child psychiatry fellowship.

It is not easy for parents to transcend their narcissistic wounds, overcome the temptation to protect themselves by subscribing to the seductive notion that emotional problems are chemical in nature and therefore have nothing to do with family experience, and bring their child for psychotherapeutic assistance rather than for pills and nostrums. Their doing so does not mean, however, that they are free from hurt and pain or that they are unencumbered by shame and guilt. It should not really be surprising that they mobilize a host of defenses that then constitute a barrier to smooth and easy, trustful cooperation with the person to whom they are turning over their child for care. The very fact that they have to engage a professional to do for their child what they feel they *themselves* should be able to do tends to be experienced as a narcissistic wound.

The professional who evaluates their child tends not infrequently to be perceived unconsciously both as the bearer of extremely unwelcome, bad news about their child and as the outside judge who pronounces them responsible for the child's problems. Feelings of resentment and hostility, however unfounded, get in the way in such circumstances of cooperating with the very person to whom they have come for help. It is only when these interferences are recognized and dealt with effectively by the professional that an effective therapeutic alliance can be established with the parents that will enable treatment to proceed. Psychotherapy with adults can succeed only if a good working alliance, both on a real relationship level and on a transference relationship level, can be established and maintained between therapist and patient. With children the working alliance has to be established not only with the child but also with the parents. Winnicott observed that there is no such thing as a baby without a mother. In the treatment of children, at least at the outset, there is no such thing as a child without the parents. It is not only the child who has to be evaluated as to the genetics• and dynamics of the illness, the pain the symptoms are causing, motivation for change, the capacity to tolerate the impact of therapeutic regression and withstand. the rigors of treatment, the transference potentials, the configuration of the defenses and the kinds of resistances that are likely to emerge, the life situation and the likelihood of its impinging positively and negatively upon the . treatment that is being planned, and so on. The parents (and, where they play a significant role in relation to the treatment, grandparents and other significant individuals) also need to be evaluated with regard to these critical matters.

Parents bring a number of fears with them when they bring their children for assistance. They often are afraid that the treatment will not help. They may have known of children who have not been helped by various forms of treatment. They certainly are not encouraged in this regard by what they have been reading in the popular press. Care needs to be taken to dispel unwarranted pessimism, but it also is necessary to include the parents actively in the evaluation and planning process' and to describe the kind of treatment that is being proposed and its likely outcome clearly, understandably, and in realistic terms, without undue pessimism but also without embellishment or overambitious promises.

Another fear that parents frequently harbor is that their child will become overly dependent upon the therapist; that is, that they will lose their status as the primary love objects upon whom the child relies for care, protection, nurturance, and love. They consciously or unconsciously worry that the child will develop a greater affection for and allegiance to the therapist than to them. This stems from their unconscious guilt for not having protected their child from developing emotional problems in the course of their development or even for having contributed to their emergence. Their unconscious fear is that in the course of treatment the child will come to blame the parents for his or her troubles and turn away from them. This is an outgrowth from, and exaggeration of, the difficulty parents have in general in coming to terms with their own limitations and human deficiencies. Children need to idealize their parents initially as omnipotent, omniscient, perfect, even exalted beings and to de-idealize them only gradually as they develop their own strengths, capacities, and ability to tolerate the imperfections of life and of the human species of which they are a part. Parents, in their participation in the child-parent interaction that takes place, not only try to live up to their idealization but tend to find the de-idealization process painful. This is so both because of the narcissistic blow that is entailed and because it connotes the passage of their own importance to their child and hence the ebbing of their own strength and vitality, the movement on in their life cycle toward eventual enfeeblement, superannuation, and death. Therapists need to be very sensitive to this latent set of anxieties in parents who bring their children for treatment, so that they can inculcate a sense of trust in the therapist as an ally who will not blame them, take over their role in the child's life, or strip them of their sense of primary strength, power, importance, and respect in their child's heart and mind.

It is also necessary when working with parents at the outset of evaluation and treatment of a child to be sensitive to the possible . presence of secret (conscious) worries and of unconscious worries about their child's health derived from historical, familial factors, which they may not initially be able to share because of excessive shame, guilt, or fear. Parents may worry, for example, about having passed on to the child a serious genetic disturbance they believe might run in their family or a genetic trait they secretly fear they may themselves harbor. There may be a history in themselves or in close family members of what they believe might be a link to manic-depressive illness or some other serious psychotic disorder. They may harbor the secret, painful belief that they may have passed on a learning disability, or they may worry about the possible implications of a past history of severe adolescent turmoil or a childhood behavior disorder. A family history in near relatives of psychopathic traits, alcoholism, suicide, homosexuality, neurologic disorders, or other conditions they may fear are genetically transmitted may be frightening them. If they are afraid of revealing such things or believe that it is best to let sleeping dogs lie and are afraid of therapy stirring up things that are better left untouched, there may be a serious impediment to possible treatment. Such latent concerns need to be gotten to and dealt with sensitively, patiently, and cautiously, while building up a good, trusting, working relationship with the parents. The same is true of any secret, guilt-ridden history of past episodes of loss of temper with the child on a parent's part, or of overly seductive or overly stimulating behavior that a parent is concerned may have played a part in generating the child's problems.

A particularly difficult issue to deal with is the presence, which more often than not is not readily apparent at the very beginning of treatment, of an unconscious reluctance on the part of one of the parents or at times both parents, namely, of unconscious reluctance to give up certain practices that are contributing to a child's neurotic disturbances. This may be so because the practices are gratifying to the parent or parents, or because they are necessary to sustain a particular family equilibrium that would be upset if those practices were to be given up. A parent may be reluctant, for example, to stop bathing with a child. Or there might be a family practice of walking about nude or scantily clad, rationalized as offering the children a "positive" attitude toward interest in the human body as something to be viewed as natural and free from guilt and shame. A parent may surreptitiously, and without conscious awareness of the ulterior motives involved, encourage a child to come into the parents' bed at night or insist that one of the parents sleep with the child because the parent wishes to be prevented from being able to engage in an intimate, sexual relationship with the marital partner. Parents may give one message to the child, usually verbally, while giving a very different, contradictory message via their actions and subtly communicated attitudes.

These kinds of active, unconsciously motivated and implemented contributions to the very problems for which the parents are bringing their child for help need to be approached and dealt with very differently in different instances. Sometimes it may be possible to ally oneself, patiently and progressively, with the parents' rational desire to help their child, with the result that the parents come to trust the therapist, reveal what is taking place, reflect on it with the therapist, and decide to make sacrifices necessary to facilitate the child's recovery through treatment. Sometimes they prove capable of carrying out their resolve. At other times, however, parents may ask directly, or accept a referral, for consultation with someone else that leads to the conscious decision to give up a gratifying practice that is not in their child's best interest, only to replace it with a more disguised form of the behavior involved. I once analyzed a youngster, for example, whose learning problems stemmed in part from the need to cloud his mind and be unable to grasp the import of what his senses perceived in response to his very attractive and seductive mother's habit of permitting him to periodically observe her nude or only partially dressed. She consulted another child analyst about it after I had expressed some reservation about what she was doing. When he recommended to her that she discontinue the practice, she dutifully complied. Sometime later, however, I learned from her son that although she no longer openly exposed him to her unclad body, she periodically carried on a conversation with him while he stood in her room watching her towel herself after a shower, via the mirror that was mounted on the bathroom door that stood slightly ajar.

At times, it is necessary to guide one or another parent into treatment of his or her own in order to permit the treatment of a child to have any chance of succeeding. This was so with regard to the mother who could not stop herself from holding her son's interest in her by surreptitiously exposing herself to him despite her conscious awareness that it was necessary for her to discontinue it. At other times, it becomes evident that there is so much irremediable, neurotic acting out within the family or so much irreducible turmoil that although intensive psychotherapy or psychoanalysis clearly is indicated for a youngster brought for treatment, it has to be postponed until later on or replaced altogether by one form or another of family therapy.

A 7-year-old girl, for example, was brought for treatment because of phobic preoccupations and a behavioral disturbance that took the form of temper tantrums and of clinging, demanding, abusive behavior with her mother at night and in the morning. Although evaluation of the child clearly pointed in the direction of intensive psychotherapy for her largely oedipal, neurotic conflicts in the presence of favorable motivation and a strong, core ego organization, she insisted on her mother being present during all her sessions after the initial, evaluative ones. It soon became clear that her neurotic struggles were intricately interwoven with a dysfunctional family interaction in which an overwhelmingly powerful sadomasochistic interaction between her parents had become organized around disputes between the parents over their relationships with her. Her father was insisting that she be in treatment "to stop creating the distress and turmoil in the family" that actually stemmed primarily from what was going on between the parents. A complex family therapy approach, involving a shifting pattern of sessions with individual family members and various combinations of family members, emerged out of what turned out to be a protracted evaluation process. To have collaborated with her parents in forcing this little girl to undergo intensive psychotherapy for what was viewed as "her problems" without involving her parents (who would not accept referral to another therapist) would have been detrimental in that it would have given an authoritative stamp to a fictional attribution to her of responsibility for the family troubles.

The ways in which the individual, neurotic struggles of a child brought for treatment fit in with and interdigitate with the family dynamics always need to be elucidated at the beginning of treatment. The importance of the child's struggles, as reflected in the presenting symptoms. and their underlying dynamics, in the overall patterns of interaction within the family is an essential ingredient of the initial evaluation. It is necessary to determine not only how the family dynamics are influencing the child's dynamics, but also how changes in the child's dynamics are likely to affect the family dynamics and therefore the ability of the parents to accept changes in the child without having to oppose or interfere with further change.

Two dramatic examples involve an 8-year-old girl who was brought by her parents for assistance because of incapacitating phobic and phobic-obsessive symptoms of which her parents wanted her cur d, and a 17-year-old girl whose anorexia and school phobia caused her parents enormous grief. When the 8-year-old girl expressed powerful motivation to enter psychoanalysis, it quickly emerged that her parents had an enormous investment in her being ill to distract them from their • intense hostility toward each other and to pull them together on her behalf instead of being so enraged at each other that they harbored terrifying, murderous feelings toward one another. As soon as she began to settle down, feeling more secure in the knowledge that help• was on the _way, one rationalization after another emanated from the parents to interfere with the beginning of the analysis, which, of course, never could get under way.

The 17-year-old girl was referred by someone who practiced at such a distance from the family home that it was impracticable to see her more than once or, at most, twice a week. We moved toward and then into a three-times-weekly psychotherapy in which the patient began to overcome her immaturities and summon up the courage to begin to pull away from her anxious clinging to her mother, to get a job, to begin to date young men, and to think about moving out of the parental home. Her mother, who, it then became clear, was extremely unhappy in her marriage to the patient's father, began to place one obstacle after another against the treatment, despite all the efforts expended by patient and therapist alike to work with her so as to save the treatment situation. The mother soon broke off the treatment, with the support of the patient's father, and brought her back to the initial therapist for twice-weekly treatment, rationalized by an argument he accepted. That treatment too was disrupted, predictably, 6 months later, with the rationalization that traveling that far for treatment interfered too much with activities that were necessary for the girl, who agreed with her mother at that point to quit her job, break off with the boyfriend of whom her mother disapproved, enter a local college, and live at home.

Even where there are no formidable resistances on the part of the parents against intensive treatment that leads to major change in the child and within the family dynamics, careful assessment of the family patterns and of what is going on psychologically within the parents is invaluable in pointing the way toward appropriate technical decisions during the opening phase .of a psychoanalysis or intensive psychotherapy. This is illustrated by the contrast between the opening phase of the psychoanalytic treatment of a 5-year-old boy with a gender identity disorder and that of a 6-year-old girl with intense phobias, obsessions, and panicky temper tantrums. The boy's mother had bonded to him initially in a highly ambivalent manner that had interfered with his capacity to achieve a secure, safe sense of his own identity and intactness and had contributed to a burden of enormous guilt that aggravated her deep distrust of and ambivalence toward males in general. Following signs from both the boy and his mother that the opening phase had to include the two of them, who had not psycho- logically differentiated from one another but were ambivalently inter- locked with one another, the analyst agreed to have the mother present during the psychoanalytic sessions, which were gradually increased in frequency, for 6 months before they were ready to shift to sessions for the child alone.

The little girl, in contrast, was brought for analysis after the mother had been advised by her own therapist to shift from twice-weekly psychotherapy to psychoanalysis four times a week, which her mother was very reluctant to do. It became evident during the evaluation that the mother, whose own mother had become irreversibly psychotic during the mother's childhood, had been terrified of the recommendation for psychoanalysis for herself because of the unconscious fear that she would respond to the regressive impact of psychoanalysis by becoming psychotic. She had unconsciously decided to bring her daughter to a psychoanalyst for evaluation and treatment instead of placing herself in analysis, to try it out on her, as it were. It became clear that psychoanalysis was indicated for the little girl, but the analyst was mindful of the circumstances in which the treatment had been initiated. When this patient, with subtle encouragement from her mother, sought to have the mother join her for the opening sessions of the analysis, the analyst did not agree to the request but made it clear that the treatment • was for the little girl alone and that he would wait for her to become able to leave her mother to join him in the playroom. It took less than a week for her to do so, and the analysis went on to a very successful psychoanalytic and therapeutic conclusion, after which her mother entered analysis for herself.

In summary, it is essential to view a child brought by parents for intensive psychotherapy or psychoanalysis as but one element in a family constellation that has to be carefully and often patiently evaluated to assure that an accurate determination is made of the feasibility of undertaking such treatment, and that such a treatment will begin on a sound basis. Parents are as much a focus of the initial evaluation, planning, and initial implementation of such a treatment as is the child.

CHAPTER 16

INSECURITY AND FEAR OF ATTACHMENT IN A TROUBLED ADOPTION: A CLINICAL EXAMPLE

[(2004). Journal of Infant, Child & Adolescent Psychotherapy, 3(3):313–328.]

A case is presented of the psychoanalytic treatment of a four-year-old girl who had been adopted in traumatizing circumstances that interfered with the development of secure, healthy bonds of attachment between her and her adoptive parents. This led to severe interpersonal and behavioral problems. The analysis was dramatic and emotionally intense for child and therapist alike. What emerged in the course of the treatment can help illuminate the psychology of adoption as well as that of healthy and pathological attachment between children and their parents. The case also illustrates the way in which intensive (psychoanalytic) treatment of a young child needs to conform to the unique requirements dictated by the child's history, psychological makeup, and family situation. It trenchantly demonstrates the way in which a therapist intensely treating a severely traumatized, distrustful, rage-filled young child, one who is terrified of allowing herself to get close to someone and fall in love with and yearn to be loved by that person, has to be able to withstand the intense emotional storms that can be expected to erupt in the course of treatment. The excellent result obtained from the treatment also demonstrates, however, that the emotional stress is well worth experiencing.

The illusion of inviolable safety and security enjoyed for nearly two centuries by the American populace was shattered on

September 11, 2001, when a destructive, murderous attack on the World Trade Center demonstrated that an ocean on either side and a friendly nation above and below could no longer protect us from attack by elements hostile to the United States. It remains to be seen whether the government to which we look to provide us with care and protection can restore a sense of reasonable security to the citizens of our country. To do so, it will have to show not only that it has the resolve to do so, but also the strength, the integrity, and the means with which to restore faith among our populace in those who in a larger sense are in loco parentis with regard to our citizenry.

The events of September 11 and what has transpired since then have been testing the faith of American adults in the capacity of the government to ensure the safety of the citizens of our nation. For American children, these events are a test of their parents' and, by extension, the adult generation's capacity to keep *them* safe and secure. As President of the Association for Child Psychoanalysis, I reviewed materials being promulgated to parents looking for help in assisting their children to cope with what had occurred and was occurring. They did not come across as being as fully adequate as they might have been, so I prepared some terse guidelines for parents1 that among other things stressed the need for children to perceive their parents as sensitive to their feelings and to their needs and as brave, strong, and ready to provide realistic means of protecting them and keeping them safe. Children need to know that their parents love and care about them and are prepared not only to nurture and protect them but also to rebound and recover from failures to provide them with a wall of solid protection.

What do children need to feel reasonably safe and secure? Certainly, they need to feel loved, cherished, and wanted by their parents and other significant family members. Only then can they develop the capacity to love and cherish other human beings, beginning with their parents and extending beyond them into the world beyond. Life experience is imperfect, however. Disappointments, frustrations, and hurts cannot be avoided even in the best of circumstances. For healthy, secure attachment toward parents to emerge, it is necessary for the child and the parents to be able to recover from disruptions and breakdowns in the positive relationship that has been building between them. And disruptions and breakdowns inevitably occur.

CLINICAL MATERIAL

In this article, I focus on the adoption theme in the analysis of a child who had been adopted in circumstances that seriously interfered with the development of secure attachment between the child and her adoptive parents. For reasons of economy, I focus mainly on my work with the child and therefore say relatively little about my work with the child's parents, even though that aspect of the work was extremely important in determining the outcome of the treatment.

Let me begin with some brief general comments about child analysis. Anna Freud has urged that we search for the *core fantasy* that underlies and organizes the neurotic problems that bring a child to psychoanalytic treatment. Good psychoanalytic technique grows out of the recognition that every analysand is unique and that a unique genetic and dynamic constellation is generating the disorder with which we are confronted when we work with any particular patient. At times, this dictum illustrates itself in dramatic fashion in the course of an analytic treatment.

Jackie was just four years of age when her analysis began. Her teachers in nursery school were extremely concerned about her. Her extremely oppositional and defiant behavior frustrated and alienated them. With other children, she was so controlling, demanding, and, at other times, rejecting of them that they did not want anything to do with her. This distressed her enormously, but she was unable to change the way she interacted with them.

At home, the situation was no better. She would not listen to her mother, and they fought constantly. She demanded her mother's attention, and threw temper tantrums when she did not get what she wanted. What was most painful to her mother, however, was that she refused either to accept affection from her or to give her the affection she so much yearned to receive from Jackie. Her mother longed for a loving relationship with her, but Jackie coldly rebuffed and pulled away from her. At the same time, Jackie was extremely jealous of attention her parents paid to her two-year-old sister, a very easygoing, affectionate little girl, and she accorded her sister disdainful neglect. She alternated between wanting to spend time with her father, when he was around, and coolly ignoring him. She was not truly loving or affectionate with either of her parents. The person with whom she was most animated and affectionate was her maternal grandmother, who lived very far away and whom she saw very infrequently. This was especially frustrating to Jackie's mother, because as a child she had not had that kind of relationship with her mother.

Jackie's parents, after a struggle with infertility, had adopted Jackie through an adoption agency. They explained that the adoption laws in the state in which she was born required placement in foster care while the suitability of prospective adoptive parents was investigated. Bureaucratic delays stretched the time out to six months. Jackie reportedly was a happy, thriving baby during her stay with the very attentive, warm, affectionate, somewhat older woman who cared for her during that time. When she left foster care and came to her adoptive parents, she was in an alarming state. She refused to eat or sleep, and she howled in inconsolable torment for a long period of time. This terrified her adoptive parents all the more because the adoption would not be finalized until a year had passed, during which they were subjected to monthly scrutiny by an investigator who submitted reports as to whether they were suitable parents. Jackie eventually recovered from her initial, frantic state. With all the tension, uncertainty, and distress they both were experiencing, however, she and her mother, as her mother put it, "never truly bonded."

Jackie's sister was adopted at birth from a state with different laws. Jackie's mother and little sister easily bonded with one another, and they had a good relationship. Jackie was told from the beginning, in accordance with the advice her parents received from the adoption agency, that she was adopted and that her parents wanted and loved her very much. Her parents tried hard to convince her of it.

Jackie studied me carefully when I entered the waiting room the first time we met. Her mother introduced me to her and reminded her that I had a playroom. "Shall we go inside?" I asked. Jackie promptly turned her back on her mother and marched in to explore the playroom, which was unusual for a child her age. "Would you like your mother to come in with us, or should she wait in the waiting room?" I asked. "She'll wait for me," Jackie said. She examined the contents of the room. Then she picked up a large, plastic truck and crawled under the table. She motioned for me to come over, and, when I did so, she shot the truck out at me. She motioned for me to roll the truck back to her so that she could do again with me what she had just done. "You seem to feel that you have to be careful and protect yourself," I said. I briefly recounted to Jackie what her parents had told me about why they had asked me to help her. I said, "I'd like to help you be happier, but I'm patient. I can wait until you feel more comfortable with me." Jackie climbed out from under the table, looked up at me, and asked, "Do you know *Peter Pan?*" "I know the story," I said. "Why do you ask?" Jackie told me she had seen the movie. Then she asked, "Can we play Peter Pan?"

For the next five or six months, meeting together four times a week, we played out the story of *Peter Pan*. Jackie carefully controlled the play. She assigned the parts and was very strict in her role as director. She had us play out an opening scene in which Wendy and John, and their dog Nana, left their parents in Boston (where Jackie had been born), and flew to Neverland. There we met Peter Pan. (Jackie always played the role of Peter from this point on.) Peter told us that we could stay, but he was anything but enthusiastic. He really didn't care one way or the other, he informed us. When I wondered out loud why Peter was so diffident, Jackie instructed me that it was my job to recite the lines that were given to me. She said that I was not supposed to say anything else. "But you and I can talk, can't we?" I said. "We're being actors playing Peter Pan, but we're also two people, meeting here so we can figure out what troubles you and makes you unhappy." Jackie looked at me carefully, but didn't reply.

One session started with Jackie, playing Nana, climbing under the table. Nana curled up and went to sleep, supposedly because it had been a long, tiring trip from Boston to Neverland. When I began to speak, Nana shushed me. Jackie signaled for me to take a step toward the table. When I did so, Nana shot a toy truck out at me to chase me away and punish me for having disturbed her. I was very aware of the extent to which Jackie was defensively pushing people away from her. Identification with the aggressor seemed to be playing an important part. I told Nana that I knew that she had had a long, complicated, difficult journey from Boston to Neverland. I said that I could understand that she was cautious about letting anyone approach her and that she just

344

might not want to take a chance on getting too close to someone and too used to someone and then maybe not seeing that person again. Nana responded by coming out from under the table, ready to continue with the performance of Peter *Pan*.

Several, related themes emerged in the Peter *Pan* play. One was intense envy of those who have a maternal caretaker on the part of those who lack that good fortune. Another involved the intolerable pain experienced by someone who is rebuffed, rejected, and unwanted. The third appeared to center about self-defensive refusal to have feelings toward other human beings, or, for that matter, to feel anything *at all*.

Captain Hook was furious that he had no mother. The boys in Neverland had no mother, but they had Peter and now they had Wendy to look after them. Peter professed to have no need for a mother, but he did have Tinkerbell to love him and look out for him. What outraged Hook was that in addition to all that they had in Neverland, Peter, Wendy, and John also had Nana. He did everything he could to get them to give Nana up and then to entice Nana to leave them. All his efforts were foiled, and he grew angrier and angrier.

I played the parts assigned to me, in accordance with Jackie's instructions. I was given the part of Captain Hook. I played the part as assigned. After a while, however, I commented that I could appreciate what Hook was feeling. He yearned *so much* to have Nana. It was so *hard* for him *not* to have her. I also indicated that I was impressed with the loyalty the children and Nana showed to each other. I said that I knew how hard it is for real children when they lose people to whom they have become attached.

A bit later, I said that the play reminded me of what Jackie and her parents had been going through. Her parents wanted so much for her to love them and to let them love her, but it was so hard for her to let them do that. (I was exquisitely aware from my contacts with Jackie's parents how very much in pain they were over her rejection of them and how increasingly impatient they were for the analysis to produce changes in her in that regard.) Jackie found it difficult to have me say these things. I commented on how hard it was for her even to *hear* them being said. I could only imagine, I said, how difficult *her experience* of them had been. She gave me a sharp, but thoughtful look.

As Jackie and I worked together, I became increasingly aware that she was keeping herself extremely distant from me emotionally. This was very different from my experience with most children her age whom I have analyzed. It felt as though there was no emotional involvement with me at all. She assigned me parts to play and lines to recite, and treated me as though I were no more than an easily replaceable, journeyman actor sent to her by Actors' Equity to play secondary roles. If I entered into the play with even a modicum of enthusiasm, she appeared anxious. She herself was a model of emotional restraint and distance. When I commented that she seemed reluctant to get involved with me personally or for us to become too comfortable together, she informed me that it was my job to play the roles assigned to me. I agreed to simply follow the director's instructions if that were necessary, but I noted that we also were two people playing *Peter Pan* together, and I reminded her that I had promised to help her with her feelings. I said to Jackie that maybe we could get to know why she was so uneasy about our getting to know one another and about our getting too close to one another emotionally.

In the play, Tinkerbell (a part assigned to me to play) tried and tried to get through to Peter that she loved him, was devoted to him, and would do *anything* for him. He rejected *all* her overtures. His only interest was in fighting off the Red Indians and the Pirates who threatened repeatedly to attack and kidnap the inhabitants of Neverland. Tinkerbell grew more and more despondent. She stopped eating and sleeping, and pined away more and more until she was close to dying. I found myself becoming increasingly concerned, partly because Peter's hardhearted recalcitrance reflected Jackie's self-defeating unwillingness to let herself warm up to *anyone* in her life, but partly, too, because her parents were growing more and more frantic and less and less willing to support the analysis. I recognized, as well, that it also stemmed from my own countertransference. The degree to which I was being dehumanized and rendered lifeless by Jackie's defensive refusal to allow any human feelings to emerge either in her or in me was extremely unpleasant.

After a while, I told Jackie, "I know you're the director and I'm an actor who has to follow directions, but it's *so hard* for me to play Tinkerbell this way. Her *heart* is breaking. She's *dying*. She loves Peter, and all she wants is for Peter to love her a little, and then she'd be so happy." Jackie insisted that I just play the part of Tinkerbell the way I was instructed. I replied that I would try to play the part as directed, but I couldn't stop myself from having feelings. "I feel for Tinkerbell," I said. "She has feelings, too." "*So do you!*" Jackie said, derisively. I played the part of Tinkerbell pining away in hurt and pain and misery, as instructed. Periodically, however, I reminded Jackie that, as a human being, I was finding it very difficult to do so. I told her that I had read the book and didn't remember Tinkerbell dying of a broken heart the way she was doing in our play. I wondered, I said, what it was that had made Peter so obdurate in his rejection of Tinkerbell's expressions of love that he was punishing her so horribly. *Something* must have happened to make Peter be that way.

Jackie insisted that Tinkerbell had to pine away of heartache and die. I said that I hoped that Jackie and I could get to understand what had made Peter so hurt and angry that he did not care about how terribly he was treating Tinkerbell, so that perhaps Tinkerbell could live and she and Peter could find a way for them to be happy together. I said that it reminded me of the pain and suffering Jackie had been having and her mother had been having that had brought Jackie to me. I said that maybe after all their suffering, they could become happy together, too. Jackie asked how that could happen. I said maybe Wendy could help Peter and Tinkerbell, and maybe I could help Jackie and her mother.

Jackie decided to let Tinkerbell live. She would suffer a great deal, but then Wendy would nurse her back to health and restore to her the will to live. She was not so sure about the possibility of her being restored to the will to *love*, however. When I expressed faith in the human spirit, Jackie said, "Tinkerbell isn't human. She's a fairy." When I replied, "Maybe fairies are part human," Jackie looked very thoughtful. She seemed to know just what I had meant.

The focus shifted back now to Captain Hook trying desperately to convince Peter that he should give up Nana. After all, Hook pointed out, he had Tinkerbell to look after him. Peter merely grunted, in a way that indicated that he did not care about Tinkerbell. He also had Wendy to care for him, Hook observed. But Peter didn't care about Captain Hook. He saw no reason to let him have Nana. Captain Hook, with mounting fury, set out on a campaign first to steal Nana away and then, if he couldn't have her, to *kill* her so that no one else would have her either. I told Jackie that I was very impressed with the way Hook felt. How infuriating it was for him to see Nana with Peter and Wendy and John when *he wanted to have her.* He couldn't stand it. That must be the way Jackie felt, I said, when her teacher was with other children when she needed her or when her mother spent time with her little sister. "Don't talk about that!" Jackie said. "Just play your part!"

Hook was determined to kill Nana. Jackie turned to me and said, "You'll probably say Nana shouldn't die!" I said that I felt for Nana but that I could feel for *Hook's* pain too. He was a villain in the story, but he, too, had feelings. "You don't know very much," Jackie said, "if you can say *that!* "The action continued thick and fast. When Hook's sidekick Smee questioned whether Nana had to die, Hook promptly killed him and knocked him overboard. "Wow," I said, "I can see now how strong Hook's hurt and anger are. He can't stand it. He can't hold it in. He *has* to hit. He *has* to hurt." I was indirectly referring, of course, to the way Jackie treated her teachers, classmates, mother, and sister, and it was my impression that the message got through to her.

An incident occurred in which Peter and the boys captured the Red Indians and were about to tie them up and burn them to death. Wendy (which role I was assigned to play) compassionately intervened on their behalf. Peter immediately commuted their sentence to banishment. He made it clear, however, that he had done so not to be humane but to show Wendy how little he cared about *anyone,* one way or the other. I commented on the way Peter protected himself from hurt and pain by *not feeling.*

Hook set out to kill Peter with a bomb. The alligator, which had bitten off and ingested a part of him—his arm—and wanted the rest of him, caught up with him and did him in, gruesomely and horribly. The bomb went off, destroying them both. It was time now for Wendy and John to return to Boston. Jackie became restless and fidgety, however, and broke off the play before they could do so.

Jackie had us move out of the playroom at this time. We began to use my consulting room, where she instituted an ongoing game in which she had me twirl her around in a large chair until she would become "dizzy" and fall out of the chair. After many repetitions, she added the element of it hurting when she fell out of the chair. She would not verbally explore the meaning of the game with me. Finally, one day I said, "Jackie, it's like you're being born!" With that, she moved over to a chair by the telephone. She punched numbers at random. To her surprise, as well as mine, a woman answered. She spoke with Jackie for a minute or two and when she discovered that Jackie had called her from New Jersey, she asked her to put me on the phone. "You'd better hang up quick," she said, "I'm in Hawaii!" Jackie was impressed that she had reached a woman so far away. "You know what I think?" I said. "I think you were looking for your *first* mother." Jackie replied that when her family moved to New Jersey two summers earlier, she had to leave all her friends. "I miss *them!*" she declared.

Jackie and I returned to the playroom where for weeks she wrote letters, with my assistance, to the friends she had left behind. She eagerly awaited a response from them, and was increasingly sad that responses never arrived. She had me make a letter arrive for her, in such a way that we could pretend that it had come from one of her old friends.

Christmas was approaching, and her parents were preparing to take her and her sister away to Disney World. She was distraught at the prospect of leaving me. She became preoccupied with deciding on a Christmas present to give me. Finally, she brought in a penny. She searched and searched for a safe place for it. I had to promise that I would take good care of it and that it would not disappear. She wanted me to keep it in my pocket "always." She had great difficulty deciding what *she* wanted from *me,* however. Finally, she brought in a Polaroid camera and took a picture of me to take with her on her trip. "That's what I want," she said.

Her family was to leave for the airport immediately after Jackie had had a session with me. In the waiting room before the session, Jackie was irate. How could I agree to be parted from her? Never mind that she was leaving me. She became increasingly agitated, reached over, and bit a button off my jacket sleeve. Thinking of the alligator that had bitten off part of Captain Hook and wanted the rest of him, I said, "I think you want to eat me up, so you can have me inside of you and take me with you." "Then you can *never* leave me!" she replied. When we spoke about it in the playroom, I said, "It must feel like you'll lose me and will never see me again. I think it reminds you too much of things that happened in the past that were very painful to you."

To my surprise, I received a picture postcard from Florida, signed, LOVE, *Jackie*. When she returned, Jackie searched for the penny she had given to me and was very much relieved when she found it. She told me, however, that she lost the photograph she had taken of me. She looked for it but couldn't find it. It simply had disappeared. During the next six weeks, we explored Jackie's feelings about separation and loss, and the way they had expressed themselves in connection with her trip away from me.

While we spoke, Jackie worked painstakingly at making an elaborate Valentine's Day card to give to me when the time came. It was replete with a huge, red heart and an elegant lace border. The day before Valentine's Day, the card appeared to be finished. When the time came for her to leave, however, she kept insisting that she needed yet a little more time to complete it. The next patient (another little girl) had arrived. I commented on Jackie's difficulty leaving and her feeling that she needed yet a little bit more of me. I said that we could figure out together what that was all about but that we did have to stop. Jackie erupted in rage. She impulsively grabbed up the Valentine's Day card and tore it to pieces. "How could you do that?" I expostulated. "You worked on it for weeks!" She stalked out.

Forty-five minutes later, the telephone rang. It was Jackie.

"Hi," she said.

After a moment, I said, "Hi."

Jackie was silent.

"How come you called?" I asked.

"I just felt like it," she said. Then she was silent.

"Jackie, how could you tear up that card," I asked, "after all the work you did on it?"

"It doesn't matter," she said.

"It doesn't matter?" I replied. "It *does* matter!"

"It doesn't matter," Jackie said again. "It's only a card." Jackie paused. Then she said, "Where are you?"

"What do you mean?" I asked.

"Just answer!" she said.

"In my office, by the telephone."

"What are you wearing?" She had me describe my clothes, the room, what I saw out the window, and so on.

"You know what, Jackie," I said, "I think you got so hurt and so angry, so very, very angry at me when I sent you away to see another little girl, especially after you had gone to so much work to make me that wonderful Valentine, that you didn't just rip up the Valentine's Day card. I think you were so angry that you ripped up the picture of me you had inside your head. You were so angry with me that your anger destroyed all the other feelings you had about me. So you had to call me to build up a new picture of me. I think something like that happens when your Mommy turns away from you to spend time with your sister, and that that's part of the trouble between you and your mother."

Jackie was silent.

I said that I felt bad when she tore up the card, and that I felt bad for her and her pain when she did so.

"It doesn't matter," she said. "The card's not important."

"Yes it is," I said. "Feelings *are important! You broke my heart!*"

We analyzed this incident when we met together during the

352

next few months. Her fear of our getting close to one another, her difficulty sharing me or her mother or her teachers with other children, her fear of loving me or letting me love her, her fear of letting herself love her parents, the pain she felt when children didn't like her because of her behavior, and the fact that life is difficult at TIMES all came into focus. We were able to connect these things with the circumstances of her adoption and their impact on her and her parents. I acknowledged that the card itself was not very important, but I indicated that *her feelings were important.* Harking back to the Peter *Pan* play, I stated that it was indeed not my job to have feelings in response to what she brought to me to help her with, but that I had feelings, nevertheless, and that I could tolerate that. I said that she, too, had feelings, although at times she wished she didn't have them, and that it was my impression that she, too, could tolerate them. I invited her to face the feelings in her that had been involved in the Valentine's Day card incident. She agreed to talk with me about it.

What emerged was that I had become important to her and that, when her parents had taken her away for Christmas vacation, her feelings of loss had painfully stirred up feelings inside of her connected with earlier losses, of her original mother during the adoption process, of her friends when the family moved, and of her mother when her sister was born. The Valentine's Day card had epitomized her longing for the idealized, wonderful, perfect mother she felt was out there somewhere (like the pleasant-sounding woman in Hawaii she had reached from my office). When I sent her away to see another child, her hopes of finding that special mother through me were dashed, and the rage that she was feeling destroyed all hope of having me as the incarnation of her wishful dream. It also became clear to us that, as an adopted child who had suffered losses and abandonment, Jackie felt entitled to be especially loved to make up for what she had suffered. An oedipal theme emerged, involving a yearning for her father to choose her over her mother and sister, while her mother suffered rejection and loss this time instead of her. Jackie made it clear that she experienced her father's business trips and his backing away from the tense atmosphere in the house as a personal rejection. There were allusions to the lack of consanguinity with her father heightening her oedipal tension by lowering the incest taboo between them: "I *can* marry my daddy. I'm not *really* his daughter." It became possible to point out to Jackie that her misbehavior at times was designed to invoke punishment to relieve unconscious guilt.

While we talked, we played games (for the first time) or Jackie preoccupied herself with writing love notes to her mother, Mother's Day and Father's Day cards, and hundreds of invitations to her maternal aunt's wedding that was coming up in the near future. She was beginning to express affection toward her parents, and her behavior improved both at home and at school. She began to speak with me about frictions and conflicts at home instead of fighting with her mother and mistreating her sister. She began to look at herself in the mirror when she came to see me. We addressed this in terms of a growing interest in how she looked, both to others and to herself, and in terms of not looking like her parents and sister because she had been adopted.

Jackie was able now to let her parents go away together for a week. She came in looking pale and drawn. She paced back and forth, distractedly. "You're thinking about your parents, aren't you?" I said. "I think about them all the time." "You miss them." "I miss them very much!" Jackie complained about being hungry (which she had never done before). The babysitter had forgotten to provide an after-school snack. She pleaded with me to get her something to eat. How could she talk to me if all she could think about was being hungry? As she spoke, she stroked the breasts of an African figurine of a naked woman with a naked child on her back that she had picked up from my desk. She became so agitated that I went out and brought back some strawberries and a tangerine. Jackie wolfed down the tangerine, and then sat stroking the tangerine peel the way she had stroked the breasts of the figurine. "You know what I think?" I said. "I think you'd like me to grow breasts and become a Mommy for you." *"Could you?"* she exclaimed. I said that I wished it could be that simple but that her feelings about her mother were the important thing. We could feel together and talk together about her feelings so that I could help her deal with them better. Jackie listened attentively.

I said, "I think you're afraid they're not coming back. You're not *sure* of them, the way you weren't sure the penny you gave me would still be there when you got back from Disney World. You weren't sure I'd still want to see you when you got back. You're not sure your parents *want* to come back. "

"They said they *miss* me."

"When?"

"On the phone."

"But you're not sure they mean it. I think you're afraid they're glad to be away, and you miss them."

"They *said* they miss me."

"But you think they miss Katie [her little sister] more."

"They *do* miss Katie more," she said. "She's *nice*."

"And you're not able to be nice."

"They'll come back," said Jackie.

"But it's hard to wait," I said.

"It's *very hard*."

"I'll help you wait," I said. "I'll help you the best I can."

Jackie looked up at me and said, "I know."

The analysis led to a very useful result for Jackie and her family. And when she left, I missed her.

DISCUSSION

Every analysis is unique, because every person is unique. Jackie was not merely an adopted child. She was an adopted child who had been abruptly taken away, at the age of six months, from a warm, caring, nurturing, foster mother to whom she had bonded closely. She went on at this point to her permanent family, but with two developmental burdens: the imprint of the wrenching loss she had just experienced and the ongoing effects of devastating, bureaucratic interference in the otherwise natural process of bonding that then had to take place between her and her adoptive parents. Instead of taking place in an ambience marked by peace, tranquility, and security, the bonding process had to occur in an atmosphere of tension, uncertainty, and mutual disappointment, fear, and anger.

Her adoptive mother tried hard to connect with Jackie, relieve her of her initial, intense distress, and establish herself as a new source of emotional sustenance, but this was very hard for her to do. Jackie was so distraught that she simply could not be comforted. And her mother-to-be felt so anxious and insecure, enveloped as she was by the bureaucratic Sword of Damocles that hung over her, and so frustrated and defeated by her inability to meet Jackie's needs, that she could not break through the barrier that was created by Jackie's seeming refusal to accept her as the all-giving, all-nourishing, perfect mother she wanted so much to be for her. She received too little assistance from those around her, and she felt increasingly discouraged and hopeless.

By the time Jackie entered analysis, she was enmeshed in a self-defeating neurotic pattern in which she not only pushed her mother away, despite her desperate longing for closeness with her, but she pushed everyone away from her as well. She reproduced this in the analysis, in which she made it increasingly clear that she hungered to get inside of me and for me to get inside of her, but was so terrified of making herself vulnerable by loving and being loved that she had to vigorously deny her need for me. She had to prove that she could get along without me or anybody else and had to dehumanize me so as to make it impossible for a loving relationship to develop.

This was played out graphically and dramatically in the opening, Peter *Pan* phase of the analysis. It became increasingly clear to me during the Peter *Pan* play that merely putting her actions into words would not suffice. With Jackie moving farther and farther away from me rather than closer, and with her parents growing increasingly frantic and impatient with what might be accomplished in analysis, it became more and more evident that something dramatic and intense was called for. Like Eliza Doolittle in My Fair Lady, Jackie was telling me, "Words are not enough; *show me!*" If Jackie were to be convinced that she should allow herself to have feelings, I would first have to demonstrate that I, too, was willing to have feelings, however unpleasant or uncomfortable they might be.

During the next phase, Jackie oscillated between holding fast to an unconscious fantasy of being reunited with her *idealized first mother,* as revealed in the birth play that was followed by making contact with the kindly older woman in Hawaii she reached on the telephone and then trying to contact her old, long-lost friends, and taking a chance on letting herself slide into a new, loved and loving relationship with me. When I demonstrated that I was willing to join her in her pain and distress, while I was putting what she was expressing on an action language plane into verbal language, this facilitated her summoning up the courage to take a chance on falling in love for real, in the present imperfect. What transpired between us around the Christmas break demonstrated both sides of her dilemma.

What happened after that was pivotal. Jackie relaxed her guard enough to let herself grow closer to me, both as *a person* she let herself like and love and as *her analyst* whom she allowed to help her tackle her problems. As we worked together, she lovingly constructed an elaborate Valentine's Day card, only to fly into a rage and destroy it when I insisted on sending her away the day before the holiday to be with another little girl in her place rather than remaining with her *as long as she needed me!* When she telephoned me a little while later, to reestablish contact with me, she had to have me provide her with the building blocks she required to rebuild the mental image of me she had destroyed along with the Valentine. In doing so, she indicated that she had enacted with me, on a primitive, organismic, transferential level, a core fantasy she had been carrying within her for a long time: that she was so enraged at her original mother (s) that she had destroyed her (them) and needed to destroy her (them) again and again until her *Urmutter* finally would be restored to her in an indestructible, idealized form that never would disappoint her or leave her again.

When I told Jackie that, in her hurt and rage, she had ripped up not only the Valentine's Day card she had made for me—her love-gift to me—but also her picture of me that she carried around inside her, she did not reply. She remained silent, apart from me, absent, nonexistent as far as I was concerned. She did not hang up the telephone, however. She remained there, away from me and away from the verbally organized inner self that I had addressed, waiting, I felt, for me to reconnect dramatically with her, like the kindly, older woman in Hawaii who had responded so cordially when Jackie had reached out into the void and met up with her.

By imperatively pleading with me to provide the detailed, descriptive, building blocks she needed to rebuild the internal representation of me she had destroyed in her rage, she had indicated that it was insufficient for me merely to *talk about* her feelings of loss, pain, rage, and so on. She had indicated that she needed me to *give her what she needed* in the way of external and internal building blocks for her to become able to do that. She had communicated, it seemed to me, that she needed me to give of myself, genuinely, emotionally, and spontaneously. So I responded by telling Jackie, with genuine feeling, that it troubled me that she had destroyed the Valentine's Day card she had worked on so hard and long, to which she replied that it did not matter because it was "only a card." When I replied, in turn, "Your feelings *do* matter. *You broke my heart!*" an enormously fruitful discussion opened up that remained open for the duration of the analysis.

The unique details of Jackie's neurotic dilemma and of the forces that had created it dictated the form and substance of the way in which we had to interact and communicate with one another in the analysis. Jackie was enabled to give up the counterproductive neurotic patterns that had been causing her so much grief and holding her back so enormously in her relationships and in her development. She—and her parents—now had a chance to create a good life.

Section IV:

Psychoanalytic Treatment of Adult Patients

CHAPTER 17

COUNTERTRANSFERENCE AND THE MYTH OF THE PERFECTLY ANALYZED ANALYST

[(1985). Psychoanalytic Quarterly 54:175–199]

ABSTRACT:

Countertransference is an inevitable feature of every psychoanalysis. Psychoanalysts are (and need to be) only human; psychoanalytic work is arduous and replete with stresses, strains, and deprivations; analysands tend to probe for vulnerabilities in their analysts that can be exploited in the interest of acting out neurotic wishes instead of analyzing them; and a training analysis cannot completely immunize a psychoanalyst against countertransferential reactions that impede analytic progress. Psychoanalyst must be vigilant to the emergence of countertransference reactions so that they can analyze and overcome them. Two illustrative clinical examples are provided.

The emphasis of my remarks will be upon the inevitability of countertransference in psychoanalytic work and upon the need for psychoanalysts to be ever vigilant to its emergence. Although some analysts have viewed countertransference as a necessary and desirable source of information about what is going on in the patient, it is my firm impression that it always signifies that something has gone awry in the analyst's use of himself as an analyzing instrument.

When a psychoanalyst is working effectively, he makes use of a combination of empathic, emotional receptivity and cognitive validation that permits him to read the unconscious messages which underlie the analysand's conscious communications—in part directly and in part by understanding their effects upon his own psychological sensors. He does this by permitting himself, in a special manner that is under more or less continuous ego control, to respond emotionally to the patient's communications in small ways that can be detected as signals of the unconscious emanations from the patient. Knowledge of his own self and control over his own inclinations to seek gratification of his instinctual urges through interaction with others, gained during his training analysis, protect him against the danger of misreading his reactions and succumbing to the temptation to use the patient as an object of his own instinctual wishes.

It is not possible, however, for a psychoanalyst to maintain this optimal analytic stance indefinitely. Psychoanalysis can only be carried out by two human beings, the analyst being no less human than the analysand. An analyst is able to tolerate the strains, frustrations, importunate demands, and emotional assaults that are so much a part of his daily experience not only because of his professional understanding of their necessity but also because of his human and humane interest in facilitating his patient's achievement of improved emotional well-being. As Jacob Arlow once put it to me, a psychoanalyst needs to be softhearted as well as hard-headed.

Anna Freud (1954) stated that a psychoanalyst ideally should be no more than a blank screen reflecting back to the analysand what is being projected onto him, without introducing anything from his own feelings and attitudes, but, of course, she stated, none of us can do that. An analyst cannot be guided primarily by self-interest, but must have feelings for his patient as a troubled, struggling, fellow human being. The danger is ever present, however, as Anna Freud emphasized, for him to be drawn into complicity with the patient in a surreptitious, joint acting out of the wish to obtain gratification of each other's repressed infantile wishes. If the analyst is indeed immersed in the intense emotional interchange that the analytic situation is designed to provoke, he is subjected to powerful pressures to abandon his analytic neutrality. He is bombarded by a stream of complaints, supplications, subtle seductions, bitter accusations, and ingenious bits of blackmail from his patients. He is also subjected to an intense pull from within his own being to ease his burden by obtaining some measure of instinctual gratification from the analytic experience to make up for the deprivation and abuse to which he has given himself up. The analyst is continually drawn to do more than analyze, and his very humanness makes it difficult for him to invariably resist all the temptations.

The very nature of the psychoanalytic task makes it impossible to avoid the periodic emergence of countertransference reactions in the place of analytic empathy if the analyst truly is doing his job. It is of fundamental importance that the analyst be ready to recognize that this is taking place and to overcome it so that analytic empathy can be restored. Most of the time, when things are going well, this can be carried out quickly and smoothly. There are other times, however, when self-analysis needs to be carried out to correct a situation in the analyst that is interfering with his ability to do his work effectively. If countertransference reactions arise that transcend his ability to eliminate them via self-analysis, then a period of reanalysis with another psychoanalyst will be necessary.

For reasons that are intrinsic to the psychoanalytic method, no analyst can be entirely free of the tendency to develop countertransference reactions. The psychoanalyst who believes himself to be so "well analyzed" that he is immune to countertransference reactions as he undergoes the emotional dislocations required of him in the almost "impossible profession" of psychoanalysis may be the most vulnerable of all to their development. Such an analyst is at serious risk of developing well-disguised, well-rationalized, subtle countertransference reactions that will limit or destroy his efforts to help his patients to overcome the neurotic problems that are preventing them from realizing their potential in life.

THE ANALYTIC SITUATION

Psychoanalysis is a two-person enterprise that aims at gaining access to the unconscious conflicts that generate neurotic behavior. One participant, the analysand, is encouraged to give himself over to the free verbal expression of associatively linked derivatives of unconscious emotional strivings, but this is countered by unconscious defensive maneuvers that underlie his neurotic symptoms and character traits. The other participant, the analyst, strives to adopt a freely hovering attentive state in which he is receptive, emotionally and intellectually, to the analysand's utterances, gestures, and postural expressions in such a way that he is free to grasp their unconscious as well as conscious import without filtering, disguising, rejecting, or utilizing them for his own personal gains.

The analysand's attempt to restrict himself to verbal free association inevitably is outweighed by the inclination to direct his repressed instinctual wishes toward the person of the analyst in the hope of gratifying them. The analytic setting, by fostering regression and making the analyst available as a kindly, helpful, attentive, accepting object of the patient's drives, encourages the transference of unrequited infantile longings, libidinal as well as hostile, onto the analyst in place of the representationally internalized, original objects of their expression. The central core of psychoanalytic work consists in the analyst's painstaking, interpretative delineation of the analysand's transference resistance to free association. The patient, in other words, is drawn inevitably toward insisting that the analyst gratify his neurotic wishes (Calef and Weinshel, 1983), while the analyst holds him to his agreement to gain understanding of the infantile roots of his demands by interpreting them as regressive transference resistances.

The analyst, being no less human than the analysand, is also inclined toward the utilization of an available object for the discharge of repressed infantile longings. The counterpart of the analysand's tendency to shift from free association of derivatives of unconscious neurotic strivings to acting them out in the transference is the analyst's tendency to slip from analytic empathy to countertransferential (including counteridentificatory) acting out of his own unconscious neurotic strivings with the patient. In two early papers, Freud (1910), (1912) cautioned that the only way for a psychoanalyst to avoid or to minimize the latter danger is to protect himself by undergoing analysis of his own neurotic tendencies. His first recommendation (1910) was for erstwhile analysts to undergo self-analysis, as he himself had done (Freud, 1887-1902), (1900). Later he recommended that the would-be analyst undergo a training analysis so that he might resolve his resistances and thus "become aware of those complexes of his own which would be apt to interfere with his grasp of what the patient tells him" (Freud, 1912, p. 116).

In "Analysis Terminable and Interminable" (1937), however, Freud expressed serious reservations about the ability of anyone, including a future psychoanalyst, to so thoroughly analyze all the neurotic propensities within him in the course of an analysis that he could completely eliminate them. He concluded that one of the main functions of a psychoanalyst's own analysis is to prepare him for the ongoing self-analysis that must be a central part of his work throughout his career. He further advised that every psychoanalyst be prepared, if necessary, to undergo periodic reanalysis with another psychoanalyst, without shame and without regret. Beiser (1984), in a recent communication, described an experience of resolution of a countertransference blind spot via successful self-analysis, in the course of which she discovered that her own analyst had possessed a blind spot similar to the one which she later had to overcome herself.

As the analyst permits himself to drift freely in response to the patient's free associations, he allows himself to undergo a regressive emotional reaction. This produces, via the controlled utilization of introjective and projective processes, a trial identification (Fliess, 1942) with the patient and a limited emotional response to the patient's expressions in the interest of grasping what is going on within the patient. As the analyst permits his intuitive and empathic abilities to bring him into resonance with derivatives of the analysand's powerful unconscious passions and desires, he is inevitably carried to the very line that lies between apperception of what is emanating from the patient and the evocation of his own latent passions and desires. The latter are ready to take advantage of the analysand's availability (either directly or vicariously, through identification) as an object of their expression and fulfillment. When the analyst's cognitive abilities are brought to bear upon the emotional stirrings within him, as must be done for empathy to be *analytic empathy (Beres and Arlow, 1974)*, it is only too easy for him to rationalize indications of his own pursuit of drive gratification or of defense against it (acting out with the patient or defensive blind spots) by formulating what he observes in terms of emotional reactions within the patient rather than recognizing his own countertransference. The working analyst repeatedly hovers between apperception and misperception. Therefore, he needs to be continuously vigilant to that which emanates from him rather than from the patient.

A dimension of the analytic situation that has received insufficient attention is that the analyst is not the only one who uses his empathic sensitivities to perceive derivatives of unconscious neurotic conflicts in the other participant. The analysand, too, uses his intuitive and empathic abilities to detect evidence of emotional conflicts in the analyst that can be played upon in the attempt to obtain transference gratifications. Patients are quick to recognize and to utilize the analyst's vulnerabilities in their efforts to obtain gratification rather than understanding of their unconscious desires, or in their efforts to externalize and ward off disturbing unconscious contents rather than gaining insight into their defensive operations. It is sometimes difficult for the analyst to be certain that he is accurately perceiving the unconscious meaning of what is being conveyed to him. He may instead be falling prey to the implantation of misleading views by an analysand who is playing upon the analyst's biases and personal inclinations to lead him astray. The ability of certain patients to subtly but skillfully produce desired feelings in and reactive responses by their analysts can be impressive. It seems to me likely that this has contributed significantly to the Kleinian concept of projective identification, to the tendency of some analysts (including Freud) to give credence to extrasensory perception and thought transmission, and to the tendency among followers of Kohut's later concepts to abandon defense analysis in favor of "empathic" kindness and acceptance of their patients' projective attribution of total responsibility for their neurotic disturbances to parental abuse and failure.

CLINICAL ILLUSTRATIONS OF
COUNTERTRANSFERENCE PROBLEMS

It is well known that the presence of countertransference reactions can be signaled by the appearance in the analyst of boredom, sleepiness, vague malaise, irritability, excessively positive or negative feelings toward the patient (or toward the patient's past and present objects [Jacobs, 1983]), difficulty in grasping the meaning of the analysand's communications, dreams about a patient, parapraxes, and various forms of acting out of neurotic inclinations with the patient. A less obvious sign of countertransference interference can be the failure of the analysis to progress satisfactorily despite seemingly proper technique and seemingly accurate understanding of the analysand's communications. The following is offered as an illustration of such a situation.

A woman in her early forties came for reanalysis after her first analysis of seven years' duration had come to an end when the analyst retired from practice. The picture she painted of her first analysis was curiously replete with internal contradictions. On the one hand, she described her first analyst as hardworking, essentially on target in his interventions, and genuinely interested in helping her overcome the frigidity (which began immediately after her marriage to a man with whom she had been very enjoyably orgastic until then), the work inhibitions, and the recurrent, severe premenstrual depression for which she had entered analysis. On the other hand, she stated that she never had felt at ease with him, never had felt that he empathized with her, and never had felt that they had gotten anywhere. Although she had "followed the rules," had worked hard, and had learned a good deal about herself, her symptoms had not changed in any way, and she felt that she had not made any fundamental changes in herself. She was astonished, in fact, that she had stayed in analysis with him for so long, since she had not achieved any meaningful analytic gains. Despite her pain, sadness, anger, and intense disappointment over what she considered an unsuccessful, long first analysis, she expressed a great deal of thinly veiled excitement when she spoke of her first analyst. She began her second analysis with clear allusions to hurt and puzzled disbelief that he had left her without having provided the love, adoration, baby, and penis she somehow had excitedly felt he had promised her if only she were an obedient, hardworking, pleasing analysand. Her first analysis, she indicated, had centered on the themes of penis envy, envy of her brother who was favored by her father, and her reactions to having grown up with an exciting, unpredictable, irascible father who had alternated between being physically and emotionally overstimulating (libidinally as well as aggressively) and being remarkably disappointing, frustrating, and infuriating. He also had presented her with a model of intermittent dishonesty and exploitation in his business practices.

Analysis of the residual transference to the first analyst, which, although quite ambivalent, appeared to center on a longing for him as a well-meaning, exciting doctor who helped her by performing painful operations on her (a recurrent dream representation of him), gradually became intertwined in the second analysis with a slowly evolving but then persistent theme that preoccupied her frequently. She became agitated and anxious when her husband requested that she change an analytic appointment to attend a function with him to which he very much wanted her to go and which she herself would have enjoyed attending. When she summoned up the courage to speak with me about the possibility of changing the appointment, she was astonished that I responded by granting her request. Her first analyst had impressed upon her the importance of adhering to the schedule of their appointments and had refused to make a change the few times she had requested it early in her analysis.

As the first winter approached since the beginning of her second analysis, she wondered repeatedly whether she would be charged for sessions she might miss when severe winter weather might prevent her from driving to my home/office. Her first analyst, whose office was also in his home, had "rigidly" charged her for every missed session, even when heavy snowfalls or ice storms had made the roads virtually impassable. She literally had risked life and limb to drive to his office on occasions when prudence clearly had dictated that she stay off the streets. She finally had refused to pay for a session that she missed on a day when the roads were absolutely closed to all vehicles. She was surprised that may policy was to hold her responsible for missed sessions in general, but not to hold her financially liable on occasions when weather conditions were such that no one could be expected to drive to my office.

She expressed surprise, in fact, that my policy, which I described to her when we started our work together, was to make reasonable appointment changes when possible and to free her from financial responsibility when I could make alternative use of canceled time, although it was in her interest to miss as few sessions as possible. Her first analyst had never made an effort to reschedule or to make other use of the sessions she had (infrequently) missed. He always had charged her for them, explaining that it was in her interest to be held strictly accountable for the arrangements upon which they had agreed and to analyze her feelings about his charging her for the missed sessions. She also spoke about other differences in the way he and I seemed to work. She always had bridled at his opening the waiting room door, turning on his heels, and "marching" back to the consulting room, leaving her to follow him and to close the doors behind her along the way. I let her close the waiting room door behind her, but I held the door open for her and *followed her* into the consulting room. I raised no objection to her opening my morning newspaper and reading it, while he had objected to her looking through the books and records in the den that also had served as his waiting room. She was surprised when I questioned her fearful, apologetic tone as she spoke of something she had read in *The New York Times* about feminist psychologists who had expressed some new ideas about female development that were at variance with "classical" psychoanalytic theory. Her former analyst had instructed her not to read psychoanalytic literature, lest she use what she had read as an intellectual resistance to searching within herself. They had spoken about her resistances a good deal; although she felt that her analyst sincerely wanted her to make progress, she always felt guilty about "resisting" and always felt somehow that he wanted her to overcome her resistances so that she would do a better job and be a more satisfactory patient for him. While she felt that I was incisive, hard-headed, and took pride in my work, she had a somewhat different feeling about my aims and purposes. She felt that I was there as her assistant, to help her carry out whatever *she* wanted to accomplish, whereas with her former analyst she always had felt that she had to carry out the tasks *he* expected of her.

As we were exploring these matters, she associated them with her childhood fear of her father's explosive temper and her anger at him for repeatedly frustrating and controlling her by never being on time for her. She recalled many incidents of falling and ending up with splinters in her buttocks. These memories led her first to recall of the repeated enemas her mother had given her and then to other recollections: her mother holding her down, kicking and screaming, while the doctor gave her a penicillin shot in her behind; her father spanking her on her bare bottom; her mother terrifying her with stories of spiders coming out of the faucets as she ran her bath water; her father holding her nose so that she would have to open her mouth and let her mother put food into it, etc. The last few items, she indicated, she either never had shared with her first analyst or had mentioned tangentially on a single occasion, after which she had never returned to them.

At one point in this phase of the analysis, I commented to her that if she wanted to get at and resolve the matters within her that contributed to her problems, she would have to be willing to feel uncomfortable along the way. "You make it sound like an enema," was her reply. The realization that I had indeed permitted myself to be seduced into a countertransferential identification with her at times intrusive and assaultive parents helped me both to return to my stance as "the observing, evaluating, analyzing outsider" (Reich, 1966, p. 347) and to understand better what had happened during my patient's first analysis. It seemed evident that her former analyst had succumbed to the invitation to engage in a covert, permanent transference-countertransference interaction with her. They talked about the right things, but on an emotional level they carried out an ongoing sadomasochistic interaction. This was probably well rationalized by the analyst as adherence to "classical" psychoanalytic technique, but he seems to have been satisfying her wishes for neurotic gratification on a regressed sadistic-anal level, rather than empathically perceiving the meaning of what was taking place and analyzing it. In the second analysis, when the countertransference tendencies the patient sought to elicit could be restricted to a signal level that permitted them to be recognized, understood, and overcome, the transference resistances could be analyzed and the psychoanalytic process could lead the patient into a transference neurosis that could be analyzed and resolved.

Psychoanalysis can aptly be characterized as a venture in which the patient goes to a doctor to be cured of a distressing illness and then fights tooth and nail against being cured. In the course of this, the patient utilizes every opportunity and every tool to defeat the doctor's curative intent. This includes (perhaps especially so) making use of the doctor's very techniques and approaches. A number of years ago, I heard Peter Neubauer say that "it is a parent's solemn responsibility to set rules and to enforce them, and it is a child's solemn responsibility to break them;

development takes place in defiance, not in compliance." The analytic corollary of this is that it is a psychoanalyst's responsibility to provide analytic arrangements (not "rules") that promote analysis of, rather than acting out of, the analysand's unconscious neurotic conflicts. It is inevitable that the analysand will struggle against that intent and will use those very analytic arrangements in the effort. The analyst will be able to adhere to the analytic task only if he is continuously vigilant to the analysand's need to do this. He must also be alert to the patient's tendency to sound out the analyst's human weak spots in order to induce him to abandon his posture of analytic empathy in favor of subtle countertransference that will dovetail with the patient's transference wishes and unobtrusively gratify them. To expect that the analyst will always be entirely immune to this process is to misunderstand what psychoanalysis is all about.

Fortunately, the most common countertransference reactions are not of the permanent, ongoing type that posed such a problem in the case described above. They tend rather to be temporary and reversible, as exemplified in the vignette that follows.

A man in his early twenties was referred because of depression, anxiety, and masochistic trends that had so interfered with his functioning that, despite superior intelligence, he had had to withdraw from college with failing grades. Although his well-to-do father had offered him a place in the family business, he had spurned the offer and had pointedly renounced his father's affluent way of life in favor of a simple life in service to others. In keeping with this, he worked at menial, semi-rural jobs through which he supplemented the small salary his wife earned. After an extended consultation, he decided to enter analysis. Since he was adamant in his determination to pay for his treatment through savings and his own earnings rather than accepting money from his father, the analysis had to begin at a considerably reduced fee.

He entered a local college and eventually graduated with high honors. He took a series of jobs that more appropriately suited his talents, did very well in them, and advanced rapidly each time. When he felt that he had proved himself on his own, he returned to the family business, although not without trepidation. There, he took on increasing responsibility and contributed in a significant way to the company's rapid growth.

Analysis of his preoedipal and positive and negative oedipal conflicts enabled him to increasingly overcome the passive-dependent and passive-aggressive attitudes that had been inhibiting him from assertively pursuing his personal goals. His wife gave up her job. They bought a house (despite his father's strong objections) and started a family. He gradually recognized that he had adopted a passive-feminine, outwardly submissive but actually provocative, passive-aggressive, ambivalent attachment to his father in order to ward off his anxieties and accomplish certain neurotic aims. He worked hard to analyze this so that he might overcome it.

By the time the patient entered his sixth year of analysis, he had become a respected, self-respecting, outwardly successful young man. He liked the results of the redecoration my office had just undergone, but found himself tense and anxious as he worried about what it had cost me, and he was concerned that the redecoration must have interfered with my August vacation. In association, he thought of his envy of his parents for lavishly redecorating their home. He reported that his competitive anxieties had grown more intense, and he puzzled over his conflicted attitudes toward money. He was plagued with thoughts of being attacked, robbed of all he had, and left to starve. With embarrassment, he confessed to thinking, despite all his previous egalitarian assertions to the contrary, that a man is measured by the amount of money he has and makes. He worried about the stock market and thought about the invitation he once had extended to me to join him in buying stock in a company he knew about through his work. I had refrained from doing so, of course, in the knowledge that it could only have led to significant problems in the analysis whether I made or lost money in the venture. The stock had gone on to be the leading gainer on the New York Stock Exchange for that year, and my patient made enough money to buy two horses and to cover the costs of their keep for several years to come. He now reflected on his reasons for having given me the stock tip and concluded that he had wanted us to be "in the same bed" together, either making money together (although he was afraid that I might make more than he) or sharing the pain of loss together.

When his sister's stormy marriage finally dissolved and she entered the family business, he reacted with a series of dreams and fantasies either of being pursued and devoured or of being a predator chasing and devouring his prey. He wrestled with thinly disguised, murderous fantasies toward his father and siblings, aimed at eliminating the rivals who prevented him from being "king of the hill," only to retreat from them to bitter envy of his sister for being "kept" and lovingly provided for by his father without working for what she got. He was outraged that she actually put in very little work for the enviable salary she received.

In the midst of all this, he let me know that he had become bold enough to set plans in motion to buy a new house that undoubtedly was a good deal more expensive than mine. He was obtaining this house for himself at the very same age—in fact, a year earlier—at which his father had bought his own "big house." He gradually permitted me to discover the full range of details connected with his purchase. He did this with a subtle talent (that I had had no inkling he possessed) for deftly building the effect via small, understated, and therefore dramatically incisive, well-timed increments. He not only had raised his income far beyond the minimal subsistence level at which it had been when he first came to me for treatment; he was now so successful in the business I had helped him enter and build that he was making much more money that I was, with every expectation of making a great deal more in years to come. The house he was buying at an excellent price (which was five times more than I had paid for mine) and at an excellent mortgage rate stood on the top of a mountain on several lush acres, with a swimming pool, a tennis court, and a barn for his horses. He told me little stories about the wildlife and the bird feeders he installed, since he believed (correctly) that I loved such things and he wanted to "share his pleasure" with me. He toyed excitedly with the idea of bringing me a striking aerial photograph of his house and had repeated fantasies of inviting me to share his enjoyment of his wonderful new house and to play tennis with him on his new tennis court. The last reminded him of previous fantasies of playing tennis with me, which had turned out to be quite ambivalent, and he wondered if he didn't also want to beat me. He was able to see that alongside his gratitude toward me for helping him obtain so many enjoyable things was also the transference wish to outdo and humiliate me as he had wanted to do to his father all the time he was growing up. He expected me to react, he realized, like a fire-breathing dragon, the way his father always seemed to react to any forward step he dared to take.

He became aware that behind his wishes to share his good fortune with me and even to "feed" and take care of me was the wish to get rid of me so that he could have the money he paid me to use toward the house and land he was buying. He reacted by pulling back cautiously. When his fear of getting close to me was called to his attention, he expressed the fantasy that if he let himself get too close to me, he would kill me. He associated his childhood wishes to get rid of his father and siblings in order to have everything—money, power, and his mother—to himself. A fantasy of murdering his father terrified him. He could not imagine how anyone could get close without envy, jealousy, and fighting. He feared becoming ruthless, vicious, and rapacious like his father, though he began to wonder to what extent he had projected his own tendencies into his perceptions of his parents. He became increasingly teasing with me by continually hinting at being on the verge of sharing important, exciting things that never quite materialized. He would hint at wonderful money-making opportunities he could tell me about but never did and would sporadically mention that it probably was in order to consider raising the fee he paid me, only to quickly drop the idea and change the subject each time.

As I sat and listened to all this, I at first found it fascinating and felt pleased with all the signs of analytic progress and with the productive way my patient was working and we were working together. Gradually, however, I found myself growing irritable, impatient with the "repetitiveness" of the working through process I was observing, and tired of the "slow pace" into which my patient had settled after his initial flurry of rapidly productive hard work. I found it increasingly difficult to get up for our very early morning sessions and noticed that I was beginning, for one seemingly plausible reason or another, to keep him waiting for a few minutes before we started.

It did not take a great deal of self-scrutiny for me to realize that I resented my patient's teasing me by dangling offers to reward me for my labors, which indeed had been of enormous assistance to him, but then pulling back short of fulfilling them. He had been teasing me by accelerating his progress toward a good analytic result and by hinting at using some of the greatly expanded income I had helped him obtain, via an analysis that had proceeded for a long time at a low fee, to pay me more money, only to put the brakes on each time I became interested.

I thought of my own childhood, with its extremely modest financial circumstances, and of all the years of near poverty and accumulating debts as I went through college, medical school, psychiatric residency, and psychoanalytic training. And I thought about having treated this wealthy young man at a reduced fee because he had preferred not to avail himself of the plentiful funds that always had been there for him. But I was far from starving, I thought. I was not rich, but I was earning a good income. And although the fee had been low for a long time, it was quite acceptable now, though a little below my current minimal fee. I had not made all the money I would have made had I followed up on that stock tip, but after all, I knew about the rigors involved in being a psychoanalyst when I chose the profession, and I loved doing psychoanalytic work. Anyway, I was not interested in owning horses or even in riding them. Still, it was ironic that I had agreed to reduce my fee considerably for a long period of time to help someone overcome an inhibition against accepting from *his father* what I always had wished I had had an opportunity to receive from mine.

My thoughts led from here to a number of details involving my actual and fantasied relationship with my father, in the present as well as in the past. As a result of these self-analytic conversations with myself, which stretched over a number of weeks (and then, intermittently, over several more months), I realized that much more was involved than money and the provision of material things. My inability to deal quickly and easily with certain aspects of my emotional involvement with my father, which had been stirred by the analysis I was conducting, had been blocking me from sustaining the consistent, empathic, insightful attention to my patient's communications, of which I had been capable until then. It became clear to me that my patient's tantalizing provocations represented a seductive invitation

380

for me to act out a negative oedipal fantasy with him by attacking him "from behind."

This was clearly discernible in the communications that were emanating from the analysand. For example, after several weeks of expressing obsessive fears of getting mud on my new couch, he finally managed to splatter it with mud. I interpreted this as a warning to me that he could play dirty. He admitted at first only to wanting to "make his mark" and projected his competitive, murderous rage onto me by perceiving me as a "butcher": I had replaced my benign desk with a "butcher block" table along the wall. He accused me the next day of eliminating the stains he had left on the couch in order to "obliterate his individuality." He was wheezing and coughing as our next session began. He said that he wished I could "surgically remove the organs" that made trouble for him. "I want you to make me a eunuch … masculine ambitions are dangerous." He reported that he coveted the twenty acres of beautiful land available behind his new house and had said to his wife, "If my father died and I had his inheritance, I could buy all of this." He recognized that this had not been his adult self speaking, but had been a residuum of something he had felt "way back" when, as a little boy, he had wanted his father out of the way so that he could "take over his business and his wife, control the babies, everything!" He went on: "He was an ogre. I was afraid of him, afraid if he knew what I thought and felt … he'd kill me. He was power hungry and didn't want to share or make concessions. It's better to surgically remove what gets you into trouble. Hmmmm! The concession I have to make here is to share everything with you. It makes me mad. I don't want to share with you! I want it all! Sharing is giving away, ending up with less." He contemplated his rage at his father and his wish "to be the young Turk, the tough one, instead of the turkey my father wanted to pluck!" As I noted before he left, his wheezing had disappeared in the course of his emotional outburst.

He sold his old house (at a considerable profit) and closed on the new one, which cost him the same amount that his father's house was valued at for tax purposes. He paid me promptly, as usual, and thought about paying me "month after month after month." "Protection money," I said. He vociferously agreed. He was terrified that his inclination to be ruthless and destructive would put him and others in danger, and he expressed a wish for me to keep him a "castrated, safe, controlled eunuch." He expressed fear of his envy of his father, whom as a boy he had perceived as a cruel, tough lord and master over his mother and over everyone else. He was afraid of his voracious wish to have "unlimited power and all that goes with it." He stated, "I'm afraid that buying that estate is setting in motion the vicious pursuit of the realization of all my dangerous fantasies!"

He continued to analyze and work through his oedipal conflicts, in the course of which he excitedly but anxiously perceived himself as moving toward symbolically "castrating" his father by taking over the business and drawing more money than he did (as his father had actually done with his own father), with fear of retaliation. He became excited when he saw a television show about whales and discovered that, so very different from humans, two males court one female and then it doesn't seem to matter to them which one impregnates her. He ruminated unhappily about being (a bit) overweight and made a parapraxis in which he meant to say that killer whales pose a danger to whales but instead said that they were dangerous to humans. He became confused, thinking that he may have underpaid me the previous month, to which he associated having gone from paying me a reduced fee for a long time because his income had been so small to reaching a point, with my help, at which he earned more than I did and expected to earn more and more. He anxiously mentioned the possibility of raising the fee he paid me, but quickly recanted. He expressed highly conflicted attitudes, ranging from wanting to provide for and take care of me, with affection and gratitude for my having helped him become a much happier person, to wanting to outdo and humiliate me and leave me to starve. He was as fearful of exposing tender, affectionate feelings toward me as he was of revealing fantasies of robbing and killing me.

He realized that he fantasied having obtained what he had by "stealing" from me. He was flourishing as the result of an analysis that had begun with a low fee and in which he had tried to get results passively, as gifts, rather than working for them. He expressed gratitude to me for "standing firm" and "patiently" waiting for *him* to obtain results from the analysis through his own efforts. "I'm no longer inhibited and noncompetitive," he said. "I've gotten balls, masculinity, from you. Or did I have them all the time? I watched you and tried to find out how *you* do things, and be like you. But you're smarter than I am. You wouldn't show me, and you wouldn't fight with me. You decided you'd rather wait ten years if necessary for *me* to find it in myself. I always used to fake it. I never believed I had the balls. I always thought I had to get them or imitate someone who did. I didn't really get my balls from you. I had them all the time. But I was afraid someone would take them from me, the way I wanted to take them from everyone who looked like a big man with big balls... I don't *need* to sulk and act like a little boy—which always enraged my father—and I can use my balls with a woman. You're not jumping and screaming and angry. And I bet you don't feel I've taken anything away from you! And don't think I haven't wanted to! I wanted your balls! But I don't need your balls. Where would I be if I had *your* balls? Back where I was ten years ago: hiding my balls and wanting to get yours so I wouldn't lose my own. I'm nervous ... I'm a bit scared."

After the patient closed on his new house, he became more and more aggressive and assertive in his daily life. But he still suffered from anxiety lest he become a "destructive monster," a "prick," like his image of his father. And he still envied his "masochistic" sister for being female, having a baby, and being "kept" by his father. He made effective use of free association, which permitted him to gain insight into his envy of women: their breasts, an enviable source of "supply," and their mouthlike vaginas give them the means, he felt, to get loved and to be given sexual pleasure and babies. He came to see that in a childish way he wanted to have "it all, to have what father gets and what mother gets, to be male and female both. I couldn't compete with my father as a boy, but I couldn't hold a candle to my mother!" To candle, he associated flame, passion, and penis. If he couldn't have his mother one way (sexually, as a man), he realized, he would have her another way (identify with her as a woman, an identification modeled in part on the observation that his father dominated her as well as the children). He recalled my periodically confronting him about his insistence upon feeling miserable and feeling that he did not have enough no matter how much he had. He said: "What am I so unhappy about? That I can't have a baby? That I can't measure up to my mother? To my father? That I can't be a woman! So absurd!"

In the weeks that followed, this theme was worked through intensively, mainly within the setting of the transference. He gradually came to see that as frightening to him as it was to think of violent, bloody battles between us, it was just as frightening to find that he wanted me to love and protect him. He recalled that as a boy he had furtively stolen money from his father's pocket. He had done this not only out of competition and anger but also as a derivative of his wish for his father's love. He felt that he was repeating this by paying me less than he could. But he avoided any discussion of increasing the fee. It gradually became clear, via dreams and other forms of expression, that he was afraid I would not simply ask for more money, but would "gouge" him and "take away everything." I noted his dangling the money before me tantalizingly, *inviting* me to attack him and take it away. "It is a fear and also a wish," he replied. His next thought was that he had heard about a man who had gone into his son's room to investigate a noise, only to have his son shoot him in the belief that he was a burglar. When I connected this with his provoking me to go after him for his money, he recalled his resentment of his father's intrusions into his bedroom when he had been growing up and his repeated fantasy of blowing his father's head off with a shotgun.

At this point in the analysis the patient began to withhold not only money but his thoughts as well. His free associations dried up and were replaced by a dreary, repetitive, staccato recital of complaints about the slow progress of his treatment. He wheezed a bit as he related his difficulty in speaking freely to the fear that what he shared with me was lost to him. He challenged me to come after him and "dig" the thoughts and feelings out of him.

He continued to subtly encourage me to lose my patience and demand more money from him. He didn't like to see me incurring the expense of repairing the sidewalk in front of my office, for example. The money he gave me should go for food only and nothing more, he said. He deftly contrasted this with his own ambitions. In business, he said guiltily, he presented himself as a plodding, soft-spoken, scrupulously fair and honest man who impressed everyone with what a good loser he could be as he trudged along unaggressively, yet he "somehow" landed most of the lucrative contracts he pursued in competition with rival companies. He was on the brink, in fact, of obtaining exclusive rights to a product that could give him an edge over his competitors, which would cut them out of the market altogether. And this was in a branch of the business that he had just developed into something very profitable, much to his father's surprise.

He connected all this with his feelings about the analytic fee. He probably should pay me more, he said, but he wasn't about to offer it himself. He couldn't understand why I didn't insist on a fee increase, though he expected that he would be very angry if I did. He fantasied my attacking him, "beating the shit out of him," and "dumping him, bleeding, on the doorstep," although somehow he would end up the victor rather than the vanquished. He was not sure how, but he felt this was connected in some way with his childhood wish to have his mother to himself. I called attention to his allusion to the idea of provoking me into raping him anally and making him bleed like a menstruating woman; although outwardly he was picturing himself as being treated like a woman, his plan was to come out of it a masculine winner rather than a loser. In subsequent sessions, he confirmed this, via multiple corroboratory fantasies and lines of thought, and he struggled to understand it.

He pondered over his conflicted attitudes about paying me, in the course of which I called attention not only to his wish for me to castrate him and take everything away from him but also to his wish to be freed of his neurotic anxieties "at no cost," i.e., without having to give up the infantile strivings that underlay them. Mindful of what he had teasingly attempted to provoke me to do, I interpreted his behavior with me in terms of the attempt to buy me off; he wished to get me to accept money from him in lieu of analytic work through which he would lose not only his neurotic anxieties and inhibitions but his neurotic sources of infantile gratification as well. This led to very fruitful work, in which we came to understand the transference-countertransference transactions in terms of his wish to act out exciting but terrifying primal scene fantasies (with both positive and negative

386

oedipal identifications) with me instead of analyzing them. It was only after we had accomplished this, nearly a year after he first mentioned the idea of a larger fee in accordance with his greatly improved financial circumstances, that we finally increased the fee. Had I been unable to recognize the countertransference traps into which I had been so cleverly led and had permitted myself to press him quickly for a fee increase rather than holding firm to the analytic goal of working with him first to understand what was involved, we would have acted out his neurotic conflicts together instead of analyzing them.

CONCLUSION

I have attempted to explicate the impression that countertransference is an inevitable feature of every psychoanalysis. I see it as inevitable because of the very nature of the psychoanalytic process and because of the impossibility of any analyst's gaining so thorough an understanding of and control over his own unconscious inclinations from his training analysis that he will be completely impervious to the skillful efforts of his analysands to draw him into acting out their neurotic conflicts with them rather than analyzing them. Two clinical examples have been presented. In both, the very arrangements and "rules" of analysis were implicated in the transition from understanding to enacting the unconscious inclinations.

Annie Reich (1951), (1960), (1966) addressed herself cogently to this aspect of psychoanalysis. As she pointed out, countertransference always represents an interference with analytic progress, just as the analysand's transference always represents a resistance to it. The analyst's ability to recognize, analyze, and learn from it, so that he can return to analytic empathy and cognitive understanding, is as necessary as is analysis of the patient's transference to the analyst of his neurotic inclinations. A psychoanalyst needs to be vigilant to the emergence of countertransference reactions so that he can become aware of them, without shame and without feelings of inadequacy or failure. He can then employ self-analysis (or a period of reanalysis with another analyst if necessary) to understand and overcome them. As Annie Reich put it at the end of her last paper (1966) on the subject, "The possibility of gliding from a controlled, aim-directed use of one's unconscious into being run by it, is always there. Who is so free of guilt that he may throw the first stone?" (p. 360).

The importance of self-analysis in the work of the psychoanalyst has been given increasing recognition (e.g., Baum, 1977)[and in Panel, 1974]; (Beiser, 1984);(Calder, 1980); (Fleming, 1971); (Gardner, 1983). It is only one avenue, however, of several that are available to help psychoanalysts remain alert to their countertransference inclinations so that they can maintain control over them. Another is an ongoing communication with their analytic colleagues, who also are struggling with this difficult dimension of psychoanalytic work, a communication that is afforded by involving themselves in study groups and by teaching, writing scientific papers, and participating in panels such as this one.

REFERENCES

BAUM, O.E. (1977). Countertransference and the vicissitudes in an analyst's development. *Psychoanal. Rev.* 64 539–550.

BEISER, H.R. (1984).. An example of self-analysis. J. Am. Psychoanal. Assoc. 32:3–12.

BERES, D. & ARLOW, J.A. (1974). Fantasy and identification in empathy. *Psychoanal. Q.* 43:26–50.

CALDER, K.T. (1980). An analyst's self-analysis. J. Am. Psychoanal. Assoc. 28:5–20.

CALEF, V. & WEINSHEL, E M. (1983). A note on consummation and termination. J. Am. Psychoanal. Assoc. 31:643–650.

FLEMING, J. (1971). Freud's concept of self-analysis. In *Currents in Psychoanalysis ed.* I. M. Marcus. New York: Int. Univ. Press, pp. 14–47.

FLIESS, R. (1942). The metapsychology of the analyst. *Psychoanal. Q.* 11:211–227.

FREUD, A. (1954). Problems of technique in adult analysis In *The Writings of Anna Freud Vol. 4 Indications for Child Analysis and Other Papers, 1945–1956,.* New York: Int. Univ. Press, 1968 pp. 377–406.

FREUD, S. (1887–1902). *The Origins of Psycho-Analysis. Letters to Wilhelm Fliess, Drafts and Notes*: 1887–1902. New York: Basic Books, 1954.

———— (1900). The interpretation of dreams. *Standard Edition* 4/5.

———— (1910). The future prospects of psycho-analytic therapy. *Standard Edition.* 11.

———— (1912). Recommendations to physicians practising psycho-analysis *Standard Edition.* 12.

———— (1937). Analysis terminable and interminable *Standard Edition.* 23.

GARDNER, M.R. (1983). Self Inquiry Boston/Toronto: Little, Brown & Co.

JACOBS, T.J. (1983). The analyst and the patient's object world: notes on an aspect of countertransference. J. Am. Psychoanal. Assoc. 31:619–642.

PANEL (1974). The analyst's emotional life during work.. R. Aaron, Reporter J. Am. Psychoanal. Assoc. 22:160–169.

REICH, A. (1951). On counter-transference. *Int. J. Psychoanal.* 32:25–31.

———— 1960). Further remarks on counter-transference. *Int. J. Psychoanal.* 41:389–395,

———— A. (1966). Empathy and countertransference. In *Annie Reich: Psychoanalytic Contributions* New York: Int. Univ. Press, 1973 pp. 344–360.

CHAPTER 18

CLINICAL MATERIAL

[(1987). Clinical Material. In: *How Theory Shapes Technique: Perspectives on a Clinical Study.* Edited by Sidney E. Pulver, with Philip J. Escoll & Newell Fischer. *Psychoanal. Inquiry,* 147–166.]

Miss K., 25 years old, was referred for analysis by a psychiatrist with whom she had been in psychotherapy in college in another location. She showed sexual and social inhibitions, masochistic tendencies, and chronic, neurotic depression. Throughout her childhood and adolescence, she indicated, she had been unhappy, restricted in her self-expression, and a homebody who clung to her family. She had always felt unappreciated and mistreated, both at home and outside of it. The details which she presented amounted to a litany of complaints and grudges over injuries and slights she could neither forget nor forgive. Her parents had gone away together on frequent business trips each year during her childhood, including her birthday, which still infuriated her. Her father and older brother always had had a special, intellectual relationship with one another, centering largely on word games and word play, from which she had been excluded, since she was too young to keep up with them. She had always considered herself "dumb," even though she had been an excellent student in elementary school.

Her father was an emotionally restrained man with a quiet but quick temper. He had a way of explaining things unclearly but was impatient with her and intolerant when she failed to understand him. She had developed a kind of pseudostupidity with him so that she found herself incapable of answering even his simplest questions and ended up in tears. She had looked up to and loved her father, with whom she had subjected herself to repeated disappointments and pain. She described her parents as angry people who compensated for resentments, insecurities, and low self-esteem, stemming from unhappy childhoods, by derogating and disparaging other people, whom they perceived as their inferiors. Miss K. described her older brother as a pampered, favored child who in her parents' eyes could do no wrong. He was condescending and disparaging with her, when he paid her any attention at all. Miss K. had always loved, revered, and hated her older brother.

She always had clung to her mother while complaining bitterly about her favoritism toward her older brother. She repeatedly expressed hurt and disappointment at her mother's dependence upon her father and her failure to appreciate herself as a woman.

Short in stature until a growth spurt in mid-adolescence, and one of the youngest in her class, she always had been quiet and painfully shy. She was an unhappy, brooding, angry child who felt lonely and different from her peers. She had once plucked up enough courage to approach a popular boy, but he rejected her and she never got over it. In adolescence she had been pursued by a kind, gentle, ambitious young man, who eventually asked her to marry him. The vehemence with which she rejected his proposal astonished her and hurt him to the quick. At college and thereafter, she recoiled from young men's advances.

The analysis at first proceeded in a slow but encouraging manner. She worked at exploring her feelings, attitudes, relationships, dreams, and daydreams, past as well as present. She showed an apparent capacity for workable, analytic transference and for analyzing the resistances that inevitably arose. She greatly expanded her access to the unconscious depths of her psyche. She became less masochistic and self-defeating in her everyday life, more socially active, and more self-respecting, with improved self-esteem. She moved out of her parents' home into an apartment of her own. She went on a diet, began to dress more attractively, and became involved with a man who appeared to be very interested in her.

Several years into the analysis, however, her father's health deteriorated dangerously and her older brother married. Her progress not only came to a halt; she shifted into reverse. She backed away from men, put back the weight she had taken off, found herself "forced" by circumstances to enter the family business, found herself unable to meet suitable men, and settled into what began to look like an interminable analysis in which she would intellectually explore and understand her conflicts, but would make no real changes in herself or in her way of life. A transference neurosis appeared to develop, in which she expected me, as her analyst, to serve as a quasi-parental, idealized, yet perennially disappointing love object who would care for, protect, and excite her at a controlled, safe distance for the rest of her life, rather than courageously pursuing an uncertain, unpredictable, inevitably imperfect, and therefore partially disappointing real life in the real world.

The analytic work during the year preceding the sample sessions to be provided centered around the analysis of this transference impasse. By means of painstaking analytic work, Miss K. was helped to see that she had elected to transform her analytic relationship with me into a neurotic substitute both for real life and for resolution of the defensive constellation with which she perpetuated the neurotic compromise-formations that had been impeding her from achieving a truly adult, self-expressing, reasonably satisfying life. For several months leading up to the sample sessions, she had struggled to be aware of and explore excited feelings and fantasies about me, in the course of which she remembered and grappled with exciting transference dreams of beds and bathtubs, entered the bathroom at my office for the first time ever, and tried hard to express rather than suppress her feelings during sessions. We were able to connect her transference dreams to early primal-scene experiences and baths with her brother. She had agreed, after an initial flurry of distress, that it was in her interest to complete her analysis and make a real life for herself. She had resumed dieting, had taken in someone to share her apartment (a personable young woman who was actively involved with men), and had begun both to avail herself of opportunities to meet men and to respond more freely and warmly to them than ever before. At a singles weekend, she had met an exciting, young man she liked very much. She agreed to have him travel in to spend a couple of days with her, but was humiliated when she found herself waiting for hours at the appointed spot without his ever showing up. She tried to analyze the experience, to determine whether and how she might have contributed to having been stood up.

The week that ended with the first of the sample sessions began with an account of an "intimidating" tennis lesson with a tall, strapping, handsome tennis pro. She found that she could not understand him no matter how he phrased and rephrased his instructions. She fleetingly recognized that analytic transference feelings were involved in her strong reaction to the tennis pro, in that she comes to me to "learn" about herself and for "lessons" in living. The next day, she was "mad" at me, presumably for commenting on her having come for her Monday session wearing makeup and dressed attractively. She insisted that she always wears makeup and had not dressed any differently that day than on any other day. She was so angry that she was not inclined to talk to me or work with me. Her associations led her to her anger that her roommate repeatedly is noticed and taken interest in by men, while they do not respond to her. "It's not fair," she insisted: "what's wrong with me?" She approaches men at singles dances, but they do not respond. A man meets her for a drink and never calls her again. She cannot believe that she drives them away, although she does put weight on again each time she loses some. And it is not fair that her older brother got praised by her parents for doing them a minor favor while no attention is ever given to what she does.

On Thursday, the day before the first sample session, she was feeling hurt and angry because her father had berated her for saying too much to a salesman who had called. He had never made clear exactly what she should and should not say to salesmen, but she did not protest when he berated her. She answers the phone to relieve her father of the burden of doing it, and she accepts his chastisements, however unfair, without complaint for the same reason. She lets her father intimidate her and doesn't say anything when he gives her ambiguous instructions and then berates her for not having done what he wanted her to do. She used to get tongue-tied and was not even able to answer him when he asked the simplest questions, thinking he was out to trap her. She reflected on my observation that she was extremely hurt and angry at her father for not recognizing her loving willingness to sacrifice for him, and that, in her struggle with her ambivalent feelings, she had offered her *own* self up to be hurt, erotizing the pain so that she was paradoxically excited by her father's "abuse." It was difficult for her, she said, not to reject my observations. She loved and worried about her father. He always acted strong, seemed strong, and claimed to be strong—the whole family did that—but he actually was not a strong person and leaned on her mother. She did not know what to do.

The Sample Sessions

My thoughts during the sessions are in parentheses. My verbalizations to the patient, marked by "I speak:", are also in parentheses.

Observations about the patient's affect or about background data are in brackets.

Friday

The rain woke me up early this morning. It was beating down on my air conditioner so loudly it woke me up. I looked at the clock. It was 5:30. I thought in an hour I have to get up to come here. I didn't want to come today. I've been mad at you all week. It's not that I'm mad at you. I wanted to stay away from all this stuff I think I feel here. I also got angry at R. [her roommate] yesterday. In the bathroom, she takes two towel bars and a hook. And I just have one towel bar. I didn't say anything for a long time. I finally got up the courage and told her we have to change the arrangements in the bathroom. It sounds so silly. I get so worked up over such little things. I get so angry. *She* was talking about being all worked up because someone called her for a date. She hardly listened to what I was saying. She's so self-centered. Her boyfriend came, and he was there two minutes and he asked about my cousin. She never asks about my cousin. She only thinks about herself. I thought of saying "thanks for asking" to him because I was so grateful he'd asked, but I decided not to say it. Because I'd have been calling attention to her never asking. I get so mad at her. I thought about something else in the car on the way here. I went to have my hair cut and it was to be cut at seven o'clock. But I had to wait and wait till nine o'clock. I got angrier and angrier. I told the girl when I paid (she'll get a bill from me in a few days, and it's the end of the week and she has to wait two days to see me again on Monday—like the two hrs. for the hairdresser—and in two weeks I leave for vacation, and she'll have to wait a month for me) that I was angry. I told her that I can go to someone else to get my hair cut—or I can wait for him. I don't like either alternative. I don't even know why I go there. I don't fit in. They're mostly older women. But I didn't say anything to *him*. I'm intimidated by him the way I'm intimidated by M. [the tennis pro]. I don't know why. He's not big and tall like M. He's good-looking, but he's not my type. He's married and has children (so does her father). He has their pictures up. With M., I think it has something to do with my knowing nothing about tennis and his knowing so much about it. And I couldn't understand when he was telling me what to do. "Hold it this way" and "turn that way," and I couldn't understand anything he said. It was just like with my father all my life. He thinks he gives such good directions and clear explanations, as I said yesterday, but he doesn't. I get intimidated with men. I always feel that they know they have the knowledge. They have the brains, and I'm dumb. And I always feel like I don't know anything and I can't understand and I get intimidated. It's the same thing here. I keep feeling like asking you, "What does it mean?" I always feel like you know. I feel like asking you now. I know you've told me you don't know anything until I've told it to you, but I don't feel that way. I feel you're always a step ahead of me. You *know,*s24 because you're smarter than I am and all the training and experience you have. (I speak: I don't think that's what it is. I think you feel I know because I'm a man, that as a woman you don't have the brains.) I get intimidated by men. [anxiously] Do you think I signal it to them and that drives them away? So they think, "Who wants her!" I think it started in a way when my father said to me, "Every man is going to want the same thing from you." I got so angry. Why? Why would he expect that of me? What right does he have? I heard R. and her boyfriend kissing just outside the door. She *likes* it! When my father said what he did, first I was mad at them for wanting sex eventually, and then I got mad if I thought they wanted to kiss on the first date. Then I started getting mad that they'd *ever* want to kiss. I got so *angry*. I'm such an angry person. (I speak: As you've said, you get mad to push away other feelings.) With A. [the young man she had met on a singles weekend trip, at which she had relaxed her usual guarded stiffness and had danced and smiled and joked, and who had become interested in her and arranged to come in from out of town to spend two days with her only to stand her up when she went to meet him] I told him when he said he would come down here that he could stay at my apartment. And he got all excited about it and eager to come. And then I got frightened about what I'd said to him, and I said, "Wait a minute," and I made it clear to him I meant he could sleep over at my apartment—on the couch—not with me. [with emotion] Do you think that's why he didn't show up? Did *I* chase him away? Men intimidate me. It's like with my father. It's a mixture of excitement and pain and hurt and fear. But wait a minute. It's not only men who intimidate me, I get intimidated about money. Paying and tipping intimidates me. I avoid it if I can. Until lately, when I've been thinking about it here and trying not to avoid the things I tend to avoid. When I left the hairdresser's I looked for the girl who'd shampooed my hair to give her a dollar. But I'd have avoided it if I could. If they had a can with tips in it I would've put it in there. I was too intimidated by the hairdresser who cut my hair and I was intimidated about tipping the girl who shampooed my hair. Why? [slight pause] I can't figure it out. There's no rhyme or reason. I don't understand it. (I speak: So long as you take that attitude, so long as you don't think it out and find out the rhyme and reason …) Well, *he* cut my hair. He *cut* me. But she just put her fingers into my hair. I don't understand. (I speak: He stuck scissors into your hair and she stuck her fingers into your hair. You were talking before that about avoiding sexual excitement. Scissors and fingers into your hair *sounds* sexual. You turn away and avoid the excitement, pain, and hurt with men, and when you turn away from men altogether and turn toward a woman you get scared all over again.) Yes. But there's something that doesn't fit. I had no problem about tipping the woman who gave me a manicure. And she massaged my fingers. And that didn't get me anxious. I like it. It's relaxing. I thought of something. I told you about it a long time ago and then I dropped it and avoided it. It's a masturbation fantasy. [Now her voice changes, becomes more hollow, tending toward a chilled monotone, drained of all emotion. She speaks this way for much of the remainder of the session, constantly pausing between words. I found her slow, start-and-stop delivery agonizing, and have tried to convey it on the page by the use of dashes to indicate her briefer pauses, reserving the word *pause*, in brackets, for the longer ones.] There's—a doctor—a mad scientist—and his nurse and—he ties me down to—do things to me. I don't know what this has to do with being intimidated by the hairdresser and feeling inhibited tipping the girl who washes my hair but not the manicurist. It makes no sense [pause] (I speak: You've blocked yourself from hearing the answer you gave: the hairdresser sticking scissors in your hair and cutting you; the young woman preparing you for the haircut; they're the mad scientist doctor and his nurse.) The fantasy had to do with—something—it had to do with getting bigger breasts. It's foolish—I feel sheepish [pause] It's so silly [pause] (I speak: There's nothing silly about it; you mobilize those feelings to push away and avoid looking into the fantasy and the feelings.) I'd try not to think the fantasy. I didn't want to dig into it. You're right. I feel sheepish to push it away. (I ask: And what happens to sheep?) They get sheared, their hair cut off. (I say: And so do "fallen women".) In old times, they did. I know about that. The hairdresser was cutting *my* hair off. Maybe it was my "crowning glory." And sheep certainly get their hair cut off. When I was in New Zealand, I saw the sheep getting sheared. There was one brown one I remember. They held it and sheared it, and piled the wool, and all that. (The emotion's gone from her voice; she's shearing the sheep to pull the wool over our eyes.) (I speak: You're getting away to avoid uncomfortable feelings.) You're right. That fantasy makes me very uncomfortable. The mad scientist would do something to give me bigger breasts. I wanted bigger breasts very much [pause]. (I speak: Notice you're interrupting yourself, stopping yourself?) I don't want to talk about it, think about it; I'm afraid you'll think I'm foolish. I had to submit to the mad scientist, like I was his slave and he was my master. When I'm intimidated by men, it's like I have to put up with anything, like I'm a slave and he's a master and it makes me angry [pause] That slave and master theme in relations between women and men gets me mad (Her voice changed again.) (I speak: Notice you switched from uncomfortable thinking about the wish for the mad scientist to give you bigger breasts to the slave and master theme?) [back to working voice] There's something about—it's not called S&M—something and bondage—in porno—people waiting to be tied up and things done to them [pause]. (I speak: I notice you keep interrupting yourself and stopping yourself.) You've told me several times that you couldn't promise that this would always be easy—I'd be uncomfortable at times—If I could be comfortable, I could talk about these things—I could look into them—and understand—but—it's—too hard—[There's tightness in my belly, and I'm getting irritated at her excruciating stopping and starting and hesitating.]—if I could find a way to do this without feeling so uncomfortable [pause] (I speak: You want me to make you do it. You're having all that trouble talking about, thinking all those thoughts about pain and hurt, S. & M., bondage, because of a wish to enact the fantasy with me rather than think and feel it out and understand it. You want *me* to be the mad scientist doctor forcing and hurting you and making changes in you.) I want you to use your knowledge and your understanding to change me. Instead of working at this myself and making changes. I want you to do it. But you say it's because I want you to be the mad scientist of my fantasy, that if you force me and hurt me it's exciting. I have to reject that. I can't agree with you on that. That would mean I don't really want to change. But I do want to change. I have to think about it. Maybe I'm undecided and that's why it's so difficult and uncomfortable. I'll have to think about it. (The thing with the tennis teacher was on the weekend; here's another weekend; in a few weeks I'll leave her not just for a weekend but for a month; absence makes the heart grow fonder; she also wants to kill me for leaving her, for not being crazy about her so I can't bear to be without her; masochistic transference; transference neurosis.)

Monday

I had an interesting weekend. I told you about that personal ad I answered from *New York Magazine*, in a whacky mood. The phone rang Friday and it was that man. He's 39 years old and has joint custody of a seven-year-old. He thought my answer to his ad was funny and he wanted to find out about the one who wrote it. It was wonderful. I didn't do anything Saturday, except take a tennis lesson, which was pretty good! It was fun. I have good hand-eye coordination, which helps. It was good for my ego. Saturday night I got up the oomph to go to a singles dance, with Linda, who was wearing an outfit I thought was whacky. A guy walked right up to her and asked her to dance. She left early. I guess she wasn't crazy about him. I got to talking to him. He was a nice guy, though not really my type. But I have a date with him Saturday night. I thought, it's been so long, I want to see what it's like again. I told him about going up to three guys and asking

401

them to dance and being refused. He said maybe they were getting even. I said, yeah, maybe, getting even for all the rejections they had gotten going up to girls. I spoke to two other guys about it too, and they said it wasn't right. They said I'm attractive and there's no reason to turn away. I asked Frank, the guy I have the date with, as a scientific experiment, why he went up to Linda first rather than to me. I thought maybe it was her whacky outfit. If so, I'd incorporate it into my routine. I didn't like his answer. He said maybe because she was closer to him, and he went up to the first one. A guy asked me to dance at one point, and I didn't like the music they were playing so I said, "Not right now." After he walked away, I thought, "Dope, why didn't you say not now but ask me again a little later." Maybe I can stop cutting them off! Be more open and responsive. That guy whose ad I answered said he was embarrassed to say he got 80 answers to his ad. I think of putting in an ad, but how do you do it without describing yourself as God's gift to the universe? Linda left with a guy who she later said is 40 years old and married. He put his arm around her as they left. The guy I took the tennis lesson from told me to relax. I'm not relaxed. All the guys I meet I react to by not being impressed. A. was the first one I got excited about. This guy Saturday night, my first reaction is he doesn't have two heads but I'm not excited, no pizazz. But I told myself, give yourself a chance. Go out with him. Maybe he's different on a date. With A., I kissed with him in the car, and I liked it. It was new. Most of the guys I meet at these dances—just have no pizazz. I'm looking for someone with something more. That's why I answered that ad in *New York Magazine*, with the note about Don Quixote. ["Stop chasing windmills and come to your Dulcinea," she had written.] I was sitting in the waiting room and thinking that I didn't do much more on the weekend. Wanted to be alone. (I'm going away in two weeks and leaving her alone.) Friday, here, I

opened up and went into something, and now I hear myself ram-
bling about the dance and nothing consequential, not about what
I opened up on Friday [pause]. (I speak: You sound undecided
about looking further, thinking and feeling further, into what
you opened up on Friday.) I'm thinking about watching—once
more—*Now Voyager* (The movie about a *doctor* rescuing her
from her mother.) I am undecided—I'm uncomfortable—uneasy—I'm thinking about the past—"what if" genre—[her voice
is restrained, suppressing emotion] I'm thinking —what if—if it
could've been different [pause] now I'm silent completely—because some emotion is beginning to come out and I'm nervous.
(I speak: And thinking of what you expressed Friday, there's also
a wish for *me* to urge you, push you, make you.) Perhaps, there's
a desire for you to push me through the tunnel, out into the light
[pause] I have to push myself—to take tennis—to go to dances—
to mix—I get into a problem that's rife in my family—what my
father calls "instant gratification"—impatient—begin to take
tennis lessons and right away want to be playing. The guy I took
a tennis lesson from said after 15 minutes I did as much as it usually takes him 45 minutes to get across. I listened and learned. I
could understand what he wanted; he's different from M. It's not
just that M. is big and hulking. In school, if I related well to the
teacher, I learned. I guess I'm saying I look to you as a teacher,
someone I'm learning from. I want you to take a more active role.
(She wants me to be her teacher—about men and sex?) Guide
me. Tell me. Talk about this and that. I guess make it easier for
me, so *I* don't have to do it, which is more difficult. I liked the
depiction of a psychiatrist by Claude Raines [in *Now Voyager*] I
liked the way he talked to troubled Bette Davis. (I ask: "What did
you like about the way he talked to her?") He said, "People have
to make decisions in life, and I'm there to say not this way but
that way." In one of the early scenes, he sees the problem about

the domineering mother and sees the ivory carving she's doing. He's soft spoken, all-knowing in a quiet way, not dominating, but giving her the time, not hurrying her. (I speak: You're undecided whether you want me to steer you, guide you back to what you were looking into in yourself on Friday but that you're uncomfortable, uneasy, nervous, thinking and feeling about, or be more patient, gentle, give you time.) You're right; I feel time is running out. I want to goad my father and make him mad. I don't want to make you into my father. [pause]. (I speak: Your idea of my "pulling it out" of you can also be part of the fantasy that you permitted to surface Friday and began to look into and were also pulled to enact with me. Mad means two things. If you can goad me and make me mad, as you did with your father, you get me to be the mad scientist doctor making you and forcing you to doing something to you that, as you put it, gives you bigger breasts, pulls bigger breasts out of you.) When I get so mad, it's a substitute, I'm beginning to see, for being sexually excited. I get mad a lot as part of it. Maybe that's what attracted Frank to Linda first. She has bigger boobs. She wears tops that accentuate it. It's what attracts men. If you don't have them, you don't have what it takes to attract them. It gets me mad. I watched some of the women on the dance floor who were bottom heavy. They moved, for want of a better term, so sexy. Why can't I move like that? Because I'm so uptight I can't move like that. I think of my friend X., who's married, and flat as a board, and of friend Y, who has a live-in boyfriend, and she's flat as a board. So it's not all that. But there's my roommate and Linda who I see guys attracted to. They are so more well endowed than I. I don't have the knockers. I'm so mad and jealous. I can't help thinking what could men see in me. I wish I could get over it. And stop feeling like that. But maybe it's something I cling to, something I hold on to. (I speak: Maybe we can find out *why* you cling to it.) (So *Now Voyager* has something to do with a daddy doctor taking her away, carrying her off with him, leaving mother behind. So I'm supposed to cure her by being her idealized, loving father, leaving my wife/her mother, and marrying her; the mad-scientist doctor giving her bigger breasts is really giving her her mother's breasts? Finding her more attractive than her mother? She repeatedly brings up *Now Voyager*. Is that the script for the analysis? For her secret, unconscious desire here?)

Tuesday

I know I have to go back to where I was yesterday. But it's so hard to take the plunge. I began thinking about other things: everyday occurrences that don't mean anything. There's something, a fetish; we've talked about my being overweight as taking out on my body my anger at my body, though if I were enormously angry, I'd be a blimp. But I keep myself unattractive. I'm angry at my mother for lying to me, saying when I got my period this would happen and that would happen. I used to make jokes, for instance, that I'm flatchested because when my mother was driving she used to fling out her arm when she stopped. (I speak: The joke implies that your mother didn't want you to be attractive.) But my mother used to tell me I was pretty, cute face, and everything. But I never believed her. Maybe because she wasn't the one I wanted to hear it from. I wanted to hear it from myself. I'd look at myself in the mirror and see ugly glasses, always felt unattractive. Wanted to be taller, have bigger breasts, be a model, but not tall enough. Wanted to be a model or a stewardess, glamorous; heard that they're just a glorified waitress, but heard stories of their meeting men, passengers they traveled with and marrying them, but no, not good enough, and said wanted to be a nurse but told (by mother) that too much science, and accepted it instead of saying "so there's science." I wanted to be more attractive, but did nothing to have it. Remember going shopping for a culotte dress and excited because this jumper I bought was on the cover of *Seventeen* magazine. I'm sure I took the magazine to school with me to show everyone: "Look, the dress I'm wearing is on the cover." Next best thing to being on the cover myself. Fame by association. Through girl scouts, I got my name in the local newspaper. It was exciting. I lived vicariously through my fantasies. I was excited and very angry: dirty tricks against me. I got my period very early and was excited: thought there would be changes. There were a few; got a shape, hips, though more than I wanted. I think I thought if I ate more it would land on my chest (She's back to the mad doctor fantasy), but it went south, to my derrière. My mother used to say things to make me feel better, because she knew how bad I felt. She said she was flat-chested till after she had children. She meant well, but it only fed false hopes. I felt men would be attracted to women with bigger breasts than I had. (I speak: Like your mother.) Like my mother, but she by no means has big breasts, though more than me. I found it embarrassing to go shopping for bathing suits. They had a preshaped cup and I couldn't fill it out. It was embarrassing and I hated it. I felt a lot of anger, and it was easier to blame my lack of success with men on what I looked like. (She's facing her defenses. She can do something for herself.) I felt somehow persecuted. I was at that awkward, gangly age where I was neither here nor there. Short hair. Once when I worked at Z I had a haircut (Haircut again. She's working here.) and makeup session, and next day no one recognized me at work. I began to feel better. I don't know what specifically about me changed. [pause] I had such a negative attitude about myself as a whole. I thought I was stupid, unattractive, and those were the days I was thin. I wasn't popular. I was shy. (Reconstructing her adolescence is important, but she's getting away from what's here with me.) I was not terribly together.

I think back to kids I wanted to fit in with and be popular, but I just didn't fit in. (I speak: And you wanted to be different.) I wanted to be queen of the hill. I wanted there to be something so special about me I'd be famous, a famous actress or singer, not blah as I perceived about me. If you were a cheerleader in high school or in the marching band, you were automatically popular. But I didn't try out for anything. (And she doesn't try, actively, now; afraid of rebuff, failure.) In junior high I tried out for cheerleader, but was a dismal failure, though I have to give myself credit for going all through the classes and the tryouts for cheerleader [and I need to], given my hesitance to get up before people. I was a nervous wreck, but I did it. I wanted desperately to be the center of attention. But I didn't do anything about it, like the class clown who got attention making people laugh. I just had secret wishes and would go home and have heavy sessions of wailing self-pity, telling my mother I was unpopular, no one liked me. I felt I didn't belong and I wanted desperately to belong. I was talking to someone recently at those dances I've been going to. I feel I don't belong. It sounds snobbish, but I'm too sophisticated, too attractive even, and it scares them off. (She also mean me?) Maybe that's what I'm after, to keep people away, though I said I want to be popular. Do I want the satisfaction of being by myself and crying? Emotional satisfaction of self-pity and unhappiness. (Narcissistic defenses) There are lingering memories of times I started to feel good about myself and then got slammed in the face for it, and it made it that much harder to try the next time. I was excited about meeting A. and then I got shot down in flames again. It's hard to try all over again. (She means me.) Either I'm a glutton for punishment and that's why I keep going back to these dances or I'm trying to change things (Where's this going? How do *I* help her? It's about how I help her!) (I speak: And you very much want me to effect changes. What you've been saying these past few days reflects poignant hopes about *my* part in changing things for you.) Maybe it's like Annie Sullivan and Helen Keller. I'm moved by stories of handicapped people overcoming their handicaps. I see myself as a handicapped person. (retreating) (I speak: Or maybe it's more like Claude Raines and Bette Davis, and the male passenger on the trip the stewardess meets and marries.) She had strong, fond feelings for the psychiatrist. He helped her turn her life around and get free. I relate to her. There she was, fat, dumpy, having a nervous breakdown, and is transformed into a sophisticated woman who begins to enjoy life instead of hiding from it. I fantasize that happening: I'm going to be transformed. (I speak: By me.) Who else? And there'd be Paul Henried waiting for her. But I wasn't satisfied with whom she ended up with. He had a baby and he returned to his wife and baby. (I speak: You weren't satisfied with whom she ended up with.) I was satisfied with whom she ended up with, but not the situation. I know what you're getting at, that I wanted her to end up with her psychiatrist, and the same with me. He had to be noble and go back to his miserable wife! Enough for her, but not for me. In the middle of the movie, it wasn't her psychiatrist who gave her courage to go on, but Paul Henried, who sent her flowers when she was trying to get the courage to leave her mother. *He* helped her. (She's retreating and covering.) (I speak: You have difficulty putting into words your feeling she should've ended up with her psychiatrist, and the same with you.) I have difficulty—there was affection between her and her psychiatrist; in the movie—she went to the hospital after her mother died and saw Paul Henried's daughter. Her psychiatrist said, "I thought you came here to have a nervous breakdown," and she replied, "I decided not to."—I liked the bantering between them (I speak: The way you'd like that kind of bantering between you and me.) I *would* like that. I'm never completely relaxed here. That's why all that with the bathroom and the door. I'm never completely relaxed here. (Her voice is tense. She's trying, but it's difficult.) (I speak: Because your feelings make you nervous.) I guess so. Maybe that's why I keep bringing up that business with A. Because there were new feelings that I let come up, that I felt uncomfortable with. Whatever part I had in botching that up had to do with my fear of my feelings. I was afraid of the feelings I felt with him and how strong they were. (I speak: And you're afraid of your feelings and how strong they are here with me.) I think so; must be so. (I speak: Including your feelings about being here with me at specified times during the week, then being alone on weekends, your feelings about not wanting me to leave you on weekends and leaving you at vacation times, as I'm doing in a couple of weeks, presumably with someone else, which feels like by-passing you and going to someone else, like when Frank went to Linda, but to stay with you instead. You don't want me to help you merely to make changes in yourself so you can summon the courage to leave your mother and her protection and find a Paul Henried. You want me to change you by demonstrating to you *personally* that you're attractive by by-passing others, preferring *you*, loving *you*. If you're Bette Davis, I'm your Claude Raines, and you want your psychiatrist to change you and make you happy *directly, personally*. But let's interrupt here.) [Looks at me smilingly as she leaves.] (I'm not happy with what I said. Too many words. Am I being too cautious? Too gentle? Taken in by the narcissistic defenses? Afraid of hurting her? I should've been more direct, more concise, especially more precise. Not careful and choosing my words carefully to not "bruise" her. Am I afraid of my sadism she's masochistically inviting? She spoke of S & M last week. She erotizes pain. Watch out. Being too careful not to give her pain means transference-countertransference, silent gratification. Let's see what happens next.)

Wednesday

No session scheduled.

Thursday

Calls in sick with an intestinal virus.

Friday (condensed):

Angry, sulky, tightlipped, and almost inaudible as she complains about having been ill; states that she had pushed to come in today lest she miss two sessions to punish me for going away and leaving her at the end of next week; speaks derisively and bitterly about hearing about others being ill with the same thing after coming down with an illness —"It's going around." (She's defending against an imagined accusation that she wasn't really ill, looking for a fight.) Relates having had to cancel a doctor's appointment because she was ill and responding to the nurse's "If only you'd let us know earlier" with a nasty "Look sister, I didn't know I was going to get sick!" (Angry she missed her doctor's appointment with me.) (I ask: How come so angry?) The nurse got me so mad, etc. (I speak: You use anger to push away other feelings?) Called in to tell father that sick and unable to work, and he just said, "OK, I'll get the mail." Know it's difficult for him for me to be out at this time, already shorthanded. So mad [Silence] I'm not talking—That guy I met at the singles dance called. He was boring. I didn't know what to say to him. I'm not talking to you. I don't know what I'm pushing away. (I speak: Maybe from what we were looking into together on Tuesday.) I don't remember. What were we talking about? [pause] About *Now Voyager*—about my looking to you to be my teacher—teach me how to act differently. [pause] (I speak: You're diluting it; you

410

were speaking about not being satisfied with my helping you change things for yourself but for *me* to change things for you.) I'm angry, jealous. Everything seemed to go right for my older brother. He seemed to have everything. Smart, had friends, and I never saw him work for it if he did. My mother would say I didn't work for things. That's just an expression. I'm angry about my life, that things come easily to other people and not to me. (I speak: So you sulk.) I've always been good at that! What was I good at when I was younger? I was good at running. (I speak: You're still running.) Yes. I'm running away. What from? [pause] My father and older brother withheld their emotions (sounded like "motions") and were constipated. (I speak: You're angry your father didn't show more interest and concern and feelings for you when you called in ill, and you're angry you haven't gotten from me what you wanted from me, and you're withholding from me what you think I want from you.) And I'm spending my whole life sulking and angry, excited and nervous and unable to deal with big, strong tennis players and bored with unexciting little accountants. My father didn't give me what I wanted from him and I got mad and reacted by taking it out on all men and turning on and turning away from all men; and then I met you and I got mad at you for not giving me what I wanted from him and want from you, and I'm taking out on you what I feel about my father and all men! You're going away and leaving me, and I'm angry and sulking and insisting on being miserable! Am I going to spend my whole life angry and sulking?

CHAPTER 19:

THE ANALYST'S RESPONSE

[From: *How Theory Shapes Technique: Perspectives on a Clinical Study,*
Edited by Sidney E. Pulver, with Philip J. Escoll and Newell Fischer.
Psychoanal. Inquiry, 277–288.]

Sydney Pulver's request that I provide material to serve as a springboard for a panel on the influence of models of the mind on clinical work seemed to afford an opportunity not only to contribute something useful to psychoanalysis but also to obtain the consultative assistance of a group of thoughtful, experienced psychoanalysts that might be helpful to me in my work. I welcomed the opportunity to present material from an ongoing analysis to four (later expanded to eight) dedicated and esteemed colleagues. I elected to present a series of hours from my work with the first patient I was to see the next day (though I had to settle for the second patient, because the first one was going through a largely silent phase in his analysis). Although my aim was to present random analytic material, I was not unaware that I would be obtaining the benefit of observations on a very difficult case, a case which I believe any psychoanalyst would find very difficult.

As I understand it and make use of it in my work, the structural model utilizes a multidimensional, multifaceted approach to human psychology that is broad enough to cover an extremely wide range of normal and pathological phenomena, yet is sufficiently specific and consistent to do so coherently and comprehensively. It emphasizes the concepts of innate libidinal and aggressive drives; heuristic division into id, ego, and superego as systematized, mental and emotional operational groupings; progressive ego development that in part is conflict-free but in very large part is conflict-derived and defensive in nature; emotional development through more or less well-defined developmental phases and subphases; and relationships with people that derive from the confluence of internal desire and external impingement.

My clinical experience, with children as well as with adults, leads me to appreciate the enormous significance of the Oedipus complex, not only in neuroses but in most other conditions as well, including psychoses. I do not, however, scant the importance of preoedipal, as well as postoedipal, development (see Silverman, 1980, 1981, 1982, 1985a, 1986b), nor do I look at clinical manifestations that are recognizable as preoedipal in their form and content as deriving solely out of regressive retreat from oedipal conflicts. I do not see, in fact, how the Oedipus complex can be understood without taking into account the pre-oedipal configurations that precede them and out of which, in part, they epigenetically arise (see Silverman, 1980, 1986a, 1986b). The Oedipus complex does not suddenly spring up out of nowhere, without connection to its emotional antecedents.

One advantage of the structural model, it seems to me, is that it is broad enough to apprehend a very wide range of psychological configurations, without necessarily requiring undue emphasis upon any one of them to the exclusion of all others. It is my impression that the ideas offered by my colleagues *highlight various dimensions* of a very complex case. No one of them, in my estimation, offers one convincing, unitary conceptualization of the analysis that overshadows all the others in importance.

I am reminded of an experience I had almost 20 years ago, when I was very interested in Piaget's observations on the successive stages of cognitive development in childhood and adolescence and replicated some of his experiments with children of different ages.

I presented a four-year-old girl with pieces of cardboard of different colors—yellow, green, and red—that I had cut into a variety of shapes—squares, circles, and triangles. There were several of each of these color and shapes, but there also was a single rectangle of a color—blue—that was not to be found among any of the shapes present in multiples. I asked the little girl to sort the various items into "families." She enjoyed the game, and at first had no difficulty carrying out my request. She did so in a fashion that is quite typical of the preoperational, transitional cognitive organization of the four-year-old. She used shifting criteria of shape and color to link and group the items, correcting herself repeatedly and using various techniques to create a manageable field, until she had sorted all but one into intersecting, overlapping "families." The single rectangle of a unique color was beyond her capacity to fit into the various sets, however, because she was not yet able to comprehend and deal with a class containing a single member. She repeatedly frowned and puzzled over it, with deep concentration and effort.

Suddenly, she looked up from her work toward a place above my left shoulder and pointed to the window behind me. "What's that?" she asked, in a surprised voice. I looked back at the window, but saw nothing remarkable. "I don't know," I replied, "What did you see?" "Oh, never mind," she replied, "I just thought I saw something." She motioned to the cardboard shapes before her, beamed, and told me that she was finished. I was puzzled at first. I knew something was wrong, but I couldn't tell what it was. Then it struck me. The rectangle was missing. "Where's the blue rectangle?" I asked. *"I hid it,"* she replied.

What reminds of this experience is that human complexity can be approached in two different ways. One can approach it in an open, explanatory, searching fashion that is informed by a preexisting model or set that, although it inevitably influences the way in which the data are organized and understood, is broadly inclusive enough and is mindful enough of the variability and multiplicity that characterizes human functioning that it is not closed and monolithic. Such an approach ideally would contain enough tolerance of uncertainty (and I very much agree with Schwaber that dogmatic adherence to a narrow, confining point of view that rigorously precludes all others is inimical to the tradition of unbiased, inquiring psychoanalytic investigation) and enough willingness to discover new things and learn from new experiences that one would be able to continually improve and refine one's skills unceasingly throughout a psychoanalytic career.

Another approach is to reduce the complexity of the field by focusing upon only a part of it while setting everything else aside. This approach permits the elaboration of a much simpler, more parsimonious, but incomplete clinical and theoretical model, for it sets aside or ignores data that do not fit easily within it. Such an approach offers a degree of uncertainty about one's point of view that is comfortable but spurious, and it precludes the possibility of learning from experience and of learning from others. What the various panelists have offered seems to me to constitute a group of partial truths in danger of being elevated to whole fictions.

While I cannot agree with everything offered by the various panelists, the vast majority of their observations and conjectures are compatible with my understanding of the case. Like most of the panelists, I find convincing evidence of positive and negative oedipal conflicts in the patient, associated with primal-scene interest and excitement, and exhibitionistic anxieties that in part bear qualities that are typical of a child in an early so-called phallic phase of development.

It is not my impression, however, that the oedipal conflicts are of primary importance in the evolution of the patient's psychopathology. My understanding of the significance of the oedipal problems approaches that of Modell and of Burland in that it is my clinical impression that preoedipal, narcissistic problems carried forward into the oedipal period made it impossible for her to engage and resolve the triadic conflicts she experienced during that developmental phase. It seems to me that she hastily retreated from them to an ambivalent, sadomasochistic, preoedipal form of ambivalently clinging to preoedipal transference objects, from whom she hopes for magical deliverance from the perpetual disappointment, pain, defeat, and disillusionment she experiences, even as she conducts her life in such a way as to evoke just the kinds of responses to her of which she bitterly complains.

I agree that the central issues in the structure of the patient's character neurosis are a profound sense of defectiveness, inadequacy, and powerlessness and an inability to establish a separate, independent sense of self that provides sufficient self-esteem and confidence to sustain a forward developmental thrust and to pursue independent pleasures, achievements, and satisfactions. There are intensely conflictual, ambivalent merger fantasies which are linked with the belief that she cannot function on her own. She dares not reveal her personal strivings, goals, aims, or ambitious lest she suffer from inevitable and intolerable rejection, disparagement, and narcissistic injury. She has great difficulty recognizing that she assiduously seeks to evoke just such reactions from people, in the interest of passive-into-active pseudomastery and justification for nursing her grievances and sadomasochistically wreaking self-inflicted revenge upon the objects with whom she has oral-incorporatively identified.

One of the prominent ways in which this is expressed in the analytic transference is that, no matter what I do and do not do, what I say and do not say, to what I direct my attention in my interventions and what I elect at the moment to ignore, she responds by feeling misunderstood, mistreated, insufficiently cared for, and inadequately taken care of. This is very wearing on the analyst, who is repeatedly drawn to the edge of departing from his analytic, interpretive stance into a confrontative, prodding one, behind which is an element of intermittent discouragement and weariness that plays into the invitation to join into a sadomasochistic, transference-countertransference enactment with her. Something of this was going on in the week's sessions I presented that was quite apparent to me, as I believe I indicated by sharing my thoughts during and after the sessions. I am indeed surprised by Gill's belief that I was not aware of this core dimension of the analytic process even, as I am grateful to him (as I am to Modell) for his useful suggestions as to tone and wording of analytic interventions. The patient does indeed want to change and is hopeful of somehow finding a way to make use of me as an analytic assistant rather than as an inevitably disappointing, idealized transference object. This is the lifeline that provides hope for a potentially satisfactory analytic outcome despite the factors that threaten to draw the analysis to an interminable stalemate.

In this connection, let me share my impression that the encouraging, self-exploratory efforts that were evident during the early years of the analysis impress me as having represented a compromise-formation. formation between genuine efforts to grow and change, associated with a hopeful, idealizing transference, and an attempt to please a powerful, largely pre-oedipally perceived transference object (with elements of an idealized father of whom she was ambivalently in awe and whom she envied, and from whom she hoped to receive a magical cure of her ills even as she resented his possession of the power she attributed to him, and of an idealized phallic mother and grandmother who lurked behind this imago). Mason accurately perceives the patient's powerful idealization of her father and his phallic equip-ment, associated with the wish to be penetrated sexually and forcibly made into a woman. Her profound sense of defectiveness and the impact of years of her father emotionally distancing him-self from her and pushing her away in a continually impatient, seemingly unappreciative, disparaging way, however, appears to have contributed to attitudes of despair and hopelessness. This led to a solution that centered about attachment of herself to a powerful, phallic protector by whom she wishes to be overpow-ered, although she is terrified at the prospect, and who she hopes will provide the magical solutions to which McDougall refers, but from whom she expects only disappointment, hurt, and re-jection. She settles for transference relationships in which she remains permanently attached, at a carefully controlled, safe dis-tance, from which she controls her hurt and pain by actively evoking them and controls her vengeful, destructive rage via dis-tance and self-victimization.

I find Brenner's conceptualization of the oedipal conflicts ac-curate, but my clinical understanding of the case leads me to conclude that the psychopathology cannot be adequately ex-plained by consideration of her Oedipus complex alone. The preoedipal, narcissistic problems seem to me to play a central role in preventing full engagement in triadic, oedipal conflicts so that the latter can be worked out. I find Burland's conceptualization of the pre-oedipal problems oversimplified and framed too narrowly in terms that fit them to Mahler's ideas about the rapprochement crisis within the process of separation-individuation, and I find Modell's utilization of Winnicott's ideas about true and false self too confining and narrow as an organizing concept. Nevertheless, I agree strongly with them that years of analytic attention to the narcissistic character defenses, self-disparagement, and provoca-tion of a transference-countertransference re-enactment of a sadomasochistic, frustrated and frustrating pseudo-oedipal inter-action (without blame being cast upon anyone and with consideration together of the participation of analysand and analyst alike, as Fenichel [1939] and Greenson [1967, 1978] have empha-sized) has to precede the emergence of a true oedipal transference. This indeed is the approach I have employed with this patient.

For a number of months leading to the specimen sessions, Miss K. appeared to have begun, in response to all the careful attention to the preoedipal, narcissistic, sadomasochistic elements in her character neurosis, to explore her conflicted, sexual fantasies about me as her analyst and to connect them meaningfully with her past masturbation fantasies and her past core object relation-ships. My interventions during the specimen sessions were consciously informed by my impression that the long-term goals of the analysis would be best served by acknowledging her sexu-ality, her sexual fantasies, and her developmental strivings. I did not believe that I was interpreting oedipal fantasies and conflicts as though they were in the forefront of the analysis at that time. That my interventions were couched in terms that could be taken as such, derived, I think, from two sources. First was a counter-transference desire on my part to guide her forward developmentally, as a good mother, especially with the long sum-mer vacation just ahead. Second was my desire to fulfill Pulver's request that I provide illustrative material that could serve as a springboard for discussion of so-called "classical" structural the-ory, in which the Oedipus complex plays an organizing role.

By the end of the week of the sessions I shared with the pan-elists, I realized that my awareness of the fact that the sessions with Miss K. were to be used to "help psychoanalysis" was affect-ing my conduct as an analyst.

Looking further into myself, I realized that associated with my eagerness to give to psychoanalysis as a worthwhile science and profession was eagerness to give something to my patient as a worthwhile human being that might help her to get beyond her masochistic, self-defeating retreat from the narcissistic vulnerabilities, anxieties, and guilts so that she might realize some of her developmental potentials. She had been struggling unsuccessfully to venture into the sexual, oedipal arena that for so very long had been too terrifying for her to more than gingerly enter before beating a hasty retreat. It became apparent to me that I had been attempting to encourage, urge, and prod her into summoning up the courage to move ahead in life. In doing so, I had been succumbing to the wish to be a good father and, especially, a good mother who would help her to stop clinging to me as a preoedipal protector, and, instead, to pursue her potentials, ambitions, aims, and desires for a full life as a woman, even if it meant being the object of contentions, negativism and attack upon me as an oedipal parent.

The various discussants have given very little attention, in fact, to the maternal transference-countertransference issues in this analysis, although these are, in my estimation, of enormous importance. The need to respect privacy and confidentiality precludes the presentation of a great deal of historical data that would be very useful in shedding further light on the case, but I can say that self-denigration as a striving person and as a woman on her mother's part, with genetic seeds in her mother's relationship with her own mother, and her mother's inability to foster a self-reliant, secure, self-appreciative, independent, positive self-image in her as a girl were extremely important determinants of my patient's emotional difficulties in life.

Although she had to struggle with all the ordinary problems with which a woman has to contend in modern times, I certainly cannot agree with Levenson that my patient's problems are merely the ordinary problems of a modern woman. Her neurotic difficulties go far beyond those of the average woman. Mason's hunch that the patient's phallic envy is associated with the fantasy of obtaining entry into her mother's world and into her mother's very self "through the father's penis," strikes me as an allusion to his perception of a wish (with preoedipal and idealizing components) to obtain closeness to and merging with her mother as a pathway to becoming a woman, which I believe is present and is extremely important. I have reservations about the advisability of making the kinds of interpretations he suggests, however. My inclination is to approach this in a very different way. I have difficulty commenting on Goldberg's remarks, for I find them inaccurate, distant from the clinical facts, and not very helpful.

Like Modell, I am concerned that the formidable problems presented by the kind of solution my patient has adopted in her efforts to resolve her emotional difficulties poses the threat of a limited analytic result or even of an interminable analysis. There are some hopeful signs, however, which Lichtenberg has aptly summarized in his closing remarks, and there are good reasons to press forward in an effort to accomplish the goals he outlines. I can only express my heartfelt gratitude to my colleagues for the thoughtful assistance they have provided me in my attempt to do so.

Twenty years of experience as a psychoanalyst has demonstrated to me that while psychoanalysis is not an impossible profession it is not an easy one either. The individuality and complexity of each human being not only make our work exciting and fascinating, but also make it extremely challenging. People are enough alike that we are able to know a good deal about general developmental sequences, about the probable impact of certain kinds of early experience, and about certain patterns of maladaptation that permit placement of a person into certain categories of emotional disturbance rather than into others. They are different enough from one another, however, that no patient fits neatly into any category, and every analysis is a unique experience that rigorously tests our observational, empathic, and therapeutic skills.

Our patients attempt to utilize us to help them explore and resolve the unconscious sources of their overt symptomatology and of the restrictions, inhibitions, and self-defeating tendencies that block them from realizing their realistic ambitions and obtaining the satisfactions and achievements which would otherwise be available to them. This effort conflicts, however, with a very different aim, of which they are not consciously aware but which is as strong as the conscious one and at times much stronger. They seek, without realizing it, to reestablish with the analyst the same wishfully passionate but disappointing, dissatisfying, insufficiently fulfilling, and even painful relationships with the key persons of their past (and present) lives within which their core problems formed and jelled. They do this not only in a quest for mastery and for a hopefully new and better outcome but also, as Gill emphasizes in his discussion, in the hope of obtaining active control over what they previously had experienced passively and helplessly.

The analyst's task is twofold. He has to permit himself to be utilized in two different ways, at times alternately and at times simultaneously. He uses his emotional sensitivities and intellectual capacities to recognize both currents. He seeks to help the patient, via verbal interventions that are suitably framed and properly timed, to employ the former to render them conscious, so that mature (and maturing), rational, reflective thought can be used to resolve and overcome them.

In so doing, as I have discussed elsewhere (Silverman, 1985b), the analyst utilizes freely hovering attention and a more or less controlled emotional regression that employs trial identification and an emotional response to the patient that optimally serves signal functions, although it brings him repeatedly to the brink of counteridentification and countertransference. It is his ability to monitor these shifts and movements within himself and make corrections in his responses that permits him to "read" the patient without falling into permanent identification-counteridentification and transference-countertransference enactments that can contribute to an analytic stalemate. He is enabled to do so by the self-awareness and self-regulation obtained through a training analysis followed by ongoing self-analysis. No analysis, including training analysis, is perfect. The perfectly analyzed analyst is a myth. And our analysands tend to be very adept at sensing out the vulnerabilities and soft spots within us as they oscillate between the poles of seeking understanding and mastery, on the one hand, and reestablishing the conflicted relationships of the past within which their problems developed, on the other. We need to be ever alert to the emotional currents both in our patients and in ourselves. We need to read *both* participants in the analytic process, and this is a formidable task.

Psychoanalysts tend not to be content, therefore, with struggling alone with all the complexities and intricacies they encounter in the course of their work. They read, write, present, and discuss psychoanalytic papers. They attend psychoanalytic meetings. They discuss cases, especially difficult cases, with their colleagues, individually and in workshops and study groups. Self-confidence and humility go hand in hand with one another. A psychoanalyst who feels that he knows everything and has total, perfect command over all that goes on in his work with patients, and has nothing to learn from his colleagues is in the wrong field. None of us is so wise and wonderful that he cannot gain something useful from someone else.

REFERENCES

FENICHEL, O. (1939). *Problems of Psychoanalytic Technique.* Albany, NY: Psychoanalytic Quarterly, Inc..

GREENSON, R.R. (1967). *The Technique and Practice of Psychoanalysis.* New York: Int. Univ. Press.

——— (1978*). Explorations in Psychoanalysis.* New York: Int. Univ. Press.

SILVERMAN, M.A. (1980). A fresh look at the case of Little Hans. In *Freud and His Patients*, ed., M. Kanzer & J. Glenn. New York/London: Jason Aronson, pp. 95–120.

——— (1981). Cognitive development and female psychology. *J. Amer. Psychoanal. Assn.* 29:581–605.

——— (1982). The latency period. In *Early Female Development: Current Psychoanalytic Views*, ed., D. Mendell. New York/London: SP Medical & Scientific Books, pp. 203–225.

——— (1985a). Progression, regression, and child analytic technique. *Psychoanalytic Quarterly* 54:175–199.

——— (1985b). Countertransference and the myth of the perfectly analyzed analyst. *Psychoanalytic Quarterly* 54: 175–199.

——— (1986a). Identification in healthy and pathological character formation. *Int. J. Psycho-Anal.* 67:181–191.

——— (1986b). The male superego. *Psychoanal. Rev.* 73:427–444.

CHAPTER 20

DISCUSSION OF: "WHAT IS THIS MOVIE DOING IN THIS PSYCHOANALYTIC SESSION?"

Marshall Edelson

[(1998). *Journal of Clinical Psychoanalysis* 7(1):54–66.]

I was very pleased when Sydney Pulver (1987) invited me to participate in a panel on "The Relationship of Models of the Mind to Clinical Work" which he was organizing for the May 1985 Annual Meeting of the American Psychoanalytic Association. I very much enjoyed my work as a psychoanalytic practitioner. I was grateful for the excellent training I had received at the Psychoanalytic Institute at New York University Medical Center, and I had been able to help a good number of people through what I had learned there. I was ever ready both to give something back for what I had received and to avail myself of the opportunity to learn more from my analytic colleagues. I was well aware that psychoanalytic theory and practice are and always will be imperfect, that I and my fellow psychoanalysts are human beings so that we too are and always will be imperfect, and that free and open exchange of ideas among inquiring and thoughtful psychoanalysts is vital for the discipline to grow and evolve and for individual practitioners to continually improve and develop their skills.

Human psychology is extraordinarily complex; psychoanalytic work is challenging; and there is always more to learn. As I stated at the close of my response to the other participants in the expanded version published as Volume 7, Number 2, of *Psychoanalytic Inquiry* in 1987:

A psychoanalyst who feels that he knows everything and has total, perfect command over all that goes on in his work with patients and has nothing to learn from his colleagues is in the wrong field. None of us is so wise and wonderful that he cannot gain something useful from someone else [p. 287].

But Syd did not merely invite me to participate. He asked me to present process notes of a week of sessions with one of my analytic patients to representatives of various schools of psychoanalytic thought, each of which purportedly employed a model of the mind and an associated model of psychoanalytic technique that was very different from those that guided the other panelists. And some of the people he had in mind for the panel could be forceful and stentorian in espousing their views. The proceedings could be expected to be quite lively. He asked me, furthermore, to present material that would illustrate classical, Freudian psychoanalysis organized around a structural model of the mind. This was necessary if a baseline were to be provided in apposition to which approaches deriving from alternative views of the mind could be presented.

There was enough in the charge presented to me to give anyone pause. For one thing, although there appeared to be considerable, potential heuristic value in the project, it seemed to me to have inevitable, built-in flaws that would limit what could be achieved. It would be impossible, for one thing, to obtain clinical data that would be free from distortions imposed by the very structure of the project. I do not ordinarily take notes during sessions with my patients. Taking notes would be a departure from my ordinary way of working, which would have to affect my work. It also was inevitable that I would not be able to maintain the usual kind of concentrated, undivided, clinical focus that ordinarily informs my work. The knowledge that I would be recording a week of sessions that was going to form the basis of a discussion at a scientific meeting of the American Psychoanalytic Association could not help but be a formidable distraction. I do not subscribe, furthermore, to a strict "classical Freudian model" in my work. My understanding of psychoanalytic theory and practice is that psychoanalysis is a continually changing and evolving discipline in which the gathering of new data and the accumulation of a widening range of clinical experience dictates ongoing refinement and correction of the ideas that influence our work. Sigmund Freud was the first to recommend such an attitude about psychoanalytic ideas.

For a number of years I participated in the teaching of a course of "Alternate Schools" at a psychoanalytic institute. In this course, I emphasized to each group of candidates that the various schools of thought we were to be examining deserved careful attention because each derived from effort expended by serious, intelligent investigators into significant problems that existed in "classical" psychoanalytic theory and practice.

The request that I present material that would illustrate a "classical" model conflicted with my own, to my mind updated and current, approach to clinical psychoanalytic work. I wanted to fulfill the needs of the organizer of what impressed me as a very worthwhile panel at the same time that I did not want to do anything that would impair my ability to be a good analyst to my patient. I was quite aware that my desire to provide material that would usefully serve the purposes of the panel could very well affect the way I worked during the sessions with my patient, despite my efforts to prevent or minimize that from happening. Introduction of significant, nonclinical parameters into the clinical situation has to deform what takes place within it to a greater or lesser degree. It is the Heisenberg principle raised many degrees.

Psychoanalysis is carried out under conditions that isolate the analysand and the analyst from outside view in order to maximize the degree of freedom of fantasy elaboration and of verbal expression that is afforded the two participants. When we undertake to examine what is taking place in order to study the process, we necessarily alter the very structure of what we are attempting to examine. We thus are faced with an unavoidable dilemma, one which is quite evident in the supervisory situation, in which it is clear that what candidates present to their supervisors reflects not only what is taking place between them and their analysands but also what is taking place between them and their supervisors. I could not possibly avoid being influenced in my work with my patient by my note taking and by the knowledge that what would take place between my patient and me would be grist for more than one mill.

Psychoanalysts, furthermore, as my own analyst observed to me during one of my analytic sessions, are merely "people who went to school." Their analyses have not transformed them into ideal, narcissistically well-balanced, conflict-free paragons of virtue and equanimity. They are no less subject than other people to petty jealousies, rivalries, vindictiveness, sadistic impulses, and all the other human foibles to be found in the population at large. The perfectly analyzed analyst is a mythical being (Silverman, 1985). It was very possible that one or more of the panelists commenting on the material I would be providing would eschew the opportunity to collaborate in a collegial, mutually respecting, productive exchange of views in favor of utilizing the platform to derogate everyone else as he or she stepped forward as a proponent of the one and only, true way of conducting a psychoanalytic treatment. Would I be contributing to a useful and productive exchange of ideas or would I be facilitating a fruitless exercise in sterile self-advertisement?

Someone once told me that she had left a meeting of a psychoanalytic society, back in the 1930s, together with Heinz Hartmann. She saw that he was scowling fiercely and asked him what was the matter. "Psychoanalysts," he replied, "are *Altklugeskinder*; they think they know everything about everything!" I do not believe that this has changed. Not only can psychoanalysts wax arrogant in their belief that they and only they have the final answers, but they can (defensively, no doubt) fall prey to the conceit that *everyone* can be analyzed—if only *they* are the analyst. There are analysts who cannot admit that not everyone can benefit from analysis, that the best of analyses are necessarily imperfect and incomplete, and that excellent work cannot always lead to optimal results (see Schmideberg, 1938). They can derogate the work of others regardless of the demonstrable value and effectiveness of what has taken place. They can blithely deride the work of all others, even as they take care not to expose *their own work* to scrutiny.

But it is necessary in life to be optimistic and to have a reasonable degree of trust in one's friends and colleagues. There was a good chance that at least the majority of the other participants in the panel (and then in the expanded panel that was assembled for the issue of *Psychoanalytic Inquiry* on "How Theory Shapes Technique: Perspectives on a Clinical Study" [Pulver, 1987]) would be wise enough to recognize that the clinical material provided would not be free of artifact and would utilize it for productive purposes rather than for personal, narcissistic gain.

The possible deleterious effects of outside intrusion into the clinical situation was likely to be offset by the opportunity it provided for consultation with eminent, thoughtful clinicians who might be very helpful to me in my management of the case from which I would be extracting the clinical record I would be presenting. I had recently been named a training and supervising analyst, and it was likely that the proceedings would provide the additional benefit of shedding light upon the supervisory process in which I was very much interested. So I prepared the material, which I drew from a case at random, and made my contribution to the science I loved and cherished.

The outcome demonstrated the value of the enterprise. The panel was very well attended and the *Psychoanalytic Inquiry* issue has proved to be of considerable educational value. The latter continues to be very widely used in the curricula of psychoanalytic institutes. I continue to receive expressions of gratitude for its availability. It is gratifying, in fact, that such eminent colleagues as Marshall Edelson continue to be interested in it and to draw upon it to assist them in making their own contributions to the psychoanalytic literature.

The participants in the original enterprise for the most part came through admirably. They were serious and thoughtful and a very useful exchange of ideas was developed. One facet of what emerged that was quite striking to me was that each of the participants focused largely upon one aspect of the case, to the relative exclusion of other aspects. Put together, their observations added up to a montage that depicted a complex, multidimensional neurotic constellation in a complex human being whose treatment required the deft application of psychoanalytic skills.

When I was a candidate in training, Bill Console gave us a course in which he demonstrated that careful examination of a single session can yield such a wealth of data that it is possible to construct a surprisingly rich picture of the analysand's psychology from that single session. It cannot, however, dictate a clear and accurate prescription for analyzing the patient from start to finish. Human beings cannot be analyzed by formula. And this, I believe, offers a framework for examining and responding to

Edelson's paper. He has studied my account of the week's sessions, artifact-ridden as it is, developed certain ideas about my patient's problems and about what he thinks was taking place between her and me at that particular point in the analysis, and has utilized his perceptions as a framework for promulgating certain ideas he has about how *he* feels analysis *should* be carried out.

For the most part, I am quite in agreement with the general principles which he espouses. I fully agree that what transpires between the patient and the analyst, the transactions that occur between the two participants in the analytic process, is the most important aspect of that process. The way in which psychological conflicts in each of the two participants, the ways in which they are dealt with in each of them, their personal strengths and weaknesses, their character traits, and so on, express themselves in the here-and-now of the analytic interaction are of primary importance, both in the way they shed light upon the past of each of them and as a vehicle for effecting change in each of them. These dimensions of the two participants derive from their past developmental experiences and also represent the current, *continually changing facets* of their existence. The developmental process proceeds throughout life; everyone is continually evolving.

I do not see how effective psychoanalytic work can take place without ongoing scrutiny on the analyst's part of what appears to be taking place within the patient, what is taking place within the analyst, and what is taking place between them. Self-analysis has to take place simultaneously with and, in fact, as a part of the analysis of the patient if the analyst is to be able to use himself or herself as an analyzing instrument. I tried to demonstrate this by including references to my own thoughts and feelings in the protocol I provided for the purposes of the panel. (I could only do this, of course, in an artificial way that made observations that pointed to the way I work in the analytic setting rather than

433

actually presenting it as it occurs. No one thinks in the telescoped way I "recorded" my thoughts in the protocol when he or she is working in analysis. I generally *feel my way along with the patient, allowing feelings, thoughts, memories, and fantasies to emerge from within myself,* keeping track of them during the session, and only subliminally formulate my ideas in words—when I am free to float in tune with my patient, unencumbered by the need to serve as an amanuensis recording the proceedings in which I am taking part.)

At the point at which I recorded the week's sessions that were to be the focus of the panel, the analysis had been going along for a considerable length of time. The work that had been done focused largely upon Miss K's timidity, fearfulness, and inhibition, and upon her perception of herself as weak, helpless, and lacking what she needed to fend for herself in the world. It focused too upon her low self-esteem and derogated self-image, upon her clinging to her mother to nurture and protect her while she idealized her father and older brother at the same time that she furiously resented them for apparently possessing the self-assurance and self-confidence which she lacked. It focused upon her terror of her capacity to become enraged, and upon her fear of allowing herself to enter into a more than distant, platonic relationship with a man.

When Edelson, apparently for the sake of exposition, posits a reluctance on my part to recognize Miss K's tendency to cast me into the role of a nurturing mother to whose breasts she might attach herself, he is overlooking the observation I made in my response to the panelists that I was surprised that they had paid scant attention to the maternal transference-countertransference issues in the analysis (p. 284). This had been a major focus in the analysis. The sessions that were recorded covered but a single week out of a very long analysis. Every analysis, whether the analyst is male or female, casts the analyst into female as well as male roles.

I once analyzed a little girl, for example, who had been adopted in circumstances that promoted insecurity rather than security in her relationship with her mother. The first time she was to be separated from me for a considerable length of time, she expressed intense distress and fear that we would forget what each of us looked like. During the last session before she went off on vacation with her parents, in an agitated state, she bit a button off the sleeve of my jacket. "It looks to me," I said, "like you want to eat me up so you can take me along with you on vacation."

Several months later, she allowed her parents to go away on a trip without her, the first time she had been able to do so. When she arrived for a session with me, she was distracted and dis-traught. She expressed enormous pain at being separated from her parents, and became increasingly distressed. She told me that she had not had a snack after school and complained about in-tolerable hunger. With mounting agitation, she implored me to find something for her to eat. When I brought her some straw-berries and an orange from the kitchen, she ignored the strawberries but devoured the orange greedily. As she sat strok-ing the orange peel, I said to her, "You miss your parents *so* much that I think you would like me to grow breasts and feed you the way a mother does with a baby." *"Could you!?!"* she burst out, with her eyes opened wide and a hope-filled expression on her face. Adults tend to be more subtle and subdued in the expres-sion of their wishes, but the wishes are the same.

When Edelson attributes the attention I paid to Miss K's terror of the involvement she was beginning to have with men and of her destructive feelings toward them (how else, for example, are we to understand her reaction to scissors versus fingers in her hair and the fantasy of the mad scientist, which she related with excitement mixed with terror, with which her reaction was associated?) to a theoretical bias, he is creating a convenient straw man to demolish. Far from drawing upon theoretical ideas in an arbitrary fashion, I was going by what Miss K herself had communicated to me.

She had recalled among other things adolescent and young adult masturbation fantasies, derived in part from an exciting movie she had seen in which Roman soldiers attacked and slew their enemies in bloody combat, of punishing her brother and other males for spurning, insulting, and humiliating her by castrating and decapitating them (scissors in the hair?) with a sword. She also had connected her overeating and making herself unattractive to men to her intense excitement as a child when she saw a cartoon in which a pig defeated and obtained revenge over a mad scientist who was punishing her for her passionate desires, by eating so much that she exploded like a bomb. It is pertinent that, as she herself observed, both her father and I were identifiable as scientists. These memories occupied our attention repeatedly, both before and after the sessions that I recorded for the panel.

As a result of the work we had done together, Miss K had become able for the first time in her life to move beyond her clinglingly ambivalent attachment to her family and to summon the courage to become involved with men. She was already into her thirties and wanted to give herself a chance at a full life. She was terrified, however, by her fears of rejection and humiliation and by the rage at men that was mobilized by her excitement and by disappointments which she encountered. It was this that I was attempting to help her with during the week upon which I reported. I was not addressing a sterile, theoretical issue. Her reaction to my impending vacation, as we went on to consider together, was related to a large extent to her sense that she could not deal with her conflicts in this regard without receiving continual infusions of maternal and paternal strength from me, without which she felt inadequate and helpless. And, of course, she did not expect to be given what she needed unless she masochistically seduced, provoked, and forced me to provide it to her. Hence, we were led into the kind of enactments that were recorded in the protocol and that we went on to identify, examine, and understand together. Anyone who has analyzed someone who is struggling like Miss K to get beyond the angry, masochistic, self-derogating, righteously indignant, smolderingly suffering constellation that brought her into treatment will recognize what she and I were experiencing and working upon together.

I certainly agree with Edelson as to the usefulness of closely following the minute details of the patient's (and, I might add, the analyst's) verbal and nonverbal expressions, "the microdynamics of the here-and-now in the psychoanalytic situation." I also agree, however, with Ted Jacobs that Paul Gray's (1973) recommendation:

> [T]hat the analyst track shifts and changes in the patient's mental processes, particularly his defensive maneuvers, implies a kind of alert, focused attention that is very different from the open-ended, non-directed listening . . . that [permits] the analyst [to] attain the kind of free-ranging, unfocused mind-set that allows for . . . subjective reactions to rise freely to the surface—another of the analyst's important functions [Jacobs, 1997, pp. 111–112].

Psychoanalysts need to carry out multiple activities, some of which compete with others, in a finely tuned, coordinated fashion that is far from easy to carry out. If one becomes too enamored of one facet of the analytic process, one runs the risk of losing sight of other important aspects.

Similarly, there is general agreement that analysis of the analytic transference (i.e., the transference-countertransference interaction) is central in the psychoanalytic process, as Merton Gill (1982), among others, has emphasized. It can be a serious error, however, to focus exclusively upon this dimension, overlooking extra-analytic transferences and the real life functioning of the analysand. Working within the analytic transference needs to take place within the context of what is actually taking place in the patient's life.

Miss K had lived her life largely through fantasy rather than through active involvement with people. Named for the exalted heroine of a romantic escapist novel that had stirred her parents' ardor, Miss K lived vicariously through novels and films. (I read the novel during the course of the analysis and she and I addressed it repeatedly and intensively.) There was another powerful pull toward films that was an important part of her family history. *Now Voyager* (1942) was only one of many films, books, and stories she brought into the analysis. Unlike Edelson, I was not familiar with the movie before she made reference to it. My responses to the film during the sessions I recorded were based upon what *she* had told me about it. It is not at all uncommon for analysands to bring in stories, books, and films as readymade fantasy vehicles for expressing their emotional struggles. While I agree with Edelson that analysts need to allow themselves the freedom to make use of their own feelings and thoughts in connection with such material brought in by the patient, it is my impression that caution is warranted lest one stray too far from what *the patient* focuses upon and associates to in the material. In this respect, the principle involved is the same one that holds for ftlinedealing with the manifest content of dreams and daydreams.

Miss K had just begun to refer to the film *Now Voyager* to any extent, and it was during this week of sessions that, going by what *she* was saying in connection with it, it began to occur to me that *with this particular film* she might have been presenting the script *for the analysis.* When I eventually saw the film, I found myself far more impressed with the potential significance of the way the film ends, in contrast with Edelson who was intrigued with the way the film begins. As she and I explored at length, both in its transference signification and in reference to her life in general, it was very meaningful that in the film Charlotte only appears to individuate herself from her mother. She rejects the offer of marriage that Tina's father makes to her and in essence adopts Tina as her child, devoting the rest of her life to living out the very mother-daughter duality, from which men are excluded, which she had tried to escape from in the first place. She determines to be a better mother to her adopted daughter than her own mother had been to her, but she does not give herself the full life of a grown-up, mature woman for which she has yearned.

The Monday morning quarterback is always right. How could he or she not be? The plays which he or she would put into the game are entirely theoretical and hypothetical. There are no teams on the field. There is no way to test what the outcome would be with the use of those plays. It is not possible to replay the game. Professional football teams make use of game films to learn from, so that they can try to improve their future performance. The material I provided for Sydney Pulver's panel in 1985 is the equivalent of a small segment of such a game film, albeit artifact-laden because of the circumstances of its filming. It seems to me that *that* film and the making of the film are very pertinent foci in regard to the discourse of which Edelson's paper and my response are parts.

Edelson had the luxury of being able to run the entire film segment repeatedly and to examine and reflect upon it at leisure. In his paper, in fact, he responds to the first session by associating at length to the film *Now Voyager,* which did not appear until the second session that followed it! He had the luxury of being able to reflect upon the first scene with the advantage of possessing material that did not appear until the second scene. We do not have that advantage while playing the actual game. (Football is a game; and games are to be enjoyed. Any psychoanalyst who does not enjoy his work as an analyst is in the wrong profession.)

To return to something I stated earlier, psychoanalysis is a difficult profession and we are all imperfect. We can all learn and we can all continue to improve and sharpen our skills. When I look back over sessions I have had with my patients, including the sessions with Miss K which I recorded in 1985 (and I was startled to see how much I had been affected by the request to be a "classical Freudian"), I too can see ways in which I might have improved upon what I have done. I am sure that this is true for everyone, and I know that we can all learn from one another. I should like to make a plea for our communicating with one another in this regard in a spirit of friendship and mutual respect. Edelson reminds us early in his discourse that, "What a patient says at the beginning of a session sets up expectations, as a tonic chord in music does. It alerts me to possibilities, prepares my mind to receive, my ears to hear" (p. 7). At the very beginning of his paper he refers to the analyst who "ignores, misplaces, or misconstrues," who "dismissively treats things the patient says," who uses "dubious approaches to listening and interpretation," etc. He employs words like *unempathic* and *off-the-mark,* albeit in language that disavows applying such adjectives to the analyst who provided the material he is utilizing. To paraphrase the title Edelson chose for his paper, "What Are These Words Doing in This Psychoanalytic Paper?"

If we are truly to engage in useful dialogue from which we might learn from one another, we need to address each other graciously and in a spirit of cordiality. We need to be willing to expose our work to

one another and to expect that we will be rewarded by receiving responses from our colleagues that will be informative and fruitful.
That is the way in which we can each grow and our science can grow.
When I chaired the Child Analysis Section at the Psychoanalytic Institute at NYU Medical Center, I instituted a course in which I
presented one of my own cases to the candidates. I titled the course
"Warts and All," and I encouraged my coteacher and the candidates
we were teaching to be open and frank in their response to the material. One of my principle aims was to dispel the myth that seasoned
analysts are paragons who have attained a state of perfection.

I recently came across the following in a book on genetics:

Textbooks (including this one) tend to be glib in their accounts of scientific achievements, presenting a smooth continuum of success after
success; rarely do readers learn about the intervening false starts, dead
ends, misinterpretations, or outright failures. And as Stephen Jay
Gould (1986) points out in a review of Nobel laureate Peter Medawar's engaging autobiography (1986), the same is true for articles in
scientific journals, whose standard writing style: ... misconstrues,
even falsifies, the actual doing of science. ... The epitomized logic of
inductivist accounts—from introduction, to materials and methods,
results and conclusions—omits the basic human dimensions of hypothesis, confusion, error and collegiality. The false starts are in the
wastebasket, not in the *Science Citation Index*. By focusing the text on
the frustrations, the errors and the bullheaded approaches, until
kicked in the pants by data or good advice by colleagues with other
perspectives, Medawar has illustrated his favorite themes by honestly
discussing his own work [Mange and Mange, 1990, pp. ii–iii].

When are we in the science of psychoanalysis going to temper arrogance with humility and professional rivalry with collegial
generosity?

REFERENCES

GILL, M.M. (1982). Analysis of Transference, Vol. 1. *Psychological Issues* Monogr. 53. New York: International Universities Press.

GOULD, S.J. (1986). Reflections from an interior world. *Nature* 320:647–648.

GRAY, P. (1973). Psychoanalytic technique and the ego's capacity for viewing intrapsychic activity, *J. Amer. Psychoanal. Assn.* 21:474–494.

JACOBS, T. (1997). Response to the contributors to "Essays inspired by Theodore Jacobs's 'The use of the self.'" *Psychoanal. Inq.* 17:108–119.

MANGE, A.P., & MANGE, E.J. (1990). *Genetics: Human Aspects*, 2nd ed. Sunderland, MA: Sinauer Associates.

MEDAWAR, P. (1986). *Memoir of a Thinking Radish: An Autobiography.* New York: Oxford University Press.

NOW VOYAGER (1942). *Screenwriter, C. Robinson, from the novel by O. H. Prouty, dir. I. Rapper*, prod. H.B. Wallis. Warner Brothers.

PULVER, S.E. (ed. with P.J. Escoll & N. Fischer) (1987). How theory shapes technique: Perspectives on a clinical study. *Psychoanal. Inq.* 7:141–299.

SCHMIDEBERG, M. (1938). After the analysis . . . *Psychoanal. Q.* 7:122–142.

SILVERMAN, M.A. (1985). Countertransference and the myth of the perfectly analyzed analyst. *Psychoanal. Q.*, 54:175–199.

———— (1987). The analyst's response. *Psychoanal. Inq.* 7:277–287.

CHAPTER 21:

PSYCHOANALYTIC ETHICS AND PSYCHOANALYTIC COMPETENCE: LESSONS FROM THE BIOGRAPHIES OF MASUD KHAN

[(2007). *Psychoanalytic Quarterly* 76(3):1019–1026.]

Psychoanalysis, as Renik (2006) has recently emphasized, is not an intellectual exercise or an aesthetic indulgence pursuing insight for its own sake, but a form of *therapy*. It is a treatment modality that aims at helping unhappy, troubled, and at times emotionally damaged people to wrestle with their internal conflicts, overcome the deleterious effect of unfortunate life experiences, build the strengths they need to contend successfully with "the slings and arrows of outrageous fortune" (Shakespeare 1603, III, I, 58), and become more capable of realizing their potential for enjoying life, personally and interpersonally. It is not carried out for the benefit of the analyst but for the benefit of the patient, who is willing to undergo the rigors of analytic treatment and to pay a good deal of money for it in the hope of obtaining benefits that will justify the effort and the expense the treatment entails.

Two biographies of Masud Khan by Roger Willoughby and Linda Hopkins, reviewed in the preceding pages of this issue of *The Psychoanalytic Quarterly* by Manasi Kumar and Howard Levine, respectively, describe in distressing detail how easily the true purpose of psychoanalytic treatment can be lost sight of, with devastating effects for all concerned—the analysand, those with whom the analysand is interacting and will interact in the future, and the analyst. Salman Akhtar's thoughtful introduction, as well, describes how an analyst "of towering stature" can "turn into a fallen angel of disgrace."

Why am I putting all this in the present tense when the events involving Masud Khan occurred so long ago? And why have two such detailed, thoroughly researched, lengthy biographical books only recently appeared in print? I use the present tense because the kind of defects, deficiencies, loss of perspective, boundary violations and transgressions, and exploitative mismanagement of the analytic treatment process described in these two books do not belong only to a bygone era. These thorny issues are a proper focus of examination in the present—both within the profession of psychoanalysis and within the larger mental health field, of which psychoanalysis is a relatively small but highly influential component—as much as they are a part of history.

There is much to learn from Khan's story that is applicable to issues in present-day currents and ferments in the field of analysis. At the time that Khan arrived in England, seeking analytic treatment for himself, psychoanalysis was a young discipline encumbered by all the uncertainty and insecurity (compensated for by authoritarian arrogance) that not infrequently characterizes a novel, groundbreaking venture into scientific and intellectual inquiry. Psychoanalytic observations and revelations about human nature were creating enormous stir in the world, but were in some ways so unsettling or even disturbing that they elicited considerable hostility and derision. Since so many of the earliest psychoanalytic pioneers were Jewish, defensive antipathy toward this new discipline became swept up, furthermore, in the anti-Semitism that was rife in Europe and elsewhere. World War II had just ended, in fact, and a good number of the leading figures in the field in Great Britain had arrived there in flight from Nazi oppression.

There was also a considerable amount of competitive struggling between rival camps within British psychoanalysis. Such struggles were not limited to the well-known and heated rivalry between those who considered themselves loyal to Anna Freud and those who were favorably impressed by the observations and ideas of Melanie Klein. Additionally, the object relations investigations of Fairbairn, Guntrip, Balint, Bowlby, and others were being conducted by outspoken and/or charismatic luminaries who had their own ambitious investment in becoming the leaders of an important psychoanalytic school of thought.

And is it so very different at the present time? Psychoanalysis is once again under attack. We live in an anxious age in which overpopulation, global warming, powerful economic and social threats presented by global geopolitical change, and the threat of nuclear annihilation are shaking the foundations of the sense of security and safety that were once extant in the Western world. It is an impatient era, in which quick and efficient, simple solutions tend to be sought; managed care holds sway; and skepticism tends to prevail about the value of treatments that are slow and steady, thorough-going, and unavoidably lengthy.

The pendulum tends to swing in a wide arc. In reaction to the authoritarian, seemingly omniscient approach of far too many analysts sixty years ago, the tendency within the field of psychoanalysis has been to move toward humanization and egalitarianism within the analytic frame, away from the expectation that the patient will submissively accept the analyst's presumed wisdom and authority. It is widely recognized at present that analytic treatment is a two-person rather than a one-person process. McLaughlin (2005), for example, presented a well-reasoned, albeit cautious argument in favor of viewing psychoanalysis as a two-person process in which both participants gain something personally.[1]

There has been a growing tendency to shift the central focus in analytic work away from the acquisition of insight into the genetic

---

[1] See also Chodorow 2007.

and dynamic, unconscious roots of neurotic conflict, and toward the curative effects of the here-and-now relationship between analyst and analysand. As laudable as is the recognition of this dimension of analytic work, it would be unfortunate if we were to throw out the baby with the bath water. Each of our patients does have a unique set of past experiences that have influenced his or her emotional development. Each patient brings the shadow of her or his past relationships into the arena of analytic interaction. Our patients need us to appreciate the power of their past internalizations in shaping their inner worlds and to help them free themselves from the deleterious impact of certain aspects that those internalizations have had upon them. As Kumar emphasizes in her review essay, Khan's analysts' apparent lack of adequate appreciation of his cultural background contributed to the difficulty they seem to have had in understanding his problems and recognizing what he needed from them.

As we work with our patients, we are confronted with the task of resisting our own internal pull toward transcending the boundaries between a professional and a personal relationship. Analysis is a complex and demanding process that entails courage and is fraught with risk. Analysts at one time believed that they needed to maintain a distant stance from their analysands. They believed that they could and should limit themselves to doing no more than mirroring back to their patients what emanated from them. Menninger (1958) depicted this deftly when he cited "an untraced poem by one Tom Prideaux":

> *With half a laugh of hearty zest*
> *I strip me off my coat and vest.*
> *Then heeding not the frigid air*
> *I fling away my underwear.*
> *So having nothing else to doff*

I rip my epidermis off.
More secrets to acquaint you with
I pare my bones to strips of pith.
And when the exposé is done
I hang a cobweb skeleton.
While you sit there, aloof, remote
And will not shed your overcoat [p. 62].

We know now that it is impossible for us to remain as anonymous and personally uninvolved as early analysts thought was indicated. But all advances bring their own risks and hazards. At the time Khan entered the analytic scene, it was becoming evident that more active interventions than merely "making the unconscious conscious" were needed by some or even many analysands. The way in which imperfect understanding of the pitfalls involved in this contributed to Khan's post-analytic personal and professional problems is described vividly in Willoughby's and Hopkins's biographical works.

We have come a long way since then, but we have not entirely left behind the dangers faced by analysts sixty years ago. As we participate in the analytic task, we can all too easily carry self-disclosure so far as to blur the boundary between human interaction and professional restraint. We have learned a great deal about countertransference as a source of valuable information about our patients, but *everything* an analyst feels or thinks is not a direct and reliable message from the patient's unconscious. It has also become evident that enactment of emotional conflicts is a more or less inevitable occurrence in every analysis, and that we need to vigilantly keep track of our own input as we involve ourselves in our patients' lives. It is incumbent upon us to take care lest we use our patients to act out our own issues with them.

The definition of psychoanalysis has tended to be broadened so as to make it more palatable to its critics and to widen the patient pool (see, for example, Meadow 2003). We need to exercise caution, however, as we participate in this. When the analyst of a number of analysands simultaneously treats them in group therapy, treats them and their spouses in marital therapy, or provides supervision to them, this can lead to a variety of problems. Is it not similar to what took place between Winnicott and Khan?

When Khan—a brilliant, engaging, articulate, charismatic, as well as wealthy and aristocratic scholar from a distant and exotic corner of the British Empire—arrived in England in 1946, according to his biographers, he was looking for personal treatment rather than for training as a psychoanalyst. His various attributes must have greatly impressed his interviewers at the British Psychoanalytical Society, who "mistakenly" enrolled him as a student. Despite his history of having suffered painful losses of close family members, he was successively placed in analysis with two seriously ill training analysts, each of whom died after a short period of time. After two additional attempts at obtaining analytic treatment failed to work out, Khan gravitated to Winnicott, who himself was brilliant, charismatic, and ambitious, and eager for fame and prominence. Winnicott was innovative, adventurous, and willing to undergo considerable risks (to himself as well as to others) as he undertook the treatment of seriously disturbed individuals (see Rodman 2003).

Winnicott made useful contributions through his at times heroic efforts in this regard, but as Levine (2006) explains in his review of Rodman's 2003 biography of Winnicott:

> There is ... a darker side to Winnicott's advocating the management of the manifestations of severe pathology by action rather than interpretation.... There is an uncertain delineation and a potentially

slippery slope between Winnicott's proposals for "management," his sometime failure to maintain the treatment frame, and overt boundary crossings and even violations. [pp. 587–588].[2]

It becomes clear in reading the recent biographies by Willoughby and Hopkins that Khan both benefitted and suffered from his treatment with Winnicott. He became able to mirror his analyst and mentor—with whom he developed an ongoing, complex relationship as analysand, collaborator, editor, champion, and friend—in making real contributions to the field as a writer, reviewer, and editor. Unfortunately, he also mirrored Winnicott's personal and professional deficiencies, even outdoing him in these respects. He went on to commit major transgressions in his work with patients, grossly violating boundaries and acting out his own neurotic issues in clinical interactions. It is no less important now than it was sixty years ago for analytic institutes to exercise caution in selecting training analysts.

Do personally ambitious, politically adept people necessarily make the best clinical analysts—or the best training analysts? Considerable debate is taking place in our field about the whole idea of the *training analysis*. There are those who question the entire concept, others who press for personal analyses to largely precede or otherwise be divorced from the formal training process, and still others who advocate that the personal analyses of candidates be carried out elsewhere than at the institute at which the candidate trains (see, for example, Berman 2004; Reeder 2004). We also need to be knowledgeable and thoughtful if and when we provide guidance to a candidate who is in need of a personal analysis.

The phenomenon of the articulate and charismatic analyst who gathers a coterie of followers or even myrmidons while

---

[2] See also Sabbadini (2003) and Silverman (2006) for more on Winnicott's treatment of his colleagues—and their treatment of him.

seeking to vault to prominence as a leading, influential force did not end in the early days of psychoanalysis as a field of endeavor. Adherents of various analytic schools vie loudly and vociferously with one another to declare themselves as the one, true, effective representative of psychoanalysis. Developmentalists, ego psychologists, interpersonalists, intersubjectivists, Kleinians, Lacanians, and self psychologists each proclaim to have the real story. True, there have been those who have sought to foster useful integration of what have been recognized as the various parts of the psychoanalytic elephant (see, for example, Schafer 1997a, 1997b, 2003; Smith 2005), but they have been minority voices.

Perhaps the time has come when psychoanalysts will be able to stop bickering rivalrously among themselves, learn from one another, and settle down to the pursuit of the proper occupation of treating suffering patients and training capable psychoanalysts and psychotherapists. The most salient feature of psychoanalytic ethics is psychoanalytic competence.

REFERENCES

BERMAN, E. (2004). *Impossible Training: A Relational View of Psychoanalytic Education*. Hillsdale, NJ: Analytic Press.

CHODOROW, N.J. (2007). Review of *The Healer's Bent: Solitude and Dialogue in the Clinical Encounter,* by James T. McLaughlin. *Psychoanal. Q.* 76:617–629.

LEVINE, H. (2006). Review of *Winnicott: Life and Work,* by F. Robert Rodman. *Psychoanal. Q.* 75:585–591.

MCLAUGHLIN, J.T. (2005). *The Healer's Bent: Solitude and Dialogue in the Clinical Encounter*. Hillsdale, NJ: Analytic Press.

MEADOW, P.W. (2003). *The New Psychoanalysis*. Lanham, MD: Rowman & Littlefield.

MENNINGER, K. (1958). *Theory of Psychoanalytic Technique.* New York: Basic Books.

REEDER, J. (2004). *Psychoanalytical Institutions: The Dilemma of a Profession.* New York: Other Press.

RENIK, O. (2006). *Practical Psychoanalysis for Therapists and Patients.* New York: Other Press.

RODMAN, F.R. (2003). *Winnicott: Life and Work.* Cambridge, MA: Perseus Publishing.

SABBADINI, A. (2003). The Gaddini-Winnicott correspondence, 1964 to 1970. *Psychoanal. & History* 5:1–69.

SCHAFER, R. (1997a). *Tradition and Change in Psychoanalysis.* New York: International Universities Press.

——— (1997b). *The Contemporary Kleinians of London.* New York: International Universities Press.

——— (2003). *Bad Feelings.* New York: Other Press.

SHAKESPEARE, W. (1603). *Hamlet.* Oxford, England: Oxford Univ. Press, 1992.

SILVERMAN, M.A. (2006). Review of "The Gaddini-Winnicott Correspondence, 1964 to 1970," ed. A. Sabbadini. *Psychoanal. Q.* 75:1220–1226.

SMITH, H.F. (2005). Dialogues on conflict: toward an integration of methods. *Psychoanal. Q.* 74:327–363.

CHAPTER 22

THE PSYCHOANALYST AS A NEW OLD OBJECT, AN OLD NEW OBJECT, AND A BRAND NEW OBJECT:
Reflections on Loewald's Ideas about the Role of Internalization in Life and in Psychoanalytic Treatment

[(2007). Psychoanalytic Quarterly, 76(4):1153–1169]

INTRODUCTION

Hans Loewald is one of the most important contributors whom the field of psychoanalysis has had. In a relatively soft-spoken way, he has been a seminal voice in effecting the transition that has taken place—away from the authoritarian, complacent, overly certain, theoretically narrow, and reductionistic form in which psychoanalysis tended to be understood and practiced during the first half century of its existence, and toward the increasingly open, egalitarian, fallibilistic nature of psychoanalytic art and science that has characterized it during the past fifty years.

What has made Loewald's contribution all the more remarkable is that he never succumbed to the temptation to belittle or scoff at the achievements of his predecessors in order to elevate himself to a position of preeminence or superiority. Unlike those who move from apotheosis to apostasy, he always remained appreciative of and respectful toward the pioneers who established the foundations of our discipline, while he allowed his patients to educate him and his colleagues to inform him from the vantage points of their particular investigative interests. Harold Bloom (1975) once observed that his graduate students, eager to make their mark as new writers, assiduously read and studied the works of the great authors who had come before them so that they could learn from them—and tear them down so that they might surpass and replace them as the leading figures on the literary scene. Loewald never fell prey to that all-too-common human tendency.

Via a limited number of presentations, papers, and book reviews, Loewald deftly articulated a rationale for viewing psychoanalysis as a two-person rather than a one-person psychology, a view that has become a central feature of the *Weltanschauung* that currently prevails in our field.[1] In doing so, furthermore, Loewald has been clear-headedly attentive to the principles of child development and to the biopsychosocial framework that defines human existence.

Loewald's Conceptualization of the Superego

Loewald's 1962 paper "Internalization, Separation, Mourning, and the Superego" addresses the topic of superego formation in accordance with traditional Freudian structural theory. In actuality, however, it goes far beyond that. Most saliently, it examines the development of psychic structure in toto, particularly with respect to its emergence out of the interaction between the baby (with its innate, genetically programmed potentials) and what Winnicott (1965, 1971) designated as the (more or less successful) facilitating environment. Loewald, however, goes even further than Winnicott in his depiction of parental input as not merely facilitating, but also shaping, molding, and building the child, not only in infancy but throughout the child's entire development.

The child's side of the interplay between it and its parents, Loewald emphasizes, is characterized by an ongoing conflict between a powerful need to maintain the illusion of oneness with

---

[1] The work of McLaughlin (e.g., 2005) admirably exemplifies this development within psychoanalysis.

the primary parental figure (at first the maternal one, but then an increasingly more inclusive figure) that is gradually, albeit reluctantly, recognized as separate and apart from the child, and to break away from the extreme emotional dependence upon the parent(s) that is increasingly experienced as an oppressively stultifying obstacle to the child's sense of internal cohesion and integrity as an independent and self-reliant being. The parents' side of the interaction, Loewald indicates, is one of oscillation between the exercise of power and authority that inherently resides within them as bigger, stronger, and better equipped to exert influence over their initially weak, helpless, utterly dependent, more or less malleable offspring, and the acceptance of responsibility for both allowing and assisting the child to increasingly take over command and ownership of its own powers and self-determination.

In his earlier, more well-known, and more frequently cited paper, "On the Therapeutic Action of Psychoanalysis" (1960), Loewald clearly indicated that he viewed drives as not merely innate, instinctual, constitutionally determined imperatives, but rather as psychological end products that emerge out of the interaction between the infant's potentials and environmental shaping:

> The understanding recognition of the infant's need on the part of the mother represents a gathering together of as yet undifferentiated urges of the infant, urges that in the acts of recognition and fulfillment by the mother undergo a first organization *into some directed drive.* . . . These acts are not merely necessary for the physical survival of the infant but necessary at the same time for its psychological development, insofar as they organize, in successive steps, the infant's relatively uncoordinated urges [1960, p. 237, italics added].

Loewald emphasized, not only in his 1962 paper but throughout the corpus of his written work, that via a process of intermittent but ongoing detachment from, opposition to, giving up of, and losing of one's parents, accompanied by feelings of loss, sadness, and mourning of the parents as idealized, perfect providers, vital aspects of parental images and the interaction with them are incorporated as structure-building components of the child's independent self system. The very process of facilitation of structuralization and building of strength is internalized, so that the child increasingly becomes its own parent as it undergoes psychological development that mediates movement toward becoming an autonomous adult.

Loewald remains true to Freud's structural conceptualization of human psychology in his 1962 paper,[2] but he develops it and brings it much further by expanding Freud's one-person, child-focused configuration of id-ego-superego into a two-person, developmentally oriented schema that centers upon the concept of an increasingly internalized process of bidirectional interaction between self and other, between the child and its primary objects of affection as well as of resentment, of love as well as of hate—not only in early life but throughout the life cycle.

For the time at which this paper was written (as indicated on the first page, earlier versions had been presented in 1959 and 1960), Loewald begins traditionally enough by citing Freud's concept of a two-step process of the development of the superego as a structural agency within and to one side of the ego—an agency that serves to watch over the self and render favorable or unfavorable judgments, admiring or critical ones, that are intended to guide the attitudes and behavior of the child in a more or less helpful manner. The first step is a preoedipal one in which the child incorporates images and

---

[2] Editor's Note: In this article, page numbers from Loewald 1962 refer to the numbering in the republication in this issue, not to the original *Quarterly* publication of 1962.

communications from its earliest libidinal objects via "introjections and identifications" that contribute to the development in of the ego. The second step occurs in the course of (at least temporary) dissolution of the Oedipus complex in recognition by the child of its inability to win a battle for which it is as yet inadequately equipped, and which at best would be a Pyrrhic victory anyway, given the love the child feels toward its parents and its recognition that it still needs them for its very survival. The child's acceptance of the reality of its inability to fend for itself in the world is a central feature in this process.

The child incorporates the images of the oedipal objects that are "relinquished as external objects, even as fantasy objects, and are set up in the ego, by which process they become internal objects cathected by the id,—a narcissistic cathexis" (Loewald 1962, p. 11142). This second step creates the superego proper. Loewald emphasizes that "the early ('ego') identifications take place during stages of development when inside and outside—ego and objects—are not clearly differentiated," while the "later type of identifications, the superego identifications . . . are identifications with differentiated objects of libidinal and aggressive cathexis,—objects which themselves cathect in such ways." Loewald makes the further observation that "in actuality, of course, there is a continuum of stages between these two types and much overlapping and intermingling of them" (p. 1114). Like Freud before him, he does not clearly distinguish between ego as agency and self as identity, apparently viewing them as integrally connected with one another.

The Analyst as a New Parent

Loewald then directs his attention to certain important similarities that exist between what takes place in the interaction between parents and their children and what takes place between analysts and their analysands. In an analysis, significant internalized object relations are reexternalized onto the person of the analyst, who is prepared to interact with the analysand in a manner that in certain ways is not at all unlike what parents do with their children. Two aspects of the internalization process that contribute to childhood psychological development also make it possible for analysis to be successful. One is that internalization of parental objects, and of the interactional experience with them, does not necessarily involve losing them in the same way that this occurs with the internalization of someone who is lost through death or through permanent disruption of a romantic relationship later in life. The child continues to interact with its parents in an ongoing process of internalization that provides ongoing opportunity for revision, change, and growth in the child's inner world. In addition, as the child matures and develops, it becomes increasingly capable of parenting itself.

Loewald emphasizes that a good analyst, like a good parent, appreciates and respects the patient's need both to internalize the analyst and what the analyst provides in the way of growth-facilitating assistance, *and* to reject and push away from what the analyst offers in favor of shaping her or his development to her or his own specifications.

The Child's Ambivalence Toward the Parents and the Analysand's Ambivalence Toward the Analyst

Loewald observes that in the developing child—and again in the course of an analysis—separation is desired as well as dreaded. The dialectic tension between the two can be resolved, when things go well, via an interaction in which the parent (or the analyst) provides child-oriented (or analysand-oriented) assistance that permits internalization of useful *aliment*—to use Piaget's

458

felicitous term—from the analyst as a *new object,* at the same time that stultifying, incestuous, oedipal relational involvement is given up in favor of true independence. As Loewald (1962) puts it:

> Emancipation as a process of separation from external objects . . . goes hand in hand with the work of internalization which reduces or abolishes the sense of external deprivation and loss. Whether separation from a love object is experienced as deprivation and loss or as emancipation and mastery will depend, in part, on the achievement of the work of internalization [p. 1120].

All relationships, he emphasizes, are ambivalent because of . . . the polarity inherent in individual existence of individuation and "primary narcissistic" union .... Separation from love objects, while in one sense something to be overcome and undone through internalization, is, insofar as it means individuation and emancipation, a positive achievement brought about by the relinquishment and internalization of the love objects. The change of function taking place here is that a means of defense against the pain and anxiety of separation and loss becomes a goal in itself [pp. 1120-1121].

Loewald stresses the importance of differentiating between preoedipal and oedipal desires—although this is not an easy task, given the developmental relationship that still in part exists between them. The oedipal identifications that contribute to the formation of the superego proper, he points out, are:

> . . . new versions—promoted by new experiences of deprivation and loss—of identifications which precede the oedipal situation. The narcissistic cathexis, replacing object cathexis in internalization, is secondary and is founded on an older, "primary" narcissism of which it is a new version. [p. 1121].

This is so, furthermore, for aggressive as well as libidinal aspects of oedipal identifications. Internalizations are always, in part, re-internalizations of aspects of self, powered by intrinsic drive energies, that have been externalized onto need-fulfilling and desire-fulfilling external objects of those needs and desires—but they can never again be the same as they originally were, since they have now acquired characteristics of the objects. Loewald elaborates:

> Figuratively speaking, in the process of internalization the drives take aspects of the object with them into the ego. Neither drive nor object is the same as before, and the ego itself becomes further differentiated in the process. Internalization is structure building [p. 1122].

At first, Loewald emphasizes, there is nothing defensive about the processes of internalization and externalization. Inside and outside are not distinguished from one another, initially, but very quickly, beginning soon after birth, they are increasingly demarcated via boundary creating—projective-introjective mental activities that promote differentiation. This at first takes place merely as a result of simple sensorimotor activity, outside of emotional conflict (Silverman 1971), but as a result of the increasing complexity of the interaction that takes place with the outside world—which at times is soothing and gratifying, but at other times is disappointing or frustrating, even in the best of circumstances—it inevitably becomes colored by internal conflict.

Winnicott's (1965, 1971) observations about the importance of good-enough mothering and of early experience in shaping the true self versus the false self are pertinent in this regard. Bion's (1962) observations on the importance of maternal holding or containing, and Balint's (1968) concept of the *basic fault*, are also meaningful in connection with what Loewald is addressing here. Equally significant are Lacan's (1977) observations about the mirror stage in development, during which the child's perception of itself as a defined entity crystallizes out of what its parents reflect back to it about who and what the child is to them.

The Significance of the Oedipus Complex

The relinquishment and internalization of oedipal objects represent a continuation and a "resumption on a new level" of these differentiating and "boundary-creating processes" (Loewald 1962, p. 1122). Loewald accepts Freud's concept of superego formation as deriving from incorporation of the image of the child's controlling and inhibiting father, who threatens castration as punishment for oedipal rivalry, but he adds to it and goes beyond it in an important way. The child, he maintains, is forced to give up oedipal strivings not only out of a fear of punishment (and of failure), but also because these strivings threaten the integrity of the child's sense of its boundaries as a separate self. It has to give up its genital sexual longings in order to prevent dissolution of the differentiation and demarcation it has made between inside and outside, between self and non-self, which it acquired during separation-individuation, as eloquently described by Mahler (1972a, 1972b; Mahler, Pine, and Bergman 1975). Reider (1959) also elaborated on this aspect of the significance of the Oedipus complex.

Observers of infants and toddlers can only be impressed with the degree to which these little ones experience intense frustration over the degree of utter helplessness and dependence on others, imposed by humans' secondarily altricial state at birth. Equally impressive is the degree to which they are delighted, even intoxicated, as they acquire the capacity to turn over, push up on all fours, feed themselves, crawl, walk, run, make their wants known via language, obtain items on their own, and so on (Silverman 1986).

It is noteworthy that Loewald retains Freud's drive-defense and structural models as descriptively and developmentally useful, even as he increasingly appears to doubt that these suffice to fully explain what transpires within the child as it traverses the various phases and stages of interaction with its parents. Loewald appears to firmly believe in preserving the usefulness of early formulations, rather than dispensing with them altogether as we move on to new and novel formulations. This belief is clearly demonstrated in his 1966 review of Arlow and Brenner's *Psychoanalytic Concepts and the Structural Theory*, in which he warmly embraces the authors' championing of structural theory for its utilitarian usefulness, while chiding them for overlooking the continuing usefulness of the topographical model. Again, in his 1973 review of Kohut's *The Analysis of the Self*, Loewald praises the author for contributing to our understanding of certain disorders of self organization, but criticizes him for scanting aspects of the "more mature integration of the personality" (p. 348) in favor of an emphasis instead on the significance of more primitive self object issues. Loewald also criticizes Kohut for being "biased in favor of the analysis of the archaic ego [while he] . . . neglects the analysis of ego defenses" (p. 349).

Loewald's uneasiness with inclinations to discard earlier formulations and models in favor of embracing new ones is quite in keeping with his view of psychological development as taking place as the result of continual and ongoing incorporation of new input that contributes to steady revision and modification of that which has already been internalized and developed, rather than destroying and replacing what is already there.

Facilitation of Independence and Autonomy

Loewald makes two important observations in this paper that

pertain to our understanding of the developmental process, and also to our understanding of the way psychoanalytic treatment works. One observation (not fully developed) is that, in the course of interacting with their children, at least in favorable circumstances, parents themselves also grow and develop emotionally, just as analysts do in working with their analysands. The other is that ambivalent feelings are inevitable between children and their parents, just as they inevitably arise in the course of analytic work—in the analyst as well as in the patient.

In discussing this, Loewald harks back to Freud's use of the terms *ideal ego* and *ego ideal*:

> The ideal ego, by identification with the parental figures—perceived as omnipotent—represents, in Freud's view, a recapturing of the original, primary narcissistic, omnipotent perfection of the child himself. It represents an attempt to return to the early infantile feeling of narcissistic sufficiency, so rudely disillusioned by the inevitable frustrations and deprivations inherent in the conditions of extrauterine existence [1962, p. 1125].

The child at first clings to the illusion of "symbiotic" union with the mother, and then to "reliance on the seeming parental omnipotence" (p. 1125), Loewald continues. In fact, "both the child and the parents can be said to have fantasies—some would say illusions — about the other's state of perfection ... or at least ... perfectibility" (p. 1126). Such illusions are very difficult to maintain, however. The child inevitably finds itself disappointed by and angry with its parents (and vice versa) for thwarting its aims to exert dominance and control. These experiences, so long as they remain within the bounds of tolerability, lead to an increasingly realistic appraisal by the child of the parents and by the parents of the child, along with increasing maturity and effectiveness within the egos of both. Self psychologists, in particular, have come to focus analytic treatment heavily upon past failures of helpful, empathic attunement, and upon the mutative effect of the repair of these breaches of empathy.

Loewald (1962) emphasizes that:

> The parents are to be the guides in this process of clearing and resolving which leads to a more rational mutual relationship externally, as well as to a reasonably balanced internal relationship within the ego-superego system, in so far as the internalized demands lose their archaic insistence on narcissistic perfection [p. 1127].

He uses Ferenczi's observations on "sphincter morality" as a superego precursor to illustrate how parental failure to be "in tune with the maturational stage of the child—a lack of empathic interaction . . . interferes with internalization" (Loewald 1962, p. 1128). When parents are tuned in to the child's maturational stage and are aware of what the child needs to negotiate that stage, the child internalizes the parental assistance it receives, including its perception of what the parents favor and disfavor, approve and disapprove, and transforms it into something internal that it can continue to use to enhance and expand its effectiveness in dealing both with its own impulses and with the outside world. Loewald emphasizes that this process takes place throughout the life span, and that it is its continuing operation that allows psychoanalysis to be successful later on.

With each significantly disappointing loss, there is an experience of something that is somewhat similar to the way that children and adults mourn someone who is actually lost to them:

> Elements of the lost object, through the mourning process, become introjected in the form of ego-ideal elements and inner demands and punishments [that] . . . over long periods of time . . . may be found to

be progressive, so that eventually what was an ego-ideal or superego element becomes an element of the ego proper and is realized as an ego trait rather than an internal demand [pp. 1128–1129].

In other words, the taking in of external restraints and prohibitions in the service of facilitating realistic adaptation to the external world promotes autonomous self-regulation and self-control, as well as a more mature relationship with the object world. By inference, the analyst's appropriate and well-timed deprivation of gratifications, and/or expressions of disapproval of inappropriate behavior, is necessary if an analysand is to receive maximal benefit from analysis.

Loewald indicates, finally, that analysis affords the analysand opportunities to project or externalize superego elements onto the person of the analyst. This enables the analysand—as Loewald discussed in "On the Therapeutic Action of Psychoanalysis"—to utilize the analyst as a parent figure:

[This is] representative of a higher stage of organization [that can offer] . . . integrative . . . experiences of interaction, comparable in their structure and significance to the early understanding between mother and child . . . which in its full implications and in its perspective is a radical departure from the classical "mirror model" [1960, p. 239].

The analyst is thus afforded an opportunity to utilize the power conferred by the analysand to become a new preoedipal and oedipal parent—that is, to function as a guide and assistant who is perceived simultaneously and alternately as an omniscient, omnipotent being whom the analysand desperately needs, and/or as a de-idealized equal who can be questioned, doubted, criticized, competed with, at times defeated, and ultimately given up as no longer needed. And the analyst needs to be able to recognize when it is important to accept and go along with the use that the analysand is making of him or her at a particular time.

Loewald appears to recognize the duality of what takes place within an analysis, but he nevertheless focuses more on what occurs in the child than what occurs in the parent, and more on what is taking place in the analysand than what is taking place within the analyst. As Wesley (2000) points out, Loewald was "distinctly modern" in his belief that "early life experiences caused later psychopathology," but "postmodern" in his "emphasis on the relational factor in psychoanalytic cure—Loewald's idea of the analyst as a 'new object'" (p. 401), even as he "fashioned his quite radical innovations within the terms of classical psychoanalytic theory" (p. 404).

Loewald notes that a parent is only human, and so is a psychoanalyst. Both are still evolving, and both bring to their interactions their own needs, biases, struggles, conflicts, ambivalent feelings, and limitations. Every parent and every analyst oscillates between being helpful and facilitating independent growth, on the one hand, and pursuing his or her own needs and desires in ways that are not necessarily in the other's best interests, on the other. The myth of the perfectly analyzed analyst is just that—a myth (Silverman 1985).

Loewald (1960) expressed caution about the power the analyst has in influencing the process of rebuilding "the core of himself and 'objects'" (p. 229), which the analysand allows to emerge during the analytic process: "If the analyst keeps his central focus on this emerging core, he avoids molding the patient in the analyst's own image or imposing on the patient his own concept of what the patient should become" (p. 229).

Wesley (2000), similarly, expressed hesitancy about certain aspects of a recent tendency to emphasize the real relationship in the course of analytic interaction with the patient:

But what exactly does "more self expression by the analyst" mean in practice? . . . If we abandon the goals of neutrality and abstinence, what are the dangers at the margin? Does awareness of our subjectivity become a license to impose our personal views on an analysand, who, because he or she is a patient, is vulnerable to such impositions? Has a technical problem in psychoanalysis been transformed into a technical recommendation? [p. 408].

Such challenges—apt to face the analyst daily—are epitomized in the following vignette, shared with me by a colleague:

A 14-year-old patient, P, announced at the beginning of an analytic session that her dog had just died, apparently of cancer. The analyst, Dr. R, spontaneously reacted by being sympathetic and comforting. The patient, however, drew back from this, and indicated that she did not at all find it helpful to be soothed and comforted. She expected to talk to friends about what had happened, she said, and was certain that *that* would make her feel better.

In thinking about this, Dr. R realized that P's negative response to being comforted probably stemmed in part from her adolescent need to move away from adults and toward her peers for solace and assistance. Her response could also be viewed in light of the fact that her divorced mother had not only gone through a period of not liking P (connected with the mother's unsatisfactory experiences with her own parents), but had also held back from allowing herself to get close to P, while the patient's father, who had suddenly reappeared on the scene, threatened to take P away from her.

Dr. R also realized that she had responded to P in the way she did in part because she was being reminded of a time a number of years earlier when she had gone through cancer surgery and chemotherapy herself, and, overwhelmed by physical and emotional distress, she had not been able to adequately help her own daughter cope with the threat of possible maternal loss. Dr. R further realized that, in the past, her own mother had failed to help her deal with the fact that the mother was herself undergoing cancer treatment—just as she had failed to help Dr. R with childhood issues of growing up, many years earlier.

The analyst was exquisitely aware of the need to "disentangle the intertwined" issues in her patient and in herself, if she were to be able to help P effectively, and to refrain from an inclination to use the interaction over the illness and death of the dog for her own purposes. During the sessions that followed, aware that she would have to wait until P might be ready to delve into what had been stirred within her by the loss of her dog, she was able to largely sit and listen, without being unduly intrusive, while P continued to mourn this loss. The patient subsequently indicated that she had felt helped and was grateful to Dr. R.

Conclusion

In sum, the analyst plays a triple set of roles on the analytic stage. She allows the analysand to externalize and to project upon her the imagoes of past objects of the patient's own loves and hates, with all their positive attributes as well as their defects, deficiencies, and disturbances. The analyst must allow this to happen even when it makes her feel abandoned, dehumanized, or misused. In this role, she needs to weather the barrage of—at various times—puerile demands, complaints, and vilifications that she can expect the analysand to heap upon her, and she must do so without complaint, demurral, or seeking any retribution.

The analyst, secondarily, permits the patient to invest her with the powers, realistic and unrealistic, that previously resided in the analysand's parents, as well as in siblings, other relatives, teachers, doctors, and all the other significant figures who populated the analysand's world while she was internalizing them and their interactions with her, in the process of building her inner world and developing her own self as a person with power and emotional strength. In this regard, the analyst must provide the kind of responses that assist with the definition of self and other—the reactive as well as spontaneous emotional expressions that convey recognition and appreciation, in addition to the intermittent admonitions, cautions, and prohibitions that the patient received, and/or should have received, from parents and other players on the patient's stage during childhood and adolescence.

Furthermore, the analyst must exercise the self-restraint necessary to resist straying too far from the qualities exhibited by the original models upon which the dramatic role she is being asked to play are based. Otherwise, the analyst will be experienced as too far from the original models to be usable as an assistant, as the patient resumes the internalization process through which her psychological structure was constructed, so that the patient can continue to build and be rebuilt. It is vitally necessary, for example, as Busch (1999) and Goldberg (2004) have stressed, for the analyst to hear the music as well as the words, and to be on the same page as the patient in the analytic drama that is unfolding.

Finally, the analysand needs the analyst to be a brand new object, different from the original objects and able to present a new model for dealing with people. In this role, the analyst must be herself, and must be spontaneous and real as she interacts with the patient. This role may be easier and more comfortable than the other two roles, but imposes its own stresses. It requires the ability to be sensitive about how far to go, and how far not to go, in functioning as an altogether new object. Care must be taken not to intrude upon the analysand's agenda or to use the patient for the analyst's own emotional ends.

Psychoanalytic work entails clear-sightedness, deftness, and the ability to know when and how to play each role, at times more or less sequentially and at times simultaneously. Hans Loewald, in the paper spotlighted in this commentary and in his other contributions, has been extremely helpful in assisting us in carrying out this task, by greatly clarifying the second role mentioned without losing sight of the first one, and casting important illumination on the third role as well. For this we can be grateful.

REFERENCES

BALINT, M. (1968). *The Basic Fault: Therapeutic Aspects of Regression*. London: Tavistock.

BION, W.H. (1962). *Learning from Experience*. London: Heinemann.

BLOOM, H. (1975). *A Map of Misreading*. New York: Oxford Univ. Press.

BUSCH, F. (1999). *Rethinking Clinical Technique*. Northvale, NJ/London: Aronson.

GOLDBERG, A. (2004). *Misunderstanding Freud*. New York: Other Press.

LACAN, J. (1977). *Ecrits, trans. A. Sheridan*. New York: Norton.

LOEWALD, H.W. (1960). On the therapeutic action of psychoanalysis. In *Papers on Psychoanalysis*. New Haven, CT: Yale Univ. Press 1980, pp. 221–256.

———— (1962). Internalization, separation, mourning, and the superego. *Psychoanal. Q.*, 31:483–504.

———— (1966). Book review and discussion of *Psychoanalytic Concepts and the Structural Theory*, by Jacob A. Arlow and Charles Brenner, 1964. In *Papers on Psychoanalysis*. New Haven, CT: Yale Univ. Press 1980, pp. 53–58.

———— (1973). Book review of *The Analysis of the Self. A Systematic Approach to the Psychoanalytic Treatment of Narcissistic Personality Disorders*, by Heinz Kohut, 1971. In *Papers on Psychoanalysis*. New Haven, CT: Yale Univ. Press 1980, pp. 342–351.

MAHLER, M.S. (1972a). On the first three subphases of the separation-individuation process. *Int. J. Psychoanal. Psychotherapy* 53:333–338.

———— (1972b). Rapprochement subphase of the separation-individuation process. *Psychoanal. Q.* 41:487–506.

————Pine, F. & Bergman, A. (1975). *The Psychological Birth of the Human Infant. Symbiosis and Individuation.* New York: Basic Books.

MCLAUGHLIN, J.T. (2005). *The Healer's Bent: Solitude and Dialogue in the Clinical Encounter.* Hillsdale, NJ: Analytic Press.

REIDER, N. (1959). Chess, Oedipus, and the mater dolorosa. *Int. J. Psychoanal. Psychother.*, 40:320–327.

SILVERMAN, M.A. (1971). The growth of logical thinking. Piaget's contribution to ego psychology. *Psychoanal. Q.* 40:317–341.

———— (1985). Countertransference and the myth of the perfectly analyzed analyst. *Psychoanal. Q.* 54:175–199.

———— (1986). Identification in healthy and pathological character formation. *Int. J. Psychoanal. Psychother.* 67:181–191.

WESLEY, P. (2000). Modernism and postmodernism in psychoanalysis—an essay on *Kohut, Loewald, and the Postmoderns: A Comparative Study of Self and Relationship,* by J. G. Teicholz. *Psychoanal. Q.* 69:397–409.

WINNICOTT, D.W. (1965). *The Maturational Process and the Facilitating Environment. Studies in the Theory of Emotional Development.* New York: Int. Univ. Press.

———— (1971). *Playing and Reality.* New York: Basic Books.

CHAPTER 23:

PSYCHOANALYSIS AND THE TREATMENT OF PSYCHOSIS: *TREATING THE "UNTREATABLE"*

[(2010). Psychoanalytic Quarterly, 79(3):795–817]

A Book Review Essay on: *Healing in the Realms of Madness.* By Ira
Steinman. (London: Karnac, 2009. 207 pp.)
and
The Psychotic Wavelength: A Psychoanalytic Perspective for Psychiatry.
By Richard Lucas. London/New York: (Routledge, 2009. 335. pp.)

When I was a first-year resident in psychiatry at University of
Rochester Medical Center, I spent a four-month rotation at the
Rochester State Hospital to learn about chronic, severe mental
illness. One of my responsibilities was to interview 250 of the
long-term patients housed there and write a "six-month progress
note" on each of them. (I use the term *housed* because, although
everyone seemed kind and caring, resources were scarce and the
patients received little or no definitive treatment.)

One of the patients I interviewed was a regressed, disheveled,
schizophrenic man in his late thirties who wore a wild stare and
displayed palpable physical tension. I was informed that he had
not spoken an intelligible sentence in a very long time. I introduced myself, asked how he was doing, and asked if I might be
able to help him in some way. He spewed out an emotional tor-
rent of disorganized, disconnected verbiage that was utterly
incomprehensible. I tried hard to discern some kind of thread in
the profusion of words he was spraying in my direction, but was

unable to make out anything at all. After a while, I said: "I'm sorry, Mr. Adams. I've tried to understand what you're telling me, but I just don't know what you're saying."

What happened next startled the psychiatric nurse who was accompanying me—to such an extent that she stumbled backward and knocked over a cart laden with instruments and medication containers, which fell to the floor with a loud clatter. Mr. Adams had spoken his first intelligible sentence in seven years! "You're the first honest psychiatrist I've ever met," he said to me. "What do you mean?" I asked. "The others *say* they understand me," he replied, in an increasingly agitated tone of voice, "but they—" and here he erupted into a flurry of word salad. He flew into a sputtering rage and had to be led off by a big, burly aide who had been standing nearby.

Before he departed, I said, in all innocence and naiveté, calmly but firmly: "Look how angry you are! Maybe that's part of your problem. Maybe you get *so* angry that it scares you—and then you speak in a way that makes sure that no one can understand you and everyone stays away from you." He only growled and muttered as the aide led him away.

About ten days later, as I was standing in the hall talking to some nursing students whom I was expected to teach, I felt a tap on my shoulder. It was Mr. Adams. "Hi, doc," he said, "how are you?" We chatted for a while, during which he told me that he had thought about what I had said to him about his fear of his anger, and had concluded that I was right. He asked if we could talk about it.

From that point on, Mr. Adams and I spoke for a while almost every day. He told me about experiences he had had with people in the past that still bothered him, and we came to understand the self-protective function served by some of his psychotic symptoms. Although he was by no means "cured," the hypercritical voices that had been tormenting him for years eased up in their relentless attacks upon him, and his condition significantly improved.

A few days before my rotation was to come to an end, Mr. Adams walked by me and snarled, "I heard you're leaving; I don't care!" 'Yes you do," I said, "You do care." His physiognomy softened, and he said, 'You're right. I do. Thanks for your help. I'll miss you." I did go back and visit him a number of times.

There have been other psychotic patients—during my stint at the state hospital, when I was at Strong Memorial Hospital, and throughout my clinical experience since then—with whom I have been able to work psychodynamically. The vast majority of them have been able to make good use of this work and have made significant gains in their struggles with illness. I am fortunate to have had a first-rate psychiatric residency at a time when psychoanalytic understanding was valued in most psychiatric training programs. It has been sad for me, as it has been for many of my colleagues, to observe the shift that has taken place in psychiatric training away from a psychodynamic orientation and toward a predominantly pharmacological and behavioral one.

It was delightful, therefore, to come upon Ira Steinman's wise, wonderful, lively, and engaging book, *Treating the "Untreatable": Healing in the Realms of Madness*. Steinman has dedicated himself to working psychodynamically with severely ill, schizophrenic, bipolar, and multiple-personality patients. His description of his work is clear, hard-headed, convincing, and inspirational. *Treating the "Untreatable"* is filled with rich clinical detail that is both fascinating and a distinct pleasure to read.

Steinman begins by observing that humane institutions that employ judiciously administered medications together with group and individual psychotherapy are not only few in number at present, but are rapidly disappearing. Even in the best of them, furthermore, the treating personnel do not generally delve deeply into the meaning of psychotic delusions and hallucinations. For many years, he has worked intensively on an outpatient basis with psychotic patients, a large number of whom previously spent years in one or more of those institutions without achieving a major change in their condition. His approach has revolved around the expectation that helping these patients understand the origin and functions of their psychotic symptoms is the most effective way of helping them become able to relinquish them.

> Not only is the symbolic meaning to the patient of the content of delusions and hallucinations explored, but a rigorous attempt is made to try to figure out how, why, and when psychotic thinking began, and under what emotional and life circumstances [p. 20].

The "defensive retreat from psychological conflict, painful reality, and powerful affects" is made clear to the patients, so that they can come "to accept and work through the chaotic feelings of neediness, fear, fury, guilt, and despair which often preceded the development of delusions and hallucinations" (p. 29).

Steinman emphasizes the value not only of helping the patient understand his or her need for these psychotic mechanisms—especially "to diminish loneliness and assuage terror" (p. 29)—but also of reaching back with the patient to when and where these mechanisms began to be employed. He makes the cogent observation, furthermore, that even when there are neurophysiological deficits and disturbances that predispose one to the development of psychosis, the symptoms that develop always have genetic, historical significance and centrally important dynamic meaning.

> Crucially important is the knowledge—to be gleaned through repeated interactions—that even psychotic patients transfer the past to

the present and repeat past developmental stages and interactions in their relationships, delusions, and schizophrenic productions. If anything, the psychotic patient's transference reactions are more dramatic and extreme . . . [and they] . . . can be dealt with by the usual therapeutic technique of exploring and dynamically understanding these intense phenomena [pp. 30–31].

What is brought to the surface in the course of exploring the origin and meaning of psychotic manifestations can be terrifying to the patient, and can lead to chaotic outbursts and suicidal impulses. A therapist who carries out this kind of treatment has to stand by the patient very closely during difficult times, although this can prove extremely demanding on both participants in the treatment process. Steinman appreciates the value of antipsychotic medications, but he tries to wean the patient off them as quickly (or at times as slowly) as possible. He is also prepared to rehospitalize patients at times of crisis, although he attempts to keep the hospital stays as short as possible.

Most of the pages of this book are filled with clinical examples that dramatically illustrate the author's therapeutic approach (one possible cavil is that the book is quite short on general and theoretical explication). Daphne, for example, a 50-year-old woman diagnosed as schizoaffective, was unable for years to hold a job because of erratic, eruptive behavior, which alienated even her children from her. She had been hospitalized thirty-five times and had made a number of serious suicide attempts before Steinman began to work with her. She often sat mutely, staring into space, during their early sessions.

Daphne was very surprised when Steinman asked her to please tell him what she was staring at, as no psychiatrist had ever asked her that before. They explored at length the meaning and origins of her intermittent, delusional communication with an imaginary companion who had been part of her life since early childhood. "Mary" was a "good" friend who had accompanied her when she dissociated away from her depressive, at times abusive mother and from the alcoholic father who repeatedly molested her from the time she turned four years of age. At other times, Mary was a "bad" friend who encouraged her in childhood to try to do away with the baby sister who stole the meager attention she received from her mother, and who periodically pushed her to try to kill herself.

The treatment was prolonged and stormy. Suicidal inclinations emerged, which necessitated four brief hospitalizations. Despite this, Daphne made such good use of her intensive, dynamic psychotherapy that she "returned to work, had ten good years with her husband before his death, and was reconciled with her children" (p. 59). She remained "essentially delusion-free" (p. 60) during the twenty-five years that led up to the publication of this book. Her previous psychiatrist-psychoanalyst was "chagrined" that he had not pursued the kind of vigorous treatment Steinman described; he regretted having maintained the erroneous belief that "one had to treat severely disturbed patients with kid gloves, not with intensive psychodynamic psychotherapy" (p. 60).

Some of the vignettes in the book are tantalizingly brief, leaving the reader yearning to know more about the patients described. Also, Steinman's interventions tend to sound perfectly timed, crisp, and dramatically on target. I should have liked to read about his struggles to grasp what was going on, about the interventions that did *not* hit the target, and about the slow, difficult, groping efforts to make emotional contact with the extremely mistrustful and wary patient population on whom he reports—which I know from experience had to play a huge part in his work with them.

I should also have liked to hear about the role of empathy, understanding, compassion, and human caring in contributing to good results. The patients the author describes were hungry for safe human contact. What he does tell of his clinical work very much points to the important role played by his coming across to his patients as decent, caring, and above all respectful—not only of them as human beings, but also as capable individuals whom he believed in. Many of these patients had had prior experiences with mental health professionals who seemed to view them as helpless, defective, and hopeless.

I found myself somewhat startled by Steinman's accounts of several severely regressed, very poorly functioning, long-time schizophrenics who apparently gave up their psychotic symptoms in just six to eight months of treatment, and who maintained their gains for years thereafter. I cannot help but wonder whether some of them may have hidden their psychotic symptoms rather than truly given them up. On the other hand, I have treated some extremely paranoid individuals who were able to get over their paranoid delusions after twelve to eighteen months of treatment and remained free of them for years afterward. None of these patients appeared to be schizophrenic, however.

This brings me to another important dimension of working with very seriously disturbed patients. Steinman correctly observes that the therapist's goals may not necessarily coincide with those of the patient. A reduction of symptoms may be as wonderful a result for some people as total removal of them is for others.

Occasionally, a markedly delusional patient comes along who is both so intelligent and so intractably paranoid that the best that can be hoped for in the course of a short-term psychotherapy is a type of therapeutic impasse, where the patient saves face and insists on the correctness of paranoid beliefs, while clinical improvement occurs.

Such a stalemate is unsatisfactory for the therapist, but may be of crucial help to the patient in terms of work, relationships, and
involvement in life [p. 74].

I am reminded of another experience I had at Rochester State
Hospital. The superintendent of the hospital was a warm, humane, wonderful man who truly cared about the patients. When
I arrived, he gave me a list of seven patients in whom he hoped I
would take particular interest. He felt that they had potential for
much more clinical improvement than they had been showing,
and he hoped that something might click with one or more of
them that might enable me to be of real help to them. Unfortunately, none of them showed any indication of an interest in
working with me while I was there. To my great surprise, however, one of them approached the superintendent after I had left,
saying that he thought I might be able to help him. Arrangements
were made for Mr. Brown, as I shall call him, to enroll in the outpatient clinic at Strong Memorial Hospital (my next rotation site)
and to begin twice-weekly psychotherapy with me. He paid the
minimum fee of one dollar per session and walked the two miles
between the two hospitals each time he came, even during Rochester's harsh winters, in order to save the bus fare.

The treatment went very well for six or seven months, during
which Mr. Brown—a man in his early thirties who had been hospitalized for about ten years with a diagnosis of chronic,
undifferentiated schizophrenia—worked with me at trying to
understand the origin and meaning of his extreme anxiety, social
isolation, and subtly paranoid symptoms. He became less and
less withdrawn and isolated, and more and more interested in
intellectual pursuits, than had been possible for him for many
years. He began to make home visits for the first time in a long
while, and started to look up some old friends from the past.

Then everything seemed to come to a halt. Mr. Brown became increasingly hesitant and even silent during his sessions. We tried together to figure out what had happened, but seemed to get nowhere. Finally, something dawned on me. The next time we met, I told him I had an idea: "When you asked to come into treatment with me, [the superintendent] was excited and hopeful, and I was flattered. You thought I might be able to help you. I also got excited—I was going to cure you of your schizophrenia. But I never asked you what *you* wanted. I think that might be the problem."

"I'm glad you mentioned that," said Mr. Brown. "That *is* the problem. You want me to get out of the state hospital. But I'm never going to leave the hospital; I'm going to spend the rest of my life there. What I want is for you to help me become less anxious. I'm anxious all the time—all I do is pace all day. I started making a rug in O.T six months ago, but I've only been able to finish two inches of it. Please help me so I can feel better and be able to do more . . .but I'm never going to leave the hospital."

A subsequent visit to me by the patient's parents made it clear that they did not want him to be discharged either, and they had no intention of letting anyone make them change their minds about this.

Mr. Brown and I adjusted our sights, and progress resumed in the treatment. I scaled back my therapeutic zeal, and he, to his credit, allowed me to encourage him to raise his own goals to a meaningful extent. By the time his treatment ended, about a year later, he had finished his rug and two others, was taking a greatly reduced amount of medication, was elected president of the patient council, and had become the regular left fielder of the hospital Softball team (which competed in a league whose teams were not all hospital based). He also convinced his parents to agree to regular, biweekly weekend visits back home with them, and got them to assist him in looking for some kind of part-time work.

A large number of the patients Steinman describes in *Treating the "Untreatable"* eventually revealed to him that they had been sexually, physically, and/or emotionally abused as children. When he helped them recognize that there was an understandable genetic and dynamic link between these experiences and the content of their delusions and hallucinations, they could see that these disconcerting symptoms actually made sense, rather than being bizarre, foreign, or incomprehensible. Steinman's willingness to side with them in feeling anger at their abusers enabled them, furthermore, to regain ownership of the human emotions from which they had been desperately fleeing for many years. He was then often able to help his patients recognize that the psychotic mechanisms they had been using did not truly contain or reduce the terrors that bedeviled them, and that much more effective ways with which to deal with them were available. He also helped them understand that the delusions and hallucinations themselves contributed significantly to the loneliness and isolation from which they suffered, even though the delusions and hallucinations gave the illusion of connecting these lonely patients with other people.

I found myself, as I read the clinical vignettes recorded in this book, wondering to what extent the success of the treatments derived from gains that the patients—some of whom had been ill for a very long time—had obtained from various earlier treatment experiences that had enabled them to summon the courage and the will to end their withdrawn isolation and definitively tackle their problems. I also wondered to what extent it was Steinman's enthusiasm, courage, and determination that inspired them to succeed. My inevitable conclusion, of course, is that no one factor suffices on its own, and that a combination of things must have helped his patients. At times, furthermore, enlisting the assistance of an equally courageous, caring, and determined family member also played an important part in facilitating progress in treatment.

Once again, I find myself thinking back to Rochester State Hospital, to a young male patient in his early twenties who was mute and catatonic. Charles could not speak to me, but—being an artist by vocation—he demonstrated his desire for help first by showing me paintings he had already done, and then by producing more paintings to show me. I hazarded guesses from the content of the paintings about the emotions swirling within him, behind the impassive mask he wore. Gradually, Charles began to speak and we could have more conventional therapy sessions.

One day, he was moodily silent and then angrily blurted: 'You're the only person who sees my real self! Everyone else only sees what I show them. You're stealing my soul!" From that point on, he objected to having sessions with me, but I refused to give up on his treatment. I even traveled back to the state hospital to see him for sessions after I rotated to another hospital.

In an attempt to get away from me, Charles misbehaved in order to get himself transferred to units for more and more seriously disturbed patients. He finally ended up in what was known in the hospital as "The Snake Pit," where patients paced naked, masturbating, frothing, and growling in rage, guarded by the biggest, burliest aides in the institution. An aide would lock up the two of us in an interviewing room when I came for his therapy session, in order to keep me safe from the other wild and dangerous patients.

At this point, Charles gave up his flight from treatment and resumed working collaboratively with me. He rapidly improved and became well enough to leave the hospital within another six months. He expressed deep gratitude for my belief in him and for my persistent refusal to give up on his treatment. Seeing these attributes in me, he said, had enabled him to appreciate his own self and to fight against his illness. Interestingly, I met Charles again by chance a year after the treatment ended, at an art show, where he was exhibiting some of his work. Two of the paintings I saw there, each with a "sold" tag on it, were ones he had done as part of our work together.

I include references to my experiences as a psychiatry resident in this essay because of my deep appreciation that those who trained me, at a general hospital and at a state hospital, viewed psychotic patients as human beings who were often just as capable as nonpsychotic ones of participating in intensive, dynamically oriented psychotherapy that could lead to a successful outcome. Training based on this viewpoint enabled me to go on to successfully treat a good number of such patients over the course of my career as a psychiatrist and psychoanalyst.

At times, Steinman was able to apprise his patients that the very paranoia that expressed their anxious distancing from their families and from people in general simultaneously kept them connected to others. George, for example, had been ill for a quarter of a century, and had spent ten years in a leading psychiatric hospital, where the consensus opinion was that he would have to reside there for the rest of his life. Steinman enabled him to recognize that his paranoid conviction that his father had enlisted the aid of the Mafia to observe and control his every move served surreptitiously to provide him with the illusion that his father had not abandoned him, but was actually maintaining constant, vigilant contact with him.

> Even though George was convinced he perceived the world as it was, I [indicated to him that] . . .our task was to help him understand how he got to see things as he did. I told him that I didn't expect him

automatically to give up his beliefs, since they must mean something to him. Wasn't it curious, I went on, that he was so lonely and cut off from his family and friends, yet believed that "the Family" and his father followed his every move? Could the extent of his paranoid beliefs be a reflection of his loneliness? Could the paranoia be his way of trying to maintain contact with his family or other people? [p. 123].

George was dubious at first, but then agreed to explore the possibility that Steinman was correct. Not surprisingly, they discovered that behind George's fear of his father was rage toward him—a rage that terrified George. When the two of them explored George's powerful delusions—first, that a television personality was in continuous personal contact with him; then that a famous movie star was in love with him; and then that a female psychiatrist who had once treated him was not only in love with him, but was even prepared to leave her husband to marry him—George finally realized how empty these beliefs were. This led to his giving up his delusional solution to preoedipal and oedipal conflicts in favor of healthier, more reality-bound solutions—although his first reaction to the debunking of the delusional connection he felt with the television personality was to fill the emptiness within himself with alcohol and drugs, necessitating a hospitalization for detoxification. (This episode graphically illustrates Steinman's willingness to take risks, as well as the consequences that can follow when a treatment misfires.)

In the course of their trip toward a healthier level of functioning for George, Steinman accompanied him on an exploratory peregrination through the world of "Georgeland," in which George was the favored child of a fatherly "Unconscious God" who even at times loved him, unlike his ever-critical and unappreciative actual father. He came to recognize that the Christ-like suffering to which he had subjected himself was not really appreciated by his father.

George was doing whatever he could to hold on to the experience of love he felt when held by "God the Father." If not his father's most loved child, he was his god's favorite. . . . Slowly, he began to see that the "Unconscious God" devoted to George was a compensation for his perceived position of being less favored in his family. . . . More and more clearly, George began to see that he had been following his own promptings and wishes for a close relationship in his own family, and that he had not been following the dictates of an "Unconscious God" [pp. 134–135].

George became able to progressively abandon the delusional alternative world to which he had retreated in order to escape the pain he experienced in the external world of reality. George continued in outpatient therapy with Steinman during the fifteen years that led up to the writing of this book. During that time, he established a good relationship with his father and stepmother and lived almost exclusively in the real world, retreating only briefly to his delusional one at times when he was under great stress. He was not "cured," but he was greatly improved. How many of our neurotic patients do better than that?

It is important to note that the author does not arrogate to dynamic psychotherapy the sole, or even always the central, role in the treatment of psychosis. He recognizes that antipsychotic medication is necessary most of the time, and that social support, work with patients' families, and hospitalization are necessary for many psychotic patients. What he laments is the tendency to underestimate the capacity of a large number of psychotic patients to make use of intensive, exploratory psychotherapy to understand and gain control over the terrible illnesses from which they have been suffering.

It is one thing to diagnose and medicate and treat with supportive psychotherapy and social technique. But if this is not enough, and it certainly was not enough in George's case, one must unwind the threads that entwine the patient's delusions. The skein, the warp and weft of encircling and debilitating intrapsychic yarn must be unraveled . . . . Why was this method, in conjunction with the judicious use of antipsychotics, not employed in [his] many years in treatment settings? I believe that it has to do with our field having become convinced that antipsychotic medication is all we can do for severely psychotic patients: at best, we can medicate, reality test, and help with social adjustments. Furthermore, young psychiatrists have no experience treating such patients with psychodynamic techniques, and older colleagues (who for the most part have not tried it) doubt that it can be done. [p. 143].

Steinman can be critiqued for only scantily addressing the literature on psychodynamic treatment of psychotic patients and for the lack of a rich theoretical section in his book. Nevertheless, his effort to demonstrate the effectiveness of psychodynamic psychotherapy for psychotic patients by providing multiple, convincing clinical examples is quite successful, and we can be very grateful to him for it.

Fortunately, *The Psychotic Wavelength: A Psychoanalytic Perspective for Psychiatry,* also appeared in 2009. Written by the British psychiatrist and psychoanalyst Richard Lucas, who has himself devoted a lifetime to working with psychotic patients, this book contains the extensive literature review and theoretical perspective that is lacking in Steinman's book, so that the two volumes complement each other admirably. Lucas, too, is determined to facilitate understanding of the effectiveness of treating severely disturbed people with psychodynamic psychotherapy.

In *The Psychotic Wavelength,* the author stresses the wide variation among psychotic patients in the ability to successfully participate in intensive psychotherapy—a variation that is, of course, just as wide among neurotic patients. Lucas's experience confirms for him the correctness of Bion's (1967) observation that there is a more or less powerful, non-psychotic dimension within psychotic individuals to which a therapist can speak, and which can be engaged in the struggle to overcome the dominance of the psychotic dimension within the individual's psychological organization. He strongly disagrees with those who believe that psychotics are unable to think logically and are incapable of working with dynamic principles to wrestle with their emotional problems, and he presents multiple clinical vignettes to demonstrate the cogency of his contention.

Lucas, like Steinman, contends, furthermore, that much more can be accomplished in the treatment of psychotic patients than what he perceives as the very limited or even spurious results obtainable from cognitive-behavioral therapy. He seriously questions the assertion that people can be induced to give up entrenched, intensely self-protective delusions in ten formulaically programmed sessions. When that seems to occur, he maintains, the delusions have merely gone underground. He quotes Britton (2009), who, in a volume coedited by Lucas, "distinguishes between beliefs that have merely been surmounted and those that have been worked through and relinquished" (p. 41).

Lucas also points out that CBT outcomes can often be understood via the observation that "many psychoses resolve through a flight into health, by identification with an idealized parental figure" (pp. 42–43). This mechanism dovetails with something else about psychosis to which the author gives emphasis in this book, namely, that "the commonest symptoms of schizophrenia are not auditory hallucinations or paranoid delusions, encountered in some 60% of cases, but denial and rationalization, found in over 95% of cases" (p. 30). Intensive therapy is required to obtain meaningful, lasting results.

Lucas provides a condensed summary of the theoretical un-
derpinning of intensive psychotherapy of psychotic patients as it
tends to be viewed in Great Britain. He describes Klein's (1975a,
1975b) concept of lifelong oscillation between paranoid-schizoid
projection of "phantasized" envious, destructive, spoliating attacks upon the maternal sources of all good things, so that they
are perceived as persecutory (organizing the structure of paranoid delusions), on the one hand, and depressive, guilty, self-
accusatory attacks upon the self in punishment for those destructive inclinations (generating the suicidal inclinations of
schizophrenics), on the other hand.

Klein as well as Segal, Lucas indicates, stressed the importance
of manic defenses that produce grandiose "feelings of triumph,
control, and contempt. . .to protect the individual from experiencing severe underlying anxiety of psychic pain, whether
predominantly persecutory or depressive in nature" (p. 67). The
concept of manic reparation can help explain instances of sudden, apparent recovery from a schizophrenic or major depressive
decompensation. Segal (e.g., 1981) also distinguished between
true, metaphorical symbolism and concrete "symbolic equation"
of internal reality with actual external reality.

Rosenfeld (1965) observed that psychotic patients experience
transference reactions, although they tend to be concrete in nature, and that these transference expressions can respond to
analytic interpretation. He emphasized, however, that the paranoid-schizoid splitting and projection that occurs in psychotics is
greatly confused, so that the patient has much difficulty distinguishing between self and other and between good and bad.
Steiner (1993) emphasized the significance in psychosis of a desperate retreat from intense, overwhelming anxiety and pain to an
idealized, delusional world that protects against the threat of dis-
integration and annihilation (Lucas, p. 79). Enormous therapeutic

effort is required, therefore, to convince the patient of the necessity of leaving that world.

Lucas puts great stock in the importance of Bion's (1967) emphasis upon distinguishing between the psychotic and the nonpsychotic self and upon strengthening the latter so that it can deal more effectively with the psychotic self. Lucas cites Bion's view that:

> The psychotic part cannot think (lacks the capacity for symbolic thought); it can only fragment and expel. If the expelled parts come back, individuals experience this as an assault by actual objects. The more they aggressively fragment the particles coming back at them, the more they experience them as increasingly hostile. [Lucas, p. 91].

It is necessary to promote emotional strengthening and integration, and to advance to higher-level, symbolic thought, in order to empower the psychotic patient to apprehend and deal with destructive forces emanating from the psychotic part of his or her psychological structure. Bion (1967) believed that everyone begins in early life with a psychotic part that aggressively attacks and attempts to destroy all disturbing elements, both internal and external, with initial inability to distinguish between what is internal and what is external. A nonpsychotic, reality-oriented part develops, beginning very early, that grows larger and larger over time, with increasing divergence between the two, until the gulf between the two parts becomes so great that it is unbridgeable. (Unbridgeable except, perhaps—it seems to me—in certain controlled ways in exceptionally talented, creative, artistic individuals.)

In those who will eventually become psychotic, the nonpsychotic part does not develop sufficiently enough to dominate, control, and adumbrate the psychotic part—but there is always, to a greater or lesser extent, *some* nonpsychotic structure, and it is this which the therapist must address (Lucas, pp. 91–93). Bion also made reference to the nonpsychotic part of a patient being concerned with neurotic conflict while "the psychotic personality was concerned with the problem of repair of the ego" (Lucas, p. 161).

Lucas briefly summarizes Bion's theoretical explanation of hallucinations, derived from his clinical experience, by picturing an infant who expects the arrival of a nurturing breast but encounters a "no-breast" or absent breast. The author posits an infant who is unable to tolerate this experience and therefore evacuates the painful image of "bad breast" in the form of a hallucination of it—in contrast to the emotionally stronger baby who develops increasing tolerance for frustration, associated with the development of thought; i.e., this baby comforts him-or herself by thinking of a (good) breast. The mother plays a crucial role. A mother who accepts split-off, bad contents and detoxifies them via her reverie, according to Bion, facilitates the child's increasingly capability of reaccepting and reinternalizing the detoxified elements. Without this process of maternal containment of hostile projections, the infant experiences *nameless dread*. The implications for therapeutic technique are clear.

Lucas also applauds the clinically derived conclusions about schizophrenia made by Freeman, Cameron, and McGhie (1959). At the core of this illness, according to these three co-authors, is dissolution of the personality, with regression to early, primitive modes of psychological functioning, dominated by primary rather than secondary processes, to deal with stress and overload. Lucas agrees with Freeman, Cameron, and McGhie that biological factors play a major role in schizophrenia, necessitating the administration of antipsychotic medication. Although psychotherapy is necessary to mitigate and control psychotic mechanisms, it is unrealistic to subscribe to the concept of a neurotic-psychotic continuum that might support the idea that a "cure" can be obtained from psychotherapy.

Lucas draws in particular upon the work of Henri Rey at the Maudsley Hospital to distinguish, albeit in a somewhat oversimplified manner, between borderline and schizophrenic patients, with respect to what they look for from therapy. The former, he indicates, search for a helpful container for their extremely needy and destructive inclinations, and if they find it in a therapist, they worry about losing it again. The latter, in contrast, fearfully reject the container in the external world in favor of retreating into an internal delusional world of their own making. (The catatonic young artist I worked with at Rochester State Hospital dramatically epitomized this.)

Rey believed that:

> The only safe position for [borderline] patients is the border between the depressive and paranoid-schizoid positions. If the demand for perfection experienced in the depressive position becomes too much, the pain is split off and projected, and the patient reverts to a paranoid-schizoid mode ... [and] ...the border is the only safe position where both depressive pain and persecution from the paranoid-schizoid position can be avoided [Lucas, p. 132].

Lucas embraces Steiner's emphasis on the need to employ analyst-centered interpretations ('You experience me as ..." or "You are afraid that I ..."), rather than patient-centered ones, with borderline patients. This view stems from Steiner's observation that these patients "are more concerned with what is going on in the analyst's mind rather than in their own" (Lucas, p. 133). It might be said, it seems to me, that this applies as well to other classes of patients who are narcissistically extremely sensitive and vulnerable.

Lucas distinguishes clinically between what he terms *borderline states* and *a major psychotic disorder,* with respect to the kind of transferences that can develop and to the patient's ability to participate in a psychodynamic treatment process. With patients in borderline states, there are intense transferences, the ability to work psychotherapeutically (albeit with hypersensitivity and a tendency to experience narcissistic injury from the analyst's interventions), a sizable nonpsychotic self, and only brief, intermittent psychotic episodes. By contrast, in patients with what Lucas calls *major psychotic disorder,* there is no transference, because splitting and projection are so intense that all that is bad is ejected, and the capacity to feel the ambivalence necessary for entering into relationships is lacking; the nonpsychotic self is miniscule; and there is constant psychosis (although it can be disguised and hidden), due to the patient being on a constant *psychotic wavelength* covered over by denial and rationalization, rather than having frank delusions and hallucinations. With the latter group of patients, the therapist must depend heavily on working with family members, on environmental manipulation, and on assistance with socialization, as well as on the major use of powerful medication.

There is probably something of a continuum between these two groups of more or less accessible psychotic patients, however. Steinman, for example, describes very difficult but ultimately quite successful work with a number of patients who would appear to fit easily into Lucas's more seriously disturbed group. Some of the patients who did well in psychodynamic outpatient therapy with him had been delusional and hallucinatory for many years, and/or had had lengthy hospitalizations before he began to work with them. Giving up too quickly, or too hastily labeling patients "untreatable," can be a very unfortunate error.

Lucas, too, describes a case in which he often felt like giving up during a lengthy treatment that eventually turned out to have a happy ending. He provides a relatively detailed account of his heroic attempt to analyze a severely manic-depressive woman who had to be repeatedly hospitalized for florid manic episodes—in which she was flagrantly psychotic—that alternated with deep depressions. He persisted doggedly, although he was frequently on the verge of despair, until she finally made a significant and lasting clinical improvement (after the death of her mother, whom she hated).

Unfortunately, Lucas provides relatively little detail about his own interventions during his work with this patient; he prefers to speak mainly about his conception, in Kleinian terms, of what seemed to him to be taking place within the patient, which included an ambivalent, hostile "identification with an all-powerful mother figure" (p. 192), "clinging to pathological object relations" (p. 198), and "manic defense and manic reparation . . .in order to defend against underlying persecutory and depressive feelings . . .characterized by triumph, control, and contempt" (p. 199).

In connection with his work with this patient, Lucas cites Rey's belief that:

> In depression, the maternal breast, as part-object, represented the destroyed mother, and through identification, the subject felt depressed. In contrast, in manic states, the identification was with the penis as the object of reparation, with a magical ability to re-create the mother's attacked babies and breasts, that is, through phantasy of making her pregnant and refilling her empty breasts with milk (Rey 1994) [Lucas, p. 194].

Lucas emphasizes further that:

> The depressive phase is dominated by dependence on a tyrannical object, which demands total obedience and suppression of individuality. . . . Hidden resentment builds up gradually and silently . . . .

These feelings of resentment gradually tighten the spring until eventually it unwinds explosively in the manic phase [pp. 201–202].

The division of patients into groups labeled *borderline states* and *major psychotic disorder* somewhat troubles me, however. It can be heuristically useful to distinguish between the characteristics of those who are more accessible to psychotherapeutic intervention versus those who are less so, but there is a danger here. It seems to me that therapists can too easily fall prey to a tautological tendency to apply the rubric *borderline* to patients with whom their therapeutic efforts prove to be relatively successful, and apply a term like *major psychotic disorder* to those who do not respond well to treatment. This is similar to the tendency among some analysts to label patients who do not do well in analysis as *borderline* rather than *neurotic,* in order to explain inadequate results. In actuality, there is a wide range of variation among neurotic as well as psychotic patients in the ability to participate in an intensive treatment endeavor, and an individual analyst or therapist is not likely to be able to do well with every patient who lands on his or her doorstep.

It is also clear that Bion's heuristic division between the psychotic self and the nonpsychotic self is not be taken literally. *Everyone* is developmentally uneven, full of contradictions, different from day to day and from circumstance to circumstance, and unique in the details of the balance between rational and irrational. I am reminded in this regard of Bishop Berkeley's rejoinder, in response to John Locke's assertion that "beasts abstract not," that—as Carl Sagan quotes him in *The Dragons of Eden (1977)*—"if the fact that beasts abstract not be made the distinguishing property of that sort of animal, I fear a great many of those that pass for men must be reckoned into their number" (p. 113).

Greenspan (1997) wrote an interesting book on the topic of building ego structure in developmentally stunted, emotionally and intellectually primitive, but nonpsychotic individuals in order to enable them to participate in psychotherapy—just as Fonagy and his co-workers (2002) emphasized the necessity of assisting borderline and developmentally stunted but nonpsychotic patients in developing a capacity for mentalization before they can be expected to make use of traditional modes of psychodynamic psychotherapy.

Lucas's tendency to focus almost entirely on his conceptualization of what is going on within his patient psychologically, without providing as much detail of his own participation in the therapeutic work as I would have liked to have seen or of the interchange between them, can convey the impression that he is applying theoretical concepts to what is emanating from the patient rather than extrapolating understanding from it, although I am aware that this might be an artifact of shorthand expression. Examples include such statements as:

> When she was severely depressed, Mrs. L would also report a sensation that she had swallowed two tablets of stone that lay heavily on her stomach, i.e., the unresponsive stone breasts of her mother. The image also evoked [an image of] the Ten Commandments, not to be disobeyed [p. 213].

Another such example involves a man in a withdrawn, psychotic state who suddenly threw bleach into the face of a woman who was waiting to pick up her child from school.

> He said at the time that his aim had been to scar her. His action could be understood in terms of the wish of the psychotic part of his personality to avoid any reflection on his current mental state. Mr. R envied

the child, who seemingly had no problems, as he was totally looked after by his mother. The psychotic part of his personality wished to ensure that any current self-criticisms were projected and disowned into the mother, so that he could remain in an omnipotent state of mind. [p. 257]

Lucas provides a longish account of supervision of a therapist working with an extremely depressed, frequently suicidal woman, in which the central point seems to be that the therapist needed help recognizing that her patient required something specific: that is, assistance in realizing that her (the patient's) guilt about seeking care and attention by being ill was only the surface manifestation of her problem. The patient's self-deprecation actually stemmed from the attacks of a brutal superego that had developed out of an internalization of intensely hypercritical parental figures who could never be pleased, and who had convinced her that she was incorrigibly bad and sinful.

In psychotic depression, Lucas emphasizes, the patient is:

> ...totally identified with an idealized ego-destructive superego, which remains tyrannically in control .... There is a pull to remain in identification with the absolute in order to avoid all the confusing mixed feelings towards the ideal that result from starting to experience separateness [p. 278].

Lucas, following Rosenfeld (1987), stresses the need to speak both to the (sadistic) psychotic and the (timidly tortured) nonpsychotic parts of the patient's personality, in the interest of "furthering the move in the sessions from a monologue to a dialogue ...thereby moving them away from a total domination by a relationship with an ego-destructive superego" (Lucas, p. 277). This is quite consistent with Steinman's approach to such patients.

In the last section of the book, Lucas addresses a number of practical issues concerning the treatment of psychotic patients, including those that arise during hospitalization. These include risk assessment, the management of violent outbursts and (especially) of suicidal inclinations, working with family members, and the need for education of mental health professionals and auxiliary personnel about psychosis and about the challenges presented by psychotic patients.

These two books by Ira Steinman and Richard Lucas dovetail and complement one another in very useful ways. They convey the joint message that psychotic people are not necessarily untreatable, so long as psychotherapists understand what is taking place within them, are able to tune in to what Lucas terms the *psychotic wavelength* within them, and are able to speak to and establish a constructive alliance with the non-psychotic dimension of the personality. If these therapeutic aims can be successfully carried out, it is possible to engage many patients with a psychotic condition in such a way that they can collaborate effectively in psychodynamic psychotherapy, which in turn can lead to extremely welcome clinical results.

These two books inspire and inform. They deserve a place in all mental health training programs.

REFERENCES

BION, W.R. (1967). *Second Thoughts*. New York: Jason Aronson.

BRITTON, R. (2009). Mind and matter: a psychoanalytic perspective. In *The Organic and the Inner World*, ed. R. Doctor & R. Lucas. London: Karnac.

FONAGY, P., GERGELY, G., JURIST, E. & TARGET, M. (2002). *Affect Regulation and Mentalization: Developmental, Clinical, and Theoretical Perspectives*. New York: Other Press.

FREEMAN, T., CAMERON, J.L. & MCGHIE, A. (1959). *Chronic Schizophrenia*. London: Routledge, 2003.

GREENSPAN, S.I. (1997). *Developmentally Based Psychotherapy*. Madison, CT: Int. Univ. Press.

KLEIN, M. (1975a). *Love, Guilt, and Reparation and Other Works, 1921–1945*. London: Hogarth.

———— (1975b). *Envy and Gratitude and Other Works, 1946–1963*. London: Hogarth.

REY, J.H. (1994). *Universals of Psychoanalysis in the Treatment of Psychotic and Borderline States*. London: Free Association.

ROSENFELD, H.A. (1965). *Psychotic States: A Psychoanalytic Approach*. London: Hogarth.

———— (1987). *Impasse and Interpretation*. London: Routledge.

SAGAN, C. (1977). *The Dragons of Eden: Speculations on the Evolution of Human Intelligence*. New York: Ballantine.

SEGAL, H. (1981). *The Work of Hanna Segal: A Kleinian Approach to Clinical Practice*. New York: Jason Aronson.

STEINER, J. (1993). *Psychic Retreats: Pathological Organisations in Psychotic, Neurotic, and Borderline Patients*. London: Routledge.

CHAPTER 24

THE SORROWS OF YOUNG WERTHER AND
GOETHE'S: UNDERSTANDING OF MELANCHOLIA

[Martin A. Silverman (2016). *The Psychoanalytic Quarterly* 85:1,
pp.199–209.]

The Sorrows of Young Werther (1774). By Johann Wolfgang von Goe-
the, translated by Elizabeth Mayer and Louise Bogan. 167 pp.
In *The Sorrows of Young Werther, and Novella.*
New York: Random House, 1971.

The Sorrows of Young Werther was published in 1774, when Goethe (1749–1832) was just twenty-five years old.[1] A product of
true literary genius, it not only represents one of the greatest
works of literature ever written, but it also offers keenly intuitive
insight into one of the most terrible and, mystifying emotional
disorders that plague humankind. Well. before Sigmund Freud,
and most probably destined to become an important source of
Freud's understanding of melancholic depression, Goethe was
able to peer into the soul of those afflicted with what is now
termed Major Depressive Disorder (and some forms of Bipolar
Disorder) and see what is taking place within those who are suffering from it[2] is impressive how clearly Goethe grasped the twin

---

[1] Goethe wrote the novel as he was recovering from his own experience of an extremely depressing, hopeless infatuation with Charlotte Buff ("Lotte"), who was
betrothed to Johann Christian Kaestner. Furthermore, Goethe's close friend, Karl Wilhelm Jerusalem, had recently committed suicide.
[2] Among the nineteen references to Goethe's works in Freud's letters to Fliess (Masson,
1985) is the following: "The mechanism of fiction is the same as that of hysterical fantasies. For his *Werther* Goethe combined something he had experienced, his love for

roles played in melancholia of narcissistic object choice and extreme ambivalence toward a love object.

As the story begins, Werther, a young man who is about the same age as the author, has found a little valley in a somewhat remote area that impresses him as wonderfully idyllic. As a still unformed and floundering entity who has not yet discovered either his direction or his purpose in life, he idealizes his surroundings in the village of Wahlheim and falls in love, in an inchoately gushing and all-embracing manner, with the local inhabitants of the area. He interacts, with adolescent eagerness and naivete, with one person after another (especially very young ones, with whom he quickly and easily resonates), while he dabbles at painting and writing and is sustained financially by subsidies from his mother.

When he meets Lotte, a pretty, engaging, charming young woman who has lost her mother and has replaced her as the designated maternal figure of a brood of adoring younger siblings, he *instantly* falls in love with *her—madly* in love with her. He knows that she is unattainable, as she is engaged to be married soon to a very suitable young man, but he cannot stop himself from tumbling head over heels for her. He cannot hold back from increasingly centering his existence on her or from increasingly tormenting himself over his inability to do without her. His pain and anguish grow deeper and deeper until they take over his entire existence, blotting out all else as they *become him.*

Goethe designs the first two-thirds of the book as a series of letters Werther has written to his "dearest friend" (1774, p. 3), Wilhelm, from whom he has recently taken leave (as well as from his mother and from the young woman whose heart he

---

Lotte Kaestner, and something he had heard, the fate of young Jerusalem, who died by committing suicide. He was probably toying with the idea of killing himself and found a point of contact in that and identified himself with Jerusalem, to whom he had lent a motive from his own love story. By means of this fantasy he protected himself from the consequences of his experience" (p. 251).

has just broken by turning his attentions to her sister). He provides Wilhelm with a running account of his experiences in Wahlheim and its environs. He informs Wilhelm in the first letter, dated May 4, 1771, that he regrets having abandoned him and having hurt the young lady whom he encouraged but then betrayed. Werther asks Wilhelm to inform his mother that he *will* eventually at- tend to some business with which she has entrusted him and that upon meeting his maternal aunt he has *not* found her to be as terrible as his mother has depicted her to be (for allegedly cheating his mother out of her proper share of an inheritance).

Then he writes:

> Otherwise I am happy here. The solitude in this heavenly place is sweet balm to my soul, and the youthful time of year warms with its abundance my often shuddering heart. Every tree, every hedge is a nosegay of blossoms; and one would wish to be turned into a cockchafer, to float about in that sea of fragrance and find in it all the nourishment one needs. [1774, p. 4].

The all-consuming, love-at-first-sight passion aroused in Werther when he meets Lotte, however, sweeps away all the peace, contentment, and sense of fulfillment he has been experiencing in Wahlheim (literally, "Chosen or Ideal Home," which, we can speculate, might very well be a reference to the womb or the maternal bosom). He now races inexorably and inextricably toward disaster. What has happened to him?

About halfway through the *story*, we come upon a passage that reflects Goethe's intuitive grasp of the centrality of narcissistic object choice in the generation of melancholia. In his letter of October 20, 1771; we find the following:

503

It is true that we are so made that we compare everything with our-selves and ourselves with everything. Therefore, our fortune or misfortune depends on the objects and persons to which we compare ourselves; and for that reason nothing is more dangerous than soli-tude. Our imagination, by its nature inclined to exalt itself, and nourished by the fantastic imaging of poetry, creates a series of beings of which we are the lowest, so that everything appears more wonder-ful, everyone else more perfect. And that is completely natural. We so frequently feel that we are lacking in many qualities which another person apparently possesses; and we then furnish such a person with everything we ourselves possess and with a certain idealistic compla-cency in addition. And in this fashion. a Happy Being is finished to perfection-the creature of our imagination.

If, on the other hand, we just continue to do our best in spite of weakness and hard work, we very often find that, with all our delaying and tacking about, we achieve more than others with their sailing and rowing-and it gives a true feeling of our worth if we keep pace with others or even overtake them (pp. 78–79].

Goethe, in this brief passage, encompasses the manner in which narcissistic object choice, with its attendant depletion of the store of self- regard and self-worth that is so necessary for emotional well-being, plays a central role in an individual's fall into deep, melancholic depression, if the love object so invested disappoints or appears to be taking leave. He also recognizes that when someone invests deeply and thoroughly in the all-im-portance of the other, this empties the person of self-regard and subjects him or her to an intolerable sense of aloneness and lone-liness in the absence or threatened absence of the other.

Goethe also addresses in *Young Werther* the intensely ambiv-alent attitude toward the object of one's affection and desire that is the other hallmark of the disposition to melancholia. Very early in the book, Goethe has young Werther meet a peasant who is deeply despondent over his dismissal by the widowed mistress he was serving after he professed un- dying love for her. Werther understands and feels for this hapless young man, and he talks him out of committing suicide. He and Werther quickly become friends.

Later on, after Werther has descended into a deep funk in which he is ready to surrender Lotte to Albert, whom she has just married-at the same time that he wishes Albert were gone-he hears that a murder has taken place, disrupting the peaceful calm that usually reigns in Wahlheim. When he is told that a peasant formerly in the employ of a local widow has killed the man who replaced him in her service, Werther instantly knows who has perpetrated the horrific deed. Like a man possessed, he throws himself, albeit in vain, into trying to have this person set free, even though he knows quite clearly that the culprit must be put to death for having committed such a terrible crime. The "editor" of the book explains Werther's actions as follows:

> He considered him, even as a criminal, to be free of real guilt, and identified himself so completely with him that he was certain to be able to convince others. He could not Wait to plead for him; the most persuasive arguments rose to his lips; he walked quickly back to the hunting lodge and could not keep himself from rehearsing, in an undertone, as he went along, the defense he wanted to present to the bailiff [p. 130].

When Werther finds that he cannot possibly save the unfortunate peasant who succumbed to his murderous rage toward the man whore- placed him at the bosom of his love, Werther writes a note to himself that is eventually found among his papers. It reads: "There is no help for you, unfortunate man! I see only too well that there is no help for *us!*" (p. 131, italics added).

505

Werther decides that he, too, has to die. In a letter to Lotte to be given to her after his death, he writes that, in "a decided fashion," he has come to the conclusion that he must give up his life:

> It is not despair; it is the certainty that I have suffered enough, and that I am sacrificing myself for you. Yes, Lotte! 'Why should I hide it from you? One of us three must go, and I am to be that one! O *my* dearest, my wounded heart has been haunted by a terrible demon--often. To murder your husband! Or you! Or myself? Well, so be it [p. 141].

He goes one last time to Lotte, in order to tell her that he is leaving-although he hopes against• hope that she will leave Albert for him. She offers to remain fast friends with him, but he cannot accept such a lesser relationship with her. He impulsively throws himself toward her and showers her with kisses--just as the young murderer whom he befriended told him he had done with the widow with whom he was enamored. And like the widow with her servant, Lotte pushes Werther away. She runs into another room, locks the door, and insists that he leave. Werther tells her that she will never see him again and departs.

He subsequently requests of Albert, Lotte's husband, that he lend him his pair of pistols for his journey. Albert quickly assents, indicating that he never believed Werther would actually carry out the suicidal intent of which he had spoken, and Lotte herself hands them over to Werther's messenger, despite her qualms about so doing, Werther receives the pistols in his rooms, writes Lotte a note informing her that he has showered the pistols with kisses, is enraptured by having been given the opportunity to kill himself with the weapons that came to him from *her* hands, and looks forward to ultimately being together with her for all eternity. When the shot is heard, people rush to his side and find him bleeding to death, with brain matter extruding from his shattered skull!

Goethe includes, earlier in his story, an episode that dramatically highlights Werther's narcissistic fragility-a fragility that is illustrated in his enormous need to receive external validation of his worth and value and in the intense, narcissistic rage that erupts within him when this affirmation is lost to or withheld from him.[3] Werther accommodates Lotte's father by carrying a message to Count C., a high-ranking member of the king's administrative structure. The count is quite taken with Werther's affable demeanor and quick intelligence, and he invites him to accept a clerical position with him. Both his mother and his close friend Wilhelm have been urging Werther for some time to end his aesthetically pleasing, dilettantish idyll and engage in some form of gainful employment that might lead him onto a meaningful career path. Werther is flattered by Count C.'s high estimation of him, and he accepts the invitation to assist the count as he carries out the responsibilities the king has given to him. For a while, things appear to go rather well. Werther finds the work easy, even too easy, and enjoys how well he is able to outshine others in the count's employ.

Then something occurs that wrecks everything. He reports it to Wilhelm in a letter dated March 15:

> Something has so humiliated me that I shall be forced to leave this place, and I gnash my teeth! The devil! The harm is done, and it is *your* fault *alone—you* spurred me on, pushed and tormented me into accepting a position that was not congenial to me. Well, here I am! And you have had your way! And in order to prevent you from telling me

---

[3]W.H. Auden, in the foreword he wrote for the 1971 Random House version of this book, focuses intently on this episode, as he, ungenerously and without Goethe's compassionate understanding of human psychology--castigates Werther as being anything but admirable or heroic: "To us it reads not as a tragic love story, but as a masterly and devastating portrait of a complete egoist, a spoiled brat, incapable of Jove because he cares for nobody and nothing but himself and having his way whatever the cost to others" (p. xi).

that it was my eccentric ideas which ruined everything, I here recount, dear sir, the story, plain and simple, as a chronicler would put it down.

Count C. is very fond of me and singles me out, as is well known, and as I have written you many times. He had invited me for dinner at his house yesterday, on the very day when the whole aristocratic set, ladies and gentlemen, are accustomed to meet there late in the evening I had completely forgotten this fact; and it also did not occur to me that subordinate officials like myself are not welcome on such occasions. [p. 88, italics in original] .

Werther goes on to explain to Wilhelm that when Count C.'s aristocratic guests arrived and saw him there, "they opened their eyes wide and turned up their noses in the traditional highly aristocratic manner: As that clique [was] entirely repulsive to [him]" (p. 88), he decided to leave-but he did not leave. Instead, he stayed on and amused himself by internally disparaging their shallowness, vacuity, ugliness, garishly ostentatious display of tonsorial finery, and demonstration of no more ambition than that of ingratiating themselves to the count so that they might move another chair closer to him at his table.

The arriving guests demonstrate, unmistakably, their great displeasure at having a mere commoner—a mere functionary who works for a living—in their exalted company. Even the one young woman who had been friendly with Werther in the past, herself a member of the aristocratic clique, allowed him to see how embarrassed she was to be seen speaking with him. The next day, she would tell him that she had been roundly chastised for having had a friendship with him, and that he could expect "punishment . . . for [his] arrogance and haughty contempt toward others" (p. 92).

The count, finally recognizing what was happening that evening, took Werther aside and politely asked him to leave. Werther apologized for his social faux pas and departed, much chagrined. "Crushed" and "furious" the next day, he wrote to Wilhelm that he wanted to "open one of [his] veins and gain eternal freedom for himself" (p. 92). Within a week, he handed in his resignation to the court and left the count's employ. This experience only accelerated Werther's headlong descent into utter melancholic despair.

We have to appreciate Goethe's intuitive grasp of human psychology, and we can only admire his enormous literary skill. Reading this book is quite an emotional experience. A number of vulnerable young men in Germany and its environs committed suicide, in fact, after reading the book at the time of its publication. *The Sorrows of Young Werther* is a powerful work in more ways than one.[4]

We know that Freud read Goethe. We also know that Freud learned from what he read. Almost 150 years after the original publication of *The Sorrows of Young Werther,* he published "Mourning and Melancholia" (Freud 1917). Here Freud examined melancholia, or deep de- pression, by contrasting it with ordinary mourning. Unlike the situation of mourning, in which a love object who was cherished has been lost, a melancholic depression occurs when one is reacting to the loss of, or the experience of significant disappointment from, another or others from whom the individual has vitally needed appreciation, love, and affirmation of his or her worth or value.

To put it succinctly, in *mourning* there is loss of a largely *anaclitic*

---

[4] Coupled with *The Sorrows of Young Werther* in the Random House version (1971) is Goethe's *Novella* (1828), which reads as a moving, literary portrayal of power in its various forms—sociological, marital, political, financial, natural (fire, lions, and tigers), and familial-as a constructive or as a destructive force. Interestingly, it is love and art (in the form of music and poetry) that are depicted as having the capacity to tame raw power when it gets out of control and becomes destructive or potentially destructive. The success in this story of love and art contrasts starkly with their failure in the story of the unfortunate Werther. Melancholia is a terrible disorder indeed!

love object, while in *melancholia* there is a highly *ambivalent* attachment to a lost and/or disappointing, *narcissistically cathected* object from whom rejection or abandonment cannot be accepted. That object is retained unconsciously by regressively identifying with the object, apparently on the model of oral incorporation of food, to prevent it from getting away. Recovery from mourning is characterized, furthermore, by gradual *acceptance* of the loss of the loved object, while in melancholia there is gradual *destruction* of the ambivalently loved and hated object with whom the individual has identified. The core issues in melancholia that are emphasized by Freud are narcissistic object choice and an extreme degree of ambivalence, precisely what bursts out of the pages of Goethe's *The Sorrows of Young Werther.*

To quote Freud:

> The melancholic displays something . . . that is lacking in mourning-an extraordinary diminution in his self-regard, an impoverishment of his ego on a grand scale. In mourning it is the world which has become poor and empty; in melancholia it is the ego itself. The patient represents his ego as worthless, incapable of any achievement and morally despicable; he reproaches himself, vilifies himself, and expects to be cast out and punished. [1917, p. 246].

> There is no correspondence, so far as we can judge, between the degree of self-abasement and its real justification. A good, capable, conscientious woman will speak no better of herself after she develops melancholia than one who is in fact worthless; indeed the former is perhaps more likely to fall ill of the disease than the latter, of whom we too should have nothing good to say. [p. 247].

> If one listens patiently to a melancholic's many and various self- accusations, one cannot in the end avoid the impression that often the most violent of them are hardly applicable to the patient himself, but that with insignificant modifications they do fit someone else whom the

patient loves or has loved, or should love .... The woman who loudly pities her husband for being tied to such an incapable wife as herself is really accusing her *husband* as being incapable, in whatever sense she may mean this. There is no need to be greatly surprised that a few genuine self-reproaches are scattered among those that have been transposed back. These are allowed to obtrude themselves, since they help to mask the others and make recognition of the true state of affairs impossible. Moreover, they derive from the *pros* and *cons* of the conflict of love that has led to the loss of love. [p.248, italics in original]

Freud states further that:

The that ... narcissistic identification with the object ... becomes object-choice has been effected on a narcissistic basis, so a substitute for the erotic cathexis, the, result of which is that in spite of the conflict with the loved person that love relation need not be given up. [1917, p. 249].

The loss of a love-object is an excellent opportunity for the ambivalence in love relationships to make itself effective and come into the open. In melancholia, the occasions which give rise to the illness extend for the most part beyond the clear case of loss by death, and include all those situations of being slighted, neglected, or disappointed which can import opposed feelings of love and hate into the relationship or reinforce an already existing ambivalence. [p. 251.]

No neurotic harbors thoughts of suicide which he has not turned back upon himself from murderous impulses against others .... The ego can kill itself only if, owing to the return of the object-cathexis, it can treat itself as an object-if it is able to direct against itself the hostility which relates to an object and which represents the ego's original reaction to objects in the external world. [p. 252]

The correspondence between Freud's depiction of melancholic depression and Goethe's story is striking. Freud's observations about melancholia also remain valid to the present time. In the melancholic- patients I have treated and am currently treating, the prominent features include intolerable, exquisitely painful loss of an idealized but ambivalently regarded love object or love objects (past and present); an extreme sense of having been "rejected" and/ or abandoned; 'terrible feelings of being valueless and/ or un-valued by others; wrenching loneliness and alone- ness; visceral manifestations of pain and suffering •(severely disturbed eating and sleeping; gastrointestinal symptoms, such as abdominal pains, constipation. diarrhea, irritable bowel"); and extreme guilt and need for punishment (e.g., thoughts of deserving to be "in jail" or even "on death row"), as well as indications of feeling helpless and usually hopeless. Generally, there are plentiful indications of ex-tremely ambivalent attitudes toward those to whom the person is attached, usually accompanied by vigorous denial of rage har-bored toward those who appear to have disappointed, rejected, and betrayed him or her.

Freud's perspicacity about severe depression is impressive. Goethe's literary depiction of it is astounding. We owe each of them a debt of gratitude for elucidating this terrible affliction.

REFERENCES

FREUD, S. (1917). Mourning and melancholia. *Standard Edition* 14.

MASSON, J. M., ED. (1985). *The Complete Letters of Sigmund Freud to Wil-helm Fliess*, 1887–1904. Cambridge, MA/London: Belknap Press.

VON GOETHE, J.W. (1828). *Novella*, trans. E. Mayer & L. Bogan. In *The Sor-rows of Young Werther, and Novella*. New York: Random House, 1971, pp. 169–201.

CHAPTER 25:

ON MYTHS AND MYTH-MAKING: PSYCHOANALYTIC THEORIZING ABOUT MOTHER-DAUGHTER RELATIONSHIPS AND THE "FEMALE OEDIPUS COMPLEX"

[(2012). *Psychoanalytic Quarterly* 81(3):727–750.]

Book Essay on 3 books:

A Story of Her Own: The Female Oedipus Complex Reexamined and Renamed. By Nancy Kulish and Deanna Holtzman. Lanham, MD: Jason Aronson, 2008. 218 pp.

Electra Versus Oedipus: The Drama of the Mother-Daughter Relationship. By Hendrika C. Freud; translated by Marjolin de Jager. London/New York: Routledge, 2011. 205 pp.

The Monster Within: The Hidden Side of Motherhood. By Barbara Almond. Berkeley, CA/Los Angeles: Univ. of California Press, 2010. 265 pp.

> *Myth-maker, Myth-maker, make me a myth*
> *With just the right height*
> *And with just the right width*
> *Myth-maker, make me a Myth!*
> *Myth-maker, Myth-maker, plots need to hatch*
> *And I need a key that will push up the latch*
> *To let loose a theory for people to catch*
> *Myth-maker, make me a Match!*

The morning after I began thinking about what I might write in response to Nancy Kulish and Deanna Holtzman's wonderful and intriguing book, *A Story of Her Own: The Female Oedipus Complex Reexamined and Renamed*, I awoke singing the first line of the lyrics that form the epigraph with which I have begun this essay. I completed the first stanza as I was shaking off my nocturnal cobwebs and preparing to see my first patient of the day, but to my surprise, I still could not identify the song whose words I was paraphrasing.

It was not until I was walking to my office that I realized it was the "Matchmaker" song from *Fiddler on the Roof* that had inspired my lame attempt at writing song lyrics. I had seen the musical on Broadway and then again on a Parents' Day visit to the performing arts camp where our children were spending the summer—and it was our older daughter who sang that song from up on stage while my wife and I sat in the audience! As I recalled this, the second stanza sprang from my brow, like Pallas Athena from the head of Zeus (although, as I was aware, it still needed a bit of refining). The latter came to me after I recalled that I had recently read or heard somewhere something about an observation made by a drama critic: that he viewed *Fiddler* as a prime example of modern cultural myth-making. Such is the way in which the mind works.

Psychoanalytic theorists beginning with Freud—just like writers in general—draw upon the great myths of the ages as they struggle to create new myths that they hope will immortalize them in the minds and hearts of the reading and thinking public. Freud did not develop his concept of the Oedipus complex from his reading of Sophocles' *Oedipus Rex*, but from clinical experience, beginning with himself as a patient. Then he seized upon the mythological story of King Oedipus to provide a dramatic metaphor that might serve as a vehicle for popularizing his ideas. There is no such *thing* as an Oedipus complex.[1] It is merely a set of ideas about an aspect of human psychology that have been connected with an ancient Greek myth in the interest of dramatic emphasis.

Ernest Jones connected Freud's observations about the developmental importance of emotional conflict arising out of the emergence during childhood and beyond of the complexities of triadic relationships and intergenerational rivalry and competition with Shakespeare's more modern story of *Hamlet,* Prince of Denmark, finding it an even more suitable vehicle than Sophocles's ancient play. At that time, Freud was being met with fierce opposition to what he was presenting to the world in general, and to the Vienna medical establishment in particular, about what he was observing in his patients involving childhood sexuality, unconscious parricidal wishes, and castration anxiety in the generation of neurosis and psychosis. Linking his observations, which were being treated as unwelcome anathema, with those of highly respected representatives of the intellectually revered and esteemed classics of earlier centuries was a brilliant political masterstroke. As much as Freud appreciated and admired Shakespeare, he recognized, it seems to me, that Shakespeare was an Englishman; and Freud was well aware of the extent to which chauvinistic and xenophobic prejudice against non-Germans prevailed in the Austria of his time.[2]

It is an error, in my opinion, to reify and grant seeming objectivity to the contents of Sophocles's dramatic literary production, as though the play is a psychological textbook to be studied literally. Doing so, it seems to me, itself constitutes a kind of mythmaking that is likely to in turn generate a distorted view of child

---

[1] Bion is said to have expressed consternation about the way people talked about his ideas as though they were facts: "My ideas are only ideas," he said, "They are not *facts!*" (Heath 2010).

[2] See Silverman (2012) for an in-depth discussion of these issues.

development and of psychoanalytic principles. Kulish and Holtz-man, the authors of *A Story of Her Own*, allude to this when they state in their introduction that:

> Old paradigms resist change. Any alternative model for the female tri-angular situation presents a struggle for analysts, male or female. . . . If the oedipal myth is to be replaced with another, then mustn't this re-placement mirror the Oedipus story? Thus we are bombarded with such questions as: Where's the punishment? Where's the aggression? Where's the dramatic adventure and active initiative taken by the fe-male? [p. 4]

Leavy (1985), referring to Freud's (1892–1899) announce-ment in a letter to Fliess of his discovery within himself of love for the mother and rivalrous hatred of the father (which he be-lieved to be more or less universal in men, and which he connected with Sophocles's *Rex*), states that: "The psychological discovery was mythologized at the same time that the myth was psychologized" (1985, p. 445). Leavy goes on to say:

> The Oedipus complex remains a concept that organizes the meaning of the patient's discourse around certain focal developmental happen-ings affecting the status of the child in the conflictual milieu of the family. Over the decades the concept has undergone a loosening of its connection with the Greek myth—a demythologizing [pp. 447–448].

Leavy proceeds to lament the way in which the myth has un-dergone periodic remythologizing as analysts have seized upon other characters in Sophocles's play, such as Jocasta or Tereisias, or upon other ancient Greek myths, as they seek acceptance of ideas they wish to promulgate. As Phillips (2003) articulates, in the course of examining the tendency in psychoanalysis to give too much credence at times to the epistemological usefulness of what mythology has to offer, "Leavy … cautions analysts against being led down the path of Greek mythology and away from the person on the couch" (p. 1440). Phillips goes on to reiterate and elaborate upon this message.

Kulish and Holtzman on the "Persephone Complex"

Kulish and Holtzman understandably object to organizing psycho-analytic understanding of the way in which girls and women experience and negotiate the developmental step of moving beyond dyadic, "preoedipal" relatedness into the more complex, triadic de-velopmental phase that follows it in terms of what Freud worked out about this sequence in boys and men. They correctly observe, as have many others, that Freud's extrapolation of what he observed in him-self and took to be a paradigm for what he presumed to take place in men in general (which itself presents certain problems) to what he presumed occurs in the course of female development led him to in-evitable distortions in his views about female psychology. Little girls are not little boys and never were little boys, contrary to Freud's sim-plistically reifying extrapolation from male to female psychology.

Freud himself eventually recognized that his views regarding fe-male psychology needed correction, and he looked to female analysts to accomplish that. *A Story of Her Own* contains a brief but meaning-ful review of the debates that ensued among Deutsch (1925), who, in particular, championed Freud's views, even as she placed new em-phasis upon the importance of the girl's powerful, preoedipal bond to her mother; Horney (1924, 1926); Lampl-de Groot (1927); Dooley (1938); and others who brought fresh observations and understand-ing to psychoanalysis.[3]

---

[3] For a compilation of a number of these early papers, see Grigg, Hecq, and Smith (1999).

Kulish and Holtzman especially object to the application of the terms *oedipal* and *Oedipus complex* to what occurs in *female development* and *female* psychology. I find myself fully in accord with them when they champion the adoption of the term *triangular phase* of development—for boys and girls alike—in place of *oedipal stage* of development.

These authors go beyond this, however. They propose that we not only examine male and female development separately, but that we also abandon altogether the term *Oedipus complex* in connection with female development, and replace it with a unique but hopefully parallel term to help us define our views about what little girls go through during the triangular phase of their emotional development. They argue co-gently that words have power, as Litowitz (2002, 2003), Lerner (1976), and others have pointed out, and they object to applying a term that is associated with male emotional development to the development of females. Drawing upon the Greek myth of Persephone and her mother Demeter, they propose that we apply the term *Persephone complex* to what takes place between girls and their mothers during the triangular phase of development.

The problem, however, is that in so doing they simplify and reify what actually is much more complex than what is alluded to within either of those two myths. They fall prey, furthermore, to the same sort of mythologizing and casting allegiance to a metaphor as though it were a truth to which psychoanalysts have long done as they idealize and idolize the term *Oedipus complex* as the shibboleth for (ill-conceived) psychoanalytic orthodoxy.

Kulish and Holtzman also focus primarily upon but one (albeit important) aspect of mother-daughter relationships, while they scant other aspects of something that is actually much more multifaceted and complex than they depict it to be in their papers (e.g., Holtzman and Kulish 2000, 2003) and in this book. They

place powerful emphasis upon the very special connection between mothers and daughters that exists from birth and even
before birth, a vital connection that creates a serious dilemma for
both of them as the little girl moves on from dyadic to triadic
developmental organization. She and her mother are faced with
a dilemma when the girl progresses into triadic, competitive rivalry with her mother for her father's love and attention (and she
does so because of innate biological pressure, maturation, and
the attraction her exciting daddy exerts upon her—not because
of anger at her mother for not providing her with a penis and the
wish for compensation in the form of a penis-baby from her father, unless something is very wrong in her relationships with
her parents and siblings and in the society in which they live).
The idyllic relationship between mother and child that has existed until then becomes threatened (although in real life, it has
not truly been as idyllic as Kulish and Holtzman depict it to have
been, given the inevitable frustrations, annoyances, and power
struggles that arise even in the best of relationships).

In the myth of Demeter and Persephone, Kulish and Holtzman
find a paradigm with which to frame the dilemma they perceive to
be central in the transition from dyadic to triadic mother-daughter
relations. Stated in its simplest terms, the myth revolves around the
abduction of Demeter's virginal, nubile daughter as she is flowering
into womanhood by her uncle, Hades, lord of the underworld and
brother of both her parents. Demeter is distraught and inconsolable. To force her brother/husband, the all-powerful Lord Zeus, to
return her lost daughter to her, she ceases providing bountiful lar-
gesse, as the goddess of fertility and fecundity, to his valued human
subjects—so that not only will they starve, but they will also stop
rendering the sacrifices to Zeus that he requires of them.

Persephone, now queen of the underworld, demurely resists
Hades' advances, and she misses her mother dearly and yearns to

be reunited with her. Zeus submits to Demeter's pressure by granting her the boon of seeing her daughter again, although with the stipulation that she shall not have ingested any food while in the underworld. Via a clever tour de force, in which Persephone breaks the rule by ingesting a small number of pomegranate *seeds* (a reference to semen?) before she returns, a compromise is effected in which Persephone is allowed to spend part of the year (three-fourths in most versions, but two-thirds in others) with her mother (linked symbolically with bountiful Mother Earth?) and the rest of the year (winter) in the underworld as Hades' queen.

The Ancient Greek myth of Persephone and her mother Demeter, I might add, has inspired not only Kulish and Holtzman but others as well. The relatively recent film *Black Swan (2010)* can be seen as a modern version of the myth. It is the story of Nina, a young woman who has given up all other aspirations while she devotes herself totally and with single-minded determination to becoming the prima ballerina whom her mother longed to be but was not able to become. She still lives with her mother, in a child-size bedroom filled with stuffed animals, while her mother devotes herself fully to supporting and facilitating her daughter's ambitions in the ballet world.

Spurred on by another young—and in certain ways, older-sister-like—ballet dancer who is her main competitor for the lead in a performance of Tchaikovsky's *Swan Lake,* Nina darts out of her cocoon-like bedroom and follows her into a dark night club, where they drink and get involved with young men. The other dancer seduces her into entering the realm of adult sexuality, which until now Nina has totally avoided. Her first sexual encounters are with that other youthful, sensuous female dancer (in a dream? in reality?) and then with the womanizing male ballet master, who has earlier ordered her to masturbate in order to free up the passion needed to dance the starring role, and whose face in one powerfully dramatic scene is that of the devil.

Nina drifts dangerously back and forth between reality and fantasy as she is torn apart by twin conflicts. One is between intense, narcissistically driven, murderously competitive rivalry (with her contemporaries; with her mother; and with all prima ballerinas, past, present, and future) and the enormous guilt she experiences in connection with her wish to outdo and professionally demolish all her rivals, including her mother. The other is between her wish to grow up and away from her mother (as illustrated dramatically by her struggle to move on from performing merely as the innocent White Swan, to becoming able to perform as the sensuous Black Swan) and the guilt she feels for abandoning her mother after her mother has sacrificed everything else in life to be there with her and for her.

In the final scene, after Nina brilliantly performs the role of the black swan, with her mother weeping in the audience, she collapses backwards off the stage. It is not clear whether she has swooned in exultation and exhaustion or has died. Perhaps, in a way, it is both of these!

What could possibly be wrong with replacing the term (and concept of) *female Oedipus complex* with that of *Persephone complex?* To my mind, there are several reasons not to do so. First of all, it is misleadingly incomplete in its depiction of what is involved in the developmental advance from dyadic to triadic mother-daughter relations. When a little girl becomes competitive with her mother as she becomes entranced by and falls in love with her father, she does not necessarily have to give up her intense attachment to her "preoedipal" mother as the love of her life. With the preoperational thinking that prevails before the age of seven years or so, when the little girl focuses on one part of the whole field she loses sight of the other part because of her inability to hold on to the whole while examining a part of it (see Silverman 1971). It is within her capacity to maintain conflicting attitudes and inclinations inside herself; inconsistency is not a problem. Although conflict and sadness are to some degree inevitable, the girl and her mother will be able to negotiate the transition successfully *if the mother is able to tolerate dilution of their bond and help her daughter do so as well.* They do not necessarily need to lose each other or lose the special link that exists between them.

Second, invoking the duality of *Oedipus complex* for boys and *Persephone complex* for girls to emphasize the differences that exist in male and female development can blur the fact there are also commonalities. The first major, intense relationship for girls and boys alike, with rare exception, is with the mother. Moving on to triadic, competitive interaction with parents presents problems for both boys and girls, as well as challenges to the parents of both. All relationships, furthermore, are bidirectional and more or less ambivalent.

The way in which parents experience and respond to the child during the dyadic phase, during the triadic phase, and during the transition between them, as well as during the separation-individuation process that occurs early in childhood and again during puberty and adolescence, is as variable as it is vital in importance. Perceiving the mothers a sexual object rather than as a devoted, nourishing, care-giving one presents little boys with challenges that are different but no less challenging than those with which little girls are faced.

A number of years ago, Ethel Person and I were invited to conduct a three-day symposium on child development at the North Carolina Psychoanalytic Institute and Society. On the morning of the first day, Ethel began by saying, "A major problem for boys is that their first love object is their mother." On the second day, I began by saying, "A major problem for girls is that their first love object is their mother." Everyone laughed and many attendees nodded their heads in assent.

All children need to be loved, cherished, and valued by their mothers (and fathers[4]), and every child is shaken and challenged when triadic rivalry threatens the persistence of the illusion of oneness with and exclusive possession of its idealized and idolized mother. The need to be uniquely special to Mommy is in certain ways more crucial for girls, especially in a male-dominated world, but it is a need that is nevertheless shared by boys. Both, furthermore, are exquisitely sensitive to the impact of the mother's attitudes, feelings, and actions toward them. What is scanted in *A Story of Her Own* is the darker side of motherhood.

Hendrika Freud on the "Electra Complex"

Hendrika C. Freud, in *Electra Versus Oedipus: The Drama of the Mother-Daughter Relationship,* and Barbara Almond, in *The Monster Within: The Hidden Side of Motherhood,* address the darker side of what takes place between mothers and daughters. Hendrika Freud calls attention to the obverse of the longing for blissful togetherness between mother and daughter, as is illustrated, she feels, in the Ancient Greek myth about Electra.[5]

In plays by Aeschylus, Sophocles, and Euripides, Electra is depicted as far more outraged by the fact that her mother, Clytemnestra, has betrayed her father, Agamemnon—and far more jealous of her mother's romantic relationship with Aegisthus—than

---

[4] For many years, I have been performing psychiatric evaluations for schools as part of child study team evaluations of children with learning and behavioral problems. The vast majority of the children I have seen in this context have been burdened not only with Attention Deficit/Hyperactivity Disorder or learning disorders, but have also been *abandoned by their fathers.* Fathers are barely present in *A Story of Her Own.*

[5] Kulish and Holtzman note that, in 1915, Jung proposed the term *Electra complex as the female complement to the male Oedipus complex* (p. 24).

she is angry at her beloved father for having abandoned her and the rest of the family for ten years while he waged war against the Trojans. Overcome with narcissistic rage, Electra sacrifices everything in order to wreak murderous revenge upon her mother.

Hendrika Freud sees Electra as exemplifying a core conflict within many troubled women:

> The fear of being swallowed up by the powerful mother figure is in conflict with a desperate longing for her love and affection. . . . Paradoxical as that may sound, girls need their mother's cooperation in detaching themselves from her. Sometimes that opportunity for independence is lacking, and women have to find a way to sail between the Scylla of Electra's murderous hate and the Charybdis of total symbiosis. Both extremes lead to an unhealthy mother-daughter relationship. As always, it is only the happy medium that can progress to a healthy development. [p. 2]

Neither symbiotic illusion nor total separation is healthy and tolerable. Hendrika Freud emphasizes that the early relationship between a girl and her mother is so intense, so important, and so vital that even when she transfers her devotion to her father, she never does so fully. Her feelings and attitudes toward him, and then toward men in general, always continue to carry within them something that actually represents her continuing attachment to her mother. She desperately needs a great deal of help from her mother to emotionally detach herself even partially from her. What happens when her mother, because of her own problems, is not able to afford her that kind of necessary assistance?

Using convincing clinical illustrations, Hendrika Freud addresses multiple situations in which the mother's ability to help her daughter hold on to an intimate, dyadic relationship with her that will promote a necessary sense of security and safety, while she simultaneously encourages and facilitates independence and supports expansion of the girl's experience of love onto her father and then onto a man of her own, is compromised by the intrusion of significant emotional problems that the mother brings with her and/or experiences as a mother. One such situation involves the woman who looks to motherhood to provide her with the idealized, all-providing mother-daughter relationship that she was not fortunate enough to have had with her own mother. Her disappointment with her female child's inability to provide that for her can turn her narcissistic longing into narcissistic rage, and even into hatred of the child.

"A mother who is disappointed in her own mother," she writes, "will be more than likely to have an unusually ambivalent relationship with her daughter" (p. 5). A mother who has brought to her relationship with her daughter unresolved, intense ambivalence toward her own mother is likely to transfer clinging ambivalence onto her child as well. She is not likely to provide her daughter with a safety net of secure, loving, dyadic attachment to her mother that will enable her to venture beyond her connection with her mother into new, uncharted territory.

A mother who, like Clytemnestra, does not have a loving, attentive, giving husband to look after her and provide for *her* needs can all too often either fail to provide her daughter with what the daughter needs from her, or look to her daughter to take care of and provide for her own emotional needs. This is liable, in fact, to doubly impact the little girl:

> When the father is emotionally or physically absent and will not or cannot intervene to break through a mother-daughter bond that is too intense, when in the mother's experience he plays no role as her child's father, when her mother seeks her fulfillment in the child, the mother-child dyad will not become a triad [p. 13].

Persephone versus Electra

Demeter, in fact, in the Persephone and Demeter myth, does not have anything like a reliable, loyal, devoted husband, and she can hardly feel desirable to someone who may be her god but who neglects her and is a womanizer on a very grand scale indeed. All Demeter has is her daughter—and Zeus even wants to take that away from her! When Zeus notices that Persephone is flowering into womanhood, he arranges for her to be spirited away from her mother's orbit so that she might become the wife and queen of his brother Hades. Demeter is bereft, outraged, and absolutely furious. She cannot do without Persephone.

Is Zeus anxious to have Persephone snatched away from his own aroused passions as well? Hesiod (1914) makes this clear in his Ancient Greek presentation of the Demeter and Persephone myth. Referring to Hades, for example, he states: "So he, that son of Cronos, of many names, who is Ruler of Many and Host of Many, was bearing her away by leave of Zeus on his immortal chariot—his own brother's child and all unwilling" (p. 291). Persephone, after her return from the underworld, tells Demeter that Hades "rapt me away by the deep plan of my father, the son of Cronos" (p. 319).

In Ovid's Ancient Roman retelling of the Greek myth in the *Metamorphoses*, the author describes Jove sending Cupid to shoot one of his arrows into Pluto, in order to make him fall in love with Proserpina, whom he describes as "bent on chastity" (Mandelbaum, 1993, p. 161), and carry her away from her mother, Ceres. When Ceres pleads with Jove for Proserpina's return, he tells her:

> We must not speak of love, not injury, or robbery. We should not be ashamed of Pluto as a son-in-law if only you, goddess, would consent to that. Were he to lack all else, it is no meager thing to be the brother of Jupiter! [Mandelbaum 1993, p. 167].

Kulish and Holtzman indicate that they are somewhat puzzled by the part of the myth that has Demeter disguise herself as Doso (an abandoned, unattractive old woman who is past childbearing) and enter the home of Celeus, offering to nurture and help raise her child, Demophoon, into manhood, but instead stealing him from her.[6] As Doso, Demeter feeds the child ambrosia, "breathes sweetly upon" him, and at night hides him in the fire (in some versions, this is to destroy him, while in others it is to make him immortal so that she can keep him with her forever— which together add up to a very great degree of mother-child ambivalence).[7]

It seems to me that this element of the myth can represent an allusion to the ambivalence that all parents feel, to a greater or lesser degree, about their children growing up, maturing, and coming into the full flush of youthful power, strength, and desirability.[8] They wish this for the child and they revel in the child's ascent, but at the same time, they cannot help but feel envious because the child is at her or his peak—while they themselves are on the decline, in the process of losing their own strength, beauty, and power as they observe the child acquire those very attributes. Parents also cannot help but feel frightened when their children reach maturity. The child is full of life, but the parent is approaching death!

I also wonder if the element of Baubo seducing Demeter out

---

[6] Kulish and Holtzman expressed their inability to comprehend this part of the myth even more strongly during a Meet-the-Author session at a meeting of the American Psychoanalytic Association in January 2010.

[7] In Hesiod's (1914) words, in the form of Doso, Demeter is "like an ancient woman who is cut off from childbearing and the gifts of garland-loving Aphrodite" (p. 297)— that is, she is no longer fertile or beautiful.

[8] Hesiod expresses this poetically when he describes the flower that Persephone is picking when Hades swoops in and carries her away as "the narcissus, which Earth made to grow at the will of Zeus and to please the Host of Many, to be a snare for the bloom-like girl—a marvelous, radiant flower" (1914, p. 289).

of her doldrums (while Demeter is pretending to be the extremely unhappy Doso) by merrily lifting her skirts and showing her genitals refers to much more than merely pleasure in female exhibitionism, which is how Kulish and Holtzman choose to explain it. Could it not be a skillful allusion to the erotic, homosexual component of Demeter's intense attachment to her daughter Persephone? All relationships, especially the most important ones, are complex and multidimensional, and all relationships contain an erotic component.

Hendrika Freud, like Kulish and Holtzman, emphasizes the centrality of the mother-daughter relationship in female development. She indicates that girls never fully relinquish the intense, passionate, bidirectional bond they have had with the mother from birth, and perhaps even before then. Even when the girl discovers her father as another exciting object of her affections and her passions, he does not replace the mother in the girl's feelings, but is a new and *additional* love object. Throughout her life, a daughter's love relationships with men contain, to a greater or lesser extent, a hidden element of the dyadic love of her mother as her special Other, carried over to male love objects in order to keep the earlier, vitally important mother-daughter relationship alive.

In fortunate circumstances, the girl's mother not only continues to cherish and nurture the special bond she and her daughter have had together, but also tolerates, fosters, and facilitates her daughter's equally important movement toward separateness, independence, and autonomy. In instances when the mother—like Demeter and Clytemnestra in the Greek myths—has not had such a seemingly idyllic relationship with her own mother, and/or has not been receiving from a husband what she needs from him, it can be very difficult for her to let her daughter branch out and away from her and come into her own as a separate person with an existence that is largely independent of her.

Schmidt-Hellerau (2010) indicates that her understanding of the Demeter and Persephone myth is very close to Krausz's (1994) view; specifically, "it is Demeter's refusal to separate from her daughter, her pathological mourning, that prevents Persephone from safely expressing her desire to her husband or from wishing for a husband worthy of her feminine desire" (Schmidt-Hellerau, p. 921). As Krausz puts it:

> Demeter represents that part of every mother who cannot separate from her daughter.... Persephone was in the paradoxical trap of destroying her mother by leaving her, yet only being able to leave by literally disappearing, voiceless, into the underworld of the symbolic preconscious. Yet she reappeared each spring to enliven her mother's world with her loving.... Persephone's "death" each year rendered her invisible to her mother's world; only as an invisible woman could she safely express her desire to her own husband (shadowy though he was himself), for her own mother had not been able to tolerate the existence of feminine desire. Demeter's pathological mourning for Persephone shrouded her lost desire for her own husband: unable to be fully a woman, she displaced herself into a self-less and dedicated motherhood. A trigenerational unconscious legacy conspired to form Persephone into an eternal maiden of the springtime, a young girl innocent of desire in her mother's world, yet haunted by the shadow of death into which her feminine desire had escaped and hidden. [1994, p. 65]

Hendrika Freud provides a number of relatively detailed clinical vignettes that illustrate the kind of adherence to a symbiotic illusion of unending dyadic oneness between mother and daughter that can prevent the daughter from achieving developmental advance and consign her to an emotional hell of insecurity, ambivalence, torturous conflict, wrenching guilt, and masochistic efforts to resolve the intense, push-pull conflict between leaving her mother and clinging to her.[9]

Hendrika Freud is a proponent of applying the term *Electra complex* to this aspect of mother-daughter interaction. In fact, she wonders whether—had psychoanalysis emerged out of investigations of women by women, rather than out of investigations of men by men—would the Electra complex have become the initial rubric for framing the struggles that children go through when they enter the phase of involvement in triangular object relations, rather than the Oedipus complex? As she puts it:

> Ancient Greek and modern authors all agree that Electra's rage and loudly bellowed laments are intended as an indictment against her mother, of whom she saw herself, rightly or wrongly, as the unloved victim. It remains difficult to understand why Electra continued to such an extent to idealize her father Agamemnon, the ruthless killer, notwithstanding all the evidence of his selfishness, cruelty, and unfaithfulness. Not only had he murdered Clytemnestra's first husband and children, but he also sacrificed his daughter, Iphigenia, just to appeal to the goddess Artemis for a fair wind. . . . All this had happened when Electra was still a child. He could not have been much more to her than the myth of an invisible father. . . . As if she had split her feelings into opposite poles, she hated her mother as much as she loved her father. In his absence, she strongly identified with the father she idolized. . . . Women's stronger bisexuality—wanting to be a man and have a woman while also wanting to be a woman and have a man—is easily recognizable in Electra. . . . Her masculinity complex is in evidence when she calls Aegisthus a woman, thinking herself to be more

---

[9] The vignettes that Kulish and Holtzman provide contain rather little about the patients' mothers and almost nothing about their fathers. Nevertheless, allusions to the kind of interferences by mothers that Hendrika Freud focuses on can be discerned in some of these vignettes, although less blatantly than they are evidenced in the more seriously troubled patients described by Hendrika Freud.

of a man than he is—something that may also attest to her unspoken amorous feelings for her mother and her jealousy of Aegisthus. . . . As Electra's accusation of neglect implies, it is rather a matter of fierce yearning for the love of a nurturing mother and a desire to return to the lost paradise, the close homosexual bond from the earliest part of her life [Hendrika Freud, pp. 65–66].

The Darker Side of Motherhood

Barbara Almond addresses, in much greater detail than does Hendrika Freud, the most serious, even devastating or fatal effects of unbridled maternal ambivalence toward daughters that occurs all too often. Her book, *The Monster Within: The Hidden Side of Motherhood*, is addressed to a lay audience, which limits her ability to delve as deeply as she might have done had she had a more professional readership in mind. Nevertheless, she imparts a striking message about how devastating the impact can be when a mother's ambivalent feelings about her children are translated into action.

Almond begins by focusing on the fear many women have of producing a deformed child, as exemplified by the contents of such books and films as Mary Shelley's *Frankenstein (1818)*, which Almond (impressively) examines at length; William March's *The Bad Seed (1954)*; and Ira Levin's *Rosemary's Baby (1967)*. She states that:

> The horrifying idea of giving birth to a monster seems to be ubiquitous. The idea is usually experienced as a fear of physical birth defects, but the fear that you could give birth to a psychological monster, although often latent, may be even more disturbing. It takes the form of fearing that you will have a child you cannot love or will create a monster child *because* you cannot love it. [p. 53, italics in original].

The baby, Almond points out, can unconsciously represent a personification of the mother's own destructive aggression and/or her harshly punitive conscience, or a hated sibling who has come back to torment and be tormented by her, or detested aspects of her parents. I have repeatedly encountered these scenarios in the course of my clinical work with children and their families. The most devastating instance involved a little boy whose mother's own mother had, at least as she recalled it, largely abandoned her to devote herself to her baby brother, who was the mother's decided favorite from the time of his birth. When her own second child was born, she all but totally abandoned *him*. Rationalizing her actions by an overzealous adherence to something she had read that cautioned mothers against neglecting an older child when they turn their attentions to a new baby, she relegated her newborn, second child to spending each day out on a balcony, without any human contact, while he looked through the strings that formed a fringe to the cover of his carriage at the leaves and branches of the trees that faced the balcony.

When I met this child a few years later, he was severely autistic. He was unable to relate to people, was extremely emotionally dysregulated, and repeatedly flew into frenzies of agitation and terror. He attempted to ward off these frenzied states by soothing himself with lengths of string or strips of toilet paper, and tried to disengage himself from these states by diving into leafy shrubs! His mother's hatred of her own little brother, which had been incubating within her for years, had unconsciously been directed toward her second child while *he* was incubating within her, and it was reborn in full force when he left her womb and was born into the world.

Almond supports her thesis concerning the importance of maternal ambivalence as a factor affecting the experience of motherhood and causing trouble in the mother-child relationship with a host of personal observations, clinical experiences, news items, bio-graphical references, and literary expressions that collectively make her point in convincing fashion. She focuses on instances of mothers who smother their children by "over-mothering" them in such a way that it interferes with their innate thrust to-ward independence and self-reliance and compromises their ability to undergo separation and individuation from them. (I am reminded of patients—adults as well as children—who have spoken to me of "smother love" or have referred to their mothers as "momsters.") She devotes considerable attention to what she refers to as the *vampiric mother*, who drains the life force of her child, usually a daughter, and uses her to serve her own needs. She casts her microscope on very useful clinical material, as well as on such literary sources as Bram Stoker's *Dracula* (1987) and the novels of Mona Simpson (1986) and Joanna Trollope (1998). (I thought as well of the film *Now, Voyager* [1942], which played an important part in the analysis of one of my patients,[10] and of the book and film *Like Water for Chocolate* [1992].)

The chapters on severe postpartum depression and infanti-cide are painful to read. Fortunately, in the last few chapters of the book, Almond turns her attention and that of her readers to more garden-variety clinical examples of maternal ambivalence contributing to neurotic conflict concerning the mother-child relationship. She makes very positive observations, furthermore, about ways in which women can and might be assisted, person-ally and within societal structure, to deal with their inevitable maternal ambivalence—without denying it, rationalizing it away, being overwhelmed by it, or feeling excessively guilty about it.

---

[10] See Silverman (1986, 1987a, 1987b) for details of this clinical instance.

Discussion and Conclusions

Myths are powerful, both in their ability to embody important psychological and societal constellations of belief and aspiration, and in their ability to influence those beliefs and aspirations. They are never more than metaphorical, however, and they never reflect either historical or psychological accuracy. They reflect verisimilitude rather than verity. When more meaning is ascribed to them than they deserve, the results can create serious misunderstandings and problems that emanate from misunderstanding. Myths, furthermore, are open to interpretation that is likely to vary in accordance with the interests and predilections of the person or persons interpreting them. They can serve as more or less useful illustrations or dramatizations of theoretical constructs, but it is an error to look to them as primary source material for understanding clinical observations and developmental sequences.

It would be wonderful if psychoanalysis were to abandon mythology altogether and stay with clear, simple, descriptive terms. To speak of progression from an exclusive dyadic mother-child relationship to even more complex triadic or triangular relationships, as Kulish and Holtzman appear to favor, would make for greater clarity in psychoanalytic understanding and discourse than using metaphorical terms derived from ancient mythology, which by definition are imprecise and literary. The term *Oedipus complex*, however, has become firmly ensconced not only in psychoanalytic language, but also in the vernacular at large. It is inconceivable that it will be abandoned in the foreseeable future.

In the meantime, it is incumbent upon us to be ever mindful that the term *Oedipus complex*—an oversimplified, shorthand reference to a complex constellation of developmental issues—is not to be taken literally. Adding additional terms derived from other Greek myths, such as *Persephone complex* or *Electra complex*, to the basic psychoanalytic lexicon only contributes to additional fuzziness, especially as there is no universal agreement about what those myths might connote that would usefully apply to psychoanalytic theory and practice. I believe we are stuck with the terms *oedipal* and *preoedipal*, and with *male oedipal* and *female oedipal*, for better and for worse.

Sigmund Freud reshaped the psychological understanding of human nature and made an enormous impact upon societal structure when he established the field of psychoanalysis. His corpus of books and papers has embedded itself as a powerful influence in a wide range of academic, intellectual, and artistic areas of interest. He produced a body of theoretical ideas that made him one of the most influential people of recent times. He worked largely alone, however, did not know everything, and admittedly broke ground for something upon which many others would have to continue to work. Many of his ideas have so far withstood the test of time, but others were questioned even during his own life span.

One of the most glaring areas in this regard involves the psychoanalytic understanding of female psychology. Freud's ideas about female development, which derived—to much too great an extent—from exploration of his own psyche and that of men rather than women, have been criticized and questioned from the very beginning. He admitted that his understanding of girls and women, including and perhaps especially in regard to the crucial impact of what takes place in the relationship between girls and their mothers in the course of development, was limited and faulty—although at the same time he paradoxically carried his earliest ideas about the "female Oedipus complex" on into his very last writings.

Freud looked to female analysts to improve, expand, and correct his ideas about female psychology, and many have answered the call. The authors of the three books upon which this essay is based have made an important contribution to that ongoing effort. It is not fair to require that any one of them shall have provided a total and definitive solution to any of the problems that have plagued psychoanalysis from early on about the understanding of female psychology, female development, and the mother-daughter relationship. If we collate and interconnect what they have to say to us within the pages of these three books, however, we can be extremely grateful to them for what they have given us. Their observations and ideas are clear, concise, and cogent. Individually, they do not tell the whole story, but in combination they add up to an extremely meaningful picture of what takes place within the growing, shifting, evolving relationship between girls and their mothers as girls negotiate the developmental steps that lead them through their progression from dyadic to triadic configurations, beginning in infancy and extending through childhood, adolescence, adulthood, and senescence.

Pines (1993), among others, has studied and written about how a daughter's relationship with her mother evolves and passes through successive stages of restructuring and reorganization throughout the life span. If we wish to understand a girl's or woman's emotional makeup and the issues and struggles with which she is contending at any point in her life, we need to attend not only to her, but also to what is occurring within her mother, internally and externally, in fantasy and in reality—past, present, and future.

As Loewald (1962), among others, has emphasized, parents necessarily play multiple roles in their interaction with their children (as do psychoanalysts with their patients later on).[11] They allow themselves to be objects of their children's affectionate, erotic, and aggressive inclinations while directing their own feelings toward them as objects of their own similar inclinations. They

---

[11] For an in-depth discussion of these issues, see Silverman (2007).

teach, guide, direct, train, limit, prohibit, and otherwise give shape to their perception of and interaction with the world in which they live. Parents also serve as models for identification and for learning about others (with a small *o* and a capital *O*) in the societal structure that surrounds them.

For mothers and daughters, the situation is especially complex. They experience both a biological and a psychological oneness with one another. They face a challenge, however, in that the little girl has to balance her need for a lasting, very special, loving closeness with her mother, which she must have for her emotional well-being, with her need to separate and individuate from her mother so that she can turn her affections and her curiosity in new directions, including toward her father and toward males in general; so that she can find and form her own identity; and so that she can establish an autonomous existence in which she can develop her own unique, true, and independent self.

As Mendell (1988) put it:

> The very quality of the attachment to the mother, with its relative emphasis on sameness and diffusivity between mother and daughter, makes it even more essential for the little girl than for the little boy to establish separateness and boundary differences, even as it makes it more difficult [p. 22].

In her dual and conflicting need for and fear of separating from her mother, the little girl becomes sharply aware of real and fantasied aspects of the mother that seek to interfere with her development and to keep her dependent on the mother. Both the intensity of the attachment between mother and daughter and the inward directed nature of female sexuality contribute to the erasing of inner and outer boundaries and result in the girl's fearing she will be destroyed by her mother [p. 27].

Mothers bring with them all the baggage that persists from their past experience with their own parents. In addition, mothers vary in the degree to which they have satisfying relationships and gratifying lives in the present, apart from the role of mother. They are not all equally up to the task of helping their daughters resolve the dilemma of holding on to the mother they need while moving away from her and out into the world. Not all mothers can assist their daughters optimally in carrying out this complex, Janusian task.

If, as psychoanalysts, we are to help girls and women who are struggling in this regard, it is imperative that we, too, look in opposing directions as we think about what has been taking place in our female patient's relationship with her mother, within her inner world, and between the two of them in actuality—yesterday, today, and tomorrow. It is no easy task, and we can be extremely grateful to Nancy Kulish, Deanna Holtzman, Hendrika Freud, and Barbara Almond for collectively joining forces to guide us on our way.

REFERENCES

BLACK SWAN (2010). A film distributed by Fox Searchlight Pictures. Directed by D. Aronofsky; written by M. Heyman & A. Heim.

DEUTSCH, H. (1925). The psychology of women in relation to the function of reproduction. *Int. J. Psychoanal.* 6:405–418.

DOOLEY, L. (1938). The genesis of psychological sex differences. *Psychiatry* 1:181–195.

FREUD, S. (1892–1899). Extracts from the Fliess papers (Letter 71). *S.E.* 1.

GRIGG, R., HECQ, D. & SMITH, C. (1999). *Female Sexuality: The Early Psychoanalytic Controversies*. London: Rebus Press.

HEATH, S. (2010). Personal communication.

HESIOD (1914). To Demeter. In *Hesiod: Homeric Hymns, Epic Cycle, Homerica*, transl. H.G. Evelyn-White. Cambridge, MA/London: Harvard Univ. Press, 2002, pp. 288–325.

HOLTZMAN, D. & KULISH, N. (2000). The femininization of the female oedipal complex, part I. *J. Amer. Psychoanal. Assn.* 48:1413–1437.

——— (2003). The femininization of the female oedipal complex, part II. *J. Amer. Psychoanal. Assn.*, 51:1127–1151.

HORNEY, K. (1924). On the genesis of the castration complex in women. *Int. J. Psychoanal.* 5:50–65.

——— (1926). The flight from womanhood. *Int. J. Psychoanal.* 12:360–374.

KRAUSZ, R. (1994). The invisible woman. *Int. J. Psychoanal.* 75:59–72.

LAMPL-DE GROOT, J. (1927). The evolution of the Oedipus complex in women. *Int. J. Psychoanal.*, 9:332–345.

LEAVY, S. (1985). Demythologizing Oedipus. *Psychoanal. Q.* 54:444–454.

LERNER, H.E. (1976). Parental mislabeling of female genitals as a determinant of penis envy and learning inhibitions in women. *J. Amer. Psychoanal. Assn.*, 24:269–283.

LEVIN, I. (1967). *Rosemary's Baby.* New York: Random House.

LIKE WATER FOR CHOCOLATE (1992). A film released by Arau Films Internacional. Produced and directed by A. Arau; screenplay by L. Esquivel (author of the 1989 book *Como Agua para Chocolate*, on which it is based).

LITOWITZ, B.E. (2002). Sexuality and textuality. *J. Amer. Psychoanal. Assn.*, 50:171–198.

——— (2003). A case study in the relationship of theory to language. Paper presented at the Spring Meeting of the Amer. Psychoanal. Assn., Boston, MA, June 21.

LOEWALD, H.W. (1962). Internalization, separation, mourning, and the superego. *Psychoanal. Q.*, 31:483–504.

MANDELBAUM, A. (1993). *The Metamorphoses of Ovid: A New Verse Translation by Allen Mandelbaum.* San Diego, CA/New York/London: Harvest/Harcourt, pp. 161–170.

MARCH, W. (1954). *The Bad Seed*. Hopewell, NJ: Ecco Press.

MENDELL, D. (1988). Early female development from birth through latency. In *Critical Psychophysical Passages in the Life of a Woman: A Psychodynamic Perspective*, ed. J. Offerman-Zuckerberg. New York/London: Plenum Medical Book Co., pp. 17–36.

NOW, VOYAGER (1942). A Warner Brothers film. Produced by H. B. Wallis and directed by I. Rapper; screenplay by C. Robinson, based on a novel of the same name by O. H. Prouty.

PHILLIPS, S.H. (2003). Homosexuality: coming out of the confusion. *Int. J. Psychoanal.*, 84:1431–1450.

PINES, D. (1993). *A Woman's Unconscious Use of Her Body: A Psychoanalytic Perspective*. London/New York: Routledge, 2010.

SCHMIDT–HELLERAU, C. (2010). The Kore complex: on a woman's inheritance of her mother's failed Oedipus complex. *Psychoanal. Q.* 76:911–933.

SHELLEY, M. (1818). *Frankenstein*. Indianapolis: Bobbs-Merrill, 1974.

SILVERMAN, M.A. (1971). The growth of logical thinking—Piaget's contributions to ego psychology. *Psychoanal. Q.* 40:317–342.

——— (1986). Identification in healthy and pathological character formation. *Int. J. Psychoanal.* 41:729–742.

——— (1987a). Clinical material. *Psychoanal. Inquiry* 7:147–165.

——— (1987b). The analyst's response. *Psychoanal. Inquiry*, 7:277–287.

——— on Loewald's ideas about the role of internalization in life and in psychoanalytic treatment. *Psychoanal. Q.* 76:1153–1169.

——— (2012). Freud, Oedipus, and the reality principle. Paper presented as the Annual Freud Lecture to the New Jersey Psychoanalytic Society, May 15.

SIMPSON, M. (1986). *Anywhere but Here*. New York: First Vintage Contemporaries.

CHAPTER 26:

DEATH AS THE ULTIMATE CASTRATION

ABSTRACT:

Psychoanalysts, beginning with Sigmund Freud, have been scanting, denying, minimizing, and obfuscating the significance of fear of death in their patients and in themselves. Starting with Freud, they have tended to interpret fear of death as a displacement from other sources of anxiety, especially from castration anxiety. Conversely, some psychoanalysts and psychotherapists have denied the presence or significance of castration anxiety in their patients and in themselves. In this communication, the prevalence and significance of each of these forms of terror are examined, individually and as to their connection with one another. Considerable clinical, child observational, and literary evidence is presented that illustrates the significance and meaning of these two sources of terror within the human psyche, as well as the relationship which they have with one another.

"It's not fair!" she exclaimed. "It's just not fair!"

I asked my friend and colleague, who was sitting across from me in my office, looking haggard and drawn, and with a beaten, somewhat desperate look on her face, to please tell me what was so unfair. She had called me a few days earlier, pleading with me to see her as soon as possible—in a professional capacity. I wondered if I were the right person to see her, because we were friends, but she brushed that aside as irrelevant. The important thing, she said, was that she knew I would understand her. For a number of years we had driven together every month, from New Jersey, all the way out to Sands Point, on Long Island, in New York State, to participate in a study group that interested us. The study group, led by Milton Jucovy and Martin Bergmann, met at the home of Judith Kestenberg. It focused on the effect of the Holocaust on the subsequent generations of those who were fortunate enough to survive. My friend was one of the two members of the group who was a direct survivor of the Holocaust. She had spent the better part of her teenage years in the Warsaw ghetto, where she had participated in the 1943 uprising. She escaped by sloshing through the filth and slime of the sewers that ran beneath the city of Warsaw. After that, she went through a number of harrowing experiences, which she got through via luck and pluck, until she finally reached freedom.

"You know what I went through," she said.

You know how horrible it was for me in Poland—how I lost my family, suffered such terrible things, had my adolescence taken away from me, and barely escaped with my life. Then I got here. I had a chance to start over again. I went to school. I became a doctor. I became a psychiatrist. I got married. What the Nazis did to me, what happened to me in the Warsaw ghetto, prevented me from having children. That's been hard for me. But I have a good husband. I do work that I like doing. I have friends, and books, and music, and theater. And I live frugally. I've saved my money. I've never wanted a lot. When I was a teenager in Poland, all I wanted was to go to school and to have a little, one-room apartment in Warsaw. That's not asking for too much. Here, I've lived better than that. I've had a good life. And I've accumulated a million dollars.

"Well," I said, "that's good. A million dollars can give you a measure of security that you certainly didn't have in the Warsaw ghetto."

"You don't understand," she said. "That's not what a million dollars is. A million dollars is a penis! I was helpless in the Warsaw ghetto. I had no power. A penis is power. You should know that.

You're a psychoanalyst." I asked her to please continue. "A little over a year ago," she said, "I found out that I had cancer. I had surgery. I had chemotherapy. I thought I was cured. But it's come back—and it's spread. It's incurable. I'm going to die. My million dollars isn't doing me any good—and it's going to be taken away from me! I'm being castrated. Death is the ultimate castration!"

I've never forgotten what my friend said to me, and I get a shiver every time I recall it. It wasn't fair. Life isn't always fair. She didn't deserve any of the horrible things that happened to her. And death is horrible. It takes everything away from you—your family, your friends, your loved ones, everything you want and cherish in life. But is it castration? And what is castration, in the analytic sense? Is it the universal, terrible fear that Sigmund Freud attributed to all human beings, male and female, young and old, as the central terror of our existence? And if it is, just what is it of which people are terrified? Why is it so terrifying?

Denial of the Fear of Death and the Concept of Castration Anxiety

Freud, generalizing from what he discovered in himself, during his courageous but unassisted, self-analytic efforts to plumb the psychological depths within him, and from his desire, molded by the medical zeitgeist of his time, to find a unitary magic bullet that would cure his neurotic patients and relieve them of their emotional suffering, centered upon the Oedipus complex and castration anxiety as the keys to unlocking the mysteries of human emotional illness. He emphasized the roles of castration anxiety in males and penis envy in females in his theorization about neurotic and even psychotic illness. As he learned more and more from the patients to whom he applied his analytic method, however, he increasingly realized that, actually, much more than that is involved in healthy and in pathological human development. He realized that his understanding of the origins of neurosis and psychosis was far from complete, and he recognized that he did not understand girls and women very well. Modern analysts are indebted to him for the light he cast upon the complexities of psychological functioning and development, but as they have moved on, beyond the foundation that he provided, they have learned a great deal more than Freud was able to know at the time of his groundbreaking efforts.

To what extent are Freud's ideas about castration anxiety still relevant, however? And what might be the relevance of my twice-suffering friend's observations about the connection between castration anxiety and death?[1] No matter how much Freud refined, revised, and expanded his views about human development, he never got over his centration on Oedipal conflicts and castration anxiety. He also steadfastly insisted that human beings, children and adults alike, are unable to visualize death—that no one is able to picture one's own self as a lifeless corpse thrown into the ground and left to molder away into nothingness. Yes, he admitted, people think about death separating them from their loved ones and from

---

[1] My friend at one time had been in analytic training at a well-known and long-established psychoanalytic institute. As she complained bitterly to me one evening, as we were driving to Long Island together, her training analyst was not interested in hearing about her horrendous experiences during the Holocaust. Whenever she brought them up, apparently unable to deal with what her recollections evoked for him, he pushed them aside to focus instead on exploration of her emotional development prior to those experiences. Apparently, he was not able to face the horrors perpetrated by the Nazi death machine that she was bringing in to his analytic consulting room. She put up with it for a considerable length of time, but then she withdrew from the analysis—and withdrew from the institute. Her experience is not unique, to which, for example, Sophia Richman (2013) has recently attested.

their cherished possessions and activities. They expect to miss them. But, he maintained, people are unable to visualize, and therefore to fear, their own deaths. When such a fear is encountered, he insisted, it actually is a displacement from the much more fundamental and powerful fear of castration as punishment for oedipal competition.

Was he right about this? I do not think so, and for several reasons. For one thing, although fear of death can, at times, be the manifest expression of a warded off, unconscious fear of castration, this is not always the case—and, in fact, the very opposite can take place. That very opposite, the substitution of fear of castration for the even more terrifying fear of dying, may have played a role in Freud's own psychological makeup. Liran Razinsky (2013) has made a close examination not only of Freud's attitude toward death but that of psychoanalysts in general. He observed that:

> A thorough reading of analytic writings reveals a sort of "denial of death," or at least reluctance to acknowledge death as a constituting factor in mental life. Sometimes death anxiety is reduced to other fears and mental states. At other times, death's significance in psychic life is denied or ignored. … Freud maintained that when people are afraid of death, these fears should be understood as secondary, as indications of another "deeper" problem, mainly castration [pp. 1–2].

Razinsky made a further observation that is relevant to comprehending how not only Freud, but generations of psychoanalysts have managed to deny, minimize, or cast clouds over the significance of the fear of dying in human psychology. As he put it: "Theory creates blindness. Even useful, fruitful theories bring about a certain blindness. In illuminating reality, they ipso facto relegate other parts of it to the darkness. Concepts we use sharpen our perception of certain aspects of reality, but necessarily blind us to others" (p. 6).

Freud made a vitally important contribution to our understanding of child development when he called attention to childhood sexuality—but he was in error when he theorized that children are unable to grasp the concept of death. Direct observation makes it clear that children are quite able to do so. Children observe their grandparents growing old and dying, see their pets dying, and hear about people dying. And it does frighten them. One of my grandchildren, whom I'll call Cathy, for example, refused to be toilet trained, even though at the age of three she was dry at night and demonstrated that she had attained the ability not only to recognize that she needed to empty her bladder, but also would ask to be taken to the bathroom. She refused, however, to give up wearing a diaper while she was urinating or defecating. The mystery was solved one day when little Cathy, a very pretty girl from the time she was born, explained why she was resisting toilet training. "I don't want to be potty trained!" she declared. "How come?" "Because I don't want to grow up! I don't want to get old and wrinkled like Great-Grandma! I don't want to be ugly!" A little while before her parents began the toilet training, Cathy had attended the party that was thrown to celebrate her great-grandmother's one-hundredth birthday. Now it was clear what was bothering her! When her parents assured her that it would take a very long time for her to get to Great-Grandma's age, and that she would be a pretty girl for a long, long time, she agreed to undergo toilet training, and she succeeded at it very quickly.

About a year later, when Cathy was four years old (and still fully toilet trained), we had a wonderfully enjoyable, extended family outing that took us to the American Museum of Natural History in New York City. She took great delight in wandering through the various exhibits through which we passed. She asked lots of questions and made intelligent observations. As we were passing, relatively quickly, through the hall of early Central American

History for the second time, on our way out of the museum, she stopped in front of a replica of an ancient burial chamber that contained some human bones and shards of pottery. She gazed at it with rapt attention. She was reluctant to leave it so that she and I might move on toward the exit. "How come you're so interested in this, Cathy?" I asked. "We've already looked at this exhibit." Cathy furrowed her brow and compressed her lips together in an unhappy, anxious-looking pout. "I don't want to die!" she said, in a soft and somber voice. "I don't want to die!"

One day, during a meeting of a child development class I was teaching, we were discussing, among other things, the terrifying effect on preschool age children of learning about death, that is, about their becoming aware that their grandparents, parents, and, indeed, they themselves, will not live forever, but sooner or later will die. One of the students in the class was a priest, as well as being a professor of psychology at a Catholic university. "You know," he said, "if you think about it, the main thing that religions do—all religions—is help people deal with death." His observation stimulated us to think together about the biblical story of the expulsion of Adam and Eve from Paradise after eating from the tree of knowledge. The central point of the story, it seemed to us, is that the infantile illusion of total safety and security is shattered when we learn the naked truth about our human frailty and about our mortality.

No one wants to die. People want to live forever, like the ancient gods of Greek and Roman mythology, who were depicted as both powerful and immortal. What interfered with Freud's apparent reluctance to recognize that, because people are only mortal, fear of death plays a very large role in human psychology? Razinsky believed that Freud struggled so much with his own fear of dying that it clouded his judgment, both theoretically and in the conduct of his life. He observed, furthermore, that psychoanalysts and practitioners of intensive psychotherapy have tended to perpetuate Freud's depicting the fear of death as being displaced from more basic, trenchant anxieties (fear of separation from one's loved ones, fear of castration, and fear of punishment by the Superego) to this very day. He emphasized that they do so for the same reason that apparently motivated Freud to deny or minimize the fear of death in his analysands— that is, their need to push away from their own fear of death![2]

Is Castration Anxiety Real or Is it Merely a Theoretical Construct?

If one follows Razinsky's observations about the way in which theory can be used not only to clarify, but also to obfuscate or deny, that which is difficult to contemplate, one needs to consider not only how fear of death can be denied and attributed to displacement from castration anxiety, but also to consider the way in which the very opposite can occur. Castration anxiety (and the oedipal conflicts that generate it) can be defensively denied, explained away, or theoretically adumbrated by focusing on such other sources of major emotional distress as birth trauma or masculine protest (long ago) or as insecure (especially disorganized) attachment or narcissistic traumatization by negligent or abusive selfobjects (currently). Human beings struggle with multiple sources of conflict and anxiety, all of which are important foci of attention in psychoanalysis or in psychoanalytically informed, intensive psychotherapy. Any of them can be overlooked, and any of them can be used to deflect attention away from one of the others so as to avoid whatever is difficult to face and contemplate in ourselves. Human beings are complex indeed, and psychoanalysts are no less human than are their patients.

---

[2] See my review of Razinsky's book in The Psychoanalytic Quarterly, 2015, Vol. 84: pp. 239–247.

Is castration anxiety real, and if so, why is it real? Child analysts regularly encounter indications of castration anxiety in their young patients. Adam, for example, was an only child, the central joy of his mother's life, until she was surprised at becoming pregnant again when Adam was about three years of age. She was delighted. She was past forty and had not expected to ever have another child. Adam, however, was outraged. He was furious! How could she want another child when she had him? He insisted that his parents return it to the store from which he assumed they had ordered the new baby. When they explained that the baby was growing inside his mother's tummy, he begged them to trade the baby in for a puppy after it was born. His unhappiness about the prospective addition to the family increased progressively as the size of his mother's tummy increased. The day before his baby brother was born, he angrily burst out to her, "I hope the baby is born broken and you have to throw it away!" To everyone's horror, his wish appeared to come true. His baby brother was born with Down's syndrome, was blind, and had serious cardiac defects.[3] And he needed to be institutionalized.

Adam was beside himself with grief, horror, and guilt. To complicate matters, he developed severe, recurrent abdominal pain, which turned out not to be a psychosomatic, emotional reaction to what had happened, but to be caused by something physical. About six months after the birth of his brother, Adam, too, was admitted to a hospital, where he was delivered not of a living baby but of an almost five-pound (fortunately benign) abdominal tumor![4] It was not easy for his parents to convince him that his mother's pregnancy, which had resulted in the birth of a

---

[3] This occurred a good number of years ago, before the advent of amniocentesis as a means of determining the status of a fetus in utero.
[4] The wish by boys to have a baby, and the far from uncommon insistence that they can do so, will be the subject of another article.

damaged baby, and the growth of a tumor in his belly were unrelated. They also found themselves unable to convince him that his baby brother had not been thrown away but had been sent to a "sanitarium" where he could receive the special care that he required. Adam was a very bright youngster who already could read quite well. He informed his parents that he didn't believe them, because he had regularly seen the garbage trucks going by on the New York City streets, and they were clearly marked *Department of Sanitation*. It was only after they brought him to see his brother at the sanitarium that he began to believe that they had not thrown him into the garbage. He was glad to be brought to visit his brother a few times, although it upset him greatly each time they did so. When his brother died, at an extremely young age, he, like his parents, was relieved, as well as miserable.

Adam's guilt about what had happened to his brother did not abate, however. His conscience tormented him. One day, he decided to wreak a punishment upon himself that struck him as appropriate. After careful planning, he rode his bicycle at high speed directly into the corner of a stone bench in Central Park in an attempt to castrate himself! He required twenty-one stitches in his penis and scrotum to repair the damage he had done to himself!

Adam's parents brought him to the psychoanalytically oriented child guidance clinic at which I was spending half my time while I was training as a child psychiatry fellow. Adam and I (and his parents) worked together twice a week (at the clinic and then in my private office after my fellowship came to an end) in a concerted effort to help him deal with what had happened and how it had affected him. His guilt was formidable and all but intractable! He repeatedly found ways to punish himself or to draw punishment upon himself by others. There were times, when he was older, that he put himself at serious risk of getting maimed or killed.

When he took the examination for admission to one of the premier schools in New York for intellectually gifted youngsters, although he was quite brilliant, he astonished everyone by getting the lowest scores that ever had been recorded on that test. We discovered together that, because his brother had been born "mentally retarded," Adam had had to render himself brain damaged, rather than gaining entrance into an elite educational establishment.[5] A good number of years later, when he returned to treatment after a hiatus from it, he revealed to me that when all else failed, a particular fantasy would enable him to get to sleep. He would imagine that he was not yet born but was still in his mother's womb. "I'd be swimming around in there," he said.

> I'm sure you know that before we're born we're surrounded by amniotic fluid, which is like the ocean way back in our evolutionary history. But what is there to eat in there? The only thing to eat is your mother's other babies, who are swimming around in there. It's just like in my fish tanks, where the big fish eat the little fish. So, as I'm falling asleep, I imagine that I'm staying alive by eating all the other babies—except my baby brother. I only kicked his brains out. Oh! Is that why I got interested in raising tropical fish?

On a more positive note, Adam also entertained such reparative fantasies as becoming a neurosurgeon so that he might help people who have suffered damage to their brains—and he made me promise that I would use things I learned from working with him to help other children.

One day, in the playroom in which we met while we were at

---

[5] More about this and about his self-punitive behavior are included within a paper on the only child by Jacob A. Arlow (1972) to which I contributed material. (A typographical error, unfortunately, under-reported Adam's age at the time his brother was born by a year.)

the child guidance center, Adam picked up a "Fli-back," a wooden paddle to which an elastic string was attached that led at the other end to a small, rubber ball. He bounced the ball back and forth while we spoke. Suddenly, the string broke! The ball flew across the room, bounced from wall to wall, and disappeared into the venetian blinds. Adam, with a look of absolute terror on his face, leaped into a chair, pulled up his knees so that he was in a fetal position, and stuck his thumb in his mouth. We spent a good number of sessions trying to figure out what had happened. Eventually, I learned from Adam that his reaction to the disappearance of the ball had involved even more than resurfacing of the powerful guilt and anxiety he felt about the birth of his horrendously damaged baby brother and about the surgical removal of the abdominal tumor from his abdomen several months after that. Because he had relatively wide inguinal canals, he also periodically experienced retraction of a testicle up out of his scrotum, so that one of his testicles would disappear into his body. He was terrified that one day it would not come back down and he would lose it—even though the testicle so far had always returned, although sometimes he had to take a warm bath to get it to do so.

We learned, furthermore, that sticking his thumb in his mouth after the Fli-back ball jumped away and disappeared was related, in part, to a fear of getting excited. He explained to me that he had come up with the idea that his heart beat faster and stronger when he got excited (or when he became anxious) because his testicles jumped up, the way his penis jumped up when he had an erection, and banged against his heart, making it beat faster and stronger. He demonstrated what he was talking about by bouncing a ball briskly up and down on the floor. He got scared, he said, when the Fli-back ball snapped off the paddle, bounced rapidly around the room, and disappeared into the blinds because he was afraid that one day one of his testicles would jump so high that it would fly right out of his mouth and be gone!

"Castration Anxiety" and Male Genital Anatomy

Attention needs to be paid at this point to the role of anxiety about the testicles in what is termed castration anxiety. Strictly speaking, in fact, the word castration means loss of the testicles. Viewing castration anxiety as referring to loss of the penis is partial, at best, and confusing, at worst. I am reminded of a time when I interviewed a three-and-a-half-year-old boy as part of a research project on certain aspects of human development in which I was participating at the Child Development Center of the Jewish Board of Guardians, under the direction of Peter Neubauer. Billy, as I call him, told me excitedly about the set of tools his father had given him for his birthday. He enjoyed working alongside his father, he said, at various carpentry tasks, but it made him sad that his tools were much smaller than his father's and much less effective. He spoke to me in awe about how large and how wonderful his father's tools were, compared with the much smaller and less effective tools in his tool kit.

Then he brightened up. He had received another birthday present, which he absolutely loved. It was a mechanical steam shovel. He excitedly told me how the boom with the shovel at the end of it could go way up in the air when he pressed a button. He was puzzled, however, he said, about how it worked. What was the mechanism that made it go up like that? He asked if I could explain it to him. He was grateful to me for providing him with an explanation, but he still seemed dissatisfied. I said to him that boys often wonder about something else that goes up in the air the way his steam shovel does, namely, about what makes their penis go up in the air at times. "I wonder about that!" he said excitedly. "Can you explain that to me?" I did my best to provide him with an explanation of the spontaneous erections he experienced, but he had difficulty grasping what I was saying. "Could you draw a penis?" he asked. I drew what I thought he meant by "a penis." He was very unhappy with what I drew. I tried repeatedly to redo do it to his liking. Finally, he shouted, in an exasperated voice, "No! No! Draw the whole penis—with that fat thing on the bottom, where the weewee is holded." When I added the scrotum, and explained that it did not hold urine but that that was where his "ballies" resided, he calmed down and was very pleased—but he insisted that I explain to him what his ballies were for. He was both impressed and pleased when I told him that his testicles would enable him to father children, like his daddy, when he grew up. What Billy expressed to me about his interest in his genitals and about his pride in being like his father, although he felt painful consternation about being smaller and less powerful than his father, epitomizes what little boys tend to go through while they are growing up.[6]

The anxiety experienced by boys about their genitals and the oedipal conflicts with which that anxiety is related is epitomized

---

[6] The equivalent in girls of the distress experienced by little boys about the blow to their pride that comes from being smaller and less well developed than their fathers is epitomized in the story of a little girl who was invited by her glamorous aunt to spend a weekend with her, in Hollywood, where her aunt worked as an actor. They had lunch together at a restaurant where Dolly's aunt introduced her to other actors, who were attentive to her and who made a big fuss over her. They went shopping together for clothes, had a thoroughly enjoyable, leisurely dinner, with ice cream for dessert, and then went home to her aunt's house. "I know just what we can do to cap off this wonderful day we've had together," Dolly's aunt said to her. "Let's take a bubble bath!" They took off their clothes and got into the tub, where they were surrounded by fragrant soap bubbles. Dolly's aunt felt quite happy, but when she looked down at her niece she saw a very sad, dejected look on her face. "We had such a wonderful time today," she said. "Why do you look so unhappy?" "Oh, Auntie," little Dolly replied. "Why is it I'm so plain and you're so fancy!?!"

by what emerged during my treatment of nine-year-old Carl, who was brought to me because of intense anxiety that interfered with his performance at school and with his ability to enjoy competitive sports, although he was very bright and was a good athlete. He had terrible trouble sleeping at night. One day his mother made a casual remark to me about how Carl repeatedly disturbed his parents by making a racket in his room, which they could hear clearly and loudly through the air duct that connected his bedroom with theirs. When Carl and I thought about this together, I shared an observation with him. Because sound could travel in both directions, I said, he must be hearing what takes place in his parents' room. Carl was startled, but after a while, he told me that he could hear very clearly what was going on in his parents' room—when they were angrily arguing with each other and when they were having sex. Both of these drove him wild! It didn't let him sleep!

As we explored the competitive, Oedipal fantasies that were exciting him but also scaring him out of his wits, I learned that preparations were being made for Carl to undergo a tonsillectomy. He was absolutely terrified! He did not want to go through with it. When it became apparent to him that there was no way of avoiding the operation, he resigned himself both to its having to be done and to the need to explore his terror with me, although he was reluctant even to think about it. What emerged was that the ear, nose, and throat doctor had told him that his tonsils had to come out because they were as big as golf balls. "What if," Carl said to me in a terrified voice, and with a look of horror on his face, "after he puts me to sleep to do the operation, the doctor reaches down too far and takes out the wrong balls?" We eventually discovered that he was afraid of being punished for his Oedipal excitement, inflamed by the battles, accompanied by threats of divorce, that erupted periodically between his parents and by his father's frequent absences from home for business reasons, and being punished for the intensely competitive fantasies he entertained of taking on his father in battle and defeating him.

It also emerged that the doctor who was to remove his tonsils seemed to Carl to look a lot like his father—who had an explosively volatile temper. Carl also was terrified that, when he would be put to sleep for the surgical procedure, he would not wake up. He had heard people say that when they brought their aged and ailing pets to veterinarians (animal doctors) to put an end to their pets' lives, they were bringing the animals there to be "put to sleep." He was terrified both of being castrated and of being killed—not one or the other, but both!

Less Obvious Instances of Castration Anxiety Observable in the Treatment of Children

A child analyst is more likely to encounter relatively direct references to castration anxiety in the course of his or her work than is the analyst who works only with adults. It is not often as clear and dramatic as it was in the treatments of Adam and Billy, but it is clear nevertheless. The more common indications of castration anxiety are less directly evident, relatively fleeting when they do show themselves, and usually more or less disguised. Four-and-a-half-year-old Donny, for example, was coming for sessions, together with his mother, so that I might help them build the sense of secure attachment that had been shipwrecked by a number of things that occurred as they were setting sail on their life voyage together. I am running the risk of straining my nautical metaphor, but the treatment was progressing swimmingly. Donny and his Mommy were getting closer and closer with one another. They were becoming increasingly attuned to one another and increasingly happy together. Now Donny began to show a sensually excited, physical interest in his mother during sessions, which I had not observed before. He began, for example, to have the airplane he was flying around the room fly under her skirt, to (gently) poke a plastic knife into her shoe or into one of the holes in the knees of her designer jeans, and then between her breasts, and to create games in which they would be huddled close together and be very physically interactive in a corner of the playroom.

He engaged his mommy repeatedly in building a "home" for the airplanes he assigned to each of them, and to surround the home with soldiers and cannons to protect them from invasion by the "bad guys" who threatened to come and destroy their home. The good guys' soldiers had to kill the bad guys' soldiers before they themselves got killed. In the course of this, one day, he widened the format so as to include escaping from the bad guys by jumping into a boat and sailing away. When his mother asked him what made him think that the ocean would make him safe, he said that the bad guys had no boats, but then he grudgingly acknowledged that not all marine creatures who might be encountered in the ocean are gentle. Carl went on to talk about sharks being dangerous because of their sharp teeth (he recently had bitten his mother "by accident"). He began to show off to his mother how much he knew about the various varieties of shark that populate the ocean and what he knew about which ones are the most dangerous.

When he expressed the idea that sharks lay eggs, his mother reminded him that they are viviparous. "Oh yes," he said. "That's right." But then he alluded to uncertainty about how the babies get out of their mother's belly. When I asked him what he thought about that, he replied that the baby bites a hole in its mother's belly and swims out. His mommy corrected him, reminding him that he knew that babies are born through their mother's vagina, the birth canal. He thanked her for reminding him of that, but then he reminded her that it doesn't always work that way—he had heard about C-sections ("Sea-sections?"). He was neither impressed nor relieved when I informed him that C-sections are called that because they are named for one of the emperors of Ancient Rome, Julius Caesar, who came into the world that way. (When, in a later session, I recalled his having shared his idea that a baby shark gets out of its mother's belly by biting a hole in it, he said: "It doesn't do that. It comes out through the mother's mouth.")

One day, soon after this, Donny arrived with a brightly colored Band-Aid on his finger. When I asked him about it, he told me a story about an injury he had incurred, during which he so greatly exaggerated what had happened to him that his mother was astonished. "You didn't break your finger!" she exclaimed. "You only cut it!" (He had done it with an Exacto knife that he was using to cut a piece of material he wanted to use for a project he was working on). He pushed up his mother's skirt so that he could show me a small, largely healed scrape on her thigh. Then he looked at her and said, in a firm voice, "Daddy broke his leg!" "Yes, daddy did break his leg," she said. "But that was a long time ago—and it healed." "Oh yes," he replied, "it did heal." Then he shoved his hands down the front of his pants, as though to check on his genitals. "Get your hands out of your pants," his mother said, in a matter-of-fact tone that suggested it was not the first time she had ever said that to him. Donny returned to the play theme that was running through his treatment sessions, in which he recruited his mother's aid to assist him in building a safe home for their airplanes and surrounding it with soldiers and cannons to protect it from attack.

He introduced a boat into what he and his mother were doing together that day with the airplanes, wooden blocks, and plastic soldiers in the playroom. (Months earlier, he had made his mother into an aircraft carrier that could serve as a safe base for the airplanes he flew around during the treatment sessions and, later on, he brought in a large, plastic, toy aircraft carrier from home—after his mother objected to his covering her with metal airplanes that made her uncomfortable and sometimes scratched her skin.) The boat he made in this particular session, out of blocks, at first was a good guys' boat. Then it was a bad guys' boat. Then it became a good guys' boat again. "Sometimes it's hard to tell who the good guys are and who the bad guys are," I said. "You're right, Dr. Silverman," he replied. I connected this with the difficulty he and his mommy had been experiencing in their efforts to make the home they had created together completely safe from attack and with the puzzlement she had expressed about which soldiers were on their side and which ones were on the side of the bad guys from which they were protecting themselves. The play now became replete with lots of injury, damage, and a submarine blowing holes in the side of the good guys' boat. I commented on how difficult it is to feel completely safe from attackers, even in the ocean. Before he left, Donny drew a sailboat, which then became a submarine that blew a hole in the side of the sailboat. "Wow," I said. "The sailboat doesn't even feel safe from itself." "That's right, Dr. Silverman," he said. "It doesn't!" Donny was quite aware that his own internal impulses put him in danger no less than did external threats.

The Expression of Castration Anxiety in Adult Patients

Indications of intense castration anxiety tend to be even more layered over and disguised in adult patients than it is in children, but it is discernible if the analyst or therapist is willing to see it. Edward, for example, was a young man in his early twenties who developed spasmodic torticollis, or wry neck, when he was a bit more than halfway through a three-year job assignment he had taken in a location that took him very far from home. The wry neck was growing worse and worse, despite a variety of physical treatment approaches that were employed to treat it. His head became twisted more and more strongly to one side, making him look as though he were constantly peering backward to see something that was behind him. Edward, as well as his doctors, recognized that his symptom was emotional in origin, and he worked hard in intensive psychotherapy several times a week to figure out what might be generating it.

The following picture gradually emerged. While he was grow-ing up, in a rural area, his veterinarian father, and Edward's mother, who worked with him as his nurse, put in long hours in their clinic. This left Edward and his younger sister alone much of the time. They were not permitted to leave the house to play with other children. The two of them were isolated and lonely, and they had to lean on each other for companionship, love, and affection. They became extremely close with one another, as they necessarily fulfilled each other's hunger to be loved and cared about. They grew to mean so much to one another that an erotic element inevitably crept into their relationship.

It became clearer and clearer that Edward's torticollis was the somatic expression of a powerful emotional conflict involving the need to look away from and to get away from his sister, who had grown more and more attractive over the years, at the same time that he felt a strong pull toward her. He had taken the job overseas to get away from her, at the same time that he had an intense desire to hurry back to her, look at her, and drink in her beauty with his eyes. So this was the core conflict that was tor-menting him! Edward felt increasingly anxious as we explored it together during our sessions. It was unclear to us, however, what it was exactly that was making him so very, very nervous about the prospect of being reunited with his sister.

One day, as Edward was searching back into the details of their early relationship, he recalled a particularly frightening confrontation with his father that took place when he was about eight years of age and his sister six years of age. They were playing doctor. He asked his sister to take off her clothes so that he could examine her. His father unexpectedly walked into the room and caught them. He flew into a rage! "If you do anything like that again," he screamed, "I'll..." Edward could not remember the rest of what his father said. He could not recall what his father threatened to do to him, but it still gave him shivers to recollect the incident. Maybe his father had said that he would kill him, Edward said—but he didn't remember. It was extremely frustrating to him that he could not figure it out, but he was not about to give up trying.

Finally, after we had worked together for some time to solve the mystery, I said to Edward: "Your father was a veterinarian. What did you tell me he did to cats and dogs?" At first, he looked puzzled. Then he grew pale, his eyes opened wide, and a horrified look spread over his face. "He threatened to do that to me! That's what he said!" We continued to work together on this. As Edward wrestled with the impact upon him of his tortured, conflicted feelings toward his sister and the terror he felt about his father's threat to neuter him, his neck muscles gradually relaxed. The muscle spasms loosened, and the torticollis eventually disappeared altogether!

Another adult patient, whom I call Frank, entered analysis in his late thirties because of increasing, generalized anxiety and increasing malaise. He was very puzzled by it, because his life struck him as perfect. He had a wife whom he loved and who loved him, and his relatively small but thriving business was growing steadily. He was well liked, had friends, and was respected by his peers. The only thing he was aware of that caused him distress was that the father he loved was in the early stages of a rapidly advancing, senile dementia. It was extremely painful for Frank to watch the strong and powerful man he had long revered and admired crumble away like a sand castle at the beach as the tide comes in. He had deeply respected and looked up to his father while he was growing up, although they did lock horns at times and Frank had always competed with him intellectually, athletically, and in with regard to his future ambitions while he was growing up.

As his father's condition worsened, Frank found himself needing to assume more and more of the burdens of his father's care and needing to look more and more after his mother's needs, because his father could no longer do that. He did not mind it all that much, as he had always loved both of them and as he always had been very close with his mother (which at times had seemed to irritate his father). As much as he cared about his mother, however, he was finding himself increasingly ill at ease around her and was feeling resentful of the burdens she was placing upon him. His wife periodically expressed puzzlement about his growing irritation with his mother, because, in her perception at least, his mother was not making undue demands upon him and she actually was spending a good deal more time than he was in looking after his mother.

It puzzled Frank's wife, too, that he was becoming more and more "neurotically" worried about the welfare of their children, who actually were perfectly healthy and who took good care of themselves. She had been aware even before they married that he tended to be somewhat of a hypochondriac who worried inordinately about minor scrapes and bruises and about slight, and even imagined, indications of possible illness. She was worried, however, about how fearful he was getting that he would lose his children, so such so that his overprotectiveness was beginning to interfere with their doing all the fun things they wanted to do. She heartily endorsed his undergoing analytic treatment.

Not surprisingly, we found that Frank's anxiousness actually had begun much earlier in his life. As a youngster, he had been anxious and somewhat phobic. We came to understand a good deal about his childhood phobias and about the core fantasies that seemed to underlie them. He had been intermittently claustrophobic, with an Edgar Alan Poe-like fear of being buried alive. The fantasy continued to erupt fleetingly as he grew into adulthood. We came to understand Frank's anxieties, in part, in terms of the unconscious guilt he felt about being glad to have made it into the world successfully while potential siblings succumbed during the several instances in which his mother's pregnancies ended in a miscarriage. He was alive, but he could never feel completely safe. Death could experience regret over having overlooked him and could reach out to grab him at any time (a kind of survivor guilt). No wonder he was always afraid of getting sick. We also gradually came to understand why Frank was frequently late for his appointments; had to cancel or reschedule them on more than only rare occasions, seemingly for a good reason; and had to leave a session early from time to time, presumably for understandable business reasons. He had to control time! After all, time is life![7]

---

[7] Somerset Maugham captured this brilliantly in his short story, "Appointment in Samarra" (O'Hara, 1934). The story is set in medieval Arabia. A man wakes up in the morning and finds himself cold and hungry. His servant, who was to make a fire and prepare his breakfast, is nowhere to be found. He grows increasingly angry—but then his servant throws open the door and hurries in looking terrified. "What's the matter?" his master asks him. "I went to the market place to buy food for your breakfast," he replies. "Death was in the market place—and he looked at me. I know that he is after me." "Don't worry," his master tells him. "You've been a loyal servant. I'll save you.

Frank and I explored his fears of being seriously injured or taken seriously ill. He lived in terror, we found, of something happening to him that would take away his strength or that would stop him from succeeding in business—that would cut him down to size. His fear of something terrible happening to his children was just another form of this. They were an extension of him, after all. They were a part of him. Losing one of them would be like losing a vital part of himself. His mother, he recalled, experienced something similar when she had her miscarriages. She lost her power, as a woman, to bear a child. She was depressed each time it happened. It had to have been as terrible for her as it would be for him, he said, if he were to be castrated. He shuddered even at the thought of it. During his childhood, he indicated to me, he had oscillated between living in terror of being attacked and maimed, on the one hand, and of being an invincible super-hero, like Superman or Captain Marvel, who was invulnerable to injury.

Via exploration of his dreams and of the recurrent fantasies he recalled from childhood, such as sneaking into a theater disguised as a grownup to watch movies that were restricted to adults—and such as being an arch-villain, "The Eater," who could kill and dispose of scores of victims—we were able to trace his anxieties back to primal scene fantasies and intense Oedipal conflicts. In his fantasies, he barely escaped discovery and retribution, in the form of horrible things being done to him, to punish him for breaking the rules. We came to recognize that his theater fantasies derived, in

---

Saddle a camel and load it with supplies, and I'll send you to Samarra, where my brother will hide you." After his servant leaves, the man realizes that he is still hungry. He goes to the market place to buy food—and he sees Death there. "Why do you look at me like that," Death asks. "Why did you frighten my servant like that?" the man replies. "Oh, was that your servant?" Death responds. "I didn't mean to frighten him. It's just that I was surprised to see him. What was he doing here? I have an appointment with him tomorrow morning in Samarra."

part, from the details of the sleeping arrangements in the tiny, cramped apartment in which his family lived. We were able to trace his phobic-obsessive worries about terrible bodily harm befalling him back to his secret wish to be rid of and to take the place of his father as the man of the house. Then he would provide for his mother better than his father was able to do, and he could give her live babies to replace the ones who hadn't made it successfully into the world.

The (somewhat protracted) termination phase of Frank's analysis overlapped with his father's accelerating deterioration and, then, his death. When his father was in the final throes of fatal illness, Frank became more and more anxious and more and more in anguish over his father's condition. One day, in late December, he brought in a dream from which he had awakened feeling terrified. In the dream, he was doing battle with a cloaked figure, carrying a scythe, which we quickly recognized as Father Time. Frank seemed to be winning the battle, but then, with a swipe of the scythe, the figure appeared to slice off one of Frank's legs. At first, he was shocked and terrified. He looked again and saw that he actually was fully intact. As he raised his sword to strike back, the figure disappeared. Then the scene changed. Now he was on a giant clock, the hands of which were either swords or axes. The hands were moving slowly but inexorably toward midnight. Frank was hanging on to the minute hand, trying to hold it back. Then he awoke, soaked in sweat and feeling extremely anxious.

Frank, at first, was unable to join me in thinking about the dream. "It's only a dream," he said. "It doesn't mean anything." "Then how come you've been coming late for your sessions again so often lately?" I replied. During the rest of the session, and during a good number of sessions that followed it, each of which was a highly emotional experience for the two of us, we came to understand Frank's dream in terms of the way in which reality had seemed to catch up with his unconscious childhood fantasy of chopping his father down to size, the way Jack did to the ogre in "Jack and the Beanstalk," so that he could take his place as his mother's hero, despite guilt-ridden terror that he would be castrated or killed to punish him for having such terrible thoughts and feelings.

Little boys do dream of killing their fathers and replacing them as their mothers' favorite, but the wish is not supposed to come true! The progressive physical and mental deterioration of Frank's father, whom he loved very much, despite his unconscious, murderous rivalry with him as a child, not only led him to enormous pain and grief, on a conscious level, but it also inflamed the unconscious Oedipal conflicts that had lain relatively dormant within him and that had been reasonably contained as he was realizing his childhood wish to surpass and outdo his father as the man in the family. "Who's your Daddy?" the great Boston Red Sox pitcher Pedro Martinez screamed at the fans who were booing him, after he had just defeated the New York Yankees, the most dominating team in major league history, in a brilliantly pitched baseball game.

A Connection Between the Fear of Death and Castration Anxiety in Literature

The connection between castration anxiety and the fear of growing old and dying can be found repeatedly in works of literature. Talented poets and writers tend to be intuitive psychologists, exquisitely aware of the various facets of human nature. Henning Mankell, the enormously popular Swedish writer of murder mysteries, is best known for his series of books about a detective to whom he gave the name Kurt Wallander. Wallander is depicted in the series as brilliant and courageous, as well as swashbuckling, romantic, and impressively heroic on at least one major occasion (the episode played a central part in one of the most popular books in the series, *The Dogs of Riga* (Mankell, 2010), and it is revivified in the last one), who solves baffling crimes and is a model of probity, with outstanding personal character. Mankell indicates, in the last of the series, *The Troubled Man* (Mankell, 2011), that there will be no further appearance of Wallander in his books. In it, Wallander finds himself having increasingly frequent, frightening episodes of memory loss, just as his daughter, who admired him so much that she followed him into the police profession, reveals to him that she has acted upon a decision to become pregnant. Wallander loves his granddaughter fiercely after she is born, at the same time that she serves as a continual reminder to him that he is growing old and losing his powers. The man his daughter has chosen to be the father of her child is quite financially successful, as a broker operating at a very high level in a major financial institution. He is wealthy, and the contrast with Wallander's own very limited financial means, as a mere policeman who will leave no mark on the world when he leaves it, gnaws painfully at Wallander. He is very discomfited by the contrast between his own lower-middle class status and that of the upper-class lifestyle of the parents of the man who has become his daughter's partner in life.

The father of the man who, in essence, has become his son-in-law, a powerful, former extremely high-ranking naval officer, disappears after presenting Wallander with an ambiguously articulated but ominous-sounding expression of fear that he is being watched and is in grave danger. Then the son-in-law's mother appears to have committed suicide, although there are tiny details that point Wallander increasingly to the conclusion, as he devotes himself to investigating her death, that she was murdered. His memory lapses grow increasingly frequent, but he manages to solve the mystery (which turns out to relate to international intrigue, high-level spying, and cold-blooded murders carried out by two, national superpowers) before he lapses into total and irreversible, senile dementia and is institutionalized for a period of time until his life comes to an end.

Along the way, during his investigation into the death of his son-in-law's mother, his career comes extremely close to being abruptly cut short when he experiences an almost incredible episode of loss of control. He commits the unpardonable sin, for a police detective, of losing his gun! It is found by a waiter who served him a meal in a small eating establishment. The literary juxtaposition of aging, decline, loss of one's powers, death, and a quite transparent symbol for castration, that is, for loss of one's manhood, is both moving and disturbing to the reader of the book.

This juxtaposition is epitomized in a conversation Kurt Wallander has with his daughter, Linda, toward the end of the book. Wallander asks her how business is going for her partner, Hans, who is looking after the baby while she is visiting him. "I don't know," she says. "But I sometimes wonder what's going on. He always used to come home and tell me about the fantastic deals he'd closed during the day. Now he doesn't say anything at all." A formation of geese flies past in a southerly direction. "Are they migrating already?" Linda wonders out loud. "Isn't it too early?" Wallander says, "Maybe they're practicing."

Linda laughs and replies: "That's exactly the kind of comment Granddad [who has been dead for some time] would have made. Do you realize that you're getting more and more like him?"

Wallander "dismisses" the thought. He says: "We both know that he had a sense of humor. But he could be much more malicious than I ever allow myself to be."

"I don't think he was malicious," Linda says firmly. "I think he was scared." "Of what?" Wallander asks. "Maybe of growing old.

Of dying. I think he used to hide that fear behind his malevolence, which was often just a front."

The author, Mankell, then writes: "Wallander didn't reply. He wondered if that was what she meant when she said they were so similar. That he was also beginning to make it obvious that he was afraid of dying."

Could Henning Mankell have studied Shakespeare's masterful play, *King Lear*? It is likely so. Shakespeare, the intuitive psychological genius that he was, has given people an astonishingly perceptive, literary rendition of the way in which fear of death and dread of castration can interweave and interplay with one another in the course of a lifetime. Lear, a powerful king, is exquisitely aware that he has grown old. Death is creeping up upon him, preparing to snatch his strength, his power, his wealth, his all from him—and he knows that there is nothing he can do about it. He has no penis-bearing son and heir to carry on in his honor and take his place as an extension of him. The play opens with an exchange between the Earls of Kent and Gloster about the great value placed by a man in power on having a son to provide legitimate continuity of his male bloodline, in the course of which allusion is made to Lear's valorizing the mere possession of a son and heir far beyond consideration of the son's—or daughter's we soon learn—actual worth and character. (As the story unfolds, the illegitimate and legitimate sons of Gloster engage in mortal conflict with one another to acquire the status, power, and wealth which their father possesses. Edmund, who seethes in rage over his disempowerment, as the illegitimate one of the two sons, attempts to have both his brother Edgar and his father killed, and he is responsible for his father being blinded by the husband of Lear's oldest daughter.)

Lear, the audience learns, has decided to cheat death of its power to take everything away from him by refusing to passively give up his kingdom to an interloping successor. He will not allow it to be taken from him, as the ultimate castration, which my friend and colleague termed death as she was succumbing to the cancer she believed to have been inflicted upon her, in delayed fashion, by the radiation to which the Nazis had exposed her to destroy her ability to bear children and thereby propagate her race. Instead, he cuts his kingdom up into three parts and grants the truncated portions, each of which is but a third as valuable as his full domain, to his three daughters to rule, along with the sons-in-law with whom they connect as aristocratic, or even royal, consorts to provide them with the male power their gender lacks. (The magic number three as a symbol of masculinity does not escape us.) His older daughters, Goneril and Regan, hungry for wealth and power, leap at the chance to shower their father with false expressions of love and devotion, but Cordelia, who truly loves and cherishes her father, remains silent except for affirming the loyalty to him as his begotten child that binds her totally and ineluctably to him. She declines the invitation either to pour unctuous flattery over him or to take any of his wealth and power from him. The Duke of Burgundy withdraws his suit for her hand in marriage now that she lacks a dowry, but the French king recognizes her worth and offers to marry her even though she no longer can bring him treasure. Lear (truly a fool, as his Fool subsequently depicts him) banishes her from his kingdom, together with the equally faithful Earl of Kent after the latter tries to speak sense to him, and he divides her third of the kingdom between her two untrustworthy sisters.

As soon as than they take over the kingdom, together with their husbands, the equally self-serving and avaricious Dukes of Cornwall and Albany, they turn upon Lear with vicious ferocity. They humble him, progressively cut him down in importance and power, and do their best to transform him into a shriveled shell of his former self and to make him totally dependent upon them for whatever crumbs of care and honor they deign to toss his way. They make it clear that they have long resented their dependence upon him and upon his bounty, and that they can hardly wait to wreak revenge upon him for making them subservient and beholden to him for so long. His oldest daughter, Goneril, declares to Lear that she is cutting in half the retinue of knights that travel with him to demonstrate his royal status and his importance (she and Regan subsequently humiliate him by progressively stripping him of the remaining knights as well). He shouts, overcome with grief, and in enormous emotional pain, "That thou hast power to shake my manhood thus!" (Shakespeare, 1606, p. 981). He has, in effect, been emasculated!

The plot boils and bubbles as it devolves into a virtual bloodbath of perfidy, betrayal, intrigue, and murder. Lear's humiliating recognition of what a fool he has been and what horrendously stupid mistakes he has made drives him mad, as he is consumed by his own narcissistic rage. Now he has lost his mind, on top of everything else he has lost. All three of his daughters, the full complement of his progeny, end up dead—and then, at the age of "four score years," he, too, is claimed by death. Rule over Lear's kingdom is turned over to the Earl of Kent, who has remained totally faithful to Lear throughout all that was happening, and to Edgar, Gloster's younger and legitimate son. Lear, like Macbeth, in another of Shakespeare's tragedies, has ended up with nothing, neither a kingdom nor an heir to continue his blood line. He has truly succumbed to death as the ultimate castration and to the loss of his manhood, of his masculine powers, a horrible emotional death—just what had terrified him in the first place! The play is truly one of Shakespeare's greatest masterpieces!

That people have children, in part, to perpetuate themselves after death, and tend to fear their abandoning them before they fulfill that task, is epitomized in a little poem, titled "A Cradle Song," which was written by William Butler Yeats and published in 1890 (p. 498):

> *The angels are bending*
> *Above your white bed,*
> *They weary of tending*
> *The souls of the dead.*
>
> *God smiles in high heaven*
> *To see you so good,*
> *The old planets seven*
> *Grow gay with his mood.*
>
> *I kiss you and kiss you,*
> *With arms round my own,*
> *Ah, how shall I miss you,*
> *When, dear, you have grown.*

One also might think of the wrenching plight and desperate despair into which Demeter was thrown when her only child, her daughter Kore, later renamed Persephone, grew into the fetching, nubile, epitome of the blossoming of youthful power—but then left her to descend with her husband into the underworld, the kingdom of the dead—in the famous ancient Greek mythological story as it was recounted by Ovid (AD 8) and by Hesiod (1914; Silverman, 2012). The link between fear of castration and fear of death has been alluded to over and over by creative storytellers throughout the ages!

The Connection Between Fear of Death and Castration Anxiety

As these clinical vignettes and literary portrayals dramatically illustrate, human beings are the only creatures on Earth who are blessed and cursed with the kind of intelligence that burdens them with knowing that they are going to die, and consigns them to living lives of quiet desperation, as T.S. Eliot (1934) has put it, in which they know that, although they might have the ability to postpone it, people are helpless to prevent it from eventually taking place. People's knowledge of death comes to them when they are very young, and they live their lives terrified of dying. A subset of this, which people usually are able to push out of sight more or less while they are young, is the fear of growing old and feeble—and then dying. Growing old horrifies humans' both in its own right and because it brings them closer to death. In an important sense, aging and death are intimately connected, in that they threaten people with losing their strength and with having their powers taken away from them. Ruth Lax (2008) has captured this magnificently in her paper about the indignities of old age.

Castration, likewise, conveys the prospect of being divested of one's powers—one's masculine powers—the prospect of which is terrifying to boys and men. Power—the possession of it and the loss of it—is the crux of the matter. Being helpless is exasperating and infuriating. This is observable even in babies. The threat of being rendered helpless and powerless is an enormous threat, indeed. Herein, it seems to me, lies the answer to the question of the relationship between fear of death and fear of castration. They both connote absolutely terrifying loss of one's powers.

The connection between the horror of contemplating one's own death and dreading the loss of one's powers during one's lifetime was demonstrated in the vignettes adduced herein, along with the connection between fear of death and fear of castration.

My little granddaughter was not only terrified of old age taking away the good looks that contributed mightily to making her a princess to everyone around her, but she also was terrified of death taking everything away from her. Carl was caught up in the throes of intense Oedipal anxieties, which were fed by his parents' regular exposure to him of the sounds not only of their sex life, but also of the marital strife and threat of divorce that fueled his fantasies of defeating his father and taking his place—although he was terrified of his father's volcanic rage. When he was informed that he had to undergo a tonsillectomy, he became terrified both that he was going to be killed—"put to sleep"—and that he was going to be castrated, that is, that the surgeon would "reach too far down and remove the wrong balls." Adam literally attempted to castrate himself to punish himself for wishing that the baby growing inside his mother's tummy would "be born broken and thrown away." He also castrated himself symbolically in multiple ways, including rendering himself the equivalent of brain-damaged when he took a test for admission to a school for intellectually gifted youngsters. Later on, he subjected himself to dangers which literally put him in danger of losing his life.

Edward repressed the threat of castrating him, which his animal doctor father had leveled at him when he caught him playing doctor with his little sister. He replaced it with the idea that maybe his father had threatened to kill him. Frank exhibited multiple derivatives of intense castration anxiety (hypochondriasis, fear of his business failing, phobic-obsessive worry that his children would be maimed or killed, etc.), which greatly intensified when his father, whom he loved but with whom he had long been intensely competitive, began losing his powers because of progressive senile dementia and physical deterioration. His dread of losing his masculine powers was mirrored in his compassion for his mother who had lost babies via miscarriages. His dream of dueling with Father Time, who did and did not cut off his leg—followed by hanging on to the sword- or axe-like hands on a giant clock to keep it from striking midnight and thereby killing the old year so that a baby new year could be born—dramatically alludes to the connection between fear of castration and fear of death. (Things generally are multidetermined; the dream pointed not only to Oedipal conflicts, we discovered, but also to sibling rivalry conflicts, associated in part with his mother's repeated miscarriages.) My good friend and colleague was anguished and enraged that the Nazi perpetrators of the Holocaust in Europe had obliterated her capacity to give birth to children and now were in the process of obliterating her very life and all that she had in it that she so greatly valued. Henkell's and Shakespeare's fictional characters, Wallander and King Lear, respectively, feared both the loss of their lives and the loss of their masculine power and prowess.

Fear of death is complex. Not only is fear of dying more or less a universal, central issue in human psychology in its own right, but it also lends itself readily to serving as a displacement or substitute for other, currently even more terrible fears—including of castration as a *fate worse than death*. The Turkish officer who captured T.E. Lawrence, more popularly known as Lawrence of Arabia, had him punished for wanting to destroy the power of the Ottoman Empire not by ordering him to be killed but by ordering him to be castrated. On the other hand, the concept of castration anxiety can just as easily lend itself to serving as a displacement from or a substitution for the fear of death, as Razinsky has convincingly argued.

Human beings are clever and versatile. Self-protective, mental gymnastics can be carried out in multiple directions. The common theme of cutting off a person's strength and power lends itself easily to either the fear of death being substituted for the fear of castration or vice-versa in the minds —and in the theories—of human beings, when one or the other presents itself as being convenient. Was my friend correct in observing that "death is the ultimate castration?" I think she was. Might it also be correct to say that castration is a horrible kind of death? That also sounds right. Isn't there a saying that goes something like, "each is worse than the other?" There is a very real difference between literal and figurative fear of death. This also applies to fear of castration. At times, either one can be quite literal. At other times, either fear of death or fear of castration can serve as a metaphorical expression of a variety of other sources of anxiety (just as Grossman and Stewart, 1976, have pointed out for penis envy)— and the literal and the metaphorical often combine with one another in the human mind.

Why are the prospects of death and castration so terrifying? The unifying dimension would appear to be the terror of loss of power. Helplessness is extremely difficult for human beings to tolerate, and this is so from extremely early in our lives. Winnicott (1953, 1969), in particular, has addressed this. Because brain size has rendered human beings secondarily altricial, that is, because they are born in a still embryonic state in which they are very far from ready to fend for themselves, babies are almost totally helpless and are utterly dependent upon a mothering figure or figures for survival. At first, as Sigmund Freud, extrapolating backward from the analysis of adults, and, later on, Donald Winnicott, extrapolating forward from child observation, emphasized, an infant quickly appears to elaborate a fantasy that it is all-powerful—and, when the child is disabused of this by experience, it elaborates a secondary fantasy that it has the power to create, destroy, and recreate the mothering person who serves its needs. Neither fantasy is easily or totally within the child's power to relinquish. As the child grows older, it becomes aware that in multiple ways it lacks the attributes and the equipment to wrest power from the parents upon whom it depends. Life presents itself to a child as a perpetual David and Goliath struggle, in which, unlike the way it is depicted in the biblical tale, the child keeps losing.

When the child reaches that developmental stage in which it is both enmeshed in competitive, triangular relationships and exquisitely aware of genital sensations and the difference between the sexes—the so-called Oedipal stage of development— the awareness of its disadvantages in size and in both physical and mental capacity become focused to a very significant extent on genital anatomy and genital capacity, as child observation and child analytic experience regularly make evident. The male counterpart of the story of the little girl who is terribly saddened by her observation of the differences between her immature body and the mature body of her much better endowed aunt is a story that made the rounds when I was a youngster. A little boy was such an out of control terror in his kindergarten class that he drove his teacher to distraction. One day, he disappeared from sight. The teacher searched and searched for him. Finally, she found him in the clothes closet, urinating against one of the walls. "Johnny," she shouted at him, "you have some nerve!" "You think so?" he replied. "You should see my father's!"

I am reminded, too, of the time when my then three-and-a-half-year-old son hurried me through dinner every night so that we might put on our inflated "Socker-Bopper" boxing gloves and engage in a prize fight together. One day, I told him that I, too enjoyed our mock prize fights, but I also asked him why it was so important to him that he couldn't even wait for me to finish my dinner. "Well," he said. "You're big and I'm little. I want you to teach me how to fight. So I can knock you down!" He subsequently made it clear to me that he wanted to not only match, but excel over, me in all sorts of ways. He was overjoyed when, a little more than ten years later, he returned from tennis camp and soon made it clear to me that I could never again expect to take a set from him! But during the ten years it took him to arrive at that point, he made it abundantly clear that he did not feel at all good about having to wait to get there. It was wonderful for both of us when we eventually became able to win tennis matches together, as a doubles team.

The extent to which children chafe at being too little and too immature to have what their parents have and to do what their parents do is epitomized in the reaction of one of my granddaughters, when she was two years old and her aunt, her mother's sister, gave birth to a baby—and then her reaction, when she was four years old, to looking at illustrations in a book she asked me to read to her in which beautiful, well-endowed Barbie won the heart of a handsome prince, with the aid of a winged horse. In the first instance, she frantically insisted that she "want(ed) a baby Timothy too," and she did not rest until she was given a baby doll which she named Timothy. At first, she was reluctant to accept it in lieu of a real live Timothy, but after she resigned herself to the substitution, she carried it around with her everywhere— and she took very good care of her baby.

Her reaction, two years later, to the illustrated Barbie book was to gaze intently at one of the pictures and then to cry out, "Who stole my boobies?" I was rather startled, and I asked her what she was talking about. She looked over at her twin sister, who was playing with some toys on the floor, and said: "Cathy! Cathy stole my boobies!" "Does Cathy have Boobies?" I asked.

She looked puzzled for a minute, and then she looked toward the kitchen. "Mama!" she said. "Mama stole my boobies!"

"Oh Martha," I said to her, "Nobody stole your boobies. They just haven't grown yet. When you're a teenager you'll have boobies."

"I will?" she said. "Oh! Read the next page!"

What ties the fear of death and the fear of castration together is the way in which both of them reflect and derive from the wish for power and the fear of losing it once it is attained. They are central components of human psychology and of human development. Each consists of a basic fear that plagues people all through their lives. They intersect with one another. They can easily be substituted for one another. I do believe that my friend was correct when she said that death is the ultimate castration—*and vice-versa!*

REFERENCES

ARLOW, J.A. (1972). The only child. *Psychoanal. Quart.* 42:507–536.

ELIOT, T.S. (1934). *The Waste Land and Other Poems.* New York: Harcourt, Brace and Company.

GROSSMAN, W.I., & W.A. STEWART. (1976). Penis envy: From childhood wish to developmental metaphor. *J. Amer. Psychoanal. Assn.* 24:193–212.

HESIOD. (1914). To Demeter. In: *Hesiod: Homeric Hymns, Epic Cycle,* Homerica, transl H.G. Evelyn-White. Cambridge, MA: Harvard University Press, 2002, pp. 288–325.

LAX, R. (2008). The indignities of old age. *Psychoanal. Quart.* 77:835–857.

MANKELL, H. (2010). *The Dogs of Riga.* New York: New Press.

—— (2011). *The Troubled Man.* New York: Knopf.

O'HARA, J. (1934). *Appointment in Samarra.* New York: Harcourt Brace.

OVID. (AD 8). The Metamorphoses, transl. C. Martin. New York: W.W. Norton, 2004.

RAZINSKY, L. (2013). *Freud, Psychoanalysis and Death.* Cambridge: Cambridge University Press.

RICHMAN, S. (2013). "Too young to remember" Recovering and integrating the unacknowledged known. In: *The Power of Witnessing: Reflections, Reverberations, and Traces of the Holocaust,* ed. N. R. Goodman, & M. B. Meyers. New York: Routledge, pp. 105–118.

SHAKESPEARE, W. (1606). *King Lear*. In: *The Complete Works of William Shakespeare*. New York: Avenel Books, 1975, pp. 973–1009.

SILVERMAN, M. A. (2012). On myths and myth-making: Psychoanalytic theorizing about mother–daughter relationships and the "female Oedipus complex." *Psychoanal. Quart.* 91:727–750.

——— (2015). Review of "Freud, Psychoanalysis and Death" by Liran Razinsky. *Psychoanal. Quart.* 84:239–247.

WINNICOTT, D. W. (1953). Transitional objects and transitional phenomena. In: *Playing and Reality*. New York: Basic Books, 1971, pp. 1–25.

——— (1969). The use of an object and relating through identifications. In: *Playing and Reality*. New York: Basic Books, 1971, pp. 86–94.

YEATS, W. B. (1890). A Cradle Song. In: *The New Oxford Book of Verse*, ed. C. Ricks. Oxford/New York: Oxford University Press, 1987, p. 498

www.ingramcontent.com/pod-product-compliance
Lightning Source LLC
Chambersburg PA
CBHW062108020426
42335CB00013B/891